History in Our Hands

. . . history forming in our hand's
Not plasticine but roaring sands,
Yet we must swing it to its final course.

John Cornford, 'Full Moon at Tierz:
Before the Storming of Huesca'
(1936)

History in Our Hands

A Critical Anthology of Writings on Literature, Culture and Politics from the 1930s

Edited by Patrick Deane

Leicester University Press
London and New York

First published 1998 by

Leicester University Press, *A Cassell imprint*
Wellington House, 125 Strand, London WC2R 0BB, England
370 Lexington Avenue, New York, NY 10017-6550, USA

Introduction and editorial apparatus © Patrick Deane 1998

Contributions © as per copyright holders

British Library Cataloguing-in-Publication Data

A catalogue record for this book is available from the British Library.

ISBN   0-7185-0143-8 (hardback)
            0-7185-0144-6 (paperback)

Library of Congress Cataloging-in-Publication Data

History in our hands : a critical anthology of writings on literature, culture and
   politics from the 1930s / edited by Patrick Deane.
      p.   cm.
   Includes bibliographical references and index.
   ISBN 0–7185–0143–8 (hardback). — ISBN 0–7185–0144–6 (pbk.)
   1. History, Modern—20th century.   [1. Nineteen thirties.]
  I. Deane, Patrick.
  D720.H57   1998
  909.82'3—dc21   97–49340
                                                     CIP

Typeset by Ben Cracknell Studios
Printed and bound in Great Britain by Biddles Ltd, Guildford and King's Lynn

Contents

Acknowledgements

I am as always grateful to my wife, Sheila, for her critical acumen and passionate intellect. It was she who introduced me to the remarkable novels of Sylvia Townsend Warner, thereby ensuring that a mild interest in the literature and culture of the thirties would become a longstanding preoccupation. Andrea Cabajsky, Peter Darbyshire, Jacqui Mottl, Brian Mallette and Matthew Trebb allowed themselves to be drawn into intimacy with this material, and I am indebted to them for the stimulating insights which were a daily staple in our 1996 graduate seminar. Veronica Higgs, Sandra Margolies and Colin Hutchens have all made work on the book a pleasure; and Tom Orange has been most helpful at several crucial stages in the project.

Many other people have offered advice, assistance and encouragement, and I hope they will accept a blanket expression of gratitude. Some specific debts I must acknowledge by name: to Bert Almon, Ian A. Bell, Kristin Bluemel, Barbara Brothers, John Xiros Cooper, Samuel Hynes, Phyllis Lassner, Patrick Quinn, S.P. Rosenbaum, Antony Shuttleworth, Stan Smith, Paul Tiessen, Trevor Tolley and Joyce Wexler. That plans for the anthology have been realized is due in considerable measure to their support, and the breadth of the selection owes much to their advice. For omissions, though, only the editor is accountable.

I am very grateful indeed to the Social Sciences and Humanities Research Council of Canada for a Research Grant in support of this project.

Acknowledgements are also due to agents, publishers and individuals who have kindly granted permission for the inclusion of material in this book. The epigraph, from John Cornford's poem 'Full Moon at Tierz: Before the Storming of Huesca', is reprinted from *Understand the Weapon, Understand the Wound: Selected Writings of John Cornford*, by permission of Carcanet Press Limited. Other items are listed by chapter: **1** and **20** Reprinted by permission of Mr L. R. Leavis; **2** Reprinted by permission of Baron Ravensdale; **3** Copyright W.H. Auden 1932, 1933 and 1935, reprinted by permission of Faber and Faber Ltd. and Curtis Brown Ltd., New York; **4** Reprinted by permission of David Higham Associates and Dr Caroline Grigson; **5** Reprinted by permission of Random House UK Ltd and the Hogarth Press (*New Signatures*), and Faber and Faber Ltd. (*The Faber Book of Modern Verse*); **6** Reprinted by permission of Oxford University Press; **7, 13, 14, 24** ('Writers and Manifestos'), **28, 29, 31, 32, 33, 37** and **41** ('Two

Letters') Reprinted by permission from *The Left Review*, reprinted by Frank Cass & Company, 900 Eastern Avenue, Ilford, Essex, England. Copyright Frank Cass & Co. Ltd; **8** Reprinted by permission from *A Short Survey of Surrealism*, reprinted by Frank Cass & Company. Copyright Frank Cass & Co. Ltd; **9** Vera Brittain's article 'Can the Women of the World Stop War?', from *Testament of a Generation* (Virago, 1985), is included with the permission of her literary executors; **10** Copyright © Rebecca West 1935. Reprinted by permission of The Peters Fraser and Dunlop Group Limited; **11** Reprinted by kind permission of Susanna Pinney, copyright William Maxwell and Susanna Pinney; **12** Reprinted by permission of David Higham Associates; **15** and **21** Reprinted by permission of Carcanet Press Ltd; **16** Reprinted by permission of Rosemary Sprigg; **17** and **18** Reprinted by permission of Lawrence & Wishart Ltd; **19** Reprinted by permission of Curtis Brown Ltd, London, on behalf of Copyright © The estate of Sir William Empson, and by permission of New Directions Publishing Corp., Copyright © 1974 by New Directions Publishing Corp.; **22** Reprinted by permission of The Peters Fraser and Dunlop Group Limited; **23** © Wyndham Lewis and the estate of the late Mrs G. A. Wyndham Lewis by kind permission of the Wyndham Lewis Memorial Trust (a registered charity); **24** ('The Left Wing Orthodoxy') Reprinted by permission of Lady Spender and the Executors of the Spender Estate; **25** Reprinted by kind permission of Naomi Mitchison; **26** Reprinted by permission of Virago Press (Little, Brown); **27** Extracts from *The World and Ourselves* by Laura Riding. Copyright © 1938 by Laura (Riding) Jackson. Reprinted by permission of the author's Board of Literary Management; **30** Excerpt from *Three Guineas* by Virginia Woolf, copyright 1938 by Harcourt Brace and Company and renewed 1966 by Leonard Woolf, reprinted by permission of the publisher. In UK/EEA by permission of The Society of Authors as the Literary Representative of the Estate of Virginia Woolf; **34** Copyright the Trustees of the Mass-Observation Archive at the University of Sussex. Reproduced by permission of Curtis Brown Ltd, London; **35** Reprinted by permission of Carolyn Rowlinson on behalf of the John Grierson Archive Management Committee, University of Stirling; **36** Reprinted by permission of The Peters Fraser & Dunlop Group Ltd; **38** Copyright © 1937 by Arthur Calder-Marshall. Reproduced by permission of Greene & Heaton Ltd; **39** The Winifred Holtby articles are included with the permission of her literary executors; **40** and **42** Reprinted by permission of Sheed & Ward Ltd; **41** ('Art and the People') Reprinted by kind permission of Rosalind Hague Erangey; **43** Excerpt from *The Idea of a Christian Society*, copyright 1939 by T.S. Eliot and renewed 1967 by Esme Valerie Eliot, reprinted by permission of Harcourt Brace & Company and by permission of Faber and Faber Ltd; **44** Excerpt from 'What I Believe' in *Two Cheers for Democracy*, copyright 1939 and renewed 1967 by E. M. Forster, reprinted by permission of Harcourt Brace & Company, and by permission of The Provost and Scholars of King's College, Cambridge, and The Society of Authors as the Literary Representative of the E. M. Forster Estate; **45** Excerpt from 'Inside the Whale' in *Such, Such Were the Joys* by George Orwell, copyright 1953 by the Estate of Sonia B. Orwell and renewed 1981 by Mrs George K. Perutz, Mrs Miriam Gross and Dr Michael Dickson, Executor for the Estate of Sonia Brownell Orwell, reprinted by permission of Harcourt Brace & Company. UK Copyright © Mark Hamilton as the Literary Executor of the Estate of the Late Sonia Brownell Orwell and Martin Secker & Warburg Ltd.

London, Canada
St David's Day, 1998

FOR PETRA AND COLIN

Introduction

When Beatrix Campbell set out in 1982 to travel on bicycle and train through Coventry, Sunderland, Barnsley and Wigan, she was following – with modifications of her own – a route laid out some fifty years before by 'a posh, lanky young man' making 'a sentimental journey – it was a conjugation of the personal and the political – amidst the supposedly silent majority, the people excluded from politics who appeared as vagrants on the doorstep of democracy'. Her relationship with George Orwell, the young man in question, was a complex one:

> He was an upper-class old Etonian, a southern ex-colonial. I'm from the North, from the working class. Like him, I'm white, I'm a jobbing journalist; unlike him I'm a feminist. I grew up among the kind of communists and socialists who guided him into the working-class communities and who staff some of their struggles. Politics is to me what privilege was to him.

Campbell's *Wigan Pier Revisited: Poverty and Politics in the 80s*[1] was one of the most interesting books to come out of the Thatcher years, when pit closures and spiralling unemployment prompted recollection of the 1930s – both in those who had been alive during that decade, and in those others like Campbell who had come into possession of 'the Thirties' as a package of cultural myths and icons, political commonplaces and 'representative' texts. *Wigan Pier Revisited* was, despite itself, a tribute to certain of those myths – most notably to 'St George Orwell,' that creation of Eric Blair and his critics[2] – but it was also a determined attempt to dismantle them. In marking out the discrepancy between her class and Orwell's, Campbell raised the issue of his paternalism in *The Road to Wigan Pier* (1937) and the refractorily middle-class nature of his values. But the question was one which he had already addressed himself and, indeed, his frankness in acknowledging the visceral distaste he felt for the very people he supported ('The lower classes smell')[3] has long been, paradoxically, an intrinsic part of the myth of Orwell's saintliness. But when Campbell declared herself a feminist she signalled an approach to which his reputation as a deeply humane liberal was more vulnerable. Subsequent studies by Daphne Patai and Deirdre Beddoe[4] have begun to strain both the Orwell myth and the larger 'package' of 1930s myths by inserting into them the complex question of gender politics.

This is a development that presumably would be regretted by Julian Symons, who *did* live through the 1930s but held no particular brief for Orwell. His well-known 'anthology of comments' about the period, *The Thirties*, was first published in 1960 and then slightly revised in 1975; in 1990 he perceived, like Beatrix Campbell, that in some ways the Thatcher years demanded comparison with the 1930s, and reissued the book with a 'Postscript', 'The Thirties and the Nineties'.[5] In the latter he recalled his incredulity during the 1950s when 'lunatic theorists' were suggesting the privatization of the Post Office and the railways; now that 'the lunatic theorists have been in power for a decade,' he observed in 1990, there has occurred an erosion of state power, and the 'nightmarish logic' of the cult of individual freedom has fulfilled itself:

> We offer you freedom to choose, lower taxes and more money to spend, the siren voices say, but the freedom to choose depends on the amount of money you possess, and the extra money in your pocket turns out to be fairy gold. (Symons, p. 151)

Here is evidence for supposing that Symons and Campbell would be much in agreement. But on another issue they would certainly part company, for in Symons's view the currency of terms like *sexist* or *élitist* – and the notion of a 'splintered' society which they predicate – are indications, not of social health, but of a progressive fragmentation of society linked to the pursuit of individual freedom. I am not sure where he would lay the blame: whether on unfettered capitalism and its failure to realize a Just City in which all – men, women, gay, lesbian, rich, poor, black or white – could find justice and a united social identity (whatever that might be), or on those 'splinter' groups themselves for exacerbating the problem with their discourse of difference.

Either way, it is clear that while Campbell's revisiting of Wigan involves a conscious rejection of the homogenizing leftist politics of the 1930s, Symons's 'revolving' of the period (for the third time in as many decades) involves a reassertion of the continuing validity of those politics. In a passage which ought to remind the reader of T. S. Eliot's espousal of 'a certain uniformity of culture' in *The Idea of a Christian Society* (see below, p. 376), Symons recalls an idea 'relevant to the thirties', 'that British intellectual and artistic life took the form of a Pyramid, with a million-strong Audience at its base, Pragmatic worker bees above them, and the Artists at the top point (top in that they were the producers of books, plays and paintings, the Pragmatists often explicators or commentators, the Audience the consumers)'. In the 1990s 'the Audience has changed almost out of recognition, and in changing splintered into separate and at times hostile groups', which is how *sexist, racist, democracy* and *fascist* became 'current cant'. 'Splinters from the Pyramid,' laments Symons, 'make no acknowledgement of a common culture' (pp. 153–4).

Given that the population of the United Kingdom in 1934 was just under 47 million,[6] it is difficult to see Symons's Pyramid as anything other than the self-justifying myth of an intellectual splinter group – of a 'Culture Party', to use Christopher Dawson's memorable term proposed in *Beyond Politics* (1939).[7] If the remaining 46 million people were not at the base of the Pyramid, where were they? Were not those artists and Pragmatic worker bees merely deluding themselves when they imagined that civilization would stand or fall with the Pyramid? John Cornford, replying in 1933 to F. R. Leavis's claim that it would, said 'no' and reminded him about those pesky millions getting on with their own lives (see below, p. 16). And before leaving Symons's 1990 argument, it is worth noting that the claim he makes for the fundamental unity and homogeneity of opinion in the 1930s is betrayed by his own mention of a group of 'Thirties' Pragmatists', whose descendants he tells us exist today, eroding and undermining the belief that works of art are 'the fine flowers of a civilization whose proper glory [is] . . . free speech' (p. 154). Evidently there were those, even in the 1930s, who did not agree with Leavis and Symons that 'the possibilities of fine living at any time bear a close relation' to high achievements of the few in art and literature. In fact, as Leavis famously put it in *Mass Civilisation and Minority Culture* (1930), 'the minority now is made conscious, not merely of an uncongenial, but of a hostile environment' (see below, p. 21). Yet Symons would suggest that hostility of this sort is peculiar to the splintery 1990s, and was notably absent from the 1930s scene.

The cause of Symons's mythologization of that decade is surely no mystery. Whatever unknowable personal motives underlie his 'Postscript', it is also clear – because explicit – that he writes in reaction against the uncertainties and the malignities of recent British social history. Whereas Beatrix Campbell concentrates on the malignities, partly embracing uncertainty in the hope that it might provide an opening for revolutionary change, Symons sees poverty and suffering as causally related to the absence of certainty. In that, he rehearses the 'rage for order' of the 1930s (see below, p. 345), and his vision of that decade comes to serve him in the present as the idea of an 'organic community' served Leavis, or as Eliot's 'Christian Society' served him: as a firm basis for evaluation, judgement and 'discrimination' in an historical context which seems to deny the viability of such things.

It must be said that to the same degree that Campbell is aware of dismantling a myth, Symons is conscious of perpetuating one (not exactly the same, but a related one). The very first paragraph of his 'Postscript' is a defence of a label which he tells us he pins to his chest without reservation: 'A Man of the Thirties' (p. 145). Though he would hate to hear it put this way, there is something distinctly postmodern in that kind of self-conscious use of a cliché; and though he would approve this even less, it would be worthwhile to compare that act of self-definition with the way in which other phenomena in contemporary culture have exploited the iconography of the 1930s. Some readers will remember, perhaps, the way in which the BBC recycled images from that most famous of all 1930s documentaries, *Night Mail*, in advertising itself on television in the mid-1980s. And is it possible to look without astonishment at magazine clothing advertisements imitating the black-and-white photographs which Humphrey Spender took of working-class life in Bolton in 1936–7? Campbell includes in her book an extraordinary example of that sort of thing: a 1983 reworking of Bert Hardy's famous *Picture Post* photograph, *Wigan, 1938*,[8] faithful to the original in every way, except the dress of the figures. Where the original man wore miner's clogs and battered tweeds, his descendant in the 1980s is stylishly dressed in calf shoes (price listed at £45), 'hand-made Donegal tweed echo[ing] the romantic look of the Thirties' (suit: £225), and various other adornments of cashmere, wool and linen (total: £91). 'HARD TIMES–' runs the byline, 'SOFT LOOKS'. Even as one concedes that this use of the period is very different from Symons's, one still has to insist that there is a similarity: something is being sold in his case – not clothes, perhaps, but a political or cultural idea – and the decade is being mythologized or iconized to that end.

More than three decades ago, in the introduction to his well-known Penguin anthology *Poetry of the Thirties*, Robin Skelton noted that 'even before they were quite over, the 1930s took on the appearance of myth': 'it is rare for a decade to be so self-conscious' (p. 13). One thing of which almost all writers were conscious during those years was that they were working in the midst of a new era in which advertising, marketing and the mass media had become immensely and (perhaps) irreversibly powerful forces in the formation of social life. Some, like F. R. Leavis and many others whose work is collected in this book, defined themselves by their opposition to those forces; but even they, in what Q. D. Leavis called 'the conscious and directed effort . . . by an armed and conscious minority',[9] readily and expertly employed the techniques of advertising and marketing. 'Leavisism', for example, represents a body of thought and literary–cultural practice, naturally, but it also stands for one of the most successfully advertised and disseminated products of the academy in the twentieth century – one all the more remarkable for having been from beginning to end a kind of family business, with its board meetings held over tea in the Leavis home at No. 6, Chesterton Hall Crescent, Cambridge. The innumerable manifestos and tracts issued from almost every quarter in Britain during the 1930s testify that it was the first Great Age of Advertising, although 'propaganda' was the term preferred in intellectual circles for the marketing of ideology. Sylvia Townsend Warner saw more clearly than many of her contemporaries the way in which ideas can be – and are – commodified, and in her essay on 'Man's Moral Law' (see below, pp. 89–100) she was able to point out what, besides leather, men buy when they purchase 'dogged steadfast' boots.

In *Dividing Lines: Poetry, Class and Ideology in the 1930s*, Adrian Caesar has traced very well the recent marketing and advertising history of what is undoubtedly the 1930s top-selling cultural product – the literary–historical myth that the work of the so-called 'Auden group' was the sum of all that was great, good and enduring in that decade's literary output. Caesar attributes the continuing life of that myth in recent years to Samuel Hynes's *The Auden Generation* (1972), a rightly influential book not to be blamed for subsequent critics' failure effectively to broaden its terms of reference. Bernard Bergonzi's *Reading the Thirties*, two years later, followed Hynes in declaring that 'Auden's centrality in the literary life of the thirties seems to me unmistakable' (p. 8) – this notwithstanding the acute understanding of literary–historical myth-making Bergonzi was later to show in his analysis of Modernism.[10] There have of course been attempts, as Caesar puts it, to 'penetrate the canonical view' of the decade, notably John Lucas's *The 1930s: A Challenge to Orthodoxy* (1978), and the grand Cunningham book, *British Writers of the Thirties*.[11] But even the latter, Caesar argues persuasively, finally leaves it 'to the reader to infer that Auden *et al.* are more "central"' to the 1930s than the group of left-wing writers dealt with in the Lucas book (p. 3). A rather more satisfying attempt to construe the 1930s in a way that does not accord Auden quite the usual position of dominance has appeared since Caesar wrote: this is Janet Montefiore's *Men and Women Writers of the 1930s: The Dangerous Flood of History* (1996).[12] Auden is discussed there, but not – as would be the customary approach – as synecdoche for the whole age.

Although it is obligatory for an author at this point in an introduction to damn his precursors and describe the brave and bright new intellectual world he himself is about to open up, I cannot do that. In the first place Hynes, whom some would want to blame for constructing the 'Auden Generation' myth, drew frank attention to what he was doing. 'To write about the *literary* existence of a generation,' he wrote, 'is to accept a necessary restriction of subject: you will be writing almost entirely about middle-class members of the generation' (p. 10). In the second place it has to be said that the provenance of the myth in question is to be discovered decades before Hynes wrote about it, in the 1930s themselves. When Michael Roberts wrote to John Lehmann to say that he saw similarities between recently published poems by Lehmann himself and those of Auden and Day Lewis, perhaps it was the moment of conception. Certainly, the volume which came out of that correspondence – the famous *New Signatures* of 1934 – is conventionally taken to mark the birth of the 'Auden Generation' (see below, p. 45). Yeats undoubtedly played his part in nurturing the growth of the myth when he declared, in his introduction to *The Oxford Book of Modern Verse* (1936), that he knew of 'no school where poets so closely resemble each other' (see below, p. 53). And Roy Campbell, whose contribution to the literary history of the period would never surpass this one act, wittily joined Auden, Spender, Day Lewis and MacNeice together at the pen in his sobriquet, 'MacSpaunday'. Positive propaganda from Roberts, negative publicity from Campbell and Wyndham Lewis: such things, reinforced by Auden's own not inconsiderable powers of self-advertisement, gave rise to the decade's dominant literary-cultural myth. The process was an intrinsic part of the 1930s own self-imagining, which brings us back to Skelton's key point – that even before they were over, the decade had acquired 'the appearance of myth'. It also brings us back to Hynes's and other critical appraisals of the period, since whatever criticism one might wish to make of them must be tempered by the thought that at some level the 1930s *was* its myths and is unknowable outside of them. So Beatrix Campbell, juxtaposing the Bert Hardy photograph with its fashion-ad travesty, astutely asks: 'Which is fact, which is fantasy?'[13]

Even as one concedes the unanswerability of this question in absolute terms, one is likely still to feel the need to improve one's understanding of the relationship of one myth to others within the culture, and of these to the material conditions out of which they arise – which would not, admittedly, be to achieve an apprehension of 'fact', but a functional substitute for it. Something illuminating occurs when Campbell brings the left-wing myths of the 1930s into contact with the fruits of Tory myth-making in Thatcher's Britain: we see the naivety and culpability – yet also the humanity – of the lower-upper-middle-class Orwell; and we also grasp the complement or the inverse of that humanity in the harsh rationality of free-enterprise capitalism. It is as if when such social myths collide, or are brought into contention or dialogue with each other, they break open and reveal something of their hidden contents. Julian Symons demonstrates this, too, when presumably for reasons of his own peace of mind he actively mythologizes a 'splintered' present by asserting the existence, sixty years in the past, of an ordered, inclusive system of cultural production and consumption – a pyramidal 'common culture'. It is his very insistence on the exclusivity of 'splinter' groups in the 1990s that prompts one to interrogate his model of the 1930s, and to ask that embarrassing question about the other 46 million people who seem to have managed to survive outside the 'common culture'. Perhaps they had their own shared myths and common terms of reference, one begins to wonder, and from that point on Symons's Leavisite cosmology can seem no more a matter of 'fact' than the Ptolemaic one.

The lesson here is that the credibility of such cultural myths depends directly upon a great deal of complicating and uncooperative data being rendered – and kept – invisible. In *Robbery under Law* (1939), Evelyn Waugh percipiently commented that this form of myth-making is in fact endemic and inevitable in an age of mass media: 'When a crisis is announced,' he wrote, 'we hastily turn to our atlases and look out the new danger spot. We feel that these sudden explosions of international enmity, first in one part of the world, then another, are as wantonly strewn about the map as the bombs of the I.R.A. We have not the time to watch them as historical events in a series of cause and effect' (see below, p. 195). The same is true of 'sudden explosions' on the cultural scene, and of the way in which writers and movements are mediated to us through the vast, commercialized mechanism of publishing, reviewing, marketing, and (one of its adjunct industries) academic criticism and study. The 'Auden Generation' myth has come into its power and influence partly through the very process of abstraction from the 'series of [historical] cause and effect' which Waugh describes. This is paradoxical since a key element in the myth is the idea that the component parts of 'MacSpaunday' were, for the 1930s at least, deeply committed to history and to the politics of their time. Myths beget myths, and Auden's declaration in the 1939 elegy for Yeats that 'poetry makes nothing happen' has often been read, in the sway of presumptions about the intensity of his earlier commitment, as a kind of political apostasy. Stan Smith describes the two sorts of 'moral fable' that are then told about Auden: one concerning a decent middle-class man who falls into the 'bad company' of Marxists and Freudians, only to return to respectability after a shocking encounter with anticlerical violence in the Spanish Civil War; another featuring 'a petty-bourgeois intellectual born into the dying culture of a declining empire', who briefly identifies with the 'international working-class struggle' before retreating to the 'Christian pietism of his origins [and] emigrating to an America which was now the ascendant imperialist power.'[14] In both of those accounts the ideological freight of the teller is as obvious as it is different from the other, but the important point to notice is that the narrative structure which both project upon Auden's career involves a kind of dramatic peripeteia or reversal; and in that both contribute to the mythologization of the man, the reduction of a complex life to a 'sudden explosion'.

To plot the full 'sequence of cause and effect' in which that moment in Auden's career was actually embedded has been the task of his biographers, and the more one knows of those causes and effects the less real and dramatic does the peripeteia come to be. But while those two moral fables about him are by now effectively discredited (Stan Smith's *W. H. Auden* reveals a deep continuity in the career which makes nonsense of such views), the myth of Auden's own centrality in the decade remains surprisingly vital, notwithstanding Caesar, Cunningham and the rest. The reasons for this, as I have begun to suggest, are both theoretical and practical, and closely related to what has been said about the operation of myth in the shaping of his own career. If one dismantles the fiction of a personal peripeteia by rejecting the idea that in life 'explosions' are ever 'sudden', then perhaps it holds in some way true that a literary–critical fiction, like the 'Auden Generation', having served its purpose and begun to take on a life of its own, might usefully be dealt with in an analogous way. Put bluntly, could we not now watch what happens to that myth when we say (as Waugh said about the troubles in Mexico), 'despite what we have been told, this is not exceptional, it is part of a larger discourse'? Cecil Day Lewis comments (see below, p. 277) on certain tenacious assumptions in the English literary tradition, and I dare say even in the late 1990s it might be too much to ask that we abandon entirely the cherished Romantic notion of the artist as an exceptional individual and of that person's acts as, by definition, *extra*ordinary. Nor is it really necessary to do so, for in arguing as I do I have no interest in the question of Auden's inherent value as a writer; I greatly enjoy reading him and others of his group and find much to admire. But my concern is with the myth which has been constructed around him, and with what that myth is not allowing us to 'see' of the 1930s. Once again I am interested in those 46 million people Symons leaves out of his pyramidal paradigm, not in this instance the people specifically, but what they represent – the *cost* of myth-making, or the invisible labour, if you like, that lies behind a single heavily advertised literary product.

There is a striking passage in Orwell's *Down and Out in Paris and London* (1933) in which he records a scene in Limehouse that was typical of the period. In 'the land of the tea-urn and the Labour Exchange', there were

> Orientals – Chinamen, Chittagonian lascars, Dravidians selling silk scarves, even a few Sikhs, come goodness knows how. Here and there were street meetings. In Whitechapel somebody called the Singing Evangel undertook to save you from hell for the charge of a sixpence. In the East India Dock Road the Salvation Army were holding a service. They were singing 'Anybody here like sneaking Judas?' to the tune of 'What's to be done with a drunken sailor?' On Tower Hill two Mormons were trying to address a meeting. Round their platform struggled a mob of men, shouting and interrupting. Someone was denouncing them for polygamists. A lame, bearded man, evidently an atheist, had heard the word God and was heckling angrily. There was a confused uproar of voices.[15]

It is a world like the one Orwell would describe in *Road to Wigan Pier* – one in which women are noticeably silent, that is – but, even so, the sense of raucous diversity and vehement contention is powerfully evoked. With some qualifications I take this passage to be close to the spirit of the period, an 'uproar of voices' – sometimes confused and sometimes not, but always loud – being a kind of aural emblem for the age. Thinking again of Humphrey Spender's 'Worktown' photographs, I am struck by how often they show us people in voluble groups – in the pub, at a football match, around the front gate, on the hustings, at union meetings and even at temperance gatherings. As in Orwell's world, these discussions seem to be much about social and political issues; as Symons tells us (is he mythologizing or is he not?), 1930s disputes and debates 'always had behind them the idea of the Just City, in which we should consent to the necessary limiting of individual freedom in the service of a virtuous strictness' (p. 152).

It seems crucial to insist that Auden, who also acknowledged his desire 'to build the Just City' ('Spain 1937')[16] and who could imagine 'a *civitas* of sound' ('New Year Letter'),[17] was simply one voice in this extended and noisy conversation. And it is crucial not only for our understanding of the period, so long hampered by the hegemonic influence of the 'Auden Generation' paradigm, but also for our grasp of Auden himself. After all, both his tendency to conflate revolutionary and religious discourse and his end-of-decade return to Anglicanism will inevitably come to seem less idiosyncratic and more in line with the currents of the age when we read him within a context that includes the Christian Socialism of Eric Gill and the Catholic Idealism of

Christopher Dawson. Gill and Dawson were two prominent figures in cultural circles during the 1930s, and both pursued their own visions of the Just City, Gill going so far as to found several experimental communities and then to declare he had found 'a human city which was in some sort a holy city' at Salies-de-Béarn in the French Pyrenees.[18] Cunningham's massive study of the period mentions Gill only once, Dawson not at all – despite the fact that two of his books obliquely addressing the much-discussed 'cultural crisis' in Europe (*Progress and Religion* [1929] and *The Age of the Gods* [1933]) brought him considerable celebrity. It is one of the more interesting effects of still-prevailing myths about the period that religious movements and writers, except perhaps for T. S. Eliot, are typically left out of consideration, even when their influence may have been considerable at the time, and even when a critic's stated desire is to explode limiting paradigms. Perhaps our own age is not disposed to see the presumption of universal atheism as a limiting myth in itself. Certainly, to remove Auden from the centre of the decade will undoubtedly be easier to accomplish than to rehabilitate for study some of those religious voices which, as the passage from Orwell makes clear, spoke loudly and often.

Since I have now twice mentioned the question of Orwell and women, it would be as well to comment here on the general issue of women's place in myths of the period, and in particular on the ways in which those myths came into being in part through the exclusion of female voices. It has often been noticed that of the 287 pages of poems in Skelton's *Poetry of the Thirties*, no more than five or six come from a woman's hand – and this when the rich possibilities since included by Jane Dowson in her *Women's Poetry of the 1930s* (1996) were available. Cunningham endorses the view that women's poetry of the period was 'modest', but he also makes the more valuable point that 'the myth of the Auden Generation, in choosing by and large to leave out novelists,' drastically excludes women. 'The novel,' he writes, 'in the 1930s as in the whole period since the form established itself in Britain, was the classic medium of the woman writer'; 'the neglected sister [an allusion to Woolf on Shakespeare's sister] was finding her modern voice in the 20s and 30s, and her critical and editorial brother was still trying to stifle it' (p. 26). Undoubtedly that last point is in many ways true, but one should not lose sight of the fact that the neglected sister, in some cases, was herself an editor with considerable influence: Storm Jameson, for example, was for many years head of the British branch of Alfred Knopf, the giant American publisher. The continuing power of the 'Auden Generation' myth testifies to the efficacy with which the voices of women were stifled, but the means by which that was accomplished is a good deal more complex than Cunningham's wording implies. Certainly it had much to do with 'high' culture's valorization of poetry over prose during that and subsequent decades, but in theorizing the silencing of women writers it would be a mistake in any way to isolate that issue (like another 'sudden explosion') from broader questions of gender politics in the 1930s. For example, there is much to be gained from considering the issue of women in publishing in the light of Naomi Mitchison's 1934 essay on the home, which is included in this volume (see below, pp. 227–39); of particular relevance is her critique of the phenomenon of 'social ownership' as the cause of women's oppression in home and marriage. We speak of publishing *houses*, and Mitchison's understanding of 'ownership' within the home suggests, by analogy, ways of understanding not just the economic but also the psychoanalytic dimension of gender politics in publishing. Storm Jameson worked 'within the house', as it were, but so did Stevie Smith, who joined Sir Neville Pearson's publishing firm in or around 1923.[19] Of the two women it was Smith whose power in the 'house' was by far the lesser; yet it was also she, with many fewer publications to her credit and much less involvement in the international literary scene, who finally achieved the greater prominence as a writer. She wrote poetry, not prose, which may explain the readiness of male critics to 'own' her work, however qualifiedly, while they 'disown' Jameson's; but she also, for complex reasons, liked to play the child in the house, which might also have been a factor – and might still be one – in the making of her reputation.

It is an indication, once again, of Orwell's blind spot for women that he believed 'no decade in the past hundred and fifty years has been so barren of imaginative prose as the nineteen-thirties'. It was a decade, he commented sweepingly in *Inside the Whale* (see below, p. 389), that had produced 'practically no fiction of any value at all'. There had been 'good poems', he said in the same essay, but implied there had been no great ones, and all this presumably for the reason that 'on the whole the literary history of the thirties seems to justify the opinion that a writer does well to keep out of politics'. This is Orwell in reactionary mode, sounding self-consciously old-fashioned in his use of the discourse of a nineteenth-century-style aestheticism; just how much against the grain of his time this was becomes clear when we read such pronouncements beside Alick West's more-or-less contemporary attempt to rescue 'aesthetic feeling' from 'the bourgeois conception of aesthetic value' (see below, p. 133). For West, literature is to be judged as 'both content and form' in relation to 'humanity in its advance to socialism', and that is essentially the view taken by Storm Jameson in her novels of the 1930s, and even by the less obviously politicized Sylvia Townsend Warner in books like *Summer Will*

Show (1936). Orwell evidently saw little in those writers to applaud, and probably for the same reason – his resistance to orthodoxy – held no brief for male novelists like Walter Brierley and Walter Greenwood. If it might on that basis be argued he was gender-blind in his execrations, it is just as easy to endorse recent critical views that regard his bristly individualism itself as part of an ongoing process of masculinist self-imagining.

There is one form of writing from the 1930s which Orwell does praise enthusiastically, however, and with that we come directly to the point of this anthology. It was an age, he writes, of 'good sociological works, [and] brilliant pamphlets' (see below, p. 389). It is fascinating, as one looks over the material collected here, to notice how much energy during those years seems to have been devoted to reconceiving inherited forms so as to make them responsive to the particular demands of the time. The debate over 'proletarian writing' is a key illustration of this: What is it? Who is qualified to produce it? Who actually is able to produce it? Can 'proletarian' art have aesthetic 'value', traditionally defined? Are 'highbrows' forever shut out of the realm of true 'proletarian' art? But is that art? And so on. The answers to such questions sometimes achieve the kind of virtuoso convolutedness one expects to find in only the best self-justifying rationalizations. 'Politically-amorous' bourgeois critics (Kermode's phrase)[20] are often bent on having their aesthetic cake and eating it, too: why else should West be so reluctant to give up aesthetics as a category of literary analysis, or why must Ralph Fox 'save' the novel for socialism? At the root of this dilemma (for it is a single problem that takes on many shapes) is the fundamental inability of many of these writers to imagine literature outside their inherited if despised canons of value, however sincere their commitment to achieving what Auden in a poem of the period described as 'New styles of architecture, a change of heart'.[21] In fact, the 1930s as a whole provides a marvellous illustration of what Thomas Kuhn had to say about the self-perpetuating nature of intellectual paradigms.[22]

Yet while in critical prose and inflammatory pamphlets the writers of the 1930s struggled to come to terms with – and reverse – the declining vitality of poetry and the novel, they incidentally produced high achievements in traditionally undervalued genres. And this anthology has been assembled in agreement with Orwell's most persuasive point – that writing about literature, culture, and the interconnectedness of both with politics, was in fact what the age demanded, to paraphrase Pound, and that it is where the age – despite its own preoccupations – excelled. Now, Cunningham's point about the link between the 'Auden Generation' myth and the valorization of one genre over another is an excellent one, and this project has also been undertaken in the belief that an approach to the period through its journalism, criticism and cultural analysis will have an intellectually emancipating effect, loosening the hold not only of that one particular myth but also of others that enjoy currency and influence beyond their due. I wrote near the start of this introduction that the 1930s, strictly speaking, is unknowable outside of its own myths and those made up about it, and lest I become carried away by my rhetoric I must restate that here. The myth that places Auden front and centre in the period is the one at which most of my fire has been directed so far, but the aim of this project has not been to remove him from the scene altogether. What has been objected to here, and in this I echo what seems to be a growing critical consensus, is merely Auden's place in a totalizing vision of the 1930s, one which excludes *other* visions, silences the 'uproar of voices'. So what has been assembled in this book is a body of myths, counter-myths, and what might be called 'inter-myths' about society and culture in the 1930s, formed in the heat of those very years; and the aim is to make it possible to listen to snatches from the indeterminate, multivocal conversation which the decade conducted with itself about itself.

It has not hitherto been easy to do that, especially in the classroom, which brings me in closing to consider those 'practical' issues which I referred to at the outset, and which will further explain the genesis of this book. The factors which go into the construction and perpetuation of a myth like the 'Auden Generation' are in part at least ideological and hence intangible, and all scholars are familiar with the particular difficulties involved in overcoming such intangibles, in re-forming what is essentially intellectual prejudice. At the same time – and as several of the writers included here saw very clearly – myths as a body of ideas about literature, say, are inextricably bound to the material conditions of production: those who control the means of publication to a large extent determine the formation of whatever myths will come to dominate the field. Thus Stephen Spender: 'From a tactical point of view, there is a great deal to be said for the Left becoming respectable, for the writers' meetings being adorned by the golden features of Sir Hugh Walpole, for Cecil Day Lewis being on the Council of the Book Society, for W. H. Auden going to Buckingham Palace to receive the King's Medal. It is really simply a question of whether in the process of absorption the Left absorbs the representatives of the ruling classes, or whether they absorb the Left' (see below, p. 222). If the myth of an 'Auden Generation' began with a decision at the Hogarth Press to publish *New Signatures*, it grew in strength as its members achieved prominence first on the lists, and then on the boards, of influential publishers. Through that kind of 'absorption' into the structures of ideological and economic power, the myth achieved a hegemony all the more inescapable for its blandly practical ramifications: people, if they read poetry at all, read the poetry that is published and most widely distributed, most prominently reviewed. And while in every decade there are small presses publishing work from outside the mainstream, it seems generally true that the passage of time will efface that material long before the productions of the large houses begin to disappear from private and public shelves. In other words, time contributes to the production of literary myths simply because it progressively reduces the number of voices from a period that a scholar can hear. The problem can be solved for individuals with a visit to the archive, but what is to be done for non-specialist scholars, and for students, who need to be offered a knowledge of the period at least as inclusive as Orwell's Limehouse experience?

Cunningham rightly applauds Virago Press for trawling 'most impressively and fruitfully in the novel catalogues' of the 1930s (p. 26), and the Feminist Press in New York has made a considerable contribution to the reassessment of the decade through its publication of the novels of Katharine Burdekin.[23] Dowson's *Women's Poetry of the Thirties* is widely available as well, so it is today more possible than ever in the past to make a study of the 1930s – especially to teach a course in the period—that escapes the stultifying paradigm centred on Auden. Women are being heard again in the age's uproar; others, like miner novelist Lewis Jones or 'proletarian writers' such as Brierley, are hard to hear in practice, their books being expensive and difficult to acquire, even when technically available. But these are the genres which, as Orwell pointed out, did not flourish in the decade. Where the period *did* in his view achieve distinction – in criticism, manifestos and pamphlets – there has until now been no concerted effort at republication. And this has seemed to me and many others a glaring absence, a serious obstacle to any real broadening of understanding about the period. By 'real' I mean 'effective', but also 'widespread', because it seems obvious to me that the narrow myth of the period will continue to prevail in classrooms, despite our best intentions, so long as the material for a revaluation is not available in a convenient and affordable form. I know many instructors have tried to make this aspect of 1930s literary work available by photocopying; and that is better to do than not, but the hegemony of a myth buttressed by major publishing houses is in no way threatened by the ephemeral productions of a Xerox machine. Stimulated by what I have found for myself in the archive, and excited by the new ways in which I have been forced to conceive of the 1930s, I have assembled this anthology in the hope that it will indicate something of the multiplicity and the dialogic nature of cultural speculation during those years. Indeed, besides the general principle that I did not wish to reprint too much material that is already available, I have been principally guided in my selections by the desire to include essays which in some sense 'talk' to each other, and the lines along which those conversations run are indicated by notes. It will at least be clear, I hope, that Auden's voice was never solitary or 'inviolate'. If he can be said to 'speak for' the decade, that is only because so many other voices are to be heard in his. In this volume their words are printed under their own names.

Notes

1. London: Virago, 1984. Quotations are from pp. 1–2, 5.
2. Here see Rodden's superb book on Orwell and 'the politics of literary reputation'.
3. The famous declaration from Part II of *The Road to Wigan Pier* (Harmondsworth: Penguin, 1989), p. 119.
4. See Patai, *The Orwell Mystique: A Study in Male Ideology*; Beddoe, 'Hindrances and Help-meets: Women in the Writings of George Orwell', in Norris, pp. 139–54.
5. *The Thirties and the Nineties* (Manchester: Carcanet Press, 1990), pp. 143–84.
6. Thorpe (1994) gives figures from *Statistical Abstract* 80 (1937): 4–5.
7. London: Sheed and Ward, 1939, reprinted Freeport: Books for Libraries Press, 1970, p. 26. T. S. Eliot discusses Dawson's 'Culture Party' in an interesting note to *The Idea of a Christian Society*. See *Christianity and Culture*, pp. 59–60.
8. The picture is reproduced on the cover of Penguin's Twentieth-Century Classics edition of *The Road to Wigan Pier*.
9. *Fiction and the Reading Public*, p. 270.
10. *The Myth of Modernism and Twentieth Century Literature* (Brighton: Harvester Press, 1986).
11. Valentine Cunningham, *British Writers of the Thirties* (Oxford: Oxford University Press, 1988).
12. London: Routledge, 1996.
13. *Wigan Pier Revisited*, between pp. 114 and 115.
14. Smith, *W.H. Auden*, p. 1.
15. George Orwell, *Down and Out in Paris and London* (1933; Harmondsworth: Penguin, 1989), p. 136.
16. *The English Auden*, p. 211.
17. *Collected Poems*, ed. Mendelson, p. 200.
18. See the 'Postscript' to his *Autobiography*, especially pp. 244–9. His principal communities were founded at Ditchling, Sussex, and at Capel-y-ffin in the Black Mountains of Wales.
19. See Barbera and McBrien, *Stevie*, pp. 41–2.
20. See Frank Kermode, *History and Value*, pp. 40–1, for his rich discussion of the 1930s bourgeoisie and its 'love for the proletariat'.
21. 'Sir, no man's enemy, forgiving all', *The English Auden*, p. 36. Included by Skelton in *Poetry of the Thirties*, p. 201.
22. In *The Structure of Scientific Revolutions* (Chicago: University of Chicago Press, 1962).
23. Here see Daphne Patai, 'Imagining Reality: The Utopian Fiction of Katharine Burdekin', in Ingram and Patai, pp. 226–43.

1 F. R. Leavis *from **Mass Civilisation and Minority Culture** (1930)**

In 1930 Leavis was just beginning his long period of influence at Cambridge. *Mass Civilisation and Minority Culture* and *D. H. Lawrence* (also 1930) were the first of a series of pamphlets in which Leavis began to analyse the manifestations and causes of a broad cultural crisis into which, he argued, Britain and Europe had now come. His approach – reaching consistently outwards from literature to consider its social and cultural setting – was in many respects the natural outgrowth of the reform of the Cambridge English Tripos: as an undergraduate, Leavis moved from History to English in 1920, just three years after the reform was passed. He was later to remark that his journal *Scrutiny* (founded in 1932 and committed to 'a cultivated historical sense, [and] a familiarity with the "anthropological" approach to contemporary civilisation')[1] was 'a product, the triumphant justifying achievement, of the English Tripos'.[2]

Leavis's PhD, submitted in 1924, was concerned with issues which figure prominently in *Mass Civilisation and Minority Culture*: his dissertation title was 'The Relationship of Journalism to Literature: Studies in the Rise and Earlier Development of the Press in England'. He makes the point below that 'it is a commonplace today that culture is at a crisis', and in 1930 he conceived of that crisis in Arnoldian terms, as a conflict between the spiritually and socially redemptive force of literature on the one hand, and mass civilization and its agencies (of which the popular press was one) on the other. Anne Samson has pointed out, however, that while few at the time would have disagreed with Leavis about the existence of a crisis, 'the causes, nature and duration of this state of affairs were perhaps less easily agreed upon' (p. 36).[3] John Cornford, for example, argued the radical position that the 'crisis' diagnosed by figures like Leavis was a phantom produced by class-consciousness:

> The bourgeois writers are acutely conscious that they belong to a declining
> class, for they are the most sensitive of the bourgeois ideologists; as it were
> the antennae of bourgeois culture. Owing to their isolation, however, this
> consciousness is not interpreted objectively as the decline of their class. It
> seems the decline of 'culture', of 'civilisation'. They cling to what seems the
> one stable element in a collapsing world, their own literary tradition.[4]

Despite the many different ways in which the cultural crisis was conceived, it is interesting to notice how pervasive was the influence of *Mass Civilisation and*

* Reprinted from *Mass Civilisation and Minority Culture* (Cambridge: Minority Press [Gordon Fraser], 1930), pp. 3–11, 25–6 and 30–2.

Minority Culture: one is of course not surprised to see whole sentences from the pamphlet quoted with approval in Q. D. Leavis's *Fiction and the Reading Public* (see below, p. 181), but there are also clear echoes of Leavis in, for example, Ralph Fox's *The Novel and the People* (see below, p. 150), particularly in his concern for what the former refers to as a 'levelling-down' of the reading public. Auden, too, came for a while under Leavis's sway (see below, p. 39), and there are intersections between Leavis and other writers which are evidence, if not of his influence, at least of shared concerns: Norman Angell, for instance, is cited by Leavis below for his work on *The Press and the Organisation of Society,* and by Vera Brittain (see below, p. 71) for his views on 'the moral obligation to be intelligent'.

Leavis and Communists like Fox may not have agreed entirely on the origins of the crisis, but especially in the early 1930s there was the possibility of agreement between them over both the nature of the problem and possible solutions: Leavis was open to the idea of 'some kind of communism', although not as represented by the Communist Party of Great Britain.[5] However, when in 1933 *Mass Civilisation and Minority Culture* was reprinted by Leavis in *For Continuity*,[6] it was surrounded by other pieces ('Marxism and Cultural Continuity' and 'Under Which King, Bezonian?'), which ruled out all possibility of a meeting between Marxism and Leavisism. The history of the latter is from that point on a chronicle of increasingly intractible – sometimes embattled – individualism.

In any period it is upon a very small minority that the discerning appreciation of art and literature depends: it is (apart from cases of the simple and familiar) only a few who are capable of unprompted, first-hand judgement. They are still a small minority, though a larger one, who are capable of endorsing such first-hand judgement by genuine personal response. The accepted valuations are a kind of paper currency based upon a very small proportion of gold. To the state of such a currency the possibilities of fine living at any time bear a close relation. There is no need to elaborate the metaphor: the nature of the relation is suggested well enough by this passage from Mr. I. A. Richards, which should now be a *locus classicus*:

> But it is not true that criticism is a luxury trade. The rearguard of Society cannot be extricated until the vanguard has gone further. Goodwill and intelligence are still too little available. The critic, we have said, is as much concerned with the health of the mind as any doctor with the health of the body. To set up as a critic is to set up as a judge of values . . . For the arts are inevitably and quite apart from any intentions of the artist an appraisal of existence. Matthew Arnold, when he said that poetry is a criticism of

life, was saying something so obvious that it is constantly overlooked. The
artist is concerned with the record and perpetuation of the experiences which
seem to him most worth having. For reasons which we shall consider . . .
he is also the man who is most likely to have experiences of value to record.
He is the point at which the growth of the mind shows itself.[7]

This last sentence gives the hint for another metaphor. The minority capable
not only of appreciating Dante, Shakespeare, Donne, Baudelaire, Hardy (to
take major instances) but of recognising their latest successors constitute the
consciousness of the race (or a branch of it) at a given time. For such capacity
does not belong merely to an isolated aesthetic realm: it implies responsiveness
to theory as well as to art, to science and philosophy in so far as these may
affect the sense of the human situation and of the nature of life. Upon this
minority depends our power of profiting by the finest human experience of
the past; they keep alive the subtlest and most perishable parts of tradition.
Upon them depend the implicit standards that order the finer living of an age,
the sense that this is worth more than that, this rather than that is the direction
in which to go, that the centre[8] is here rather than there. In their keeping, to
use a metaphor that is metonymy also and will bear a good deal of pondering,
is the language, the changing idiom, upon which fine living depends, and
without which distinction of spirit is thwarted and incoherent. By 'culture' I
mean the use of such a language. I do not suppose myself to have produced
a tight definition, but the account, I think, will be recognised as adequate by
anyone who is likely to read this pamphlet.

It is a commonplace today that culture is at a crisis. It is a commonplace
more widely accepted than understood: at any rate, realisation of what the
crisis portends does not seem to be common. I am, for instance, sometimes
answered that it has all happened before, during the Alexandrian period, or
under the Roman Empire. Even if this were true it would hardly be reassuring,
and I note the contention mainly in order to record my suspicion that it comes
from Spengler,[9] where, of course, authority may also be found for an attitude
of proud philosophical indifference. For Spengler, the inexorable cycle moves
once more to its inevitable end. But the common absence of concern for what
is happening is not to be explained by erudition or philosophy. It is itself a
symptom, and a phrase for it comes aptly to hand in Mr. H. G. Wells' new
book, *The Autocracy of Mr. Parham*: 'Essentially it was a vast and increasing
inattention.'

It seems, then, not unnecessary to restate the obvious. In support of the
belief that the modern phase of human history is unprecedented it is enough

to point to the machine. The machine, in the first place, has brought about change in habit and the circumstances of life at a rate for which we have no parallel. The effects of such a change may be studied in *Middletown*, a remarkable work of anthropology, dealing (I am afraid it is not superfluous to say) with a typical community of the Middle West. There we see in detail how the automobile (to take one instance) has, in a few years, radically affected religion,[10] broken up the family, and revolutionised social custom. Change has been so catastrophic that the generations find it hard to adjust themselves to each other, and parents are helpless to deal with their children. It seems unlikely that the conditions of life can be transformed in this way without some injury to the standard of living (to wrest the phrase from the economist): improvisation can hardly replace the delicate traditional adjustments, the mature, inherited codes of habit and evaluation, without severe loss, and loss that may be more than temporary. It is a breach in continuity that threatens: what has been inadvertently dropped may be irrecoverable or forgotten.

To this someone will reply that Middletown is America and not England. And it is true that in America change has been more rapid, and its effects have been intensified by the fusion of peoples. But the same processes are at work in England and the western world generally, and at an acceleration. It is a commonplace that we are being Americanised, but again a commonplace that seems, as a rule, to carry little understanding with it. Americanisation is often spoken of as if it is something of which the United States are guilty. But it is something from which Lord Melchett, our 'British-speaking'[11] champion, will not save us even if he succeeds in rallying us to meet that American enterprise which he fears, 'may cause us to lose a great structure of self-governing brother-hoods whose common existence is of infinite importance to the future continuance of the Anglo-Saxon race, and of the gravest import to the development of all that seems best in our modern civilisation.'[12] For those who are most defiant of America do not propose to reverse the processes consequent upon the machine. We are to have greater efficiency, better salesmanship, and more mass-production and standardisation. Now, if the worst effects of mass-production and standardisation were represented by Woolworth's there would be no need to despair. But there are effects that touch the life of the community more seriously. When we consider, for instance, the processes of mass-production and standardisation in the form represented by the Press, it becomes obviously of sinister significance that they should be accompanied by a process of levelling-down.[13]

Of Lord Northcliffe, Mr. Hamilton Fyfe, his admiring biographer, tells us (*Northcliffe: An Intimate Biography*, p. 270):

> He knew what the mass of newspaper-readers wanted, and he gave it to them. He broke down the dignified idea that the conductors of newspapers should appeal to the intelligent few. He frankly appealed to the unintelligent many. Not in a cynical spirit, not with any feeling of contempt for their tastes; but because on the whole he had more sympathy with them than with the others, and because they were as the sands of the sea in numbers. He did not aim at making opinion less stable, emotion more superficial. He did this, without knowing he did it, because of increased circulation.

Two pages later we are told:

> The best people did read the *Daily Mail*. It was now seen in first-class railway compartments as much as in third-class. It had made its way from the kitchen and the butler's pantry of the big country house up to the hall table.

'Giving the public what it wants', is, clearly, a modest way of putting it. Lord Northcliffe showed people what they wanted, and showed the Best People that they wanted the same as the rest. It is enough by way of commentary on the phrase to refer to the history of the newspaper press during the last half-century: a history of which the last notable event is the surrender of the *Daily Herald* to the operation of that 'psychological Gresham Law' which Mr. Norman Angell notes:

> . . . the operation of a psychological Gresham Law; just as in commerce debased coin, if there be enough of it, must drive out the sterling, so in the contest of motives, action which corresponds to the more primitive feelings and impulses, to first thoughts and established prejudices, can be stimulated by the modern newspaper far more easily than that prompted by rationalised second thought.[14] Let us face the truth [says Mr. Norman Angell further on]; the conditions of the modern Press cause the Bottomleys more and more and the Russells and Dickinsons less and less to form the national character. The forces under review are not merely concerned with the mechanical control of ideas. They transform the national temperament.[15]

All this, again, is commonplace, but commonplace, again, on which it seems necessary to insist. For the same 'psychological Gresham Law' has a much wider application than the newspaper press. It applies even more disastrously to the films: more disastrously, because the films have a so much more potent influence.[16] They provide now the main form of recreation in the civilised world; and they involve surrender, under conditions of hypnotic receptivity, to the cheapest emotional appeals, appeals the more insidious because they are associated with a compellingly vivid illusion of actual life. It would be difficult to dispute that the result must be serious damage to the 'standard of living' (to use the phrase as before). All this seems so obvious that one is diffident about insisting on it. And yet people will reply by adducing the attempts that have been made to use film as the serious medium of art. Just as, when broadcasting is in question, they will point out that they have heard good music broadcasted and intelligent lectures. The standardising influence of broadcasting hardly admits of doubt, but since there is no Hollywood engaged in purely commercial exploitation the levelling-down is not so obvious. But perhaps it will not be disputed that broadcasting, like the films, is in practice mainly a means of passive diversion, and it tends to make active recreation, especially active use of the mind, more difficult.[17] And such agencies are only a beginning. The near future holds rapid developments in store . . .

I have said earlier that culture has always been in minority keeping. But the minority now is made conscious, not merely of an uncongenial, but of a hostile environment. 'Shakespeare', I once heard Mr. Dover Wilson say, 'was not a high-brow.' True: there were no 'high-brows' in Shakespeare's time. It was possible for Shakespeare to write plays that were at once popular drama and poetry that could be appreciated only by an educated minority. *Hamlet* appealed at a number of levels of response, from the highest downwards. The same is true of *Paradise Lost, Clarissa, Tom Jones, Don Juan, The Return of the Native*. The same is not true, Mr. George A. Birmingham might point out, of *The Waste Land, Hugh Selwyn Mauberley, Ulysses* or *To the Lighthouse*. These works are read only by a very small specialised public and are beyond the reach of the vast majority of those who consider themselves educated. The age in which the finest creative talent tends to be employed in works of this kind is the age that has given currency to the term 'high-brow'.[18] But it would be as true to say that the attitude implicit in 'high-brow' causes this use of talent as the converse. The minority is being cut off as never before from the powers that rule the world; and as Mr. George A. Birmingham[19] and his friends succeed in refining and standardising and conferring authority upon 'the taste of the bathos implanted in nature by the literary judgements of man' (to use Matthew Arnold's phrase), they will make it more and more inevitable that work expressing the finest consciousness of the age should be so specialised as to be accessible only to the minority.

'Civilisation' and 'culture' are coming to be antithetical terms. It is not merely that the power and sense of authority are now divorced from culture, but that some of the most disinterested solicitude for civilisation is apt to be, consciously or unconsciously, inimical to culture. Mr. H. G. Wells, for example, belongs, for the minority, to the past, but it is probable that he represents a good deal of the future. And he returns the compliment paid him by the minority. In his last book, *The Autocracy of Mr. Parham*, he makes his butt, a waxwork grotesque labelled 'Oxford Don', representative not only of tribal nationalism, imperialism, and The Old Diplomacy, but also of culture. There is, one gathers, nothing more to be said for art than Mr. Parham, in the National Gallery, says to Sir Bussy Woodcock. And the book ends with Sir Bussy (representative and defence-mechanism of Mr. Wells) declaring of a proposed newspaper propaganda to Mr. Parham: 'It would be up against everything you are.' 'History is bunk!' said Mr. Henry Ford. Mr. Wells, who is an authority, endorses . . .

The prospects of culture, then, are very dark. There is the less room for hope in that a standardised civilisation is rapidly enveloping the whole world. The glimpse of Russia that is permitted us does not afford the comfort that we are sometimes invited to find there. Anyone who has seen Eisenstein's film, *The General Line*, will appreciate the comment made by a writer in the *New Republic* (June 4, 1930), comparing it with an American film:

> One fancies, thinking about these things, that America might well send *The Silent Enemy* to Russia and say, 'This is what living too long with too much machinery does to people. Think twice, before you commit yourselves irrevocably to the same course.'

But it is vain to resist the triumph of the machine. It is equally vain to console us with the promise of a 'mass culture' [that] shall be utterly new. It would, no doubt, be possible to argue that such a 'mass culture' might be better than the culture we are losing, but it would be futile: the 'utterly new' surrenders everything that can interest us.[20]

What hope, then, is there left to offer? The vague hope that recovery *must* come, somehow, in spite of all? Mr. I. A. Richards, whose opinion is worth more than most people's, seems to authorise hope: he speaks of 'reasons for thinking that this century is in a cultural trough rather than upon a crest'; and says that 'the situation is likely to get worse before it is better'.[21] 'Once the basic level has been reached,' he suggests, 'a slow climb back may be possible. That at least is a hope that looks very desperate in face of the downward acceleration described above, and it does not seem to point to any factor that might be counted upon to reverse the process.

Are we then to listen to Spengler's[22] (and Mr. Henry Ford's)[23] admonition to cease bothering about the inevitable future? That is impossible. Ridiculous, priggish and presumptuous as it may be, if we care at all about the issues we cannot help believing that, for the immediate future, at any rate, we have some responsibility. We cannot help clinging to some such hope as Mr. Richards offers; to the belief (unwarranted, possibly) that what we value most matters too much to the race to be finally abandoned, and that the machine may yet be made a tool.

It is for us to be as aware as possible of what is happening, and, if we can, to 'keep open our communications with the future'.

Notes

1. 'A Manifesto', *Scrutiny* 1.1 (May 1932): 3.
2. F. R. Leavis, *Scrutiny: A Retrospect* (Cambridge: Cambridge University Press, 1963), p. 1.
3. Samson cites Alan Megill, who in *Prophets of Extremity: Nietzsche, Heidegger, Foucault, Derrida* (Berkeley and London: University of California Press, 1985) 'emphasises the length of time over which a sense of crisis persisted within European philosophy, attributing it to the collapse of historicism, and the failure of faith in progress that occurred in the late nineteenth century'. 'His analysis differs', she writes, 'from a view held more commonly in the 1920s and 1930s, and not uncommon today, which linked the sense of dislocation with the disappearance of authoritative standards in the early part of this century' (Samson, p.36). What makes a crisis, and what the sense of crisis makes occur in social, political and cultural terms, is shrewdly investigated in the second chapter of *Britain by Mass-Observation*, pp. 23–108.
4. From Cornford's reply to Julian Bell in the pages of the *Student Vanguard*, 1933. Reprinted in *Understand the Weapon, Understand the Wound*, p. 55. See below, p. 111.
5. See Mulhern, pp. 94–5.
6. Cambridge: Minority Press, 1933.
7. *The Principles of Literary Criticism*, p. 61. [FRL]
8. 'the mass of the public is without any suspicion that the value of these organs is relative to their being nearer a certain ideal centre of correct information, taste and intelligence, or farther away from it' ([Matthew Arnold], *Culture and Anarchy*). [FRL]
9. A good account of some aspects of the modern phase may be found in *The Decline of the West*, Vol. II, Chapter IV. [FRL]
10. 'One gains a distinct impression that the religious basis of all education was more taken for granted if less talked about thirty-five years ago, when high school "chapel" was a religio-inspirational service with a "choir" instead of the "pep

session" which it tends to become to-day.' (R. S. and H. M. Lynd, *Middletown*, p. 204). This kind of change, of course, is not due to the automobile alone. [FRL]

11. 'That would be one of the greatest disasters to the British-speaking people, and one of the greatest disasters to civilisation' (Lord Melchett, *Industry and Politics*, p. 278). [FRL]

12. *Ibid.*, p. 281. [FRL]

13. Cf. Q. D. Leavis on 'levelling down', below, p. 174.

14. *The Press and the Organisation of Society*, p. 33. [FRL]

15. *Ibid.*, p. 43. V. Also p. 35: 'When Swift wrote certain of his pamphlets, he presented a point of view contrary to the accepted one, and profoundly affected his country's opinion and policy. Yet at most he circulated a few thousand copies. One of the most important was printed at his own expense. Any printer in a back street could have furnished all the material capital necessary for reaching effectively the whole reading public of the nation. To-day, for an unfamiliar opinion to gain headway against accepted opinion, the mere mechanical equipment of propaganda would be beyond the resources of any ordinary individual.' [FRL] Norman Angell on the 'moral obligation to be intelligent' is discussed by Vera Brittain below, p. 71.

16. 'The motion picture, by virtue of its intrinsic nature, is a species of amusing and informational Esperanto, and, potentially at least, a species of aesthetic Esperanto of all the arts; if it may be classified as one, the motion picture has in it, perhaps more than any other, the resources of universality . . . The motion picture tells its stories directly, simply, quickly and elementally, not in words but in pictorial pantomime. To see is not only to believe; it is also in a measure to understand. In theatrical drama, seeing is closely allied with hearing, and hearing, in turn, with mental effort. In the motion picture, seeing is all – or at least nine-tenths of all' (*Encyclopaedia Britannica*, 14th edn, 'Motion Pictures: A Universal Language').
    The *Encyclopaedia Britannica*, fourteenth edition, is itself evidence of what is happening: 'humanised, modernised, pictorialised', as the editors announce. [FRL]

17. Mr. Edgar Rice Burroughs (the creator of Tarzan) in a letter that I have been privileged to see, writes: 'It has been discovered through repeated experiments that pictures that require thought for appreciation have invariably been box-office failures. The general public does not wish to think. This fact, probably more than any other, accounts for the success of my stories, for without this specific idea in mind I have, nevertheless, endeavoured to make all of my descriptions so clear that each situation could be visualised readily by any reader precisely as I saw it. My reason for doing this was not based on a low estimate of general intelligence, but upon the realisation that in improbable situations, such as abound in my work, the greatest pains must be taken to make them appear plausible. I have evolved, therefore, a type of fiction that may be read with the minimum of mental effort.' The significance of this for my argument does not need comment. Mr. Burroughs adds that his books sell at over a million copies a year. There is not room here to make the comparisons suggested by such documents as the *Life of James Lackington* (1791). [FRL]

18. Cf. other uses of 'highbrow' in this volume: p. 174 (Q. D. Leavis); p. 39 (W. H. Auden); p. 284 (C. Day Lewis); p. 122 (Christopher Caudwell).

19. G. A. Birmingham (Canon Hannay) was a member of the Book Guild Selection Committee. Other members of the panel at this time were Ethel Mannin, Hugh Walpole and Clemence Dane.

20. '. . . indeed, this gentleman, taking the bull by the horns, proposes that we should for the future call industrialism culture, and then of course there can be no longer any misapprehension of their true character; and besides the pleasure of being

wealthy and comfortable, they will have authentic recognition as vessels of
sweetness and light' (*Culture and Anarchy*). [FRL]
21. *Practical Criticism*, p. 320. [FRL]
22. 'Up to now everyone has been at liberty to hope what he pleased about the future.
Where there are no facts, sentiment rules. But henceforward it will be every man's
business to inform himself of what can happen and therefore of what with the
unalterable necessity of destiny and irrespective of personal ideals, hopes or desires,
will happen.' (*The Decline of the West*, Vol. I, p. 39). [FRL]
23. 'But what of the future? Shall we not have over-production? Shall we not some day
reach a point where the machine becomes all powerful, and the man of no
consequence?

'No man can say anything of the future. We need not bother about it. The future
has always cared for itself in spite of our well-meant efforts to hamper it. If to-day
we do the task we can best do, then we are doing all that we can do.

'Perhaps we may over-produce, but that is impossible until the whole world has
all its desires. And if that should happen, then surely we ought to be content' (Henry
Ford, *To-day and To-morrow*, pp. 272–3). [FRL]

2 Oswald Mosley *from The Greater Britain (1932)**

By the time he wrote this, Mosley had been an active parliamentarian for fourteen years – first as a Conservative member from Harrow Division in Middlesex, then as an independent representing Harrow (1922–4), then as Labour member for Smethwick Division in 1924 and 1926–31. In 1929 he formed the New Party when, as chancellor of the Duchy of Lancaster and minister assigned the task of alleviating unemployment, his proposals were rejected by the government. After the New Party failed he became leader of the British Union of Fascists on its founding in October 1932. *The Greater Britain,* his first significant piece of political writing, was in fact written some months before that date. Robert Skidelsky writes that 'apart from the autarchic bias, which only hardened into dogma after 1934, there was nothing in the economic analysis or programme of *Greater Britain* to repel the "man of goodwill". Had not [J. M.] Keynes himself advocated going "homespun"? Harold Nicolson believed that *Greater Britain* would "impress all clear thinking people"' (p. 308). Nicholas Mosley notes that 'in the second half of the book were recommendations for Britain's economic recovery which were not different from those which he [Oswald Mosley] had put forward in his New Party and Labour days – the necessity for centrally controlled economic planning within a protected home-and-imperial market'. The important part of the book, he continues, 'was its first forty pages, in which Tom outlined what he saw as the attitude and spirit of fascism' (p. 219). It is from those pages that the following extract is drawn.

The Breakdown

In Great Britain during the past ten years there have never been less than a million unemployed, and at present unemployment approaches the three million figure. In 1929 – a year which is now regarded as the peak of industrial prosperity – British trade was slack, large industrial areas were almost derelict, and only the stock markets enjoyed the semblance of boom conditions.

We have tragic proof that economic life has outgrown our political institutions. Britain has failed to recover from the War period; and this result, however complicated by special issues, is largely due to a system of *Government designed by*, and for, the nineteenth century.

* Reprinted from *The Greater Britain* (London: B.U.F. Publications, 1932), pp. 11–25.

Setting aside any complaint of the conduct or capacity of individual Governments, I believe that, under the existing system, Government cannot be efficiently conducted.

The object of this book is to prove, by analysis of the present situation and by constructive policy, that the necessity for a fundamental change exists. Our political system dates substantially from 1832. The intervening century has seen the invention and development of the telegraph, telephone and wireless. At the beginning of the period, railways were a novelty, and a journey of a dozen miles was a serious undertaking.

Since then, railway transport has risen and prospered, only to yield place to a still greater revolution of motor transport on modern roads. The whole question of power production is less than a century old, and electricity is a recent development. The modern processes of mass production and rationalisation date only from the War period. Within the last century science has multiplied by many times the power of man to produce. Banking, as we know it to-day, did not exist in 1832; even the Charter of the Bank of England and the modern Gold Standard are less than a century old. Social opinion has developed almost as rapidly as economic possibilities. Well within the last century children worked twelve hours daily in mines and workshops. Men were transported for picking pockets, and hanged for stealing sheep. Leisure and education have enormously widened the public interest in matters of Government concern. The huge expansion of commerce has made us depend more and more on one another; the building-up of popular newspapers has organised and formulated popular opinion.

From the standpoint of a century ago, all these changes are revolutionary. The sphere of government has widened and the complications of government have increased. It is hardly surprising that the political system of 1832 is wholly out of date to-day. 'The worst danger of the modern world,' writes Sir Arthur Salter in his brilliant book *Recovery*,[1] 'is that the specialised activities of man will outrun his capacity for regulative wisdom.' *Our problem is to reconcile the revolutionary changes of science with our system of government, and to harmonise individual initiative with the wider interests of the nation.* Most men desire to work for themselves; laws are oppressive if they prevent people from doing so. But there is no room for interests which are not the State's interests; laws are futile if they allow such things to be. Wise laws, and wise institutions, are those which harness without restricting; which allow human activity full play, but guide it into channels which serve the nation's ends.

Fascism – the Modern Movement

Hence the need for a New Movement, not only in politics, but in the whole of our national life. The movement is Fascist, (i) because it is based on a high conception of citizenship – ideals as lofty as those which inspired the reformers of a hundred years ago: (ii) because it recognises the necessity for an authoritative state, above party and sectional interests. Some may be prejudiced by the use of the word 'Fascist', because that word has so far been completely misunderstood in this country. It would be easy for us to avoid that prejudice by using another word, but it would not be honest to do so. We seek to organise the Modern Movement in this country by British methods in a form which is suitable to and characteristic of Great Britain. We are essentially a national movement, and if our policy could be summarised in two words, they would be 'Britain First'. Nevertheless, the Modern Movement is by no means confined to Great Britain; it comes to all the great countries in turn as their hour of crisis approaches, and in each country it naturally assumes a form and character suited to that nation. As a world-wide movement, it has come to be known as Fascism, and it is therefore right to use that name. If our crisis had been among the first, instead of among the last, Fascism would have been a British invention. As it is, our task is not to invent Fascism, but to find for it in Britain its highest expression and development.

Fascism does not differ from the older political movements in being a world-wide creed. Each of the great political faiths in its turn has been a universal movement: Conservatism, Liberalism and Socialism are common to nearly every country. An Englishman who calls himself a Conservative or a Liberal is not thereby adopting a foreign creed merely because foreign political parties bear the same name. He is seeking to advance, by English method and in English forms, a political philosophy which can be found in an organised form in all nations.

In this respect the Fascist occupies precisely the same position: his creed is also a world-wide faith. However, by very reason of the national nature of his policy, he must seek in the method and form of his organisation a character which is more distinctively British than the older political movements. Quite independently, we originally devised a policy for British needs of a very national character. In the development of that policy, and of a permanent political philosophy, we have reached conclusions which can only be properly described as Fascism.

Misrepresentation

All new movements are misunderstood. Our British Union of Fascists will without a doubt be misrepresented by politicians of the older schools. The Movement did not begin with the wiseacres and the theorists. It was born from a surging discontent with a regime where nothing can be achieved. The Old Gang hold the stage; and, to them, misrepresentation is the path of their own salvation.

Such tactics may delay, but they cannot prevent, the advance of the Movement. Nevertheless, every incident in every brutal struggle, in countries of completely different temperament and character, will be used against us. We are also faced by the fact that a few people have misused the name 'Fascism' in this country, and from ignorance or in perversion have represented it as the 'White Guard of reaction'.

This is indeed a strange perversion of a creed of dynamic change and progress. In all countries, Fascism has been led by men who came from the 'Left',[2] and the rank and file has combined the Conservative and patriotic elements of the nation with ex-Socialists, ex-Communists and revolutionaries who have forsaken their various *illusions* of progress for the new and orderly *reality* of progress. In our new organisation we now combine within our ranks all those elements in this country who have long studied and understood the great constructive mission of Fascism; but we have no place for those who have sought to make Fascism the lackey of reaction, and have thereby misrepresented its policy and dissipated its strength. In fact Fascism is the greatest constructive and revolutionary creed in the world. It seeks to achieve its aim legally and constitutionally, by methods of law and order; *but in objective it is revolutionary or it is nothing.* It challenges the existing order and advances the constructive alternative of the Corporate State. To many of us this creed represents the thing which we have sought throughout our political lives. *It combines the dynamic urge to change and progress with the authority, the discipline and the order without which nothing great can be achieved.*

This conception we have sought through many vicissitudes of parties and of men; we have found it in the Movement which we now strive to introduce to Great Britain. That pilgrimage in search of this idea has exposed me, in particular, to many charges of inconsistency. I have no apology to offer on the score of inconsistency. If anything I am disturbed by the fact that through fourteen years of political life, and more than one change of Party, I have pursued broadly the same ideals. For what in fact does a man claim who says that he has always been consistent? He says that he has lived a lifetime without learning anything; he claims to be a fool. In a world of changing fact and situation, a man is a fool who does not learn enough to change some of his original opinions.

The essence of Fascism is the power of adaptation to fresh facts. Above all, it is a realist creed. It has no use for immortal principles in relation to the facts of bread-and-butter; and it despises the windy rhetoric which ascribes importance to mere formula. The steel creed of an iron age, it cuts through the verbiage of illusion to the achievement of a new reality.

Stability and Progress

In the ranks of Conservatism there are many who are attracted there by the Party's tradition of loyalty, order and stability – but who are, none the less, repelled by its lethargy and stagnation. In the ranks of Labour there are many who follow the Party's humane ideals, and are attracted by its vital urge to remedy social and economic evils – but who are, none the less, repelled by its endless and inconclusive debates, its cowardice, its lack of leadership and decision.

These elements comprise the best of both Parties: and to both Fascism appeals. The two essentials of government are stability and progress; and the tragedy of politics is that the two, essentially coincident, are organised as contradictions. Stability implies order and authority, without which nothing can be done. It is regarded as belonging to the 'Right'. Progress implies the urge to reform without which society cannot survive. It is regarded as belonging to the 'Left'. Stability is confused with reaction and a stand-pat resistance to change: progress with ill-considered changes, or with the futile and paralytic discussions so characteristic of a timorous democracy. As a result, neither of these essentials is achieved. This is a dynamic age. Stability cannot exist without progress, for it implies the recognition of changes in the world which no political system can alter. Nor can progress exist without stability, for it implies a balanced and orderly view of the changes which have taken place. The 'Right' seeks stability, but denies the power of adaptation which makes stability an active force. The 'Left' seeks progress, but rejects all effective instruments and robs authority of the power to make decisions. The result of both systems of the two great organised Parties of the State is in the end the same. Stability confused with reaction and a resistance to change, together with progress confused with obstructive debate and committee irresponsibility, end alike in chaos. Both are instruments for preventing things being done, and the first requisite of the modern age is that things should be done.

The Farce of 1931

The final caricature of our present system may be found in the events of 1931.[3] The country, wearied by five years of parliamentary stagnation, had rebelled from the Conservative slogan of 'Safety First', and installed a Labour Government in office. For eighteen months, progress, such as it was, came under the aegis of dissentient committees and the dictation of discordant interests. As time passed, the Government fell under the spell of trade depression which it had done little to create, but which it was powerless to remedy. In the absence of any constructive policy, the Government came to the conclusion that it was necessary to reduce unemployment benefit, but was too weak to do this without elaborate publicity. The country – most of all, the Unemployed – had to be frightened: and the May committee soon produced a report fit to alarm the nation. The economies called for were duly realised, even though the achievement demanded a regrouping of political complexions. The Labour Government might have successfully purchased a little respite at the expense of its supporters, had it not been that foreign financiers had read the May report and taken it in deadly earnest. The report had been circulated to secure public approval for action which was 'necessary to save the pound'. But it exposed our weakness, and thus started the stream of foreign withdrawals from our banks which, in spite of £130 millions of money borrowed in support, forced us off the Gold Standard in September. A Government with a constructive policy would have averted the whole situation; a Government with authority would have reformed without apology: had even this been done, it is more than possible that the crisis might have been avoided.

We are faced to-day with the results of government by indecision, compromise and blether. Both political Parties, and the remnants of Liberalism as well, stand bound by the great vested interests of 'Right' and 'Left' which created them. In Opposition, there is the same profusion of promise; in office, the same apathy and inertia. In post-War England, their creeds have become platitudes; they consistently fail to grapple with the problems of the time. Their rule has led, with tragic inevitability, to the present chaos. Therefore our Fascist Movement seeks on the one hand Stability, which envisages order and authority as the basis of all solid achievement; we seek, on the other hand, Progress, which can be achieved only by the executive instrument that order, authority and decision alone can give.

Parliament

Fascism, as we understand it, is not a creed of personal Dictatorship in the Continental manner. The dictatorship of Mussolini in Italy is merely dictatorship of the revolutionary machine, consequent on the changes having been effected by a violent revolution owing to the collapse and surrender of Government. Neither is Fascism a creed of governmental tyranny. But it is definitely a creed of effective government. Parliament is, or should be, the mouthpiece of the will of the people; but, as things stand at the present, its time is mainly taken up with matters of which the nation neither knows nor cares. It is absurd to suppose that anybody is the better for interminable discussion of the host of minor measures which the Departments and local interests bring before Parliament to the exclusion of major issues. Such matters, in which the public interest is small, take up far too much parliamentary time. The discussion, too, is usually futile; most of the Bills before Parliament demand technical knowledge; but they are discussed, voted on, and their fate decided, by men and women chosen for their assiduity in opening local charity bazaars, or for their lung power at street corners. This is by no means an over-statement; when a young man asks his Party Executive for a constituency, they do not ask 'Will he be a good Member?' but 'Will he be a good candidate?'

In a practical system of government our political philosophy comes to these conclusions. Whatever movement or party be entrusted with government must be given absolute power to act. Let the people preserve, through an elected Parliament, the power to dismiss and to change the Government of the day. While such power is retained, the charge of Dictatorship has no reality. On the other hand, the power of obstruction, the interminable debate of small points which to-day frustrate the nation's will to action, must be abolished. The present Parliamentary system is not the expression, but the negation of the people's will. *Government must have power to legislate by Order, subject to the power of Parliament to dismiss it by vote of censure.* We must eliminate the solemn humbug of six hundred men and women indulging in detailed debate of every technical measure handled by a non-technical assembly in a vast technical age. Thus only shall we clear the way to the real fulfilment of the nation's desire, which is to get things done in modern conditions.

Liberty

When we propose an effective system of Government we are, of course, charged with the negation of liberty by those who have erected liberty into the negation of action. Liberty, by the definition of the old Parliamentarians, becomes the last entrenchment of obstruction.

We hear so much glib talk of liberty, and so little understanding of its meaning. Surely nobody can imagine that the British, as a race, are free. The essence of liberty is freedom to enjoy some of the fruits of life, a reasonable standard of life, a decent house, good wages, reasonable hours of leisure after hours of work short enough not to leave a man exhausted, unmolested private happiness with a wife, children and friends and, finally, the hope of material success to set the seal on private ambition: these are the realities of liberty to the ordinary man. How many possess this liberty to-day? How can the mass possess such freedom in a period of economic chaos? Many unemployed, the remainder living in the shadow of unemployment, low wages, long hours of exhausting labour, bad houses, shrinking social amenities, the uncertainty of industrial collapse and universal confusion: these are the lot of the average man to-day. What humbug, then, to talk of liberty! *The beginning of liberty is the end of economic chaos.* Yet how can economic chaos be overcome without the power to act?

By our very insistence upon liberty, and the jealous rules by which we guard it, we have reached a point at which it has ceased to be liberty at all. We must preserve the nation's right to decide how, and by whom, it shall be governed; we must provide safeguards to ensure that the powers of government are not abused. But that is far from necessitating that every act of government must be subjected to detailed and obstructive debate, and that in an assembly with little experience or knowledge of administrative problems. This fantastic system, begun in good faith as the origin of freedom, has ended by binding the citizen in a host of petty restrictions, and tying the hands of each successive government. Even in debate, the orators of Parliament no longer hope to convert one another, as they did in the days of Sheridan. The Party Whips are in attendance; a Member who disobeys will soon find himself cut off from the Party – which, incidentally, paid the expenses of his election – and his chances of keeping his seat will be of the smallest. The only useful purpose of debate is to advertise each Member in his constituency.

It is quite obvious that this system creates bad government and hampers the individual citizen. Constitutional freedom must be preserved; but that freedom is expressed in the people's power, through an elected Parliament, to choose the form and leadership of its government. Beyond this it cannot go. In complicated affairs of this kind, *somebody must be trusted, or nothing will ever be done*. The Government, once in power, must have power to legislate by order; and Parliament must have power to dismiss the Government by vote of censure.

This is the kernel of our Parliamentary proposals. To some it may seem to imply the suppression of liberty, but *we prefer to believe that it will mean the suppression of chaos*.

Organisation of the Modern Movement

The same principles which are essential to Government apply, with even greater force, to a political movement of modern and Fascist structure. Here we are dealing, not with the mass, but with the men who believe in the cause, and are devoting their energy to its aims.

We have seen the political parties of the old democracy collapse into futility through the sterility of committee government and the cowardice and irresponsibility of their leadership. Voluntary discipline is the essence of the Modern Movement. Its leadership may be an individual, or preferably, in the case of the British character, a team with clearly allocated functions and responsibility. In either case, the only effective instrument of revolutionary change is absolute authority. We are organised, therefore, as a disciplined army, not as a bewildered mob with every member bellowing orders. Fascist leadership must lead, and its discipline must be respected. By these principles, both in the structure of our own movement and in the suggested structure of Government, we preserve the essentials of true democracy and combine them with the power of rapid decision without which all semblance of democracy will ultimately be lost in chaos.

The immediate task is the firm establishment of the Modern Movement in the life of the British nation. Ultimately, nations are saved from chaos, not by Parliaments, however elected; not by civil servants, however instructed: but by the steady will of an organised movement to victory.

A whole people may be raised for a time to the enthusiasm of a great and decisive effort, as they were in the election of the National Government.[4] That enthusiasm and effort may be sustained for a long period, as it was in the War, by the external pressure of a foreign threat to our existence. History, however, provides few cases in which the enthusiasm and unity of a whole people have been so sustained through a long struggle to emerge from disintegration and collapse.

For such purpose is needed the grip of an organised and disciplined movement, grasping and permeating every aspect of national life. In every town and village, in every institution of daily life, the will of the organised and determined must be struggling for sustained effort. In moments of difficulty, dissolution and despair it must be the hard core round which the weak and the dismayed may rally. The Modern Movement, in struggle, and in victory, must be ineradicably interwoven with the life of the nation. No ordinary party of the past, resting on organisations of old women, tea-fights and committees, can survive in such a struggle. Our hope is centred in vital and determined youth, dedicated to the resurrection of a nation's greatness and shrinking from no effort and from no sacrifice to secure that mighty end. We need the sublime enthusiasm of a nation, and the devoted energies of its servants.

Notes

1. Arthur (later Baron) Salter was a career public servant, who in 1931 became a member of the British Delegation to the Assembly of the League of Nations. He was unenviably deeply involved in what Mosley refers to here as 'the Farce of 1931': 'I was to make my main speech on a Saturday on financial and currency policy. It was still the Government's policy, when I left home, to maintain the pound on its gold parity of $4.86, and it was obviously my task to support this policy and give such reasons as I could show that it was both right and practicable. I had prepared a speech accordingly. At the last moment I found that another speaker had been put ahead of me on the list, so that I would have to postpone my speech till the Monday. By this time the British Government had decided that the strain was too great, and that Great Britain must come off gold. But among those to whom the Treasury gave confidential warning of this intention they omitted . . . to include their representative at Geneva . . . Before Monday came the severance of the pound from gold was announced. It was fortunate indeed that I had not made the speech I had first prepared' (Lord Salter, *Memoirs of a Public Servant* [London: Faber and Faber, 1961], p. 229). In the same year Salter began work on a book, published in March 1932: *Recovery: The Second Effort*, cited here by Mosley.
2. 'Left' as a designation in British politics was relatively new at this time. David Thomson writes: 'Nobody supposed, until the later twenties, that it made sense in the context of British parliamentary politics to talk of "Left" and "Right".

Appropriate to European semicircular assemblies, where a party's conservatism could be measured by how far round to the right of the central rostrum it normally sat, the terms had no natural relevance in the two-sided face-to-face assembly at Westminster. A party sat on the Speaker's right if it was in office, on his left if it was in opposition: Labour, when in office, was on his "Right". Like the British rule of elections that the man at the top of the poll gets in, what mattered in Parliament was whether you were in or out of office. It was allegedly H. G. Wells who, in 1927, first used in print the word "Leftism". Certainly in these years the terms first gained the general currency which they have kept ever since.' (p. 116).

3. For an account of events leading up to the abandonment of the gold standard, see n. 1 above; also A. J. P. Taylor, pp. 295–7; Pearce and Stewart, pp. 362 and 404; and Dudley Baines, 'The Onset of Depression', in Paul Johnson, pp. 182–5.

4. On the formation of the National Government, see Taylor, pp. 292–7.

3   W. H. Auden   *from Writing (1932)**

'Writing' was Auden's contribution to *An Outline for Boys and Girls and Their Parents*, edited by Naomi Mitchison and published in 1932. Humphrey Carpenter tells us that the book had been commissioned by Victor Gollancz 'as a symposium of informed left-wing views on major topics' (1981, p. 133). A notable omission from the topics covered was Christ, which caused a considerable stir amongst persons in educational and ecclesiastical authority. As some of the entries in the present volume indicate, there was at the time no shortage of speculation on relations between Christianity and socialism; Eric Gill, for example, might have been invited to contribute, and Auden himself was by 1935 directly addressing the issue in the piece he wrote for John Lewis's collection, *Christianity and the Social Revolution.*[1] Mitchison's book, however, left Christ out of consideration; and Auden, responding to the furore, suggested to her that perhaps Christ should indeed have been included – but to be 'attacked' (Carpenter, 1981, p. 133).

Auden's 'Writing' essay is built on the premise that language grows directly out of the human desire for community and communication: 'At some time or other in human history,' he writes in the opening section, 'when and how we don't know, man became self-conscious; he began to feel, I am not I, and you are not I; we are shut inside ourselves and apart from each other. There is no whole but the self. The more this feeling grew, the more man felt the need to bridge over the gulf, to recover the sense of being as much part of life as the cells in his body are part of him' (*The English Auden*, p. 303). To speak or (later) to write, was to build a bridge, and in such acts was society constituted. One extension of this theory is that no verbal act occurs except that its very occurrence bears directly upon the nature and existence of society. Or put very reductively, as Auden does in his 'outline' for children, 'When we read a book, it is as if we were with a person.'[2] Out of that insight sprang not only the intensely ethical approach to reading and writing which characterized Auden's work throughout the 1930s (and even beyond), but also presumably his fondness for addressing his reader with terms of endearment – 'dear', 'love', etc.

Why People Write Books

People write in order to be read. They would like to be read by everybody and for ever. They feel alone, cut off from each other in an indifferent world where

* Reprinted from *The English Auden: Poems, Essays and Dramatic Writings, 1927–1939*, ed. Edward Mendelson (London: Faber and Faber, 1977), pp. 309–11.

they do not live for very long. How can they get in touch again? How can they prolong their lives? Children by their bodies live on in a life they will not live to see, meet friends they will never know, and will in their turn have children, some tiny part of them living on all the time. These by their bodies; books by their minds.

But the satisfaction of any want is pleasant: we not only enjoy feeling full, we enjoy eating; so people write books because they enjoy it, as a carpenter enjoys making a cupboard. Books are written for money, to convert the world, to pass the time; but these reasons are always trivial, beside the first two – company and creation.

Why People Read Books

When we read a book, it is as if we were with a person. A book is not only the meaning of the words inside it; it is the person who means them. In real life we treat people in all sorts of ways. Suppose we ask a policeman the way. As long as he is polite we do not bother whether he beats his wife or not; in fact, if he started to tell us about his wife we should get impatient; all we expect of him is that he shall know the way and be able clearly to explain it. But other people we treat differently; we want more from them than information; we want to live *with* them, to feel and think *with* them. When we say a book is good or bad, we mean that we feel towards it as we feel towards what we call a good or bad person. (Remember, though, that a book about bad characters is not therefore bad, any more than a person is bad because he talks about bad people.) Actually we know that we cannot divide people into good and bad like that; everyone is a mixture; we like some people in some moods and some in others, and as we grow older our taste in people changes. The same is true of books. People who say they only read good books are prigs. We all like some good books and some bad. The only silly thing to do is to pretend that bad books are good. The awful nonsense that most people utter when they are discussing or criticising a book would be avoided if they would remember that they would never think of criticising a person in the same way.

For instance, people will often say that they don't like the book because they don't agree with it. We think it rather silly when people can only be friends with those who hold the same views in everything.

Reading is valuable just because books are like people, and make the same demands on us to understand and like them. Our actual circle of friends is generally limited; we feel that our relations with them are not as good as they might be, more muddled, difficult, unsatisfying than necessary. Just as a boxer exercises for a real fight with a punchball or a sparring-partner, so you can train yourselves for relations with real people with a book. It's not easy, and you can't begin until you have had some experience of real people first (any more than a boxer can practise with a punch-ball until he has learnt a little about boxing), but books can't die or quarrel or go away as people can. Reading and living are not two watertight compartments. You must use your knowledge of people to guide you when reading books, and your knowledge of books to guide you when living with people. The more you read, the more you will realise what difficult and delicate things relations with people are, but how worth while they can be when they really come off; and the more you know of other people, the more you will be able to get out of each kind of book, and the more you will realise what a true good a really great book can be, but that great books are as rare as great men.

Reading is valuable when it improves our technique of living, helps us to live fuller and more satisfactory lives. It fails when we can't understand or feel with what we read, either because of ignorance of our own or obscurity in the writing.

It is a danger when we only read what encourages us in lax and crude ways of feeling and thinking: like cheap company (too many people only read what flatters them; they like to be told that they are fine fellows, and all is for the best in the best of all possible worlds; or they only want to be excited or to forget tomorrow's bills). It is also dangerous when it becomes a substitute for living, when we get frightened of real people and find books safer company; they are a rehearsal for living, not living itself. Swots and 'bookish' people have stage fright.

What Is a Highbrow? (1933)*

An untitled review, originally published in The Twentieth Century in May 1933. The books under discussion all emanate from the domain of Leavisism: Culture and Environment by F. R. Leavis and Denys Thompson; How to Teach Reading by F. R. Leavis alone; and How Many Children Had Lady Macbeth? by L. C. Knights. Knights and Donald Culver were the first editors of Scrutiny, joined in late 1932 by Leavis and Denys Thompson. Francis Mulhern summarizes the aim of Culture and Environment as follows: 'to trace the causal links between industrial "mass

---

* Reprinted from The English Auden, pp. 317–18.

production" and the patterns of contemporary culture. The main emphases of
their analysis fell on two aspects of the industrial economy: the mass market –
the new types of commodity displayed there and the means used to sell them –
and the labour process of the modern factory' (Mulhern, pp. 48–9).

Auden's relationship with Leavis and the *Scrutiny* circle was at this time still
reasonably good. He had contributed to *Scrutiny*,[3] and when *The Poet's Tongue*
appeared in 1935, Thompson reviewed it positively in the journal.[4] By 1936,
however, Leavis's reservations about Auden as a poet were becoming more serious
and his criticism more trenchant. In December of that year, his *Scrutiny* review[5]
of *Look, Stranger!* indicated that he was 'now under way with an anti-Auden
campaign that was to last for the rest of both their lives' (Carpenter, 1981, p. 204).[6]

What is a highbrow?[7] Someone who is not passive to his experience but
who tries to organise, explain and alter it, someone in fact, who tries to
influence his history: a man struggling for life in the water is for the time being
a highbrow. The decisive factor is a conflict between the person and his
environment; most of the people who are usually called highbrows had either
an unhappy childhood and adolescence or suffer from physical defects. Mr.
Leavis, Mr. Thompson, Mr. Knights, Mr. Pound, the author and the reader of
this review, are highbrows, and these books are a plea for the creation of more.

I think rightly. We live in an age in which the collapse of all previous
standards coincides with the perfection in technique for the centralised
distribution of ideas; some kind of revolution is inevitable, and will as
inevitably be imposed from above by a minority; in consequence, if the result
is not to depend on the loudest voice, if the majority is to have the slightest
say in its future, it must be more critical than it is necessary for it to be in an
epoch of straightforward development.

All these three books are concerned with school education. *How Many
Children Had Lady Macbeth?* is an attack on the bunk in most teaching of
Shakespeare, with its concentration on the characters and plot, and its omission
of the poetry. *How to Teach Reading* is a demand for training in the technique
of critical reading. *Culture and Environment* is a practical text book for
assisting children to defeat propaganda of all kinds by making them aware of
which buttons are being pressed.

All three books are good and will, I hope, be read seriously by all school
teachers. *Culture and Environment* is particularly excellent because it sets the
examination papers; teachers are usually hard-worked, and, while agreeing
with the importance of this kind of instruction, are either too busy or too tired
to prepare it themselves.

Also I am inclined to think that advertising is a better field than literature for such work, the aim of which, like that of psychoanalysis, is primarily destructive, to dissipate a reaction by becoming conscious of it. Advertising and machines are part of the environment of which literature is a reaction; those who are critically aware of their environment and of themselves will be critical of what they read, and not otherwise. I think it extremely doubtful whether any direct training of literary sensibility is possible,

Our education is far too bookish. To give children masterpieces to read, the reaction of exceptional adult minds to vast experiences, is fantas..c. A boy in school remains divorced from the means of production, from livelihood; it is impossible to do much, but I believe that for the time being the most satisfactory method of teaching English to children is throug^ ^heir environment and their actions in it; e.g., if they are going to read or write about sawing wood, they should saw some themselves first: they should have plenty of acting, if possible, and under their English teacher movement classes as well, and very, very little talk.

These books all imply the more general question 'What is to be done?' though, perhaps intentionally, they all avoid specifically stating or answering it. Mass production, advertising, the divorce between mental and manual labour, magazine stories, the abuse of leisure, all these are symptoms of an invalid society, and can only be finally cured by attending to the cause. You can suppress one symptom but only to create another, just as you can turn a burglar into an epileptic. Opinions differ both on cause and cure, but it is the duty of an investigator to state his own, and if possible, the more important conflicting ones. Consciousness always appears to be uncontaminated by its object, and the danger of the methods advocated in these books is of making the invalid fascinated by his disease, of enabling the responsible minority to derive such intellectual satisfaction from contemplating the process of decay, from which by the nature of consciousness itself they feel insulated, that they lose the will and power to arrest it.

Marx and Freud (1935)*

The following is a brief extract from Auden's long essay, 'Psychology and Art Today', which appeared in *The Arts To-day*, edited by Geoffrey Grigson and published in 1935. Among the other interesting and prominent figures who

---

* Reprinted from *The English Auden*, p. 341.

contributed to the volume was John Grierson, whose essay 'The Cinema To-day' invites comparison with the piece by Arthur Calder-Marshall included in this volume.

B oth Marx and Freud start from the failures of civilisation, one from the poor, one from the ill. Both see human behaviour determined, not consciously, but by instinctive needs, hunger and love. Both desire a world where rational choice and self-determination are possible. The difference between them is the inevitable difference between the man who studies crowds in the street, and the man who sees the patient, or at most the family, in the consulting room. Marx sees the direction of the relations between outer and inner world from without inwards, Freud vice versa. Both are therefore suspicious of each other. The socialist accuses the psychologist of caving in to the status quo, trying to adapt the neurotic to the system, thus depriving him of a potential revolutionary: the psychologist retorts that the socialist is trying to lift himself by his own boot tags, that he fails to understand himself, or the fact that lust for money is only one form of the lust for power; and so that after he has won his power by revolution he will recreate the same conditions. Both are right. As long as civilisation remains as it is, the number of patients the psychologist can cure are very few, and as soon as socialism attains power, it must learn to direct its own interior energy and will need the psychologist.

Notes

1. The essay is reprinted as 'The Good Life' in *The English Auden*, pp. 342–54.
2. I have discussed this theory at greater length, and in the broader context of Auden's changing attitudes, in my entry on Auden in *The Johns Hopkins Guide to Literary Theory and Criticism*, ed. Michael Groden and Martin Kreiswirth (Baltimore: Johns Hopkins University Press, 1994), pp. 53–5.
3. He reviewed, for example, Walter Brierley's *Means Test Man* for *Scrutiny* in September 1935. See 'The Bond and the Free', *The English Auden*, pp. 330–2.
4. See Carpenter, 1981, p. 168.
5. *Scrutiny* 5 (December 1936): 323–7. Reprinted in *W. H. Auden: The Critical Heritage*, ed. John Haffenden (London: Routledge and Kegan Paul, 1983), pp. 222–5.
6. For a discussion of *Scrutiny* and its attitudes to Auden and his group, see Mulhern, pp. 210–11.
7. See Leavis on 'highbrow' above, p. 21 .

4 Geoffrey Grigson *The Object of New Verse (1933)**

Grigson describes the genesis of *New Verse* in a lively chapter of his *Recollections* (1984). The decision to start a little magazine was made, apparently, at a tea-time discussion between himself (then editor of the book pages of the *Morning Post*), his wife Frances Galt ('that young post-graduate from Smith College and from the St. Louis, Mo. . . . of T. S. Eliot'), and Hugh Ross-Williamson, editor at the time 'of the impossibly bookish and frumpish old *Bookman*' (pp. 27–8). *New Verse* was – like *Scrutiny* and countless other papers of the period – founded in response to a perceived 'Situation' in the arts and culture generally: 'The public and official provinciality of the time in London . . . in spite of Joyce, Lewis and Eliot, and Eliot's *Criterion*, remained more than usually extreme. The educational establishment no less than the book pages of the Sunday papers and "serious" weeklies still conducted an elderly witch hunt against "modernism" in art or letters' (p. 26). The original purpose of the magazine was to subvert or counteract this provincialism, and its tone (as evident in this extract) was cutting, irreverent and aggressive. Looking back, Grigson remarks: 'I dislike recalling a rude and rough, if sometimes quite funny bullying which became one of its characteristics after two or three years.' Edith Sitwell was an unfortunate victim of *New Verse* in that phase (see no. 12 [December 1934]: 13–17), as was Laura Riding (see below, p. 219). While the paper held a brief for Gerard Manley Hopkins in particular and for the first generation of modernists (Eliot, Pound, Wyndham Lewis *et al.*), 'a second newness was arriving' in the persons of Auden, MacNeice, Day Lewis and Spender (p. 28). It was partly through Grigson's publication and advocacy of their work that the poets of the 'Auden Generation' came to prominence both as individuals and as a group. *New Verse* ceased publication in 1939 – the year of Auden's emigration to the United States.[1]

T he object of NEW VERSE needs expansion in no complex or tiring manifesto. Poets in this country and during this period of the victory of the masses, aristocratic and bourgeois as much as proletarian, which have captured the instruments of access to the public and use them to convey their own once timid and silent vulgarity, vulgarising all the arts, are allowed no longer periodical means of communicating their poems.

Periodicals exist into which poems are now and then allowed. Of the weeklies we name 'serious', one or two admit verse – by writers very often whose temporary credit should long have expired – and they use it to finish

---

* Reprinted from *New Verse* 1 (January 1933): 1–2.

off some lump of Elia-aping which will not fill the column, or print it under their last correspondence or under some such heading as 'Miscellany' or 'Pastiche'; and the poet who wishes room for his best poems must be content with the very few pages he can be given in the few grave and entertaining quarterlies and monthlies which contrive obstinately to continue in the poisonous and steaming Gran Chaco of vulgarity, sciolism and literary racketeering.

NEW VERSE, then, has a clear function. When respectable poems (as it believes) are being written and forced to remain in typescript, it can add itself as a publishing agent to those few publishers who bring out (with conscience money) a few books of verse. It favours only its time, belonging to no literary or politico-literary cabal, cherishing bombs only for masqueraders and for the everlasting 'critical' rearguard of nastiness, now represented so ably and variously by the *Best Poems of the Year*, the Book Society, and all the gang of big shot reviewers, NEW VERSE does not regard itself as a verse supplement to such periodicals as the *Criterion* and *Scrutiny*. There is no 'poetic' and therefore no supplementary experience; poetry by its words (to borrow a metaphor of Eliot's) and so by itself drives roots down to draw from all human experience. If the poem is only one organism in the creation of which those experiences are collected, concentrated, transmitted, it is the chief organism; and one (incidentally) in such an ulcerous period as our own which can serve magnificently. So NEW VERSE believes.

Note

1. For an interesting discussion of Grigson and *New Verse*, see Caesar, pp. 107–21.

5 Michael Roberts *Preface to **New Signatures** (1932)**

New Signatures was the first deliberate attempt to define the 'Auden Generation'. Roberts had studied chemistry at King's College, London, and then mathematics at Trinity College, Cambridge. After reading John Lehmann's first collection of poems, he wrote to the author to declare his belief that Lehmann's and the work of some other contemporaries 'belonged together . . . in spite of wide apparent differences' (see Tolley, pp. 108–21, for a full discussion of the origins and nature of *New Signatures*). Lehmann was working at the time for Leonard and Virginia Woolf at the Hogarth Press, and the anthology eventually appeared in 1932 with that imprint. By the end of the decade Roberts was committed to Anglicanism, but in the early 1930s his communist sympathies were still strong: he had become a member of the Communist Party of Great Britain in the 1920s, only to be thrown out 'after a year or two as a Trotskyite' (Tolley, p. 108). Nevertheless, it is a sign of his personal involvement in the communist cause that he chose at about this time to drop his given names, William Edward, and adopt the name Michael: Cunningham tells us that he began using the latter 'after the Russian scientist-poet Mikhail Lomosonov' (p. 253). Such acts of personal self-redefinition were of course common during the period, just as, subsequently, were also to be manifesto anthologies. In the two collections for which Roberts is principally remembered (*New Signatures* and *New Country* [1933]), he sought to redefine the literary character and direction of his generation. See also Hynes, pp. 74–83, and Annan, p. 183.

Hem, cleare your throats and spit soundly for now the pageant begins and the stuff by whole cartloads comes in.
—Thomas Nashe

The scientific theories of the past are not dead; the expert still reads Newton's *Principia* for the sake of the precision and economy, the elegance, with which it accounted for the facts then known. In the same detached way we may appreciate the elegance of poetry written by men whose sole experience was different from ours; but we cannot accept it as a resolution of our own problems. It is not only that our response to certain words and rhythms has changed; new knowledge and new circumstances have compelled us to think and feel in ways not expressible in the old language at all. The poet who, using an obsolete technique, attempts to express his whole conception is compelled

* Reprinted from *New Signatures: Poems by Several Hands*, collected by Michael Roberts (London: Hogarth Press, 1932), pp. 7–12.

to be partly insincere or be content with slovenly thought and sentimental feeling. Therefore, however good the poetry of Keats may be, the work of his modern imitators is mostly bad. Poetry cannot be elegant if it was never actual. Thus the elegance, the purely poetic merit, of a poem is distinct from, but dependent upon, its actuality. A poet cannot expect to write well, to give pleasure to his most careful critics, unless he is abreast of his own times, honest with himself, and uses a technique sufficiently flexible to express precisely those subtleties of thought and feeling in which he differs from his predecessors.

It was inevitable that the growth of industrialism should give rise to 'difficult' poetry. Because our civilisation has hitherto depended directly on agriculture, and because our thoughts have hitherto made use of images taken from a rural life, our urban and industrial society leaves us uncomfortable and nostalgic. Rural poetry in recent years has been, in general, a cowardly escape into the past, whilst urban poetry, the poetry of the machine age, has seemed, even to intelligent and conscientious critics, abrupt, discordant, intellectual. It is hard to find words relating to city life which are such powerful emotive symbols as those which poets have used for centuries, and the reader, not being swept off his feet at once by a poem, reverses the proper order and spends his time puzzling out the plain sense of a passage (which is seldom as difficult as Donne, never as difficult as Shakespeare), before he allows any scope at all to imagery and sound; he becomes 'too intellectual'.

The effect of pure science in undermining our absolute beliefs has been even more serious. At a time when technical advances and the resulting complexity of society have made it more necessary than ever before that the intellectual should guide and control those processes which he alone has studied, he has become self-conscious, and therefore unwilling to accept the responsibility of leadership, and has become a detached and pessimistic observer of the democratic process. Even the poets, who might have done something to remedy the sense of futility which is the cause of the trouble, have themselves succumbed to it. We have become too analytical, too conscious of our own motives, to react in the old way to the old symbols, and because for some purposes it is convenient to assume that poetry has, like religion, a psychological function, we distrust it as a child distrusts his medicine. We judge the 'truth' of a scientific theory and the 'reality' of a concept by the generality and economy with which they enable us to subsume the known facts, and in order that our own experience may fit the theory we treat much of it as 'subjective', something which deviates from the normal owing to the intrusion of irrelevant influences. Illogically, but quite naturally, we then take scientific 'truth' as the type of all validity, and, having learned to call our own judgements subjective, we are no longer certain what is right and good. We ignore the fact that it may be possible to find a moral hierarchy analogous to the hierarchy of authoritative scientific observers, and we are left with only an empirical knowledge that certain things make us uncomfortable.

Those poets who have in recent years attempted to satirise such a state of affairs, whilst being themselves the victims of it, were at a hopeless disadvantage; it is useless to show the futility of this or that if you believe that all alike is vanity. The poet as such may be concerned with none of these things, but it is not possible for any man of reasonable intelligence and sensibility to ignore them.

The poet is, in some ways, a leader; he is a person of unusual sensibility, he feels acutely emotional problems which other people feel vaguely, and it is his function not only to find the rhythms and images appropriate to the everyday experience of normal human beings, but also to find an imaginative solution of their problems, to make a new harmony out of strange and often apparently ugly material. To define a philosophy is not a poet's business, but in imaginative writing, as distinct from that lyrical writing which is simply precise delineation, he must make us accept willingly the strict necessity of simple ugliness and beauty in the world; and, if his work is not to end in mystical but barren contemplation, he must leave us, as Shakespeare does in *Lear*, with the knowledge that our efforts to root out ugliness and evil are also necessary and valuable.

But to be effective, a poem must first be comprehensible: a leader, though he may sometimes be compelled to go ahead to reconnoitre, must not be out of sight of his followers. The poems in this book show, I think, that we have just passed through such a period of reconnaissance. The solution of some too insistent problems may make it possible to write 'popular' poetry again: not by a deliberate patronising use of, say, music-hall material, but because the poet will find that he can best express his newly found attitude in terms of a symbolism which happens to be of exceptionally wide validity.

Meanwhile the poet, contemptuous of the society around him and yet having no firm belief, no basis for satire, became aloof from ordinary affairs and produced esoteric work which was frivolously decorative or elaborately erudite. His isolation was the more noticeable in so far as much his keenest emotion was the delight which accompanies intellectual discovery intelligible only to an educated minority.

For the poet, this isolation has serious disadvantages. A poet who does not expect to find an audience of the right intelligence, experience, and sensibility cannot write well, if at all, for he must, in writing, take his imagined audience into account: the tone which he adopts toward that audience and his intention in addressing them at all are important elements in the poem.

The poems in this book represent a clear reaction against esoteric poetry in which it is necessary for the reader to catch each recondite allusion. Even Mr. Empson, whose poetry may still be difficult, is definitely trying to say something to an audience. His poetry repays study, for its obscurity is due solely to a necessary compression, not to any use of accidental association: its order is logical, not fanciful, and his conceits are genuinely metaphysical, for there is not only a logical analogy between the parallel ideas of each conceit, but also a similarity between the poet's emotional responses to them. In Mr. Empson's poetry there is no scope for vagueness of interpretation, and its 'difficulty' arises from this merit. Apart from their elegance, their purely poetic merit, they are important because they do something to remove the difficulties which have stood between the poet and the writing of popular poetry.

from Introduction to *The Faber Book of Modern Verse* (1936)*

It is not possible to compile an anthology of serious poetry without reflecting the social and moral problems of our time; but writing may be poetic without being either moral or didactic. Poetry may be intended to amuse, or to ridicule, or to persuade, or to produce an effect which we feel to be more valuable than amusement and different from instruction; but primarily poetry is an exploration of the possibilities of language. It does not aim directly at consolation or moral exhortation, nor at the expression of exquisite moments, but at an extension of significance; and it might be argued that a too self-conscious concern with 'contemporary' problems deflects the poet's effort from his true objective. The technical merit of a poem is measured by its accuracy, not by the importance of a rough approximation to what is being said, nor by the number of people to whom it is immediately intelligible. If a poet is incomprehensible to many people, but clearly intelligible to a few, as Hopkins appeared to be when his collected poems were first published, it may be because he is speaking of things not commonly experienced and is using subtleties of rhythm and imagery not used in ordinary speech, and therefore not widely understood. If it can be shown that a poet's use of language is valid for some people, we cannot dismiss his way

---

* Reprinted from *The Faber Book of Modern Verse*, 3rd edition (London: Faber and Faber, 1965), pp. 3–6.

of speaking as mere 'obscurity' and idiosyncrasy, though we may regret the necessity for such a rhetoric as we may regret the necessity for scientific jargon and mathematical notation.

The significant point about Hopkins was, however, not that he invented a style different from the current poetic style, but that, working in subterranean fashion, he moulded a style which expressed the tension and disorder that he found inside himself. Good poetry is more likely to be written about subjects which are, to the writer, important, than about unimportant subjects, because only on subjects of personal importance to himself does he feel the need for that accuracy of speech which itself lessens the tension which it describes. Deliberately to imitate a style arising from one poet's crisis would be absurd, but something similar is likely to appear when a crisis of a general kind arouses a personal conflict in many poets. The conflict may be the product of a fractured personality or a decaying society, or, like some of the 'problems' of academic philosophy, a result of the deficiencies of language. The terms of the conflict may be intellectual, when people are torn between conflicting systems of ideas. They may be theological, when people argue that they themselves should be perfect, being the children of God, but are perplexed by the recognition that they are evil. The terms may be political and aesthetic, when people cling to some features of the existing state, but see that there can be no good future until that state is overthrown. Sometimes, as in Donne, several of these terminologies are superimposed, serving as metaphors for each other, and concentrating, intensifying, and ultimately simplifying the problems by this poetic identification. For 'problems' of this kind are seldom independent; there is a relation between the personal and moral problem and the political and intellectual.

To those who have not felt some adumbration of such a crisis, the expression and resolution of conflict and disorder must appear like the strained muscles and distorted features of a strong man pretending to lift stupendous but non-existent weights. But for those who have come near to feeling the crisis themselves, the poetry is important. Words do something more than call up ideas and emotions out of a lumber-room: they call them up, but they never replace them exactly where they were. A good descriptive poem may enable us to be more articulate, to perceive more clearly, and to distinguish more readily between sensitive and sentimental observation, than before. But a poem may do more than that: even though we may not accept the poet's explicit doctrine, it may change the configuration of the mind and alter our responses to certain situations: it may harmonize conflicting emotions just as a good piece of reasoning may show the fallacy of an apparent contradiction in logic.

But the poetic use of language can cause discord as easily as it can cure it. A bad poem, a psychologically disordered poem, if it is technically effective may arouse uneasiness or nausea or anger in the reader. A sentimental poem, which deals with a situation by ignoring some of the factors, is offensive in this way; and a poem is equally confusing if it takes into account greater complexities of thought and intricacies of feeling than the reader has ever noticed. It unsettles the mind – and by the mind I mean more than the conscious mind; and the reader expends the energy he originally brought to the poem in trivial irritation with the poet.

It is very natural that this should be the first response of many readers to 'new' poetry, but in so far as the poet is a good poet, the situation will remedy itself. The problem which worried the poet will worry other people, or the new grounds which he saw for delight and hope will become apparent to them too: perhaps their recognition of the new element will be accelerated by his writing. But in either case they will welcome the way of speech which makes them articulate. Sometimes, as in the case of Hopkins, the problem which is his today is the world's tomorrow. Sometimes his writing is significant primarily for only a few of each generation, as when it is evoked by some remote place or rare experience or an intricate thought which few can follow. Sometimes it expresses the problem of only few or many people at one particular moment. But in each case, if the writer is a good poet, good in the sense of being rhetorically effective, his writing has a value over and above that of its immediate appeal: he has added to the possibilities of speech, he has discovered evocative rhythms and image-sequences unknown before. It may happen that in some future state of society there will be no people in the position of Mr. Eliot's Prufrock, and therefore no people for whom the poem is actual. But the rhetorical merit of the poem remains: it has said something which could not be said in ordinary speech, and said it exactly, and people who are interested in effective expression will read it. Pope and Erasmus Darwin both wrote poems which were chiefly of didactic interest in their own time, but the elegance of Pope's writing keeps it alive today, whereas the poetry of Erasmus Darwin is almost forgotten. Chaucer has influenced English poetry and English language more than Langland, though Langland was, and is, the nearer to the thought and feeling of the common people.

6   W. B. Yeats   *from The Oxford Book of Modern Verse (1936)**

Joseph Hone, in his very early biography of Yeats, made the point that *The Oxford Book of Modern Verse* 'throws as much light on his own personality and development of taste as on the poetry of the period' (pp. 454–5). 'What an anthology!', Hone reports Sir Arthur Quiller-Couch as exclaiming, 'What a preface!' (p. 455). The collection was immediately controversial, particularly because of Yeats's refusal to include work by such First World War poets as Wilfred Owen and Isaac Rosenberg: 'I have rejected these poems for the same reason that made Arnold withdraw his *Empedocles on Etna* from circulation; passive suffering is not a theme for poetry' (*The Oxford Book of Modern Verse,* p. xxxiv). It was suggested, at the time, that his choices amongst recent material had been determined less by informed judgement than by his friendships. Whatever the truth of that claim, it is clear Yeats's familiarity with the work even of the Auden group was not great. Nevertheless, this passage offers striking indication of the discrepancy between his own views on poetry and culture, and those which were increasingly current in the 1930s. The communist claim that 'religion, art, philosophy, expressed economic change' – that 'the production of ideas, of conceptions, of consciousness,' as Marx puts it in *The German Ideology,* 'is at first directly interwoven with the material activity and the material intercourse of man'[1] – is in his view an inversion of the truth: 'the shell secreted the fish.'

When, later in 1936, Yeats came up to London to make his BBC broadcast on 'Modern Poetry', he deviated very little from his position in *The Oxford Book* – except to enlarge on what from the present perspective was his most interesting point: namely, that Auden and his associates should be read as the direct heirs of Owen and the trench poets. The latter, he asserted, were 'young men who felt they had been dragged away from their studies, from their pleasant life, by the blundering frenzy of old men, [and who] found the greater part of their style' in T. S. Eliot. 'They were too near their subject-matter to do, as I think, work of permanent importance, but their social passion, their sense of tragedy, their modernity, have passed into the influential poets of today: Auden, Spender, MacNeice, Day Lewis, and others' (*Essays and Introductions*, p. 500). Yeats's comments on the influence of, and close resemblance between, members of this group no doubt played a role in the growing critical tendency to equate the 'Auden Generation' with the sum of what was significant in British Literature of the 1930s.

---

* Reprinted from *The Oxford Book of Modern Verse* (Oxford: Oxford University Press, 1936), pp. xxxv–xxxviii.

Ten years after the war certain poets combined the modern vocabulary, the accurate record of the relevant facts learnt from Eliot, with the sense of suffering of the war poets, that sense of suffering no longer passive, no longer an obsession of the nerves; philosophy had made it part of all the mind. Edith Sitwell with her Russian Ballet, [Walter James Redfern] Turner[2] with his *Mare Tranquillum*, Dorothy Wellesley with her ancient names – 'Heraclitus added fire' – her moths, horses and serpents, Pound with his descent into Hades, his Chinese classics, are too romantic to seem modern. Browning, that he might seem modern, created an ejaculating man-of-the-world good humour; but Day Lewis, Madge, MacNeice, are modern through the character of their intellectual passion. We have been gradually approaching this art through that cult of sincerity, that refusal to multiply personality which is characteristic of our time. They may seem obscure, confused, because of their concentrated passion, their interest in associations hitherto untravelled; it is as though their words and rhythms remained gummed to one another instead of separating and falling into order. I can seldom find more than half a dozen lyrics that I like, yet in this moment of sympathy I prefer them to Eliot, to myself – I too have tried to be modern. They have pulled off the mask, the manner writers hitherto assumed, Shelley in relation to his dream, Byron, Henley,[3] to their adventure, their action. Here stands no this or that man but man's naked mind.

Although I have preferred, and shall again, constrained by a different nationality, a man so many years old, fixed to some one place, known to friends and enemies, full of mortal frailty, expressing all things not made mysterious by nature with impatient clarity, I have read with some excitement poets I had approached with distaste, delighted in their pure spiritual objectivity as in something long foretold.

Much of the war poetry was pacifist, revolutionary; it was easier to look at suffering if you had somebody to blame for it, or some remedy in mind. Many of these poets have called themselves communists, though I find in their work no trace of the recognized communist philosophy and the practising communist rejects them. The Russian government in 1930 silenced its mechanists, put Spinoza on his head and claimed him for grandfather; but the men who created the communism of the masses had Stendhal's mirror for a contemporary, believed that religion, art, philosophy, expressed economic change, that the shell secreted the fish. Perhaps all that the masses accept is obsolete – the Orangeman beats his drum every Twelfth of July[4] – perhaps fringes, wigs, furbelows, hoops, patches, stocks, Wellington boots, start up as armed men; but were a poet sensitive to the best thought of his time to accept that belief, when time is restoring the soul's autonomy, it would be as though he had swallowed a stone and kept it in his bowels. None of these men have accepted it, communism is their *Deus ex Machina*, their Santa Claus, their happy ending, but speaking as a poet I prefer tragedy to tragi-comedy. No matter how great a reformer's energy a still greater is required to face, all activities expended in vain, the unreformed. 'God,' said an old-country woman, 'smiles alike when regarding the good and condemning the lost.' MacNeice, the anti-communist, expecting some descent of barbarism next turn of the wheel, contemplates the modern world with even greater horror than the communist Day Lewis, although with less lyrical beauty. More often I cannot tell whether the poet is communist or anti-communist. On what side is Madge? Indeed, I know of no school where poets so closely resemble each other. Spender has said that the poetry of belief must supersede that of personality, and it is perhaps a belief shared that has created their intensity, their resemblance; but this belief is not political. If I understand aright this difficult art the contemplation of suffering has compelled them to seek beyond the flux something unchanging, inviolate, that country where no ghost haunts, no beloved lures because it has neither past nor future.

> This lunar beauty
> Has no history
> Is complete and early;
> If beauty later
> Bear any feature
> It had a lover
> And is another.

Notes

1. From Marx and Engels, *On Literature and Art* (Moscow: Progress Publishers, 1978), p. 42.
2. Turner (1889–1946) was an Australian writer and music critic, and also a friend of Yeats.
3. William Ernest Henley (1849–1903): poet and critic.
4. Anniversary of the Battle of the Boyne (1689).

7 Writers' International (British Section) *Statement of Aim, with Responses (1934)**

The British Section of the Writers' International was established at a conference at Conway Hall, London, in February 1934. Its base was Collet's Bookshop, 66 Charing Cross Road, well-known as a centre for left-wing cultural activity. The Executive Committee (John Strachey, Ralph Fox and Michael Davidson) decided that the Conference 'Statement of Aim' should be published as a pamphlet 'with comments on it – criticisms, support, additions – from members of the section and from other writers given to "dangerous thoughts"'. To this end, and with these words of invitation, they published the statement in the first issue of the *Left Review* in order to attract comment that might be included in the pamphlet. The statement was published again in the third issue (December 1934), but by then it seems the idea of a pamphlet had been superseded by the concept of an ongoing discussion – or 'controversy' – in the pages of the *Left Review*. What follows is the original statement, plus a selection of responses from the *Left Review* of December 1934 and January 1935.

There is a crisis of ideas in the capitalist world today not less considerable than the crisis in economics.

Increasing numbers of people are reading seriously, trying to get some insight as to the causes of events that are shattering the world they know, and some understanding of the reasons for men's actions. And increasingly they are being given, not insight or understanding, but 'distraction'. Journalism, literature, the theatre, are developing in technique while narrowing in content; they cannot escape their present triviality until they deal with the events and issues that matter; the death of an old world and the birth of a new.

The decadence of the past twenty years of English literature and the theatre cannot be understood apart from all that separates 1913 and 1934. It is the collapse of a culture, accompanying the collapse of an economic system.

There are already a number of writers who realize this; they desire and are working for the ending of the capitalist order of society. They aim at a new order based not on property and profit, but on co-operative effort. They realize that the working class will be the builders of this new order, and see that the change must be revolutionary in effect. Even those to whom politics are secondary desire to ally themselves more closely with the class that will build socialism.

* Reprinted from *Left Review* 1.3 (December 1934): 75–80 and 1.4 (January 1935): 125–8.

It is time for these, together with the working-class journalists and writers who are trying to express the feelings of their class, to organize an association of revolutionary writers such as the association already formed in the United States (where there is the John Reed Club with Dreiser, Dos Passos and Sherwood Anderson)[1] and in France (the A.E.A.R., with André Gide, Barbusse, Aragon, etc.).[2] Such an association obviously should apply for affiliation to the International of Revolutionary Writers, which has among its more famous members Maxim Gorky, Ludwig Renn, Romain Rolland and Upton Sinclair.

We suggest that membership of the Association should include writers,

(a) who see in the development of Fascism the terrorist dictatorship of dying capitalism and a menace to all the best achievements of human culture, and consider that the best in the civilization of the past can only be preserved and further developed by joining in the struggle of the working class for a new socialist society; who are opposed to all attempts to hinder unity in the struggle or any retreat before Fascism or compromise with Fascist tendencies;

(b) who, if members of the working class, desire to express in their work, more effectively than in the past, the struggle of their class;

(c) who will use their pens and their influence against imperialist war and in defence of the Soviet Union, the State where the foundations of Socialism have already been laid, and will expose the hidden forms of war being carried on against the Indian, Irish, African and Chinese peoples.

All those who agree with these points, we ask to join the association.

From Professor Sherard Vines:[3]

General aims admirable: something of the sort seems to be most urgently required.

But some of the language seems at first sight to be emotional rather than argumentative. 'The death of an old world and the birth of a new', 'the collapse of a culture': are these not both hopes rather than facts? Is it not probable that capitalism from the cultural and other points of view has still an alarming amount of punch? Is Fascism really a death-symptom? One would wish it to be, but is it? If it is, it is not half so dangerous as it would be were it (to borrow your metaphor) the first kick of a rebirth.

The assumptions here mentioned seem to me a little over-confident; but the aims – to combat Fascism and imposed bogus culture – are most laudable.

With regard to your category (c): 'in defence of the Soviet Union' does not mean, I presume, 'one's Soviet right or wrong': the phrase as it stands might possibly mislead.

I should like to add category (d): 'who will oppose every conceivable kind of armed force.' Complete elimination of bloodshed seems to me one of the most revolutionary measures that can be taken.

I should like to see expressed (though it is of course implicit) the aim of educating the readers and stimulating them to think; unless indeed so unpleasant a suggestion would wreck the scheme.

From Alec Brown:[4]

All normal writing has a reading public in view. The starting point of any comments on this programme must be clarity as to *for whom are we writing?* The answer must surely be that all our writing has one end in view, the revolutionary end of establishing a socialist republic, that is a working-class democracy. The second group (b) of prospective members ought of course to come first. The membership clause need be no more than: 'members of the working class or those of other classes who have crossed over and allied themselves to the working-class, who use the written (or printed) word for furthering their share in the labour of establishing a workers' republic.'

But that still is not what we are going to *DO*, and I get back to the question: *WHOM ARE WE WRITING FOR AND HOW?* The answer is that we have primarily in view the working-class reading public.

This reading public cannot afford to buy many books; and there are not many books fit for them to buy. It is up to us to tackle both these problems. As I see it the vast jellyfish of the petty middle-class is a lesser problem, though that must be the class the committee has in mind when it talks about a 'crisis of ideas'. So my suggestions boil down to three.

Suggestion 1. A special investigation permanently to be carried on to deal with the provision of the broad masses of the working-class with what constructive revolutionary literature is and will be available. I should suggest detailing a special member or members to enquire into the possibility of much more use of parallel cheap paper editions of books. It must be shown that this parallel paper edition will not lessen sales of the expensive edition and will pay. And we should do something really practical about organizing contacts between us all, and especially between those of us with a pure working-class position, and those starting with both the advantage and the serious handicap of bourgeois beginnings.

Suggestion 2. We need a permanent propaganda committee, to work towards

a. The proletarianisation of our outlook (of those of us who have bourgeois origins in our work) – and during the initial period of our magazine, most important, to carry on rigorous contemptuous criticism of all highbrowism,[5] intellectualism, abstract rationalism and similar dilettanteisms; in short, a constant goading question to be there, the single-minded question (the marxist question) *ARE WE AN ORGANIZATION OF REVOLUTIONARY WRITERS OR ARE WE NOT?*

b. OF NO SMALL IMPORTANCE, the proletarianisation of our actual language, by which I mean getting right down to spoken English in our work. No small task, because plain English folk can't understand the jargon most of us put out, and there I suggest (with apologies to rare writers like Bunyan[6] and Defoe and a few others) we have a slogan: *LITERARY ENGLISH FROM CAXTON TO US IS AN ARTIFICIAL JARGON OF THE RULING CLASS; WRITTEN ENGLISH BEGINS WITH US;* or another slogan: *WE ARE REVOLUTIONARY WORKING-CLASS WRITERS; WE HAVE GOT TO MAKE USE OF THE LIVING LANGUAGE OF OUR CLASS;* also: *ALLUSIVE WRITING IS CLIQUE WRITING: WE ARE NOT A CLIQUE.*

Suggestion 3. The middle-class search for serious literature (the 'crisis of ideas') is of course not a separate phenomenon, as the statement rather suggests. It is partly a sign of how deeply the crisis of capitalism even in imperial England is biting directly down into the complacent petty middle-class; it is also partly due to the final complete development of capitalism in book production, which naturally lowers the quality of fiction produced by the popular novelist etc. (hack of the printing and paper industry) and drives the intelligent or honest few who have not crossed to our side into a displeasing cynicism and cleverness. Our task in regard to this middle-class is to organize our destructive criticism of their morals, their religion and their rachitic ethics.

We must take advantage of the worsening position of this middle-class; those of us who write using the bourgeois channels should give earnest attention to this work. But while we do this, and assist the more intelligent and honest members of the class over to our side, we must never fail to maintain Robespierrian suspicion, we must never forget that the present distaste for Fascism and love of 'democracy' among them is with most of them merely a result of the fact that the usual petty middle-class comfort-loving squeamishness is more than generally marked in the leading imperialist country, and incidentally makes these folk, except in rare cases, the most unreliable and weak-kneed allies.

From Montagu Slater:[7]

I have a minor quarrel with the 'statement of aim'. I agree that the 'crisis of ideas' is a convenient starting point: indeed, it was the actual starting point for very many of us. But like what you call 'the decadence of the past twenty years of English literature', its importance as a separate phenomenon can be exaggerated. Your period of twenty years narrows the questions. The truth is that capitalism never found literature a comfortable ally: the bourgeoisie blunted the pen point whenever it could (more successfully in capitalist England than in France whereby hangs – critically – an interesting tale). A sense of crisis and decadence has been reflected in literature, as a permanent symptom of capitalism, for 150 years.

There is a passage in the *Communist Manifesto* which expresses indirectly the special discomforts of literature inside capitalism. 'Whenever the bourgeoisie has risen to power it has destroyed all feudal, patriarchal, and idyllic relationships. It has ruthlessly torn asunder the motley feudal ties that bound men to their "natural superiors"; it has left no other bond betwixt man and man but crude self-interest and unfeeling "cash payment". It has drowned pious zeal, chivalrous enthusiasm, and humdrum sentimentalism in the chill waters of selfish calculation. It has degraded personal dignity to the level of exchange value; and in place of countless dearly-brought chartered freedoms, it has set up one solitary unscrupulous freedom – freedom of trade. In a word, it has replaced exploitation veiled in religious and political illusions, by exploitation that is open, unashamed, direct and brutal.'

There is, I think, no question but that the arts are on the whole less fruitful under capitalism than under the conditions capitalism replaced. 'Commodity exchange begins where community life ends,' says Marx in *Capital*. 'In bourgeois society,' says the *Manifesto*, 'capital is independent and has individuality, whereas the living person is dependent and lacks individuality.' Obverse and reverse of the same medal! And when Capitalism is achieved, when man becomes an atomic unit, 'free', equal, a voter, and *unreal*, then social relations are no longer between men, but between things, or between commodities: action and passion is between Rolls Royces and macadam roads.

Art has lost its subject-matter. This subject-matter – man – can only exist in social relations: and art at least may rediscover him, not in social relations in the older *civilized* sense of the term, but in social battle, in class war, in the war to end the atomic capitalist regime.

In such a statement of position there is, implicitly, I think, a claim that we are *carrying forward* the pre-capitalist assets and the capitalist assets too. But this needs formulating carefully.

'The social productive organisms of ancient days,' says *Capital*, 'were far simpler, enormously more easy to understand, than is bourgeois society; but they were based, either upon the immaturity of the individual human being (who had not yet severed the umbilical cord which, under primitive conditions, unites all members of the human species one with another) or upon direct relations of dominion and subjugation.' In the simplicity of societies is sometimes found the explanation for the attractiveness of their literature. 'The Greeks were normal children,' says Marx in that passage in the *Critique of Political Economy*, where he finds that Greek writing and art 'in certain respects prevail as the standard and model beyond attainment'. And then Marx carries the point further. The old, simple organization of society was 'an outcome of a low grade of the evolution of the productive powers of labour; a grade on which the relations of human beings to one another within the process by which they produced the material necessities of life, and therefore their relations to nature as well, were correspondingly immature. This restrictedness in the world of concrete fact was reflected in the ideal world, in the world of the old natural and folk religions. Such religious reflections of the real world will not disappear until the relations between human beings in their practical everyday life have assumed the aspect of perfectly intelligible and reasonable relations as between man and man, and as between man and nature. The life process of society, this meaning the material process of production, will not lose its veil of mystery until it becomes a process carried on by a free association of producers, under their conscious and purposive control. For this, however, an indispensable requisite is that there should exist a specific material groundwork (or series of material conditions of existence) which can only come into being as the spontaneous outcome of a long and painful process of evolution' (*Capital*, Chapter I, Section 4: 'The Mystery of the Fetishistic Character of Commodities').

It is a long quotation but it contains a great deal. My own application is this. Capitalism, and the process of scientific enlightenment which its own greed has forced the bourgeoisie dubiously and grudgingly to permit, has carried us to the point where 'perfectly intelligible and reasonable relations as between man and man, and as between man and nature', are at last seen to be possible – at the price of the supersession of capitalism. The painful process of evolution and scientific enlightenment has been marked till now by bewildering complexity: the arts have been baffled: and in consequence the cultural legacy of capitalism has been almost entirely scientific in form. But as we, at any rate, begin to conceive the possibility of other than scientific expression: maybe the time is coming when mankind goes on from algebraic formula to poem again, re-enacting the Grecian intelligibility 'the standard and model beyond attainment' on another plane.

A final quotation from the *Communist Manifesto* sums the position up. 'In bourgeois society living labour is but a means for increasing the amount of stored labour. In communist society, stored labour is but a means for enlarging, enriching, furthering the existence of the workers.

'In bourgeois society, therefore, the past rules the present; but in communist society the present rules the past.'

In communist society the present rules the past – or, better, eats, drinks, enjoys, makes use of it. 'All history is contemporary history,' says Croce. But the statement, like the man who made it, stands ambiguously between socialist optimism and fascist fatalism. Let our slogan, then, be that we are going to utilize history (and as writers let us include literature) for the purposes of the class which is going to build socialism.[8]

I read last month's contributions to this discussion with much interest and to give particularity to my generalizations I shall add a comment or two. I think it follows from any statement of the full Marxist position that Alec Brown is mistaken when he wants us to turn with him contemptuous backs on 'the vast jellyfish of the petty middle-class'. Unfortunately it is the class to which any professional or semi-professional writer, whether he likes it or not, belongs to. (It is only in the U.S.S.R. that it is in practice possible for writers to turn from their typewriters for six months and take with a sigh of relief a six months spell in a factory.) So, since our aim is to bring writers into the fight under working-class leadership, the jellyfish has a place in our kettle.

Alec Brown is, I think, touching an important point when he demands that 'we should get right down to spoken English in our work'. The speech of the men 'at the hidden foci of production', workers and technologists, craftsmen and peasants, is the air a live literature must breathe.[9] (Incidentally, this contradicts Brown's slogan about 'allusive writing': for nothing could be more allusive than such talk.)

It is in short the strongest argument for a Writers' International that it can bring writers into touch with life. ('Life' in this context equals the class struggle – for proof of which vast claim I can only refer readers to the first part of this statement and all issues past and future of the *Left Review*.) If in making such claims our language, as Sherard Vines complains, becomes emotional rather than scientific, let practice and criticism work to amend it: but I would urge Sherard Vines to consider whether opposition to 'every conceivable kind of armed force' is not at this stage, if not the language, certainly the logic of emotionalism.

I recapitulate thus: (1) Literature concerns human relationships. Capitalism destroyed these in their primitive forms, substituting money or commodity relationships. The mere struggle to re-establish free human relationships in a non-mystical, intelligible form is among other things a fight for a better chance for literature.

(2) The working-class is necessarily the political and practical leader of this struggle. This does not mean that we start from scratch with a proletarian culture. Among our jobs is that of making the stored-up literary labour of the past usable by the present. In return we can be put in communication with (and write about) real men instead of bourgeois money-bags. But to do so we must step into the cold air of the practical world where we shall find that the fight against 'the rule of commodities' is a fight of actual men against flesh-and-blood enemies armed both with words – and guns.

Notes

1. Association of left-wing American intellectuals and artists, named after John Reed, author of the 1919 account of the Bolshevik revolution, *Ten Days That Shook the World*. When, in 1930, six workers faced the death penalty in Atlanta for protesting against unemployment, the John Reed Club cooperated with International Labour Defense and a number of notable figures – including Sherwood Anderson, Malcolm Cowley, Upton Sinclair and Edmund Wilson – to form an Emergency Committee for Southern Political Prisoners. Dos Passos was treasurer and Theodore Dreiser the Director. See Carr, pp. 276–9.
2. The Association des Ecrivains et Artistes Révolutionnaires, founded in 1932.
3. Author of several books, including *The Course of English Classicism from the Tudor to the Victorian Age* (London: Hogarth Press, 1930), which was reviewed by George Orwell in the *New Adelphi* (June–August 1930). The review is reprinted in Orwell, *An Age Like This*, pp. 22–4.
4. 1930s 'proletarian' novelist and translator – especially of Soviet texts – who published *The Fate of the Middle Class* (London: Gollancz) in 1936. His novels include *A Winter's Journey: A Simple Country Tale* (1933) [according to Cunningham, 'an obvious attempt to combine cashing-in on the Webb–Powys rurality stunt with a bit of Marxizing about landlords'] and *Daughters of Albion* (1935) ('turgidly lengthy' [Cunningham, p. 320]). He also was the author of detective novels: *Time to Kill* and *Green Lane or Murder at Moat Farm* (both 1930).

5. Cf. F. R. Leavis (see above, p. 24, n. 18).
6. One of the best pieces of Marxist criticism from the period, incidentally, takes Bunyan as its subject: see Jack Lindsay, *John Bunyan: Maker of Myths* (London: Methuen, 1937).
7. Communist writer, playwright and editor at this time of the *Left Review*. Among the pieces which I would have liked to see included in this volume – but which, for reasons of space, do not appear – is Slater's essay, 'The Purpose of a Left Review', *Left Review* 6.9: 359–65.
8. This is a very different thing from saying with Alec Brown in the December *Left Review*, 'Written English begins with us.' Fortunately it doesn't. [S]
9. An amusing example of how people of considerable political shrewdness are scared off by the literary power of such speech is to be found in the English translation of a famous passage of Stalin. Stalin warned the imperialists 'to keep their hog-snouts out of our Soviet potato patch', a powerful and lively image which in all the English translations was suburbanized into 'Keep their hog-snouts out of our Soviet garden.' [S]

8 David Gascoyne *from **A Short Survey of Surrealism**
(1935)**

When Viscount Hastings reviewed this book in the *Left Review* (2 [1936]: 186–7),
he was largely positive about the work as an outline of surrealism, if somewhat
reserved about Gascoyne's style: 'the English gives the impression of a translation
from another language.' But he could not accept Gascoyne's claims for the
movement's link to revolutionary politics. It was, he said, 'the complete
expression of bourgeois decadence'.[1] Furthermore, 'the fundamental difference
between surrealist art and Marxism, is that the theory of Freud and of the
psychoanalysts on which surrealism is based is in no way materialistic: it is an
idealistic study of thought and the emotions, largely concerned with neuroses
of the wealthy under capitalism.' When the *Left Review* took note of the
publication of that other key text of the English movement – Herbert Read's
Surrealism, 'evidently published in connection with the 1936 surrealist exhibition'
(Tolley, p. 227) – it had very similar reservations. A. L. Lloyd (*Left Review*, 2
[1937]: 897) remarked that 'it seems the significance of Surrealism in the political
field is at present rather counter-revolutionary than otherwise': 'Surrealism is
not revolutionary, because its lyricism is socially irresponsible. It does not lead
fantasy into any action of real social significance . . . [and] is a particularly subtle
form of fake revolution. It has no bearing on proletarian problems, gives no twist
towards social responsibility.'

Nevertheless, proponents of the movement continued to argue aggressively
for the revolutionary character of surrealism. Roger Roughton's journal
Contemporary Poetry and Prose, for example, was uncompromising on this
question. And when Read's book appeared, Roughton included a review by
Humphrey Jennings which 'accused Read and [Hugh] Sykes-Davies of attempting
to kidnap surrealism as a form of Romanticism, and of thus imposing limitations
on it' (Tolley, pp. 227–8). It is interesting to note, however, that while Gascoyne
wrote regularly for *Contemporary Poetry and Prose* he seems also to have
perceived that the Freudian allegiances of the movement were at odds with its
revolutionary ambitions, that the latter were subject to 'limitations'. When in
1934 Geoffrey Grigson surveyed 40 poets on the question of their debt to Freud
and of their views on political engagement, Gascoyne replied as follows:

> I have never been directly influenced by Freud in my poetry, but I have
> been indirectly influenced by him through the Surrealists. To give oneself

* Reprinted from *A Short Survey of Surrealism* (1935; London: Frank Cass and Co., 1970),
pp. ix–xiii and 131–6.

up at any time to writing poems without the control of the reason is, I imagine, to have in a way come under the influence of Freud. I no longer find this navel-gazing activity at all satisfying. The Surrealists themselves have a definite justification for writing in this way, but for an English poet with continually growing political convictions it must soon become impossible.[2]

A year after this, Gascoyne went to Paris on a commission from Cobden-Sanderson to conduct research for his *Short Survey of Surrealism*; and in 1936 he was one of the organizers of the International Surrealist Exhibition.[3] But by September of that year he was declaring in his journal, '*Nothing* I have written so far is of the least value.' His 'growing political convictions' had led him to join the Communist Party. In October, though, a trip to Spain left him disillusioned at communist treatment of the anarchists and POUM; so by the following year he was no longer a member of the Party, and – stimulated by his meeting in Barcelona with Tristan Tzara – beginning to wonder if he was not 'really a religious?'[4] Gascoyne's was in many ways a typical 1930s career, and the ambiguous form which surrealism took in England during that period was apposite to the time. Charles Madge, through whom Gascoyne later came to be involved in Mass-Observation, wrote in 1933 that 'the essential relation between the philosophy and achievement [of surrealism] should not stop us from being certain that the philosophy is, like all philosophies, a reflection of that history in which we ourselves are actors'.[5]

Confined from early childhood in a world that almost everything he ever hears or reads will tell him is the one and only *real* world and that, as almost no one, on the contrary, will point to him, is a prison, man – *l'homme moyen sensuel* – bound hand and foot not only by those economic chains of whose existence he is becoming ever more and more aware, but also by chains of second-hand and second-rate *ideas*, the preconceptions and prejudices that help to bind together the system known (ironically, as some think, by the name of 'civilisation'), is for ever barred except in sleep from that other plane of existence where stones fall upwards and the sun shines by night, if it chooses, and where even the trees talk freely with the statues that have come down for ever from their pedestals – a world to which the entrance has generally been supposed, up till now, to be the sole privilege of poets and other madmen. For it is undeniably true that the oniric[6] domain is still regarded in very much the same way as was the erotic domain during the Victorian era. That the dream is useless, as escape from reality, the dreamer a self-indulgent and lazy person, is the accepted view of an overwhelming majority. How, then, can man reconcile himself to the fact that he spends more than a third of his life on earth in sleep, and that he spends the whole time of his sleeping in a world that his conscious mind so despises?

It is the avowed aim of the surrealist movement to reduce and finally dispose altogether of the flagrant contradictions that exist between dream and waking life, the 'unreal' and the 'real', the unconscious and the conscious, and thus to make of what has hitherto been regarded as the special domain of poets, the acknowledged common property of all. So far as the surrealists themselves are either writers or painters, it is also at the same time their aim to extend indefinitely the limits of 'literature' and 'art' by continually tending to do away with the barrier that separates the contents of the printed page or of the picture-frame from the world of real life and action.

Taking this attitude as our point of departure, we are bound sooner or later to envisage a conception of imaginative expression in general, and of poetry in particular, that is almost totally different from the most widely current in present-day England and America – countries where the vital issues of surrealism have been persistently misrepresented and obscured from the moment when, not so long ago, the rumour of this strange new 'modern' movement first came to our ears.

Surrealism, profiting from the discoveries of Freud and a few other scientific explorers of the unconscious, has conceived poetry as being, on the one hand, a perpetual functioning of the *psyche*, a perpetual flow of irrational thought *in the form of images* taking place in every human mind and needing only a certain predisposition and discipline in order to be brought to light in the form of written words (or plastic images), and on the other hand, a universally valid attitude to experience, a possible mode of living. It is thus a restatement of the ancient and supposedly discredited notion of inspiration – with a difference. This lyrical element of human thought, the source of all authentic poetry, common to all men did they but realise it, is manifested in the plays of Shakespeare and in the ravings of lunatics in *Kubla Khan* and in Walt Disney's *Silly Symphonies*; in the paintings of Picasso and in popular picture-postcards. 'I say that there exists a lyrical element that conditions for one part the psychological and moral structure of human society' (I quote from André Breton), 'that has conditioned it for all time and that will continue to condition it. This lyrical element is up to this day, even though in spite of them, the fact and the sole fact of specialists.' And when it is said that the aim of surrealism is to break down the barrier separating dream ('poetry') from reality, the irrational from the rational, that is also to say that its aim is to make this 'sole fact of specialists' familiar to everyone. Here we have the answer to the problem raised by the apparent contradiction between the artistic attitude of surrealism and its declared political faith. It should by now be clear to Marxists that the surrealist attitude is totally in accord with the Communist philosophy of dialectical materialism, with its insistence on the synonymity of theory and practice, and that only the imminence of proletarian revolution allows surrealism to hope that its aims will ultimately be fulfilled. The surrealist cause is the revolutionary cause – In spite of the surrealists' bourgeois origin, in spite of the attitude of certain dogmatic Marxists towards such phenomena as Freudian psychoanalysis and the more complicated developments of modern literature and art, and in spite of such apparent compromises on the part of the Communists as the Franco-Soviet pact and the recent rehabilitation in Russia of the bourgeois conception of the family . . .

Surrealism . . . is an activity of the mind, and cannot be limited to any one particular time or place. The surrealist movement, the immediate product of certain currents of thought that happened to be more prevalent in nineteenth-century France than elsewhere, represents the very vigorous coherent effort of a number of men to develop this activity along experimental lines and to explore its widest possibilities. And there is every reason to believe that surrealism, as a movement, is only just at the end of its earliest stages. If a really wide and properly organised international co-operation can be brought about, as there are signs that it shortly will be, surrealism may become of even more importance to the twentieth century than it is already.

There will be, of course, objections to such a co-operation. In England, for instance, there will be many to protest that surrealism is foreign to the national temperament, that it cannot grow here as it has no roots in English tradition.[7] Such an objection could only result from a lack of understanding of what surrealism *is*. As a matter of fact, there is a very strong surrealist element in English literature; one need quote only Shakespeare, Marlowe, Swift, Young, Coleridge, Blake, Beddoes, Lear and Carroll to prove this contention. For a writer, or anyone else, to object to an attempt to establish surrealist activity in England, on the grounds that this would mean an 'importation from Paris', is just as stupidly provincial as a doctor would be if he objected to the practice of psychoanalysis in England because it originated in Vienna. Surrealism itself, as it is today, is by no means wholly the product of previous French culture; there is a very strong element both of German and of Spanish thought in it, synthetising as it does the philosophy of Hegel, Feuerbach, Engels and

Marx, and the distinctly southern 'lyricism' of painters such as Dalí, Miró and Picasso. For surrealism transcends all nationalism and springs from a plane on which all men are equal.

It might be as well before concluding to summarise briefly the chief preoccupations of surrealist research during the last ten years. These fall roughly into two categories: firstly, passive or subjective; secondly, active or objective.

To the first category belong automatism, spontaneous and 'pure' poetry, and the idea of the synonymity of poetry and dream. Parallel with these features, in the realm of art, may be placed *collage* and *frottage*, and the development of the idea of the element of anonymity and chance in artistic creation. From this idea of chance or hazard (which really began in the days of Dada, with the production of poems by extracting words at random from a hat) to the paranoiac system introduced by Dalí,[8] the development is much the same as that followed by Freud in his *Interpretation of Dreams* to *The Psycho-pathology of Everyday Life*, in which he advances the theory that accidents are very largely determined by psychic necessity. Objective hazard as the pivot of the surrealist conception of life, is the subject to which Breton is at present devoting his attention; and Dalí has always contended that surrealist objects 'take the form of desire'. No longer does a surrealist await the message or the image to arise from the vast unconscious residue of experience; he actively imposes the image of his desires and obsessions upon the concrete, daylight world of objective reality; he actively takes part in 'accidents' that reveal the true nature of the mechanism that is life far more clearly than 'pure psychic automatism' could.

In addition to all this we must take into consideration the unchanging political position of the surrealists in opposing bourgeois society, attacking religion, patriotism and the idea of family, and in declaring their belief in the principles of Communism and their solidarity with the proletariat of all countries.

In conclusion, tribute should be paid to André Breton, whose energy, enthusiasm and powers of leadership have been and are still of inestimable value not only to the surrealist movement but to all those taking part in it. He is one of the most remarkable men of his time, and his influence will long continue to make itself felt in modern thought.

It is my hope that the reader will have realised by now that surrealism is not simply a way of writing or of painting, but a school of thought that may very well be playing a role of historical importance. The great task of this century is that of revising the old scales of value in every field, of destroying worn-out customs and institutions and of constructing a form of society in which men may be able to make full use of all their faculties. Few poets – and poets, though still unacknowledged, continue to be the legislators of the world – have set about this task with so great a thoroughness as have the surrealists. Already they have succeeded in widening and deepening the total of human experience.

Notes

1. This was also the view of Christopher Caudwell (see below, pp. 124–9).
2. *New Verse* 11 (October 1934): 12. See also Tolley, pp. 234–5.
3. Hugh Sykes-Davies looked forward to the exhibition in 'Sympathies with Surrealism', *New Verse* 20 (April–May 1936): 15-21.
4. See Philip Gardner, 'David Gascoyne', *DLB* 20: 143.
5. 'Surrealism for the English', *New Verse* 6 (December 1933): 14.
6. Onirus was the ancient Greek god of dreams.
7. It is interesting to compare with this Mosley's attempt to rebut a similar argument made against Fascism. See above, pp. 28–9.
8. For an alternative 1930s perspective on Dalí, see Orwell's 'Benefit of Clergy: Some Notes on Salvador Dalí' (1944) in *As I Please*, pp. 156–65.

9 Vera Brittain *Can the Women of the World Stop War? (1934)**

Vera Brittain was eighteen years old when, at St Monica's School in Surrey, she was loaned her headmistress's copy of *Women and Labour* by the South African feminist, Olive Schreiner. As she was later to remark, the book 'sounded with a note that had the authentic ring of a new gospel'.[1] It was a work, as Paul Berry and Mark Bostridge observe, which 'allowed her to articulate [her natural outrage over women's role in society] and gave expression to her feminism' (p. 36). In the last years of the First World War she began also 'to think on definitely pacifist lines – though I did not then recognise them as such'.[2] While always a combative feminist, she became increasingly active in the cause of pacifism over the next fifteen years; but it was the publication of *Testament of Youth* in 1933 which brought her to prominence in and outside the movement. In 1934 Canon Dick Sheppard made his public appeal to citizens to sign a pledge renouncing war, and by January 1937 he had persuaded Brittain to become a sponsor of his Peace Pledge Union. Her acquiescence was a fillip to the cause, and it was also to have long-term consequences for Brittain herself, binding her for the rest of her life to the search for peace (see Berry and Bostridge, pp. 349–59).

During the months when this essay was written, Brittain was the exhausted victim of the celebrity brought to her by the publication of *Testament of Youth* the previous year. She was in great demand as a public speaker, and on 15 September she embarked on a book tour of the United States, where she would give more than forty lectures. After three months, on the eve of her return to England, she made a radio broadcast which summed up the message she had tried to convey throughout the tour:

> If the courage which my contemporaries once gave to the War can be used by our successors on behalf of Peace, the martyrdom of man may still lead at least to his redemption. If modern youth has realized, as I believe it has, that to live for one's country is a finer type of patriotism than to die for it, then the youth of my generation will not, after all, have laid down the best of its life in vain.[3]

The world today is threatened by the gravest danger that has confronted it since 1914. During the past eventful twelve months there have been international crises in every part of this earth – in Geneva, in Germany, in

---

* Originally published in *Modern Woman*, February 1934. Reprinted from *Testament of a Generation: The Journalism of Vera Brittain and Winifred Holtby*, ed. Paul Berry and Alan Bishop (London: Virago, 1985), pp. 216–20.

Spain, in Russia and in the Far East. Unless humanity makes a mightier effort to save itself than it has yet achieved, the civilization that we know may well go the way of Greece and Rome, and mankind be plunged into a new Dark Age.

At such a time of possible catastrophe the part which women might play in the prevention of war becomes a question of special urgency. Men have controlled the world for centuries, yet their civilized ideals are still at the mercy of their primitive impulses. Women, however, represent a new element in politics. In many countries they are still powerless, but most civilized nations have now granted them a large measure of political influence.

Can they, and will they, use this influence to prevent a repetition of that organized slaughter which between 1914 and 1918 destroyed the fine flower of a whole generation?

The other day, while preparing an address on 'How War Affects Women', I reread part of Olive Schreiner's famous book, *Women and Labour*, published in 1911. And in the chapter on 'Women and War' – written, appropriately enough, only three years before the Great War broke out, and only seven before the vote in England was granted to women over 30 – I came across these words:

> That day, when the woman takes her place beside the man in the governance and arrangement of external affairs of her race, will also be that day that heralds the death of war as a means of arranging human differences.

Today, when the largest and most influential section of English women has had the vote for over fifteen years, can we say that Olive Schreiner's prophecy shows signs of fulfilment? It is true that woman's place in politics is hardly, as yet, an equal place 'beside the man'. But it is also, I fear, too true that women have not yet exercised that strong influence on behalf of peace in which Olive Schreiner believed with eager confidence.

A few organized women, such as the members of the Women's International League,[4] are working nobly and continuously. One or two women writers – Miss Storm Jameson, for instance, whose brilliant *No Time Like the Present* was one of the outstanding books of 1933 – constantly urge upon their readers the waste and futility of war.

But a terrible, inert mass of lethargic womanhood still does nothing, and apparently cares nothing. It does not realize that a civilization in which military values prevail is always hostile to women's interests, and that our enormous expenditure upon armaments is largely responsible for the fact that women, as a sex, are still so poorly endowed and badly equipped. Because we, as a nation, spend our money upon guns and battleships, the great majority of women have to live in wretched, inconvenient houses, and manage with old-fashioned, second-rate tools. Because English statesmen are still dominated by military ideals, many mothers who might be saved continue to die in childbirth.

Let me give you one or two examples of these lunatic values. Do you know that 20,000 new houses, of the type with low rents which are so badly needed, can be built for the cost of one armed cruiser? Do you realize that our preliminary bombardments at Arras, Messines and Passchendaele during the war cost this country fifty-two million pounds, but that a National Maternity Service would only mean a yearly expenditure of two-and-three-quarter millions? For the money, therefore, which we spent upon those three destructive bombardments we could have had a National Maternity Service, with all that it would have meant in the reduction of maternal mortality, for nearly twenty years!

When I think of such facts as these, I am not so much dismayed that women have failed to put an end to war, as astounded that so few of them have even tried to do so. Because women produce children, life and the means of living matter to them in a way that these things can never matter to men. Yet too many wives and mothers make a virtue of taking no interest in 'politics', although it is only by political methods that a new and yet vaster annihilation of human life can be prevented.

The woman who today restricts her interest to her own domestic affairs and refuses to accept what Sir Norman Angell has called 'the moral obligation to be intelligent',[5] is guilty of gross irresponsible selfishness towards her children and society. It is useless to have an ideal nursery if you do nothing to prevent that nursery from being blown to bits within the next few years.

I believe that the women of the world could stop war if they ceased to be completely absorbed in themselves and their homes and their children, and began to realize that their duty to mankind extends beyond their own little doorstep.

I sometimes feel that what the women's peace campaign really needs is the sudden uprising of a movement as swift and dramatic as that of the militant suffragists, which would adopt expedients similar to theirs, such as the refusal to pay income tax for war purposes, or the interruption of military pageants and tattoos with protests still more vehement than those already attempted by Dr. Maude Royden and her supporters.[6] But as a movement of this kind requires a leader at least as gifted and inspired as Mrs. Pankhurst, and though such leaders have a habit of appearing at the psychological moment, I believe that, even without a guide of this type, women could exercise a decisive influence for peace if they adopted the right methods on a large enough scale.

The first essentials are awareness and organization. To study the influence of public events upon private lives, to follow the course of international affairs with enough intelligence to understand what type of men and women our representatives should be and how we can ensure their choice – these are duties from which no domestic preoccupations can now excuse us. And we can best employ such knowledge and the power that it brings by giving our support to peace organizations, which exist in sufficient variety to represent all shades of opinion, from the right-wing League of Nations Union to the Anti-War Movement on the extreme left.[7] We can use these, as well as the ordinary machinery of politics, to demand the expenditure of the nation's money upon the means of life instead of the instruments of death.

In addition we can take, as individuals, certain drastic steps which would have a compelling effect if universally adopted. We can refuse, for instance, to send our sons to schools which run an Officers' Training Corps, and we can ostracize any acquaintances known to have shares in armament firms or to deal with such firms on a business basis. Society has always condemned the thief and the forger, but these are less anti-social than the man or woman who grows rich from the murder and mutilation of humanity. Our country's policy would soon change if no advocate of increased armaments could get a woman to vote for him or invite him to her house.

I refuse to believe that women, who produce life, will permit mankind resignedly to accept death from the diabolical instruments of its own invention. Since men throughout their centuries of authority have not succeeded in extending the reign of law to international relationships, it is our task today to explore every method by which the heroism and resourcefulness that respond so swiftly and tragically to war can be dedicated instead to the service of peace and life.

Notes

1. 'Olive Schreiner', *Nation and Atheneum*, 23 October 1926.
2. 'What Can We Do in Wartime?', August 1939. Quoted in Berry and Bostridge, p. 121.
3. 'Youth and War', 13 December 1934, in the Vera Brittain Archive at McMaster University, and reprinted in *Thrice a Stranger: New Chapters of Autobiography*

(London: Victor Gollancz, 1938), p. 225. Quoted and discussed in Berry and Bostridge, p. 305.
4. The Women's International League for Peace and Freedom, of which Brittain served a term as Vice-President.
5. Norman Angell's 'psychological Gresham Law' is discussed by F. R. Leavis. See above, p. 20.
6. A. Maude Royden, the feminist activist, would subsequently distance herself from pacifism in the late 1930s. See Sheila Fletcher, *Maude Royden: A Life* (Oxford: Basil Blackwell, 1989).
7. The League of Nations Union was founded by Agnes Murray. Brittain lectured for the LNU between 1922 and 1925.

This essay appeared in *Challenge to Death*, a collection edited by Storm Jameson and published in 1935. Introducing the American edition of the book (in the English edition Jameson had 'with characteristic modesty' suppressed her name as editor), Vera Brittain argued that *Challenge to Death* originated as a response to the 1928 English translation – by Richard Aldington – of Julien Benda's *La Trahison des clercs*:[1] 'Had we really, as novelists, biographers, poets, journalists, dramatists or scientists, neglected some of the opportunities which we might have taken to persuade public opinion to substitute reason for passion, truth for prejudice, justice for persecution? Of what avail was our contribution to literature and art if the type of civilisation in which literature and art are possible was to come within a few years to a violent end?' (p. viii).

Such questions apparently preoccupied Storm Jameson and Philip Noel Baker when they met in 1933 in Hastings at the British National Labour Conference, at which event they conceived the idea of holding a dinner in London to which would be invited 'a number of writers who had shown themselves, by their previous publications, to be anxious to combat that "principle of death" which again and again has appeared to condemn human society to its own destruction' (p. viii). When the dinner came to pass in early 1934, Rebecca West was included in the group – seated beside Lord David Cecil, who had agreed to act as host. In *Civil Journey* Jameson notes that she was rather alarmed at playing 'bear-leader to so many noble writers, but drew what comfort I could by placing Lord Cecil between Miss Rebecca West and Miss Rose Macaulay. He looked like an eagle sitting between two – now, what vivid bird can I put here without giving offence? Never mind' (p. 181).[2] The idea of collecting into a book the views of the assembled company appears to have entered Jameson's mind as she planned the dinner, but it took more than a year and – as Brittain tells us – '174 letters [written] with her own hand' (p. ix), before the volume appeared.

I

The public mind is bound to be disconcerted at the notion of placing the decisive weapon of warfare, air power, in the hands of an international body, who is going to use it to suppress nationalist aggressions; for it believes

---

* Reprinted from *Challenge to Death*, ed. Storm Jameson (New York: E. P. Dutton, 1935), pp. 240–60.

that the nationalist spirit is what it lives by, and to a great extent it is right in
that belief. It is natural and wholesome that an Englishman, born and bred in
England, should feel towards it the same kind of deep emotional concern, of
visceral pull, that he feels towards his father and mother and brothers and
sisters, and that this feeling for his country should for the most part, just like
his feeling for his family, take a form which may reasonably be called love.
Later he may find other countries more beautiful, more romantic, or more
agreeable as domiciles, but that does not affect his basic tie. A man does not
erase the influence of his family from his personality when he falls in love
with a stranger woman. England is the first piece of life that is offered to his
scrutiny, and he will never have the same opportunities of studying any other.
So, if he is the kind of man who loves life, he will love best of all this part of
it he knows most thoroughly; and the bond will be reciprocal. His country
can help him to live as no other can, because it can give him a tradition which
is appropriate to him, which springs from the experience of men of his own
blood contending with the same environment. Of this help he must be proudly
conscious, since the world is a dangerous place and he must keep his heart
up by making an account of the defensive material at his disposal, and by
assuring himself of its worth.

The public mind is, therefore, under no illusion when it regards its
nationalist spirit as a part of itself which it could not sacrifice without grave
loss. As a general rule, if an Englishman is to get the best out of himself, he
must feel that England is a uniquely precious entity which he must protect
from the domination of others, so that it can work out the destiny peculiar to
itself and make thereby a revelation of truth which none other can achieve.
He must feel that when the foot of an invader treads on English soil there is
threatened the interruption of a sacred process. Dostoievsky describes in a
famous passage in *The Possessed* the efficacy of this mechanism. 'The people,'
he says, 'is only a people so long as it has its own god and excludes all other
gods on earth irreconcilably . . . Such, from the beginning of time, has been
the belief of all the great nations, all, anyway, who have been specially
remarkable, all who have been the leaders of humanity. There is no going
against facts. The Jews lived only to await the coming of the true God, and
left the world the true God. The Greeks deified nature and bequeathed the
world their religion, that is, philosophy and art. Rome deified the people in
the State and bequeathed the idea of the State to the nation. France throughout
her long history was only the incarnation and development of the Roman
god . . . If a great people does not believe that the truth is not to be found in
itself alone (in itself alone and in it exclusively); if it does not believe that it

alone is fit and destined to raise up and save all the rest by its truth, it would at once sink into being ethnographic material.'

So the public mind is right when it regards as a probable danger the Englishman who feels no more emotion when he sees the cliffs of Dover after a long journey than when he sees the harbour bay at Cherbourg, or the Statue of Liberty in New York Bay, and who would genuinely remain unmoved if a foreign power established itself in London and governed us. He may be the exception who can contribute most to civilisation in alien surroundings: El Greco worked very well in Toledo. But it is more probable that he is a drifter of the sort that strikes no root and bears neither flower nor fruit, that, multiplied, would make an obscure and helot people. Where the public mind goes wrong, however, is when it builds on this recognition of the usefulness of nationalism, a repudiation of internationalism; when it lets itself feel that it ought to keep all its military forces at the disposal of the nationalist spirit. And that to hand them to an international body would be to surrender them frivolously to a new and untried and unnatural invention of the ideologists. There it is treacherous to its own nationalism. For one cannot serve the national spirit merely by getting a lump in the throat whenever one catches sight of the Union Jack, or seeing red when a newspaper reports that some foreign power has acted aggressively towards England. These reactions bear the same relation to true love of country that a chance encounter between a man and a woman who meet in the street bears to a happy marriage. The test of real and valuable nationalism is to avail oneself of the tradition of one's country; and it happens that internationalism is one of the most ancient and firmly established elements in our tradition. If there is any belief which is new and untried and unnatural, it is the astonishing notion that it is safe to allow the nationalistic spirit free play without constant insistence on international safeguards.

For the English tradition is but one branch of the European tradition, which from the very beginning has recognised that nationalism and internationalism are not irreconcilable opposites but counterbalances which can keep the nations in equilibrium. Fifteen hundred years ago a genius named Augustine worked over what he knew of the political thought of the ancient world, in order to prepare from it a guide for the new world he saw coming into being around him as a result of the fall of Rome and the rise of Christianity. He could hardly be called an ideologist, for he was a practical man, closely in touch with the conduct of affairs, and a vital period of the world's history lay before his eyes. A native of Roman Africa, a visitor to Rome and Milan while their glories were still standing, he could judge of what the Empire did for its people while it was an effective power; and as time went on, and Roman Africa was pulled to tatters by the assaults of vandals and barbarians, he realised what the failure of the Empire meant to it peoples. From what he had observed of the clash between the standardising influence of Rome and the individualities of its dominated territories, he learned to value the international spirit. One of his most notable letters calls shame on an African who had ceased living according to the African genius and remade himself on a Latin model. But when he saw that the green fertility of Africa was likely to be reduced to dust by the invading hordes, he learned to appreciate the guarantee of the maximum possible amount of peace which Rome had been able to give her peoples in her greatest days. Therefore, when he sought an ideal for the political organisation of man, he looked around for a system that would tolerate the nationalist spirit and maintain the peace necessary for its development. The Empire was ruled out as an impracticable device, for it could only extend itself to the scope necessary for imposing peace by aggressions that did violence to other nations. Augustine saw that, for the protection of nationalism, it was necessary to employ internationalism, and he therefore recommended a society of small States, 'peaceful in neighbourly agreement'. He hoped for a world in which there would be such an abundance of States as there are families in a city; and just as the families in a city have to unite before municipal life can be stable and effective so, those States would have to organise among themselves to make a peaceful world. This programme for humanity, drawn up by a man of genius who had ample material to work upon, was much too simple and sensible to be forgotten by normal human beings; and it was one of the main factors in mediæval thought.

The men of the Middle Ages were unquestionably sturdy folk. They made war constantly and with magnificent courage. Certainly they were our superiors, as anyone may see who turns to their austere and solemn art, in facing the tragic elements in experience. But they were never such melancholic idiots as to persuade themselves that war was better for them than peace, that it was desirable that sound human flesh should turn to carrion on the bloody muck of battlefields, that it was anything but scandalous if the intercourse of nations exhibited the indecorum of a dog-fight and the reek of a shambles. They prayed in their churches for 'peace in our time', for 'peace and true concord', and made earnest petitions for protection in the mass 'to be said in time of war'. They admitted that war was a horror, brought down on them as a scourge for their sins, and that no one could conceive of its persistence if the good were to come to dominate earthly affairs. They were as aware as our modern economists that military victory is an illusion, that 'it costs more than it gains'. They were undismayed by those essays at internationalism which the ignorant of to-day regard as peculiarly modern and capricious experiments, and were not ashamed of Pope Innocent III, who wrote as forcibly as any of our contemporaries in favour of peace and arbitration. When friars went forth preaching peace crusades, the most virile among warriors would listen, and recognise a good doctrine, and bid their swords not respond too actively to the provocative circumstances of mediæval Europe. They would have been extremely startled if any voice from the jingoist future had warned them to beware against losing their manliness by listening to these enfeebling counsels of internationalism, because they thought of themselves as internationalists. They were proudly conscious that they were members of a great international body called Christendom. Then as now a man's relationship to his home and his people was a matter of the greatest importance to him. But to men in the Middle Ages that relationship did not seem of nearly so great political importance as the membership in Christendom.

They would have been startled, too, at the suggestion that counsels should be enfeebling because they were internationalist. There were giants in those days; and none has been born since who can make them look like dwarfs. There have been many legends invented about Charlemagne, but he was no legend. Out of the shattered ruins of the ancient world he built the modern world, and even now reflection on his feat quickens the pulse. It was an achievement as daring as any long transoceanic flight of our day, but called also for endurance lasting not hours but decades, and for adventure of the mind as well as of the body; a vast new political trajectory was described as well as a military one. Men born within the scope of his achievement came into a community stamped with the image of his lordship as if it were a coin. He had been power incarnate, and all Western European peoples knew it. But they also knew him as an internationalist. For he had founded the Holy Roman Empire, which sought to be a commonwealth comprising the whole body of Christian people in the world, regardless of their speech and race; and this was not a pietistic label clapped on a bottle of the old imperial brew. Though he was a tiger in battle he repeatedly modified the conduct and political direction of his wars in order that he might serve the cause of harmony among the nations rather than prosecute mere conquests. He did this not simply out of prudence, but because he was intellectually a convinced follower of internationalist doctrines, which he never wearied of studying in the works of Augustine. It was his habit to read again and again those pages in which political order and peace are insistently claimed as necessary preliminaries to the full development of man. 'The earthly city, which does not live by faith, seeks an earthly peace, and the end it proposes, in the well-ordered concord of civic obedience and rule, is the union of men's wills to attain the things which are helpful to this life. The body of the elect, or rather the part of it which sojourns on earth and lives by faith, makes use of this peace simply because it must, until this mortal condition which necessitates it shall pass away. Hence, so long as it lives a captive and a stranger in this earthly city, it makes no scruple to obey the laws of the earthly city, whereby the things necessary for the maintenance of this mortal life are administered; . . . and calls citizens out of all the nations, and gathers together a society of pilgrims of all languages, not scrupling about diversities in the manners, laws, and institutions whereby earthly peace is secured and maintained, but recognising that, however various these are, they all tend to one and the same end of earthly peace. For even the body of the elect, while in a state of pilgrimage, avails itself of the peace of earth, and, so far as it can without injuring faith and godliness, desires and maintains a common agreement among men regarding the acquisition of the necessaries of life, and makes this earthly peace the foundation of the peace of heaven.' So Charlemagne read and ruled. Surely there is no man sufficient of a fool to believe that our age knows so much better than the past that we would not be well advised to read what he read in the hope of ruling as he ruled.

II

Later internationalism faded out of the foreground of the common mind, but not because it had failed. There were practical difficulties which made it for the time being a difficult ideal to serve. The Church, which was the one unifying force recognised by mediæval man, fell into disorder and was itself more disunited than the nations which it had previously united, so that they competed fiercely among themselves for its control, and the nationalist spirit blazed up in all quarters. It found it could burn to some purpose, for the long decay of feudalism set loose a vast army of landless men, who would fight for any nation that paid them as professional soldiers. But it would be foolish to represent this period as one of catastrophe and pure loss to the cause of peace, for there was an impediment to the development of internationalism which man had to put out of the way. It was indicated by Franceso Vittoria, a child of the fifteenth century, when he wrote that a 'victor must look on himself not as a prosecutor but a judge, reducing to a minimum the disaster and misfortune that have overtaken the State, the more so that among

Christians the fault lies for the most part with the princes'. There had to be settled the question of the organisation of power within the nation, so that government could be guaranteed to act gravely and with regard to the security of all its people. There had therefore to be begun that research into what the rights of man may be, and how they are to be preserved, which has preoccupied Europe for the last few hundred years, and can only be prosecuted by the help of experiment within the separate nations.

This research was a necessary preliminary to internationalism; but it was natural enough that men should forget that it had this end. There can be no denying that nationalism is deeper in a man's skin and bones than internationalism, that it is a more integral part of his instinctive life. A man so rudimentary that still wore a tail would be conscious of his relationship to his own kind and his own home; and it is extremely unlikely that he would rise to any conception remotely akin to the idea of world brotherhood. We are apt, therefore, chips off the old tailed block that we are, to forget internationalism more easily than nationalism. But this aptitude is no evidence that internationalism is any less valuable to our humanity than nationalism. There are truths which we learn almost without the exercise of thought, by immediate perception, there are others we learn only by the exercise of protracted and elaborate thought and deliberate perception, there are still others that we learn only by deduction from these other truths. These first build themselves firmly into man's consciousness, the second paint themselves on it, but can be wiped off as paint can, the third are difficult to register on its surface and have to be repeatedly reinscribed by education and argument. These differences are not in the least a measure of their value to humanity. Some of the third class, most remote from primitive man, such as the necessity for a government, are the most essential to its survival. It is well to reflect that our rudimentary ancestor would have protested much more vigorously if one had tried to cut off his tail than if one had tried to take away the branches with which he was making a shelter, yet it could not be said that a modern man's coccyx plays as useful or important a part in his life as his faculty for building houses.

The pressure of present-day events has now made it impossible for us to go on splitting into two the problem of how man is to govern himself if civilisation is to persist, and neglecting the one half while we attend to the other. The concentration of Europe on nationalism has led to a situation which must be terminated, because it has already produced an unprecedented crop of horrors, and threatens to produce worse. It was obvious as the great war went along that it was multiplying the existing forms of death and pain with an obscene creative genius which made life worse than the most melancholic lunatic's dream about it. But what was not obvious to us at once was that no one was going to be able to stop the war, that in spite of the armistice and all the treaties there was going to be no return to the normal constructive life which man hopes to live in peace-time. It is a mockery of the many brave who fell in the battles of the past centuries not to recognise that war has always been horrible. 'We thronged into the city and passed over the dead bodies and some that were not yet dead, hearing them cry under the feet of horses,' writes Ambroise Paré of the battle of Turin in the sixteenth century; and later he tells unforgettably of the old soldier who 'gently and without anger' cut the throats of his four hideously-wounded comrades, 'praying God that when he should be in such a case, he might find someone who would do the same for him, to the end that he might not linger miserably'. But in those days it was possible for man to keep his right hand from knowing what his left hand did. Space and time were real barriers, one saw the scene in the tragedy in which one appeared oneself and had only broadsheet knowledge of the rest, there was a persuasion that many of the actors who suffered most were persons of a sub-creation, whose anguish was of no importance. But now we know nearly everything about our tragedy. We have the Press, the cinema, a people sufficiently educated to tell their own tale, and almost all of us know that when a ploughman's guts are poked out with a bayonet and trodden into the mud, the same wrong has been done to him and to the universe that would have been done were he a prince. It would appear that the human mind is not made to hold such a content. Since the war Europe has displayed all the characteristics of a person shattered by a traumatic experience: capricious, distracted, given to violence towards the self and others, careless of their environment, and incapable of carrying on a normal constructive life.

Such cases, both among individuals and nations, can be cured, if they are given treatment by counsellors who have a firm conception of sanity and can see at what point and for what reason the patients have departed from it. It has been made abundantly clear that such counsellors are not to be found among the exponents of nationalism, who to-day constantly utter statements far wider, far more in conflict with the indestructible facts of human nature and the conditions of life on this globe, than have ever been achieved by the most impossibilist internationalists. Again and again it is printed in books and reviews and newspapers that all sorts of aggressive action on the part of the countries placed in a disadvantageous position by the Treaty of Versailles are pardonable and defensible, because it is not right that the young men in these countries should suffer on account of a war for which they were not responsible, since it was waged by their fathers when they were children or yet unborn. It is appalling that people of the education necessary for the writing and publishing of such propaganda should not see that they are putting in circulation doctrines which would lead to the complete disruption of civilisation. The Treaty of Versailles can be attacked on innumerable scores from the point of view of both justice and expediency; but neither it nor any other treaty can be attacked on the ground that a certain portion of the population was unborn or under age at the date when it was signed. The very essence of a State is continuity. It cannot act at all unless it assumes responsibility for its actions, not for to-day or to-morrow, but for all time. Civilisation could no more continue, were this not recognised, than could commerce if all firms were able to break their contracts, not because they were unjustly procured or mischievous in the working, but because they had been signed at a date when certain members of the firm had not yet joined it.

It would seem that when lettered men can overlook such truisms as these, that man has been shocked by the war into forgetting how to be a political animal. This suspicion is confirmed by the spread of Fascism, which is a headlong flight into fantasy from the necessity for political thought. There is nothing more obvious about the post-war situation than that it is novel, springs from causes which have not yet been analysed, and cannot be relieved until this analysis is complete and has been made the basis of a new social formula. Yet persons supporting Fascism behave as if man were already in possession of principles which would enable him to deal with all our problems, and as if it were only a question of appointing a dictator to apply them. They act in this disregard of reality because they wish to return to the psychological conditions of an ideal childhood, in which they will be given every provision and protection by an all-powerful father if only they are good and obedient children. This attempt to organise the State on nursery lines gives many people a degree of emotional satisfaction far greater than they would receive from participation in political activities, and puts them into an exalted state, comparable to that of young persons in love, when the merest trifles seem of tremendous and delicious significance. A punctual train is an object which in a democratic country arouses nearly no emotional reaction in its beholders save in circumstances too particular to be taken into account; but in a Fascist country it is the cause of glowing pride and joy. But it is impossible to choose governmental systems according to purely subjective tests. There exists the passage in history, immediately preceding and contributory to the fall of Rome, when the reforms of Diocletian gave spectacular testimony to the unwisdom of dealing with a transition age by confining it within rigid forms based on the conceptions of the disappearing epoch. But even if that lesson had been forgotten, common sense should have told nationalists that the special task of the State to-day is to remain stable but elastic, so that its individuals can adapt themselves freely to changing conditions, and the new scheme of living can emerge naturally as a result of their experience. That nationalists should turn away from this conclusion, which is recommended by the whole of human history, to a solution which can promise little but emotional gratification, shows how impossible it is to think politically to-day, if nationalism is retained as a dominant principle.

But these are extreme types of nationalism. It is true that the human spirit is so robust that many people were not unbalanced by the war, and are very much where it found them. It might be that, when these excesses have calmed down, this body of stable opinion, the wiser for the experiences of the last few years, might be trusted to carry on the task of maintaining civilisation. That might be the case, provided they held views on war which would lead to its cessation, or to its conduct within limits that would not lead to the ruin of human achievement. It is difficult to find out whether that is so, for such opinion, being able to take itself for granted, is apt to remain undefined. Perhaps the easiest way of ascertaining it is to refer to the orthodox Catholic view of war; for that represents the opinion of over three hundred million people in the world, and is based on the mediæval researches which are also the foundation of Protestant thought. This Catholic point of view certainly respects the mass of mankind in holding that a man has a right to fight for certain things. It is not wrong for him to take up arms in a war provided it fulfils certain conditions. It must have been declared in proper form by the supreme authority of the State, it must have the excuse of a just cause and a right intention – namely, to avoid evil and to pursue good. The State can plead that it has a just cause and a right intention whenever its rights are menaced by foreign aggression, not otherwise to be frustrated than by war; or when there has already happened an actual violation of right, not otherwise reparable; or when it must punish a Power for threatening the security of the future. It has the right to make a defensive war, and an offensive war also, when it is truly necessary to take the initiative to forestall attack, or a punitive war. Concerning this last type of war international law has had many doubts, but there is an obvious case for it. To punish a Power that has done evil and threatens to repeat it may be the only way of achieving security. But once war is made, it must be waged moderately. The damage done must be in proportion to the right which has been violated, and the amount of retributive justice exacted must not be vindictive.

The conscientious State must be bound strictly by these conditions. It must not make war simply for the sake of trade expansion, or of exercising a standing army, or of escaping revolutionary trouble at home. Yet those points have to be thought out very carefully. It is certainly true that trade wars are impermissible, for to assume that one State has the right to make war upon another to force it to develop its own resources is to assume that each State holds its possessions in a trust for the human race at large, with a right to share in its usufruct adhering in every other State, an assumption which cannot be accepted except as part of a wholesale system of communism, as yet rejected. Yet if a State had such an overplus of population that it was in a position analogous to a starving man, and it was within its power to seize the superabundant and undeveloped territory of another State, then the Church might consider whether there might not belong to the overpopulated State such a right of self-help as belongs to a starving man, who may seize a loaf of bread if he does not deprive another person of it. It is certainly true, also, that if a State is neglecting its duty to its own people, this does not give any other State a right to interfere. Yet here again the rule must be qualified, for the neglected people then have a right of force against its government and by asking aid from abroad would communicate this right to the succouring power. When the people's wrongs are grave to the point of the wholesale persecution of the innocent with death and slavery, there can be no doubt as to the justice of the war waged for their deliverance.

Here is a code which lays down sensible rules for the moral attitude towards war. Exception after exception has to be made to them, for the sake of justice. It would be hard indeed to invent more sensible rules or more justifiable exceptions. But they do not give the slightest ground for hoping that, even when they are applied in the light of our experience of the last twenty years, they can guarantee civilisation from ruin by war. We have come to realise during the last few years – it is perhaps the most important contribution of our age to the understanding of human nature – how enormous is man's power of self-deception. No State can be trusted always to judge objectively whether it has the excuse of a just cause and a right intention, or whether it is serving its own interests. This was the case when the code was first framed, and was subscribed to by princes who believed that they must act according to it or be damned. Looking back on the Middle Ages we detect instance after instance of wars which were waged under cover of legal quibbles and trumped-up charges, to exonerate them from the charge of not being just according to the code, but which were plainly inspired by greed and selfishness. The process continues in our day, even in an exaggerated form. There are interests in every country which would genuinely benefit by war and conquest, and there are still more which believe they would do so. There are patriots who long to show their nation's strength by pitting it against another, and there are others who, though not so aggressive, are ready to accept blindly any version of a dispute between their country and another which shows their position morally unassailable and their adversaries deserving of contempt. The development of the Press floods the public mind with news about foreign countries, which is often profoundly misleading, sometimes intentionally, but more often simply because there are whole areas of reality of which it is difficult to give an account. It is interesting to reflect what superhuman powers of presentation it would have required on the part of journalists, and what freedom from prejudice and flexibility of imagination on the part of the public, for the possession of heavy gold stocks by France not to have blinded the world to the present poverty of the French people, a state of affairs which does not produce events with news value.

These perilous elements of acquisitiveness, egotism, and ignorance fuse together into ideal material for exploitation by the international interests concerned with the manufacture of armaments. For the nationalist who imagines himself free to reject internationalism is in error. He can if he likes reject the innocent internationalism which seeks to contrive peace; but the internationalism which, since its economic interests are dependent upon war, and the rumour of war, can hardly help being guilty. It is a compromising circumstance, which must mar the satisfaction of those who are proud to remember how our lads went from the Wiltshire downs and Yorkshire moors and Lincoln fens to die for England, that their deaths brought considerable financial profit to a gentleman whose nationality is one of the mysteries of our time. This international exploitation is welcomed within the State by the modern version of the landless class left derelict by the decay of feudalism, who at the end of the Middle Ages confused the morality of the nations by becoming available as professional soldiers. There are to-day many men who are offered nothing by the present economic system except drudgery and mean living, and who are born in a curious traditionless no man's land between the proletariat and the middle classes; and they will welcome any breach of routine that affords them adventure and an opportunity for personal distinction. A speaker of this type owned in public controversy some years ago that he was glad that the war had happened, because it had fetched him off a stool in an insurance office and opened the door to a more interesting life. These people cannot be blamed. They are the debtors of civilisation, which deserves to be destroyed by them if it cannot devise some way of using them for its own good and theirs. But it is also true that, in time both of civil disorder and war, they constitute a danger to all honourable human aims.

It does not appear, therefore, that nationalism has found any formula which promises to guard civilisation from ruin by warfare. It has been able to insist that a State should pause before engaging in hostilities, and ask itself whether it is moved by a just cause and a right intention. But it is so often impossible for a State to answer this question honestly that any insistence holds but little value. If we want any further hope of security we must turn to internationalism. We must hand over our arms to a tribunal which is certain not to be perfect, to be frequently repellent in its indecision and timidity, and even from time to time to break down altogether, but which offers nevertheless far more than the best possible manifestation of contemporary nationalism. For it will provide a technique for the mutual cancellation of greeds, the pooling of aspirations towards harmony, and the slowing down of aggression's headlong pace by submitting it to a delaying critical process. It will not be a weak and nerveless body, for it holds out an ideal for which men will find it worth while to die.

III

There is a certain dualism of pride and humility which is the fruit of maturity in every valuable individual. A writer could hardly embark on the serious practice of his art if he were not convinced that he alone had command of a certain aspect of reality, that if he did not do his work no one else could undertake it. He could hardly continue with it if he had not an appreciative eye for his own gifts as they developed, if he did not recognise gratefully that his imagination was rich in material and that his power over language increased with the years. But once he had come to a position when he could see the body of his work as a whole he could probably receive no more encouraging news than a revelation from above that he is the supremely great writer of the world. Knowing the vast difference between what he wants to write and what he succeeds in getting down on paper, he would feel that his craft had stopped before it had well begun; and being aware by what pains the few certainties in his work had been arrived at, and for how many other pains he had nothing to show, he would be appalled by the news that the human mind was never to behave any better. He would be immediately relieved could he learn that this revelation had been an unfortunate device of his publisher's over-enthusiastic advertising manager. Then he could take his place again as a member of a universal body of workers whose task it is to find out for man where and what he is, by analysing his experience; not merely the writer of books, which can but start a ripple in the contemporary pond, but a contributor to literature, which has set out to make a chart of the sea; the recipient of a tradition as old as time, the transmitter of that tradition to eternity. Thus it happens that great writers have in their old age either cared little for claims of greatness, or made a freakish game of them.

It is so too with all individuals. They must know their own quality so they can keep up their hearts as they go through the hardships of life. A clever man must take pride in his mind, a sensible man in his wisdom, and in youth it may give him great pleasure to be plainly the outstanding brain or character in his family, or school, or college. But later on that satisfaction must be diminished, since nature keeps the individual fairly close to the type, and he must surely have met many people who were at least nearly his equal. It is likely to be replaced by regret that he could look for so little understanding and support in his family or early friends. Only the most monstrous egotist could fail to be disconcerted by finding that he was the supreme achievement of his environment and that it could do nothing better. The saner human being will wish to be surrounded by a brilliant community which will appreciate his best ideas and help him to realise them, which will go on succeeding when he fails, which will continue after he dies, so that his work will not be wasted. Consciousness of his own personal eminence is only half his desire. It is lacking in the essential element of security.

And so it is with the nations. Each must take pride in itself. Each must be fully aware that its gods are true gods, who can work miracles, and will in the end disclose all mysteries. We are obliged, if we are going to achieve anything valuable, to be proud of Britain, and that is not difficult. Bath, and Edinburgh, and a thousand other wonderful places, such as that line of red-plastered villages lying under the white horse of Westbury, with Steeple Ashton lying farther out on the Plain; Queen Elizabeth and Wellington; English law and literature; the body of ordinary men and women, in town and country, that are patient and gentle and averse from the chief sin, cruelty, more than any other civilised people in the world – these successes are precedents which make a race feel that they are fortunate and may be able to do what they try. There is no country better than Britain. Yet there could be no more hideous prospect imaginable than that there should be no other country than England. If we suppose for a moment that the heavenly powers had been usurped by a dictator of the bulldog breed, who had abolished all other nations as unnecessary, the contemplation of our country becomes a nightmare. The limitations of the landscape present themselves as privations; our crop of great figures seems spare and monotonous, lacking a Pascal or a Napoleon, a Goethe or a Mazzini; as well as the wealth of our English law and literature we should remember the poverty of our music and painting; and the defects in our national character, such as our smugness in prosperity, our inaptitude for logic, and our indifference to serious issues, would assume an appalling significance. It would seem as if man had suffered to create the Eton and Harrow match and the Black Country, and the end would be despair. England may have been enough for the patriotic Englishman in the youth of nationalism at the close of the Middle Ages; and the Elizabethan could be pardoned for throwing his bonnet high in the air. But now Europe has come to its maturity; and it is plain that eminence is not everything a nation needs. There is essential also a society of nations which will compensate by their qualities for her defects so that these are no heavy reproach to her; which will prosper as she does, so that when she makes the political and economic experiments that are necessary in prosperity she will not be frustrated by the interference of pauper barbarians; which will go on maintaining civilisation should she fail during those periods that come to every nation when the national genius is in abeyance; which can be trusted to continue as a society even if some of its individual members should sink into obscurity, so that their culture shall never be lost. There could be no better service done to the political and social instincts in man than the creation of an international police force which, by giving each power security against aggression, will enable all to live in this useful fellowship. It might also resolve other and more deeply vexing perplexities, for it is possible that the meaning of life might be more fully disclosed if it were allowed to live itself out, that the proceedings of the nations might form a revelation of reality if they were not perpetually interrupted by violence. Whatever our conceptions of heavenly peace may be, nothing seems more probable than that Augustine was right in prophesying earthly peace as its foundation.

Notes

1. See below, p. 107.
2. See details on *Civil Journey* below, p. 311.

11 Sylvia Townsend Warner *Man's Moral Law (1932)**

Man, Proud Man, Mabel Ulrich's collection of feminist essays from which this piece
is taken, also included articles by Mary Borden, E. M. Delafield, Susan Ertz, Storm
Jameson, Helen Simpson and Rebecca West. 'Man', as used in the title of each
essay ('Man and Personal Relations', 'Man the Helpmate', 'Man and Religion', etc.),
did not designate the masculine universal, but signalled an enquiry into specifically
male myths and cultural/political practices. Borden's essay appeared first in the
collection, setting the tone and taking as its subject 'Man, the Master. An Illusion';
her opening contention was that 'the word MAN, written in capital letters,
corresponds to nothing nowadays that has any counterpart or corporal existence
in the civilized world' (pp. 11–12).

Claire Harman tells us that while, by 1933, political tracts and pamphlets had
begun to absorb Warner's companion Valentine Ackland, Warner herself 'did not
share Valentine's deep sense of responsibility towards the world nor see the
necessity to spring-clean her own assumptions and attitudes so thoroughly'
(pp. 134–5). She 'was not conscientious in following up the lists of leaflets Valentine
recommended her to read'. Nevertheless certain events in that year appear to
have caught her attention, notably the Reichstag Fire Trial and the growing
prominence of Mosley's British Union of Fascists, founded in 1932. Mulford writes
that it was against the background 'of increasing despair and hopelessness in the
political situation at home and in Europe that Sylvia and Valentine took the decision
to join the Communist Party, some time between late 1934 and early 1935' (p. 55).
Warner's political awareness is everywhere apparent after this in *Summer Will
Show*, published in 1936 and not – as is sometimes claimed – an historical romance,
but a novel of social protest.¹ But it would be erroneous to see her career before
1933–4 as one from which social and economic concerns were blissfully absent.
Opus 7 (1931) is a playful narrative in decasyllabic couplets reminiscent of Crabbe,
but with an unobtrusively socialist lesson. Indeed, even after the watershed year
of 1933, Warner's essays on social and political themes are rarely without the
sort of wit and lightness that characterize that early poem. This piece from 1932
explores an aspect of the patriarchal world-view that many feminist commentators
could see was leading Europe into nightmare, but it does so with an acute wit and
humour reminiscent of Swift. The manifestations of Man's Moral Law would appear
more malignantly in Warner's subsequent fiction, in particular in the trials of
Sophia Willoughby in *Summer Will Show*.

---

* Reprinted from *Man, Proud Man*, ed. Mabel Ulrich (London: Hamish Hamilton, 1932),
pp. 221–45.

The philosopher Kant, celebrated for having written the *Critique of Pure Reason* and practising so exemplary a punctuality that the citizens of Jena set their clocks by his afternoon walk, gave it as his considered opinion that there were two things that beat him, or, as the English translation of this saying more elegantly puts it:

> filled his soul with awe;
> The starry heavens and man's moral law.

Since Kant's day the starry heavens have lost a good deal of their aloofness. In fact, they may be said to have become a Palm Beach of the intellect. The nebulae in Andromeda are now within the grasp of quite modest ambitions, and the meanest diner-out can speak of express trains proceeding intermittently through time-space[2] with the authority of a Bradshaw. Also, telescopes have been considerably improved. But the subject of Man's Moral Law is still as imposing a mystery as it was when it baffled Kant. Science, so brisk and dauntless in her dealings elsewhere, trembles here, and veils her face. Research drops the scalpel, even women, said to be so inquisitive, lapse into silent wonderment before this massive phenomenon and have learned by experience to provoke its manifestations as little as possible.

> Non ragionam di lor. Guardate e passa.[3]

From many points of view this reverence is admirable. History and fable combine to enforce upon us the teaching that it is not good for us to know everything. As Sir George Beaumont demanded the brown tree in the landscape,[4] the human mind instinctively craves for one point of dusk and repose, one door that may not be opened, one branch whose fruit may never be plucked. Such considerations rushed into my mind when I was first requested by the Editor of this Symposium to undertake an investigation into this aspect of the male of the human species. Why, thought I, seek to lay the axe to the root of this brown tree, why invade this privacy, why imperil the majestic shade which for so long has brooded over this unknown? In a world where so little romance is left, where every *ultima thule* of the imagination has been mapped and charted and where the bison is fast becoming extinct, would it not be better to leave Man's Moral Law alone? And for a moment I experienced an abashed awe such as I used to feel as a child when my nurse would point to a local gas-container and tell me that if I were ever so wicked as to stick a pin into that vast cylindrical bulk painted a threatening crimson, an instant explosion would hurl me and the neighbourhood to disintegration.

If action is the only test of assertion, then for all I know my nurse was right; for I have never stuck a pin into that gas-vat or any other. Nevertheless, so I argued with myself, I do not now believe in the correctness of her statement, and people better qualified to speak with authority in this matter have since assured me that she was talking arrant nonsense. But how to know, so urged the more speculative and superstitious part of my mind, that this statement of hers, though actually erroneous, was not mystically true, and sent as a warning? And again it seemed to me that I had better stay my hand, and content myself with the awe which was good enough for Kant, and should surely be good enough for me. For suppose – and now my super-rational self began to talk with the utmost loudness and plausibility – suppose that Man's Moral Law were indeed what my nurse's theory of gas-vats so grossly boded forth, and might, at one unadvised and sacrilegious prod, explode, and bring about the disintegration of society. Where should I be then, meddlesome creature?

To cut a long story short, I said that Man's Moral Law was a subject which had always interested me, and that I should be very glad to undertake an enquiry into it. \

Before I begin an account of my enquiry a word or two should be said as to my qualifications. In these days of specialization the empirical method is rightly suspect, and some may wonder at me for my readiness to attack a question of which I have already confessed my ignorance. But Man's Moral Law is perhaps the only subject left to us which may be approached with any hope of profit from a datum line of incompetence. Before so dense a mystery one eye may be as good as another, and the very fact of knowing nothing may condition a valuable freedom from bias.

It is only in the strictest sense of the word, moreover, that one can say one knows nothing of Man's Moral Law. Of its origin, its constituents, its chemistry and dynamics we are indeed ignorant; but it is scarcely possible to spend an hour in the company of man without being made aware that it exists and functions, and that it is, most emphatically, a force. Our position in this respect is much the same as the position of humankind before the discovery of electricity. Though no one could say what caused the lightning, the lightning was there, sometimes latent, sometimes leaping from a cloud, a thing to be dreaded, admired, and if possible avoided. Certain conditions of weather, so experience would teach, a sultriness in the air, a certain bulginess and dis-colouration in the clouds, heralded its appearance; and in a similar way we know by experience that certain physical aspects of man, an appearance of slight inflation, a special tense quality in his silences, prelude the manifestations, more or less devastating but always impressive, of his Moral Law. To establish a connection between the lightning flash and the peculiar properties that could be elicited from amber by briskly rubbing it with a woollen stocking would seem, did we not know that it had been done, a task beyond human ingenuity. Yet little by little, by research, observation, and experiment, the task was accomplished; and there seems to be no absolute reason why an application of the same methods may not end in the disclosure of the nature of Man's Moral Law. Indeed, upon some counts, Man's Moral Law seems a more promising subject than electricity, which in its major demonstration of lightning is too swift and intermittent a phenomenon to afford a satisfactory subject for research. And though a too rash exploration of the former may provoke alarming reactions, the actual danger to life and limb is probably less than that which attends experiments with lightning. Lastly, though this may seem almost too fantastic a consideration for mention, last year, 1931, saw the centenary of the birth of Faraday; and since Man's Moral Law must be looked into some time or another, one could not begin one's investigations in a year of better augury.

We have learned from Freud what rich results may be gained from an examination of traditional idioms, idioms that have become so much a part of common speech that their import passes unnoticed. I propose to base the first part of my examination of Man's Moral Law upon three such common phrases. The first of these is the expression, *Playing the game*; the second, the often-heard reproach, *It's not cricket*; the third the exclamation, always used in a slighting or belittling sense, *Skittles!* Or, *That's all skittles.* This may seem an arbitrary choice. But in the prolegomena of so virgin a subject one must begin somewhere; and I hope that I may presently show that the choice is not quite so arbitrary as at first sight it may seem.

Let us first observe what these phrases have in common. It will be seen that while (*a*) they are all based upon pastimes, they all (*b*) convey a moral judgement; and (*c*) they are all masculine phrases. Should it be objected against this last statement that women may and frequently do use these phrases with exactly the same connotation and emphasis as they bear in the mouths of men, I must bring forward the counter-objection that women have produced no equivalent phrases drawn from the specific interests and occupations of femininity. It is absurd to suppose that Penelope or Lucretia would condemn a lapse from conjugal fidelity with the expression, *It's not needlework*; and though cookery has supplied the term of reproach, *half-baked*, this is used as a plain metaphor of semi-imbecility, and conveys none of the earnest moral censure inseparable from the male phrases above.

We now arrive at the consideration of the first common quality of these three phrases, their origin in pastimes. It may seem at first sight peculiar that the moral judgements implicit in them should be vested in a terminology proper to games, and that so serious a matter as the reprobation of vice or ill-timed frivolity should be thus connected with activities which their very generic name of pastimes announces as a method of whiling away an otherwise negligible and unoccupied duration of time. Why, one might ask, arguing upon a purely rationalistic basis, should the conduct of one who betrays a trust, sets fire to his neighbour's hayrick, or puts poison in the children's milk, be condemned by the statement that it is not a highly organized method of passing the time which demands for its full execution twelve variously-formed pieces of wood, a small leather sphere, and two opposing bands of players, each band consisting of eleven participants and a twelfth man in case of accidents, together, should the rite be performed in its most perfect form, with two umpires, and a large expanse of smooth and levelled grass with defined boundaries? Apart from the poetical excitement inseparable from the use of metaphor, would it not be actually more emphatic, more condemnatory, to say of such behaviour, It is treachery, It is arson, It is murder? – in the two latter instances offences which involve severe punishment by legal code.

Yet a small amount of reflection will show an overwhelming speech-tendency to apply terms proper to pastimes to the graver aspects of life, and always with an implied moral overtone. And further examination will show that the preponderance of these terms are drawn from games predominantly or exclusively masculine. In England cricket and football, in the United States baseball, supply a rich harvest of such terms; tennis supplies fewer; croquet – a female game – and lacrosse, none.

In this connection it will be of interest to examine the variations of sense in the word *sporting*. To be sporting or Not sporting are terms which now rival To be cricket or Not cricket in their implications of moral worth or unworth. But it is only of recent years, comparatively speaking, that *sporting* has come to bear this moral overtone;[5] and it is in the same lapse of time that its use has been transferred almost entirely from the blood to the bloodless sports. In the days of our grandparents to be sporting meant to be given to shooting, fishing, or hunting. *Good sport* expressed either an opinion that an adequate number of grouse, salmon, hares, foxes, etc., had been killed, or a friendly aspiration that it might be so. Now this sense of the word has been practically supplanted by a secondary meaning in which it expresses a favourable moral judgement upon character or actions quite unconnected with the ability to sit on a horse, reel in a salmon or bring down a pheasant with either barrel.

This bleaching, as one might express it, of the word *sport* and its derivatives – this transference from blood to bloodless sports by which it acquires at the same time a connotation of moral excellence – might suggest to some hasty humanitarian that the moral overtone implies approbation of harmlessness. Recollection, however, of the high accident rate in football and baseball – games profoundly embroiled in the sports-morality compound – should be enough to warn one off from following this specious hypothesis. Illumination must be sought elsewhere; and for that illumination we must turn to the third phrase of my three examples: the exclamation, *Skittles*.

It is at once evident that common usage has established an antithesis, as it were, between cricket and skittles. Morally speaking, whatever is skittles isn't cricket, whatever is cricket isn't skittles. Skittles is something light, negligible, despicably easy, calling out none of the better nature of man. A life that is *All beer and skittles*, however alluring such a life might sound, is in sum worthless and morally insignificant. Cricket, on the other hand, is serious, strenuous, laudable. It is in the antithesis between these two games, both alike originally devised as pastimes, and both based on the common principle of knocking down one object with another, that we must seek the clue. What quality is it, present in the one, lacking in the other, that gives rise to their opposed moral significances, and elicits this responsive gush from the mysterious hidden fountain of Man's Moral Law?

The difference is not far to seek. The merest tyro, the most inattentive looker-on at a game of cricket, is aware that cricket is a game with a great number of rules. Skittles, on the other hand, is only surpassed by rounders for lawlessness.

It seems clear, then, that it is by the absence or presence of their rules that we may expect to find games linked up with Man's Moral Law. And there is striking corroborative evidence for this conclusion in the moral import or overtone taken on by the word *sporting* as it is transferred from the blood to the bloodless sports. Necessity was the mother of the blood sports, the necessity to kill for food or self-defence; and necessity knows no law. There are no penalizing rules, except the game-laws, conditioning the bringing-down of pheasants or the catching of salmon. And though the hunting field has its conventions, rigid enough, it cannot be doubted that these would disappear should expediency demand it; and that in a Leicestershire overrun with foxes as Kenya is sometimes overrun with locusts, foxes would be attacked with machine-guns worked from motor-cycles with no one, morally, a penny the worse for it.

Compare this with the moral overthrow involved if the rules of the highly organized bloodless sports should be tampered with; if the offside rule should be discarded by a football team, a superstitious bowler insist upon the luck of a seventh throw, or a billiard player consistently pot his opponent's ball. Under such circumstances the moral value of games, so much insisted upon by every educationalist, would be utterly lost, and cricket would be, indeed, no other than skittles.

So, having established that, ethically speaking, games are good or not good according as to whether they have many or few rules, we may proceed to lay down as a first conclusion in this study of Man's Moral Law the axiom that: In any law there is intrinsically a quality of goodness; or, to put it more simply: Laws are good in themselves.

This point of view is not an easy one for women to receive. That a law may be a good law, granted; or that the law-abiding are commonly considered good, granted again. But that a law, merely by being a law, should, irrespective of any other considerations, immediately secrete a quality of absolute good-ness, must seem to the female intelligence a trifle metaphysical, to put it mildly. Yet, as far as Man's Moral Law is involved, I do not see how the truth of this axiom can be denied. It has been arrived at by the strictest reasoning, proceeding from irrefutable facts; and the light which it sheds upon many manifestations of Man's Moral Law which must otherwise remain absolutely inexplicable establishes it, at any rate to my thinking, as unassailable.

Moreover, by the acceptance of this axiom we are guided to a better understanding of the fact, so strange at first sight, that it is in metaphors drawn from games that man expresses his deepest moral judgements. For where else among male activities, except perhaps in the matter of social drapery, shall we find the arbitrary nature of law in such a pure state as in the highly organized games? It is exactly because the laws of these games are based upon no apparent reason or expediency, and because games themselves are a purely artificial contrivance for passing unwanted time, that these laws call forth the profoundest veneration.

Further, we may assume that in insisting as they do upon the tonic value of organized games our most eminently moral males are in truth bent upon insinuating into the minds of the young this very axiom that laws are in themselves good and venerable. For the young of the human species are apparently quite as devoid of the sense of Moral Law as are women of any age; and though it would seem by what we know of the taboo system of primitive man that there is in all males a natural tendency for the feeling for Moral Law to emerge at or round about the age of puberty, our educationalists rightly leave nothing to chance, but see to it by the practice of games this tendency is, as it were, schooled and initiated, young males learning, as they learn to respect and keep holy various codes of game-playing, the estimable and inherently moral quality of laws *per se*. But women, however well they may play games, and however carefully they may observe the rules, remain outside the veil. The implicit doctrine is hidden from them, and even should they make use of the male metaphors, and say of such and such an action that it is not cricket, or that it is all skittles, they speak with the lips only, not the heart. This fact is instinctively grasped by every man. And it is admirable, in the light of this truth, to observe the unflawed tranquility of the male mind before a growing female aptitude for men's games, and how, with women challenging and overcoming them in countless contests of endurance and skill, men can still say – and do – with unshaken certainty, that women will never be any good at games.

Accepting as a basis axiom of Man's Moral Law that all laws are morally good, it is clear that we must be prepared, in any further exploration of this subject, to find a mystical approbation given to qualities which in a feminine judgement would be, if approved of at all, approved of on grounds of expediency. Indeed, this element of mysticism in Man's Moral Law seems at times to extend almost to fetishism; and if we bear in mind how cloistered a life Man's Moral Law has led through the ages, how closely and esoterically guarded from rational criticism, how implicitly received and uncompromisingly demonstrated it has been, it is not altogether surprising that it should still retain an impress of a primitive method of thought. Based, as I believe it to be, upon the attribution of a positive quality of goodness to an abstract entity of law, Man's Moral Law appears to be of such a mystical constitution that it can still, without awkwardness, anthropomorphize a considerable section of the universe which reason considers purely material and inanimate. To put this more simply, as primitive man attributed supernatural powers to natural objects, and bowed down to wood and stone, man, even now, in the privacy of his Moral Law bows down to boots, and sees a possible soul of goodness in everything pertaining to himself.

This cannot be better realized than by a study of the advertisements in our Daily Press which are directed to men, and a comparison of these advertisements with those aimed to catch the eye of a woman. By such a study it would appear that man will not contemplate the purchase of wearing-apparel, shaving-soap, whisky, automobiles, purgatives, footwear, or tobacco, unless he be assured that these articles are morally satisfactory.

Here, for an example, are two advertisements, taken at random from the *Daily Mail* of September 16th, 1931. One is male, one is female; and any reader of advertisements will see that they are typical of their kind, and in no way constitute a special pleading for my point.

'We treat them rough,' the first begins. 'Wear them day in and day out in the foulest muddiest weather on the roughest of roads – these boots will "stick it" with dogged steadfast endurance.'

Boots, admittedly, should be durable; but so should lipstick. In the second advertisement, of a lipstick, the permanence of the particular brand is especially stressed.

'It holds where others smear and wear – yet leaves no trace of greasy residue. It ends that artificial smear that women have tried for years to overcome. A colour that glorifies the lips to pulse-quickening loveliness – trust the *French* for that! On sale everywhere in 4 shades.'

It is impossible to imagine an advertisement of lipstick which praised its dogged steadfast endurance – as impossible as it is to imagine men countenancing a hint of sexual appeal in their boots. Even when the same quality is urged in recommendation of a ware, the approach, so to speak, is different as chalk from cheese. For women are realists – grim realists, as is shown by that painful phrase about the greasy residue. But man at all times refers his choice to the implicit idealism of his Moral Law, and will buy no article without its sanction.

Here is another advertisement in which this fact has been so completely accepted that the real advantages of the article in question are mentioned only to whet by contrast the superior moral allure.

'It's not alone the reasonable first cost or the light fuel-consumption – it's the intrinsic quality of our material, the built-in sturdiness . . . the downright goodness of the car that makes satisfaction assured.'

One would suppose that it was not a car that was recommended thus, but a wife for a colonial Bishop – were it not that men, even Bishops, sadly aware of female non-morality, abandon, in the choice of a wife, the standards by which they choose their pipe tobacco and their underwear.

The mention of underwear occurs here with singular propriety, since it leads me on to a further conclusion. This conclusion may seem far-fetched, perhaps even offensive; but it forces itself upon me, and I should not feel justified in omitting it.

I have shown that an essential ingredient, perhaps even the mainspring, of Man's Moral Law can be summed up in the axiom that in any law there is intrinsically a quality of goodness; I have shown also that this semi-mystical point of view is extended into an attribution of moral qualities, such as steadfastness, high-mindedness, etc., to material objects not in themselves susceptible to such attributions, and that man as a purchaser is greatly influenced by this idealistic notion. No student of man can have failed to observe his preference for wearing wool next to the skin – a preference so deeply ingrained, so piously put into action, and so unconvincingly accounted for by the adduced reasons of health and comfort, that there can be no doubt that Moral Law is deeply involved in the choice. I have already, though but tentatively, glanced at the possibility that Man's Moral Law may include a certain element of fetishism. In its general outlines it presents some striking resemblances to what we know of the taboo system, being, as that is, powerful in its effect, rigid in its tradition, and esoterically conveyed to the initiates. Moreover, the distance between fetishism and idealism is not so great as it may seem; and the peculiar variety of idealism which is exhibited in a readiness to attribute 'downright goodness' to automobiles might well be a rarefied development of the primitive impulse which deifies a tree.

One of the most persistent traits of fetishist thinking is the belief that actual or attributed qualities may be sacramentally transmitted; that by drinking the blood of bulls man can become strong, or that the wearing of a necklace of tigers' teeth will bestow ferocity. It is to the animal kingdom that man turns for these supernatural transfers, feeling here a nearer relationship than with vegetable or mineral aspects of matter. Have we not here, then, an explanation of why, at the mysterious dictates of his Moral Law, modern man is faithful to wool next to the skin? It is true that the sheep is neither a powerful nor a sagacious animal; but it is proverbially virtuous; and in these days a prudent inoffensiveness has taken the place of the earlier virtues of strength and combative ability. In this sense man may truly utter the Biblical boast that righteousness is the girdle of his loins.

It must be noticed that very few animals provide a satisfactory textile. Expense makes the weaving of a lion's mane out of the question, and though both poodles and Persian cats carry coats that may be woven up, the poodle is too intelligent to be dignified, and there is something about the cat which makes it abhorrent to Man's Moral Law. We are left with the sheep, the goat, and the camel. Goats are liable to much the same objections that rule out the cat; but the sheep and the camel, animals in their different spheres so closely akin to the behaviour standards of present-day life, animals useful, moderate, and enduring, possess exactly the qualifications we might expect to find in demand, and are rightly chosen to impress by intimate contact with the epidermis their social and moral qualities.

Whether in actual fact such a transference takes place lies beyond the scope of this enquiry. In the light of modern chemistry it seems not impossible; but my concern is with Man's Moral Law, and I must leave it to the biologist to determine by observation and experiment if the wearing of wool does actually impart a sheepishness to the wearer, or if the persistent use of a camel's-hair dressing-gown results in a notable willingness to bear obligations uncomplainingly, and do without drink. My part is done if I have succeeded in displaying Man's Moral Law at once preserving the vital beliefs of fetishism and adapting them to modern conditions – a process so intricate and so obscured from unsympathetic analysis that we need hardly wonder that the system from which it springs was too much for Kant. Indeed, I must admit that in many ways Man's Moral Law is still too much for me. For example, although I am convinced that in the matter of trouser turn-ups we have a significant manifestation of its workings, I have not been able to see how it works. Phenomena such as these I must leave to other labourers in this field, only remarking that they may be compared to the properties of amber mentioned in my electrical analogy – seemingly in themselves insignificant and undeducible from the full blaze of Moral Law in its most direct and forceful manifestations, yet indubitably connected with it. And as the early researches into the nature of electricity were most profitable when conducted along the humbler lines of investigation, I venture to prophesy that the final revelation and understanding of Man's Moral Law will be most swiftly, safely, and surely arrived at by such a method as I have here, however modestly, inaugurated – an examination of its minor phenomena. Something perhaps parallel to the lightning-conductor or the system of insulation will need to be invented. Any enquiry by women into so jealously guarded a male mystery as Man's Moral Law is likely to arouse anger and ill-feeling, and I am prepared for obloquy. Yet, while enquiry may with justification hope for such rich results, it would be weak-minded to hold back; nor, on his own showing, has man anything to fear from an impartial investigation of this subject, claiming as he does, and no doubt rightly, that it is by the possession of a peculiar Moral Law that he is eminent among created things, and, while following its dictates, infallible in judgement and conduct. Accordingly, it is without hesitation, though at the risk, maybe, of calling out a temporary resentment, that I venture to indicate a line for future research which, in my opinion, is likely to yield most valuable results. In this short essay I have succeeded in carrying back

Man's Moral Law to primitive man. Such an antiquity is respectable enough; yet I believe that research should be carried a step further; and it is with confidence that I recommend to those who may come after me a patient enquiry into the conduct of baboons.

Notes

1. See Barbara Brothers, 'Sylvia Townsend Warner', *DLB* 34: 279.
2. The example of a person walking on a moving train was a popular device for explaining Einstein's Theory of Relativity to a lay audience. 'Imagine a train moving north at 60 miles per hour', writes Martin Gardner in a more recent attempt: 'On the train a man walks south at 3 miles per hour. In what direction is he moving and at what speed? It is immediately obvious that this question cannot be answered without choosing a frame of reference. Relative to the train the man moves at 3 miles per hour. Relative to the ground, he moves north at 60 minus 3, or 57 miles per hour' (*Relativity for the Million* [New York: Macmillan, 1962], p. 13).
3. *Inferno*, 3.51, translated by C. H. Sisson: 'Let us not talk about them. Look and pass on' (*The Divine Comedy: A New Verse Translation* [Manchester: Carcanet, 1980], p. 13). 'They' are 'the sad souls of those who live without occasion for infamy or praise' and those abject angels 'who did not think it worth their while to rebel/Or to be faithful to God, but were for themselves'.
4. Sir George Beaumont of Coleorton Hall, Leicestershire (1753–1827), devotee of picturesque gardening.
5. In a passage which invites comparison with Warner's argument here, Vita Sackville-West writes that 'the English man is seen at his best the moment that another man starts throwing a ball at him'; 'the love of games with its attendant character-building qualities of fair play, team spirit, generosity in victory, cheerfulness in defeat, respect for the better man, and all the rest of the platitudes is in fact responsible for many of the less offensive traits in our national make-up' ('The Outdoor Life', in Ernest Barker, ed., *The Character of England* [1947], pp. 410–11).

12 Gerald Heard *The Significance of the New Pacifism (1936)* *

According to Mowat (p. 537), the peace movement was in 1935 at its height. The results of the Peace Ballot – instigated by Lord David Cecil and conducted by his League of Nations Union – were released in June of that year. The ballot, begun the previous March, was administered with the support of both the Labour and the Liberal Parties and about a half-million volunteers, to over eleven million people (see Adams, pp. 26–7). The results, summarizes Thorpe, 'showed massive support for the League of Nations, disarmament, and the prohibition of private arms sales; and strong support for the abolition of military and naval aircraft and "economic and non-military measures" against aggressor nations. Although 6.8 million voted for the use of force against aggressors, 2.4 million voted against' (p. 178).

Gerald Heard had been literary editor of *The Realist: A Journal of Scientific Humanism* for the duration of its run from April 1929 to January 1930, in which capacity he had published commentary on social, political, cultural and scientific affairs by such people as Rebecca West, Naomi Mitchison, Aldous Huxley, J. B. S. Haldane, H. G. Wells and Herbert Read. In 1929 he brought out his own study, *The Ascent of Humanity: An Essay on the Evolution of Civilization*, followed throughout the 1930s by some ten books on natural science and culture. *Pain, Sex and Time* (1939) saw the only hope for humanity in an enlargement of consciousness, a transcendence of individuality along the lines laid out in Eastern philosophy. Graves and Hodge put it reductively that he thought 'Yoga could help Western men to reach peace within their inner selves' (*The Long Week-End*, p. 202); in fact, he argued that it is nothing less than the 'evolutionary purpose' of human beings to escape the constraints of individuality (*Pain, Sex and Time*, p. 280).

The New Pacifism, where this essay first appeared, was edited by Gerald K. Hibbert and published as no. 3 in *The Firbank Series*, 'a series of popular books intended to illustrate in varied ways the spirit of reconciliation and friendship which exists in the world and thereby encourage its growth and expansion' (from a note facing the title page). Other contributors were Aldous Huxley, A. A. Milne, Beverley Nichols, Horace G. Alexander, Carl Heath and Canon H. R. L. (Dick) Sheppard, founder of the Peace Pledge Union.

Pacifism is certainly no new thing. Indeed I believe it to be older than its ancient antagonist War. Nevertheless, to-day it enters, in its age-long

---

* Reprinted from *The New Pacifism*, ed. Gerald K. Hibbert (London: Allenson and Co., 1936; reprinted New York: Garland, 1972), pp. 13–22.

struggle, on a new phase, and perhaps a decisive one. Most people are feeling this and they realize one of the reasons: that is, the increased moral outrageousness of war. This is an important reason, but as we shall see, not the most important and decisive. We must, however, take it first because it is in men's minds. Then we can go deeper to what is in their hearts.

War is worse and has become frankly impossible to all save specialists and monomaniacs. The rest simply refuse to think what it really is nowadays. It has lost all its masks and defences. There is no chivalry in bombing from five miles high a city packed with helpless women and children and burning them to death. No one can any longer pretend that. War, too, has lost not merely its last pretence of gallantry; it has lost not merely the dimmest excuse of morality; it has lost its last pretence of sanity. All the other instruments of science have gained in precision. Bad or good, they got what we sent them to fetch with increasing exactness. War, scientific war alone, breaks and dissipates that it was meant to capture and hold.

Reparations are a byword. But that was the ineffectiveness of the last war. The next war will be incomparably more ineffective in giving anyone any gain. War to-day is attempting to put a watch right with a sledge hammer. Peace through threat of war to-day is attempting to make man moral by blackmailing him: it is attempting to make a paranoiac sane by threatening him with the very terror, the dread of which already has him on the verge of becoming a homicidal lunatic.

War, then, is deadly, and even to the man without a heart, but possessing a head, it cannot make its case. Even if there is no other reason to suppose that war is now a monstrous absurdity, physical science would have made it an anachronism; for though people may shirk the moral challenge, 'the end cannot justify the means', they cannot shirk the challenge of common sense: Why use a means which cannot attain the end in which it claims to be justified?

But there is another and even more pressing reason than the advance of science for getting rid of war. It is not so obvious, but it is even more serious. That is the growth of feeling. Feeling has grown, just as much as thought has grown. We disregard the growth of sensibility at a grave cost – at a graver peril than we disregard the growth of science. Once we thought it sufficed to let feeling grow – our sensibility would naturally prevent us from committing atrocities. We now see that is not true. He who prepares commits himself to ultimate action. Man is only free when preparing – never when once prepared. Hence our good feelings will not save us unless we act on them. Most people realize that – and with a sigh they decide such action will cost too much and so they let things slide. They are sorry; they are concerned; but if the worst comes to the worst they feel we shall all muddle through – dirtied, disgraced, damaged, but not deranged.

Yet it is just that last word which contains our real peril and doom. The next war will certainly be ghastly physically. It would be a deadly blow to deal any civilization, however tough. But to this civilization it will be fatal *because* we have advanced so far in feeling. The last war shattered belief in progress. This war will shatter belief in man. A civilization with such feelings committing acts of which a barbarian would be ashamed, cannot any longer believe in itself. It will fall into despair and neurosis. It is not the millions of bodies which will be destroyed but the destruction of the soul and will of civilization – man's belief in himself, his self-respect – which will make 'the next war' so deadly.

There is, then, a new feeling that war must go. Men are not only thinking it, but feeling it. But, further, there is a new hope that war may be *replaced*. People ask timidly, 'What other sanctions?' Now at last we can answer. This age is profoundly suspicious of religion. Religion earned that suspicion. It talked about spiritual power and leaned on weapons: of spiritual creativeness and wealth and grasped money: of the restorative power of love and depended on coercion. Religion held its voice – or rather foreswore itself – and so the stones have to cry out.

The anthropologists making contacts with strange and suspicious tribes: the tamer of wild beasts: the new practitioners in the recovery of the insane – all these experts now know the methods they were told they must use, by the 'practical' ruler – official, bishop, general – were hopelessly mistaken, wrong, fatal. On the contrary, they find the Sermon on the Mount is not 'oriental hyperbole' but the only effective method. From these specialists' successes we are beginning to learn that the same method will work with ourselves. There is, then, a new hope among socially-minded men – not a forlorn, but a scientific hope.

But, further, there is a practical realization that this is a new drive because this new movement sees its aim – the peace it will attain – as something far vaster than simply no more war. It is not merely a protest and refusal; it is an acceptance and a scheme. The new humanists or the new friends – call them what you like – are coming together in the dawn of a knowledge which shows that there is a new, radically new, way of life. Its aim is not merely the end of national armaments but a fresh relationship between men individually, socially and internationally. And as its aim is far more embracing than the old Pacifism, so the methods and means are far more thorough, dynamic, constructive, creative. Anthropologist, alienist, animal psychologist, all say that you cannot effect your purpose of 'contacting', helping, curing, taming, unless you are trained for the task. Here was the second weakness of the old Pacifism – It fatally restricted its aim, limited its diagnosis, and underrated the need of method.

Social diagnosis to-day shows war to be only a symptom of a diseased individualized civilization. But, equally, that diseased individualism and egotism – the fundamental appeal to greed and fear as the two sole compelling motives of man – that can only be lived down by a conviction equal to its own force. The appeal to 'mutual self-interest' to stop war is like relieving a dysenteric patient's sense of deadly weakness by giving him a square meal. We all live in a civilization, sociology now makes us realize, in which certain group suggestions dominate. To lift over the social organism on to other beliefs, to swing the ship on to another tack, needs intense experience of, and so conviction of, another way of living, a true way of life because it is creative and not destructive.

The new friendship aims, then, at having every pacifist trained in the initiative of social creativeness. It aims at so doing by every member joining a cell, or team, club or group in which he will constantly renew that direct sense of unlimited liability and psychological communism which make war and competition irrelevant. Then he will have the absolute assurance of 'the excellent way' because he has actually experienced it, and that experience will make him not only able to resist the counter-suggestion of those masses which cannot believe because they have not experienced anything but greed and fear, but will also call out (Lazarus-like) the ceremented soul in each and make it have the faith that it, too, can live, and so civilization be saved.

War has, we now know, a triple root. It springs from political problems and diplomatic disingenuousness, from patriotic prestige and that love of scoring over or deceiving an antagonist, which frame of mind becomes a second nature to those who have won to national power by the exercise of such emotions and exclusive reflection on such thoughts. War, however, also springs from economic problems and financial devices. Thirdly it springs from those unresolved and unconscious neuroses, those profound inner conflicts which, if we do not know how to cure, we project on the world, assuaging our misery by blaming and finally assaulting others. War cannot, then, be really cured unless all these three sources of conflict are dried up. Its causes can only be eliminated by creating neutralizing causes. Such causative action can be generated in a small group of like-minded people who are agreed – as is every modern peace-lover – on these three sources of war. For in such cells or teams active peace-lovers can have a realization of kinship which will cure their own inner conflict, permit them to live a life of unlimited liability with their company – a true co-operative commonwealth based surely on psychology which is the only sure foundation on which a just economy can rest – and give the world a demonsration of how free from anxiety and all psychoses, how sanely economic and how free of all necessity for coercion such a social life can be. Of the early Christians it was said that they had two irresistible advertisements, Love ('See how these Christians love one another') and Joy, the freedom and more than freedom from the anxiety, resentment and depression that are the by-products of the ego which can find no goal but itself. We now know from history that small units of like-minded people not only keep each other up to their first enthusiasm but help each other over times of individual discouragement. These are conscious things and, like giving each other fresh argumentative reasons for the faith that is in them, in helping each other to know the full strength of their case and the difficulties of hesistants – they are useful. They are, however, secondary to the unconscious forces which a group like-minded and regularly gathered together can and does release.

It is clear no individual can stand by himself against the invincible ignorance and the blind belief in greed and fear as the only social forces which still dominate our society to-day. He must gain practical actual reassurance that this belief is only a deadly half-truth which vanishes when the light of actual devotion is kindled against it. He can, however, no more do this by himself than a traveller who has tumbled into a bog in the dark can strike a light to see his way out. His matches are damp. Only in the group-field of fellow-believers can he rekindle his light. That, however, is itself only half the truth. History shows that small groups meeting once a week for meditation, if each member is every day meditating by himself (and by meditation is meant the spiritual exercise every sincerely religious mind recognizes as essential to the spirit) do have an experience of precipitated power. This is not only uniquely restorative, bodily as well as mentally, not only makes the members capable of real co-operative behaviour and unlimited liability toward each other, but also gives each a power to deal generously and with creative initiative with all outside. Further, by all outside it is recognized as a power of sanity, happiness and goodwill which they, too, would wish to share, and are ready to meet, if not half-way, at least far farther than they would have gone to any other approach or appeal. The new attitude to this power is empirical. It is recognized as uniquely valuable for all pacific work. Without it we can do nothing. At the same time it is also recognized as an empirical fact that this power works under definite limits which we have not discovered how to transcend. It depends for its effectiveness (1) to the degree the constituents *are* of one mind, have the same goal, (2) to the degree that they believe this power of dynamic affection *and no other way* is the approach to and power over all human beings, and all conscious creatures (to mix this method with any form of violence is to water petrol), (3) to the degree that they have learnt how to mediate (and to use silence), (4) to the degree that they find time daily to meditate by themselves and the regularity with which they meet to meditate together; and, finally, a queer but distinctive limitation which empiricists can only recognize and obey, (5) to the degree the numbers are kept to a sum not exceeding a dozen.

Following this method, this praxis, there seems clear historical evidence (and indeed everyone may try it out for himself will he find a handful of others to help) that the life of activism which eliminates self-conflict, class conflict and nation conflict can be lived. It is not easy, but it is no more exacting and far more interesting than any military discipline, and it is, of course, far more effective. It is a form of training, and so undertaking it people naturally are not afraid of discarding impediments, and as they advance such obstacles are more easily discarded. That is a reciprocal process. At the same time we must walk before we can run, and empiricism in this matter warns itself (from the sad experience of centuries) against imagining its first draft of this power as conferring either plenary inspiration or miraculous accomplishments. That is not to say such things can never be bestowed. It is only to point out that they only come after extreme training so that much work can be done even with the first yields and that nothing is gained, indeed often all is lost by rashly claiming privileges and powers, which humility would soon discover had in fact not yet been delegated. What is clear beyond a doubt is that in the 'field' of a small like-minded group trained in meditation are the powers essential to curing conflict in the self, in society and between humanity.

This, in brief, is a new move in Pacifism – a widened goal, a more thorough method; a goal scientifically demonstrable, a method scientifically applicable. The aim so comprehended and the means so adjusted in the light of these facts, there is abroad to-day a hope and faith that not only war, but all use of violence and cunning, may be superseded because we see at last not only that that way is deadly, but the practicability of the way of charity, 'the more excellent way'.

13 Second International Congress of Writers   *Manifesto (1937)**

This manifesto was published in England in the *Left Review* in September 1937. In the same issue, Edgell Rickword provided a report which gives not only background to the International Association of Writers for the Defence of Culture, but also summaries of – and extracts from – some of the key speeches given at the second congress. There were, as usual, plans to publish the full text of the speeches in a separate volume, but the editors of *Left Review* regarded it as a matter of urgency that something of the proceedings should be more broadly known. Especially interesting among those included are the words of Julien Benda, insisting that his arguments in *La Trahison des clercs* (1927; English translation by Richard Aldington, 1934) should not be taken as an indictment of intellectuals and their involvement in social issues: 'There is here a gross, and more or less deliberate equivocation, which is to confuse politics, defined in my book as submission to the basest individual interests, with morals, that is, with the defence of the highest moral values, principally those of justice and the rights of man, which include the right of all nations to a free existence, safe from the doom of slavery into which the new feudalism would plunge them' (pp. 447–8). Others whose speeches were reported included Ralph Bates (Spanish popular culture 'was doomed when the simpler techniques of production gave way to the techniques of the Machine Age'), Pablo Neruda, Nicolas Guillen and José Bergamin. Louis Aragon 'roused the enthusiasm of the huge audience in the Porte St. Martin with his impassioned claim that the defence of the nation was an integral part of the defence of culture. He tore the mask from the reactionaries who pose as the saviours of the nation when they sacrifice the well-being of the people and massacre them, if need be, to the sordid interests of a petty clique' (pp. 453–4).

Rickword comments on the background to the Association, historical circumstances, and on literary activism in England:

> When the first Congress of the Association met in Paris two years ago, the suggestion that the next Congress might be held in a European capital under fire from the planes and guns of two hostile states would have been considered a possibility by only a minority of the membership. Of that far-sighted minority, not a few have answered for their beliefs in the front line trenches. Writers, supposedly so aloof from public life, volunteering for the most dangerous tasks, and in the thick of the political struggle – is

* Reprinted from *Left Review* 3.8 (September 1937): 445–6.

this not a new phenomenon, and is it not an abuse of their function as intellectuals? As to its being a new phenomenon, we have only to read the biographies of English writers to know it not to be so. (p. 447)

In accordance with the principles and resolutions of the first Congress of their Association, the writers of 28 nations assembled for the Second International Congress which was held in Valencia, Madrid and Barcelona, and which concluded its work in Paris on July 17th, 1937:

(1) PROCLAIM that the principal enemy of the culture which they have undertaken to defend is Fascism:

(2) DECLARE themselves ready to struggle with all the means in their power against Fascism, whether it shows itself openly for what it is, or whether it adopts a disguise to pursue its destructive aims; declare themselves ready to struggle against the war-makers:

(3) AFFIRM that in the actual war that Fascism has begun against culture, democracy, peace and the happiness and well-being of mankind in general, no neutrality is possible or to be thought of, as the harsh experiences of the writers of numerous countries prove, countries where thought itself is confined to the terrible conditions of illegality.

In consequence, they here solemnly appeal to the writers of the whole world, to all those who believe deeply and sincerely in their human mission, in the power of the written word, and summon them to take up their stand without delay against the menace which hangs over culture and humanity.

They speak particularly to those who, from a lack of information, still retain the illusion that it is possible to maintain this neutrality, and also to those who still believe the mocking promises behind which Fascism masks its work of destruction and death.

And they ask of all writers that they realise their historic duty, unite with them and rally to the struggle for the good of the people as a whole and so safeguard the precious heritage common to them all.

They salute Republican Spain, her people, her Government, her army, the advance guard at the most threatened point in the struggle which they recognise has begun and from which they will not flinch. They salute in her the champion of the democracies, the guardian of culture and peace, as the Soviet Union, as well as those nations which followed its example, has nobly demonstrated in lending its fraternal aid to the Spain of freedom.

They undertake to defend Republican Spain wherever she is threatened, and to win to her cause the waverers and the misled. Finally they state here most definitely their unshakable confidence in the victory of the Spanish people.

14   Spain's Call to Intellectuals (1938)*

In the *Left Review* of April 1938, Randall Swingler used his editorial to rage against the impending European crisis in general, and against 'Chamberlain, Halifax & Co.' in particular for having 'known from the beginning of Hitler's intentions and hav[ing] deliberately stifled any attempt to hinder them'. 'Within a month', he wrote, 'the word Crisis has flared with very real meaning across Europe. Austria has been invaded and annexed, Czechoslovakia threatened, Lithuania has had to capitulate to Poland, and vast quantities of arms and men have been poured into Spain from Germany.' This was the climax of months of 'ruthless' mobilization by Fascist states, but also the consequence of British foreign policy. In one of the decade's most memorable pronouncements, Swingler declared the crisis 'the logical conclusion of Toryism, a Government loathed by the people, pursuing a policy odious to the people, to an outcome which could only be calamitous for the people'. The editorial, ending with a plea to the Government 'publicly and forthwith' to rally nations against further aggression, was signed by fifty-nine eminent persons '*and many others*'. In the same spirit – but with a focus on a particular site in the crisis – the next page carried 'Spain's Call to Intellectuals', prefaced as below with a short note.

A manifesto to the intellectuals of Spain and of all other countries was published in Barcelona on February 28th over the signatures of about 150 Spaniards prominent in literature, art, science, and other fields. Among the signatories are the painters **Pablo Picasso** and **Joan Miró**, the sculptor **Vitorio Macho**, the writers **Juan Larrea, Antonio Machado, José Bergamin, Jacinte Benavente**, the poet **Rafael Alberti** and the philologist **Tomas Navarro Tomas**.

Among the Spaniards abroad who signed the manifesto are two professors at British universities, **Rio Hortega** and **Jesus Val**.

'We have heard the message of warning and confidence broadcast by the Premier in the name of the legitimate Government which so worthily represents our country. Profoundly moved by words so clear, so courageous and so Spanish, frank and without euphemism – only possible because of the unshakable faith with which the Spanish people today support their Government – we, scientists, writers and artists wish to renew publicly and solemnly our allegiance to the Government of the Spanish Republic, and our

* Reprinted from *Left Review* 3.15 (April 1938): 896.

resolute decision to help defend until the complete victory the independence and liberty of Spain.

'We call upon the intellectuals of Spain who are silenced by fascism but who are conscious of their duty and the destiny history assigns to our country, to aid from within the enemy camp the victory of the Republic, which will bring liberation and the rebirth of Spain.

'*We also call upon the intellectuals of all countries* to work unremittingly in favour of the Spanish people who are fighting not only in their own defence but also for universal culture and liberty.

'The war has hardened us. It has also intensified our patriotic feelings. Today, more than ever, we feel an integral part of our people. We know that no sacrifice can shake the Spanish people's firm determination to win the war, by supporting and aiding the glorious Republican army.

'In school and laboratory, in whatever posts we may be placed, we will consecrate ourselves to our work with still greater ardour, certain that other workers will do the same in factory and field. This is the only reply our people can give to the calls just made by the legitimate Government through its Prime Minister to all Spaniards. We promise to respond to that appeal with all our energy. *All must unite to save Spain*, betrayed and invaded, but imperishable and certain of victory.'

15 John Cornford *The Class Front of Modern Art (1933)**

This essay was first published in *The Student Vanguard*, December 1933. Cornford had enrolled at the London School of Economics in January of that year. He was then only seventeen and waiting to take up his scholarship at Trinity College, Cambridge, in the autumn. Peter Stansky and William Abrahams tell us that 'at the outset his academic experience counted least with him' (p. 189). Although his tutor was the well-known social historian H. L. Beales, Cornford seemed to derive greatest stimulation from his extra-curricular activities, especially from his immersion in the growing student Communist movement. Shortly after his arrival he became editor of *The Student Vanguard*, as well as sub-editor of the *Young Worker*, secretary of both the Federation of Student Societies and the Labour Research Department Study Group, and member of a number of societies, including the Marxist Society and the Anti-War Committee. He joined the Young Communist League on 17 March 1933.[1] Cornford was the first Englishman to enlist against Franco in the Spanish Civil War and died fighting on the Cordoba front in December 1936.

The period of bourgeois decline in the epoch of Imperialism, marked by the end of the possibility of outward expansion of capitalism when the whole of the earth has been divided into colonies and markets, is marked by a corresponding change of position on the ideological front. The old 'progressive' materialism which served the bourgeoisie in its struggle against reactionary feudal mysticism, is abandoned in favour of a no less reactionary idealism. Economic theories of Free Trade and Free Competition are replaced by the fascist doctrine of 'national self-sufficiency'.

Psychology is more and more openly used as a class weapon – in its 'practical' form (industrial psychology) as a means of reconciling factory workers and employees to their environment in order to prevent their rebelling against it; in its more mystical forms as a new brand of opium for the people, a religion-substitute for the petty-bourgeoisie; in its more highly-developed theoretical forms as an idealist counter-attack against the historical-materialist analysis of society.[2] So also with art. This too is no longer a dynamic cultural force, but it is as much a check on the cultural development of society as the bourgeois property-relations are on its productive development.

---

* Reprinted from *Understand the Weapon, Understand the Wound: Selected Writings of John Cornford*, ed. Jonathan Galassi (Manchester: Carcanet New Press, 1976), pp. 46–50.

Contradictions

The characteristic feature of the decay of bourgeois art is the recurring concept of the contradiction between art and life.[3] This can be traced in different forms in the work of all the leading writers. Perhaps its most conscious formulation by a poet is W. B. Yeats': 'The intellectual man is forced to choose/Perfection of the art or of the life' [*sic*]. And it occurs in the romantic concept of poetry as an escape from life, as in Stephen Spender's: 'The city builds its horror in my brain,/This writing is my only wings away.' And in a highly significant passage in *The Sacred Wood*, T. S. Eliot states that literary experience is of the same validity and can be considered on the same level as other direct forms of experience, which is a more positive formulation of the same basic idea. And even where it has no conscious formulation, the same concept can be found running through the work of the leading bourgeois writers, not as a theoretical concept but as an unchallenged axiom. Ezra Pound's idealist–romantic historical poems, which are complementary to the violent but petty and *unhistorical* contemporary satires, show just the same tendency. For Pound approaches his medieval Provence through its literature and not through its history. It is an escape into the literature of the past to avoid the present reality. His criterion for the judgement of the world to-day is a previous epoch's judgement of itself.

The Artist in Society

And from the concept of the contradiction between art and life arises as the next logical step the idea of the contradiction of the life of the artist with the life of society. The fictionised autobiography of Rainer Maria Rilke, the German poet, *The Notebook of Malte Laurids Brigge*, is the classic example of this. The hero is portrayed as hypersensitive to the verge of insanity, driven almost crazy by continual neurotic introspection, sinking frequently into a wearingly abject self-pity. The life and work of the French novelist, Proust, show exactly the same super-subjectivity. Perhaps the most detailed formulation of the contradiction between the life of the artist and the life of society is Hermann Hesse's novel *Steppenwolf*, which is devoted exclusively to the subject. It is a very interesting book, because Hesse comes closer than any of the others to understanding the objective causes for this contradiction. He specifically states that whilst Steppenwolf (who represents the bourgeois writer) is antagonistic to the form of society in which he finds himself, his attempts to alter it are confined to criticism in his writings, usually from a subjective standpoint; he cannot take up a more active struggle against it *because he is ultimately dependent upon it*. Exactly the same idea is the main theme of a novel by Thomas Mann, *Tonio Kroeger*.

This seeming antagonism to bourgeois society is not in any sense revolutionary. D. H. Lawrence condemned (in words) the bourgeois; but he found the Bolshevik equally detestable. And this is equally true of his contemporaries. His disciple, Richard Aldington, writes lyrical hymns of hate against the bourgeoisie: but also thinks that class war is 'poisonous bunk'. For the idea of the contradiction between art and life is complementary to the idea of the artist as a lofty and impartial observer, standing above the petty conflicts of society. By this disguise of impartiality they attempt to conceal the fact, more honestly recognised by Hermann Hesse, that they are inactive because they have not sufficiently the courage of their convictions to be renegades of their class – with all its unpleasant and dangerous social consequences. When Louis Aragon, one of the members of the surrealist group, went over to the Communists and was imprisoned on the charge of incitement for his poem *The Red Front*, he was quickly enough abandoned by the rest of the group.

For those who realise that the class conflict in society is a struggle between the dynamic and vital forces of society against the inertial forces, the idea of the 'impartial' artist is an absurdity. To stand outside the conflict is to add to the deadweight of forces of reaction and inertia. Thus the seeming antagonism between the bourgeoisie and its artists serves only to conceal that their class interests are fundamentally the same – incidentally serving a very useful political purpose in diverting the potentially revolutionary forces among the bourgeois intellectuals into safe literary channels.

Art and Fascism

But in its final stage of crisis when the bourgeoisie is forced to abandon its veiled 'democratic' form of dictatorship in favour of its openly terrorist fascist dictatorship, all art and all science, however far they are separated by class-prejudice from an objective dialectical attitude, must be suppressed because they are potentially dangerous. It is not an exaggeration to state that fascist Italy and Germany have expelled or silenced practically every artist or scientist of any ability. The bankruptcy of the official fascist artists is so pitiful that an increasing section of the intellectuals of both countries realises more and more clearly the class-issues involved and goes over to the revolution. But in those countries where the transition to fascism through the 'democratic' state machinery is still taking place, where the simple class issue has not been presented in as brutally direct form as it was presented to the Italians and Germans, a further change of front is taking place among the bourgeois artists, an attempted adaptation to the new policy of the bourgeoisie. Ezra Pound leads the way, coming out as an open fascist and at the same time a simple-minded propagandist for Douglas credit. Wyndham Lewis two years ago wrote a book about Hitler, containing a lame apology for his anti-semitism, and the curious theory that Hitler is a man of peace because he is the 'German man'. Since Lewis appears to have relied exclusively on the Nazi press and propaganda for information about the movement, the book appears now utterly grotesque.[4] Nevertheless it represents a significant ideological tendency. T. S. Eliot also follows rather hesitatingly. When taken in conjunction with the preface to E. A. Mowrer's book in America, with its elevation of racial theory, the anti-semitic passages in *Burbank*, and *Bleistein* and *Gerontion* have more than a passing significance. But this is not a process of adaptation that will ever have time to complete itself. The historical process does not greatly concern itself with the subjective reaction of individuals to it; and it will not stand still and wait while these gentlemen attempt to define their relation to it.

Meanwhile, all over the world there is growing up a revolutionary movement in literature which flatly denies that there is a contradiction between art and life, which rejects the theory of artistic 'impartiality'. Its writers do not regard themselves as isolated and detached observers of history, but as active participators. Their work is born out of struggle. Ernst Toller, the worker's councillor of the Bavarian Soviet, who was forced to escape with a price of 10,000 marks on his head, wrote his first plays secretly in prison. Theodor Plivier, the novelist of the revolt in the German navy, took an active part as an able seaman in the events he describes. Pudovkin and Eisenstein, whose films *The End of St. Petersburg* and *The Battleship Potemkin*[5] mark the peak of revolutionary art, both took part in the revolution. And these are only a few examples of a universal movement. Everywhere a revolutionary literature is being written with a crude and violent energy comparable only to the force of the earlier artists of the bourgeois revolution, men such as Kyd and Marlowe; but with this difference, that the hero is no longer the great king or successful general, but the working class as a whole.

In England the movement is not as advanced as elsewhere, but the same stirrings can be found in some of the work of the younger poets, Auden,

Madge, and a few others. And although the very youth of these writers, and their consequent inexperience of the revolutionary movement, means that the work still has largely the content of a literary revolt against the concept of a contradiction between art and life, the only possible logical development is towards a consistently revolutionary standpoint.

In the course of its development some of its members will leave it when it becomes clear that it offers little future for a bourgeois literary career (just as the Surrealistes left Aragon), and some will lag behind the tempo of events and become mere 'fellow-travellers' with the movement. But it is not our business here to decide what part the various individuals will play in its development. It is sufficient to know that only from this quarter can come a successful struggle for free development of culture against the cultural reaction.

Notes

1. See Stansky and Abrahams, pp. 188–99.
2. 'A new factor in history', writes F. R. Leavis in a section of *Mass Civilisation and Minority Culture* which I was forced, for reasons of space, to omit from this collection, 'is an unprecedented use of applied psychology' (p. 11). Leavis's focus is on advertising, and he laments the deleterious effect on culture of any 'deliberate exploitation of the cheap response'. Although he does not quite see psychology 'as a class weapon', his analysis of its modern uses bears comparison with Cornford's, and shows why the aims of *Scrutiny* were so often taken to be compatible with those of British Marxism. Cf. C. H. Sisson's perspective on advertising and psychological exploitation in 'Prejudice as an Aid to Government', below, pp. 186–8.
3. See Caudwell's elaboration of this point below, pp. 117, 123–5.
4. Lewis's approval of Hitler was, of course, retracted in *The Hitler Cult* (1939). See below, pp. 201–2.
5. *Potemkin* was first screened in London in 1929, principally due to the efforts of John Grierson, whose own film of that year, *Drifters,* completed the bill. James Beveridge imagines 'the impact – or to be more precise, the shock – of two such films with their harsh percussive styles set against the context of contemporary commercial feature films of 1929, sugary fantasies from a world of pure escapism . . . By energetic persuasion, by screenings of imported films, and by the prestigious success of his own film, Grierson was able to inaugurate the first production programs for the British government. This development would occupy a full decade, 1929–1939.' See Beveridge, *John Grierson: Film Master* (New York: Macmillan, 1978), pp. 43–4.

16 Christopher Caudwell *from **Illusion and Reality***
*(1937)**

When *Illusion and Reality* was published in the spring of 1937, Caudwell had already been killed in action in Spain. Auden, reviewing the book for *New Verse* that May, proclaimed it 'the most important book on poetry since the books of Dr. [I. A.] Richards'; it was, he said, 'a long essay on the evolution of freedom in Man's struggle with nature . . . and of the essentially social nature of words, art and science'.[1] Given Auden's own position on 'the social nature of words' in the 'Writing' essay of 1932 (see above, p. 37), his approbation of Caudwell is not surprising – less so, even, when one considers that Caudwell shared with Auden 'the two major influences of his system – Marx and Freud' (Sullivan, p. 87).[2] In fact, Caudwell's interest in Marx was a good deal more recent than Auden's: it was only in late 1934 that he discovered and began a systematic study of Marx, Engels and Lenin. Jean Duparc and David Margolies write:

> By June 1935, supporting himself by writing pot-boilers, he was already involved in his first explicitly Marxist work, 'Verse and Mathematics', the earliest version of what eventually became *Illusion and Reality* . . . He told the Beards in November 1935 that he had found his 'integrated Weltanschauung', had started learning Russian, and intended to join the Communist Party. A few days later he contacted the small local branch of the party. As far as is known, he had never been acquainted with any Communist before. (p. 10)

Samuel Hynes has pointed to the appropriateness of Caudwell's having written *Illusion and Reality* while isolated in Cornwall, since 'he had no English tradition of Marxist criticism on which to build' and was in that sense also on his own.[3] Christopher Pawling agrees, pointing to a 'hiatus' in English socialist criticism between William Morris's *Hopes and Fears for Art* (1882) 'and the productions of people like Caudwell and Alick West' (p. 16). The *Left Review*, after all, only began to appear in October 1934, and even John Strachey's influential Marxist studies, *The Coming Struggle for Power* (1932) and *Literature and Dialectical Materialism* (1934) contained no 'broad historical sweep, nor any attempt at a "philosophical" explanation of literature's role within society' (Sullivan, p. 70). No doubt Caudwell's isolation and the lack of a sustaining and vibrant tradition of English Marxism contributed to the shortcomings and confusions which have been frequently remarked in *Illusion and Reality*. But perhaps those very

---

* Reprinted from *Illusion and Reality: A Study of the Sources of Poetry* (1937; London: Lawrence and Wishart, 1946), pp. 101–16.

disadvantages were what gave rise to the work's most distinguishing features: its sheer ambitiousness, inclusivity and erudition – its attempt to provide 'an integrated Weltanschauung' embracing art, literature, science and society.

What follows is the last part of Caudwell's long section on 'English Poets', in which he reads English literary history in relation to an evolving 'bourgeois illusion':

> knowing the essence of this illusion to be a special belief concerning 'individualism' or the 'natural man', which in turn derives from the conditions of bourgeois economy, we cannot be surprised that the bourgeois poet is the lonely man who, apparently turning away from society into himself, by so doing expresses the more strongly the essential relations of contemporary society. Bourgeois poetry is individualistic because it expresses the collective emotion of its era. (p. 71)

The next phase of bourgeois poetry is therefore that of 'commodity-fetishism' – or 'art for art's sake' – and is given in the false position of the bourgeois poet as producer for the market, a position forced on him by the development of bourgeois economy. As soon as the pessimism of Arnold and the young Tennyson, and the even sadder optimism of Browning and Swinburne and the old Tennyson when dealing with the contemporary scene, made it inevitable that the poet quit the contemporary scene, it was equally inevitable that the poet should fall a victim to commodity-fetishism. This meant a movement which would completely separate the world of art from the world of reality and, in doing so, separate it from the source of art itself so that the work would burst like a bubble just when it seemed most self-secure.

Engels in *Anti-Düring* very clearly explains the characteristic of every society based on commodity production:

> [It] has the peculiarity that in it the producers have lost control of their own social relationships. Each produces for himself, with the means of production which happen to be at his disposal and in order to satisfy his individual needs through the medium of exchange. No one knows how much of the article he produces is coming on the market, or how much demand there is for it; no one knows whether his individual product will meet a real need, whether he will cover his costs or even be able to sell at all. Anarchy reigns in social production. But commodity production, like all other forms of production, has its own laws, which are inherent and inseparable from it; and these laws assert themselves in spite of anarchy,

> in and through anarchy . . . They assert themselves, therefore, apart from the producers and against the producers, as the natural laws of their form of production, working blindly. *The product dominates the producers.*

Engels contrasts this with the older and more universal method of production for use instead of exchange. Here the origin and end of production are clearly seen. All are part of the one social act, and the product is only valued in so far as it is of use to the society which produces it. In such a society the poem as such derives its value from its collective appearance, from the effect it has on the hearts of its hearers and the impact, direct and evident, on the life of the tribe.

In capitalist production, which is commodity production *in excelsis*, all this is altered. Everyone produces blindly for a market whose laws are unfathomable, although they assert themselves with iron rigidity. The impact of the commodity upon the life of society cannot be measured or seen. 'Man has lost control of his social relationships.' The whole elaborate warp and woof of capitalism, a complex web spun in anarchy, makes this helplessness inevitable.

To the poet the bourgeois market appears as the 'public'. The invention and development of printing and publishing was part of the development of the universal bourgeois free market. Just as the development of this market (by the extension of colonisation and transport and exchange facilities) made it possible for man to produce for places whose very names he did not know, much less their location, so the poet now writes for men of whose existence he is ignorant, whose social life, whose whole mode of being is strange to him. The market is for him 'The Public' – blind, strange, passive.

This leads to what Marx called 'commodity-fetishism'. The social character of the art-process, so evident in the collective festival, now disappears. 'A commodity is therefore a mysterious thing, simply because in it the social character of men's labour appears to them as an objective character stamped upon the product of that labour . . . In the same way the light from an object is perceived by us not as the subjective excitation of our optic nerve, but as the objective form of something outside the eye itself.' In the same way the art work, once its social realisation in the hearts of society is veiled by the 'market' or the 'public', appears to the poet as something objective. This is helped by the swing-over of art from forms visibly dependent on men in association – the dance, the song, music, the spontaneous drama and *commedia dell'arte* – to crystallised records of the art process not therefore dependent on society – the written poem, the musical score, the written play, the picture or sculpture. The art stimulus becomes objective – a commodity.

Capitalist production requires for its movement – capital. Constant capital is a continually increasing part of the sum of capital. This constant capital takes the visible form of elaborate factory plant and indirectly the more highly-developed technique and organisation necessary to use this plant. The growth of constant capital and therefore of social organisation due to increasing productivity of labour contrasts with the growth of individualism in ownership and appropriation due to the increasing wealth of private capitalists. In the same way bourgeois poetry is marked by a continually increasing sum of tradition and technique, of which the poet feels the pressure, so that there is a continual contradiction between the tremendous social experience embodied in the poem and the individualistic and anti-social attitude of the poet. 'Tradition' towers up before the poet as something formidable and tremendous, with which he must settle accounts as an ego.

But the poet is not a capitalist. He does not exploit labour. To the capitalist commodity-fetishism takes the form of sacralisation of the common market-denominator of all commodities – money. Money acquires for him a high, mystic, *spiritual* value. But the writer is himself exploited.

In so far as he 'writes for money' of course he acquires a purely capitalist mentality. He may even himself exploit labour by means of secretaries and hacks who do his 'donkey-work' for him. But the man who writes for money is not an artist, for it is the characteristic of the artist that his products are adaptative, that the artistic illusion is begotten of the tension between instinct and consciousness, between productive forces and productive relations, the very tension which drives on all society to future reality. In bourgeois society this tension is that between the productive forces (the socially organised power of capitalist technique in the factories) and the social relations (production for private profit and the resulting anarchy in the market as a whole indicated by the universality of the money or 'exchange' relation instead of the direct or 'use' relation). Because this is the fundamental contradiction, the poet 'revolts' against the system of profit-making or production for exchange-value as crippling the meaning and significance of art. But as long as he revolts within the categories of bourgeois thought – that is, as long as he cannot cast off the basic bourgeois illusion – his revolt takes a form made necessary by the system of commodity production.

The exploited – of which the poet thus becomes one – are of two kinds in capitalist production: These two kinds, the labourer and the craftsman, may be regarded as descendants of the serfs and artisans of medieval days. However, the lineage is not direct. Serfs became capitalists and artisans were hurled down into the proletariat during the capitalist revolution. The exploited may be regarded as descendants of the one class of artisans. The *labourer* has been thoroughly proletarianised; the *craftsman*, for special reasons, has still retained a measure of privilege in capitalist production which gives him the illusion of belonging to the 'middle class', a class immune from and superior to the class struggle as a whole. None the less, the proletarian abyss yawns always beneath his feet. His privilege is an accident of a particular stage of capitalist production and is always being torn from his grasp. However, the historical change of capitalist production produces always new members of this class, which therefore appears always to have a certain stability and separate existence, although its actual composition is in a state of wild flux. The final stages of capitalism reveal the fallacy of even this phantom operation, and the petty bourgeoisie finds its privileges being torn from its hands.

Let us examine the main history of these two divisions in England.

(I) *The Labourer* – He is the man who works drably, monotonously and at the most-sweated wages, a mere cog in the machine. He is the proletarian proper, the unique creation of capitalism. His fight against the capitalist is most bitter and uncompromising because his work, by its very nature, is of a kind it is impossible to like, and therefore his revolt is expressed as a fight for leisure, an attempt to snatch from his employers' reluctant hands every extra hour of decent human existence outside the factory. This fight goes with a struggle for higher wages, to make those short hours of leisure as full and free as possible.

This is the only form his struggle for freedom can take within the categories of capitalist production, for in his dull task freedom expresses itself as the opposite to social activity or 'work'. Because he constitutes the majority of those from the surplus value of whose labour-power the capitalist derives his profit, the antagonism between the two classes is naked and direct. This antagonism is the real core of the class struggle in capitalist society. Each minute of his leisure or penny of his wages is so much from the capitalist's profit. His freedom is precisely the capitalist's unfreedom, and *vice versa*.

(II) *The Craftsman* – This class, as foreman, overseer, or mechanic, or in a profession as barrister, doctor, engineer or architect, occupies a special position in capitalist production because of his personal skill, technique or 'key' job. Because of his favoured position, his delight in his skill, and his higher wages, the craftsman finds himself often in opposition to the genuine proletariat. Work for him does not stand in such sharp opposition to leisure, or his freedom to the capitalist's freedom, as in the case of the labourer. Sometimes he is even in business 'in a small way' himself, not as a capitalist, but employing two or three apprentice-assistants and selling to large capitalists. This apparent cleavage of interests is expressed in these workers' organisations. The great general labouring unions – the T. & G.W., N.U.G. & M.W.,[4] and such similar unions – in their early days, led by Ben Tillett, Tom Mann and John Burns, found themselves opposed by and contending with the 'amalgamated' craft unions such as the old A.S.E.,[5] which inherited the Liberal traditions of the 'Junta' that had, at an earlier date, ousted the original militant but badly organised lodges.

None the less, the development of capitalist production remorselessly turns the craftsman into a labourer. The machine competes with and ousts the product of his skilled hands in all departments and forces him into the 'industrial reserve army' of the unemployed.

The result is at first to make him revolt against the demands of a 'commercialised' market by setting up his skill as a good in itself, detached from social causes. You will hear such a craftsman admire an old Napier car, for example, as a superb production of skilled *craftsmen*, and compare it with a modern *mass-production* Ford, which fulfils the same social rôle and is cheaper. The old skill, although more wasteful of human labour, has acquired a special value to the craftsman because it is the condition for his existence as a class distinct from the proletariat, and is set over and against the market with its criterion of profit, which is the cause of the outdating of his skill. Eventually, employed as a factory hand, he may still cherish his outdated skill by making models, by indulging in little private 'hobbies' and other socially meaningless activities that exercise his craft.

In this his attitude is fundamentally akin to that of the writer. The writer's relation to capitalism is also privileged and craft, although its 'ideal' content gives it a still higher privilege than manual craftsmanship in an age where the class division has separated thinking from doing. The writer is a *part* of upper bourgeois society, like the doctor, barrister, architect, teacher or scientist whose work has a similar theoretical content – the manual craftsman is never more than 'lower middle class'. None the less, both find themselves expressing the special aspirations and delusions of the petty bourgeoisie.

Just as the growth of capitalism tends more and more to whelm all industrial production in mass production, expropriate artisans in thousands, and proletarianise the craftsman to the level of a labourer or machine-minder, so it has the same effect in the realm of art. Mass-production art enforces a dead level of mediocrity. Good art becomes less saleable. Because art's rôle is now that of adapting the multitude to the dead mechanical existence of capitalist production, in which work sucks them of their vital energies without awakening their instincts, where leisure becomes a time to deaden the mind with the easy phantasy of films, simple wish-fulfilment writing, or music that is mere emotional message – because of this the paid craft of writer becomes as tedious and wearisome as that of machine-minder. Journalism becomes the characteristic product of the age. Films, the novel and painting all share in the degradation.[6] Immense technical resources and steady debasement and stereotyping of the human psyche are characteristics alike of factory production and factory art in this stage of capitalism. Let any artist who has had to earn a living by journalism or writing 'thrillers' testify to the inexorable proletarianisation of his art. The modern thriller, love story, cowboy romance, cheap film, jazz music or yellow Sunday paper form the real *proletarian* literature of to-day – that is, literature which is the characteristic accompaniment of the misery and instinctual poverty produced in the majority of people by modern capitalist production.[7] It is literature which proletarianises the writer. It is at once an expression of real misery and a protest against that real misery. This art, universal, constant, fabulous, full of the easy gratifications of instincts starved by modern capitalism, peopled by passionate lovers and heroic cowboys and amazing detectives, is the religion of to-day, as characteristic an expression of proletarian exploitation as Catholicism is of feudal exploitation. It is the opium of the people; it pictures an inverted world because the world of society *is* inverted. It is the real characteristic art of bourgeois civilisation, expressing the real and not the self-appraised content of the bourgeois illusion. 'High-brow' bourgeois art grows on the bourgeois class's freedom. 'Low-brow'[8] proletarian art grows on the proletariat's unfreedom and helps, by its massage of the starved revolting instincts, to maintain that unfreedom in being. Because it is mere massage, because it helps to maintain man in unfreedom and not to express his spontaneous creation, because of that, it is bad art. Yet it is an art which is far more really characteristic, which plays a far more important and all-pervasive rôle in bourgeois society than, for example, the art of James Joyce.

The poet is the most craft of writers. His art requires the highest degree of technical skill of any artist; and it is precisely this technical skill which is not wanted by the vast majority of people in a developed capitalism. He is as out of date as a medieval stone-carver in an era of plaster casts. As the virtual proletarianisation of society increases, the conditions of men's work, robbed of spontaneity, more and more make them demand a mass-produced 'low-brow' art, whose flatness and shallowness serve to adapt them to their unfreedom. The poet becomes a 'high-brow', a man whose skill is not wanted. It becomes too much trouble for the average man to read poetry.

Because of the condition of his life, the poet's reaction is similar to that of the craftsman. He begins to set craft skill in *opposition* to social function, 'art' in opposition to 'life'.[9] The craftsman's particular version of commodity-fetishism is *skill-fetishism*. Skill now seems an objective thing, opposed to social value. The art work therefore becomes valued in and for itself.

But the art work lives in a world of society. Art works are always composed of objects that have a social reference. Not mere noises but words from a vocabulary, not chance sounds but notes from a socially-recognised scale, not mere blobs but forms with a *meaning*, are what constitutes the material of art. All these things have emotional associations which are social.

Yet if an art work is valued for *its own sake* in defiant and rebellious opposition to the sake of a society which has now no use for its skill, it is in fact valued *for the artist's sake*. One cannot simply construct random poems. If their associations are not social they are personal, and the more the art work is opposed to society, the more are personal associations defiantly selected which are exclusive of social – bizarre, strange, phantastic. In this stage of the bourgeois illusion therefore poetry exhibits a rapid movement from the social world of art to the personal world of private phantasy. This leads to individualism. In revolting against capitalism the poet, because he remains within the sphere of bourgeois categories, simply moves on to an extreme individualism, utter 'loss of control of his social relationships', and absolute commodity-production – to the essence, in fact, of the capitalism he condemns. He is the complete mirror-revolutionary.

And his too triumphant proclamation of liberty at last achieved in full, marks the very moment when liberty completely slips out of his hands.

This movement into the world of 'art for art's sake' – *i.e.* 'art for my sake' – of course is well marked in England with Rossetti, Morris before he became a socialist, Wilde and to a certain extent Hopkins. But in this epoch of the final stage of capitalism the movement becomes most rapid in other countries. England, the quickest to develop methods of capitalist production, is slowest to decline. The final movement in bourgeois art is accomplished most fully in other countries.

The movement is seen in its purity in France. Baudelaire begins it: 'Il ne peut être du progrès (vrai, c'est à dire moral) que dans l'individu et par l'individu lui-même.'[10] Verlaine and Rimbaud continue it, though Rimbaud, allying himself with the Commune, passes from poetry with the collapse of the first proletarian dictatorship.

From then on the movement develops *via* the Parnassians, through the symbolists, to its climax in the *surréalistes*. With the Parnassians the word is valued for its marmoreal craft qualities; with the symbolists for the vague penumbra of emotional associations lying beyond the word – that is, for its extra-social associations; with the *surréalistes* directly for its private unconscious significance. The transition from Heredia *via* Laforgue to Apollinaire is surprisingly rapid and clear.

In England poetry at first seems exhausted. The universal movement of the bourgeois economy which is debasing all art, or making it move to *surréalisme*, is halted in England by little 'pockets' or sheltered occupations, representing the reserves of England's long bourgeois summer. The country – preserved and protected by the rich industrial capitalist who finds it better to exploit ruthlessly the colonial 'country' for raw material and keep some vestige of idyllic relations around him – is one such pocket; it gives us Hardy and a succession of less gnarled country poets such as Thomas and Davies. Oxford and Cambridge are other such pockets; they give us Housman, Flecker, Brooke, and various other 'Georgian' poets. The war closes this period. In 1929 the final economic crisis of capitalism affects even England, and English poetry too moves rapidly towards symbolism and the most logically consistent expression of poetic craft revolt – *surréalisme*.

The *surréaliste* is somewhat equivalent to the craftsman who makes trifling models and toys in his spare time to exercise his skill. This is the way he expresses his revolt and secures some free outlet for his craft, by deliberately making something of its nature useless and therefore opposed to the sordid craftlessness of mass-production. We will deal later with the aesthetic theory of *surréalisme* and the importance it attaches to the Unconscious, when we have had time to consider the real function of the instincts and of the Unconscious in art. At the moment we need only point out that, so far from the free association which is the basis of surrealistic technique being really free, it is far more compulsive than ordinary rational association, as Freud, Jung and MacCurdy have clearly shown. In rational association images are controlled by a social experience of reality – the consciousness of necessity. In free association the images are controlled by the iron hand of the unconscious instincts – and it is therefore no more free than the 'thinking' of the ant. Man becomes free not by realising himself in opposition to society but by realising himself through society, and the character of the association in itself imposes certain common forms and conventions which are the badge of his freedom. But because the *surréaliste* is a bourgeois and has lost control of his social relationships, he believes freedom to consist in revolting against these forms whereby freedom has been realised in the past. Social activity, the means of freedom, is – because its products are appropriated more completely by individuals the more social the activity becomes – opposed by a resolutely non-social activity which is felt to constitute freedom because its producers are useless to society and therefore cannot be appropriated by individuals. Of course this is an outside view of the process. Subjectively the artist believes himself to be realising an ideal freedom derived from the 'magic' qualities of art works and the unique features of the artist's mind.

At each stage the bourgeois contradiction by unfolding itself revolutionises its own base and secures fresh development of technical resources. Hence the movement from 'art for art's sake' to *surréalisme* secures a development of the technique of poetry, of which in England Eliot is the best example owing to the already-mentioned lag. But it cannot continue indefinitely. The conflict between technical resources and content reaches a limit where it explodes and begins to turn into its opposite. A revolution of content, as opposed to a mere movement of technique, now begins, corresponding in the social sphere to a change in productive relations as opposed to a mere improvement in productive forces. As a result the social associations of words will all be re-cast, and the whole subject-matter of poetry will become different, because language itself is now generated in a different society. There will be a really revolutionary movement from the categories of bourgeois poetry to the categories of communist poetry.

The *surréaliste* therefore is the last bourgeois revolutionary. To pass beyond him – beyond Milton, beyond Godwin, beyond Pater, beyond finally Dada and Dalí, is to pass beyond the categories of bourgeois thought. What politically is this final bourgeois revolutionary? He is an anarchist.

The anarchist is a bourgeois so disgusted with the development of bourgeois society that he asserts the bourgeois creed in the most essential way: complete 'personal' freedom, complete destruction of all social relations. The anarchist is yet revolutionary because he represents the destructive element and the complete negation of all bourgeois society. But he cannot really pass beyond bourgeois society, because he remains caught in its toils. In the anarchic organisation of bourgeois economy certain laws of organisation still assert themselves, and therefore can only be shattered by a higher organisation, that of a new ruling-class.

The anarchist is the typical revolutionary product of the country where industrial capitalism has developed late under 'hot-house' conditions and has resulted in the rapid proletarianisation of a large number of artisans or petty bourgeois craftsmen. It is a petty bourgeois creed. Hence its strength in 'late' capitalist countries like Italy, Spain, Russia and France – precisely the countries where the surrealistic tendency in art is also most marked.

But it is also the character of *surréalisme*, as it is the character of anarchy as a political philosophy, that it *negates itself in practice*. The difference between communism and anarchy as a political philosophy is that communism believes that bourgeois rule can only be successfully overthrown by an organised movement. This organisation, expressed in soviets and trade unions, is a direct outcome of the organisation forced on the proletariat by the general conditions of capitalist economy. The anarchist, however, has recently been a petty bourgeois, a peasant or an artisan. He has not been organised for long in an industrial and political struggle against the capitalistic class. He therefore sees revolution as an individual destruction of authority which would suffice to restore the conditions in which he enjoyed the fruit of his own small-scale labour.

But in practice the anarchist discovers that the mere destruction of an outworn society, let alone the building of a new, requires organisation. The mere necessities of the task drive him first into trade unions and then into the creation of soviets. This was seen in the Russian Revolution, when the sincere Social Revolutionaries were mostly forced, by the logic of events, to the Bolshevik standpoint, and again in Spain, where in Barcelona the anarchists have had to support a strong Central Government, help in the organisation of militia, defence and supplies, and in every way negate their own creed. Hence the truth of the old joke as to the anarchist's code:

Para. 1. There shall be no order at all.
Para. 2. No one shall be obliged to comply with the preceding
        paragraph,

and the significance of the newspaper report after the Fascist revolt in Spain: 'The anarchists are keeping order in Barcelona.'

In the same way, as a revolutionary situation develops, the *surréaliste* poets either retreat to reaction and Fascism (as many in Italy) or are thrown into the ranks of the proletariat, like Aragon in France.

In a country such as England, the final revolt of the craftsman usually takes a different form. The craftsman is not there an independent artisan or petty bourgeois whose first taste of proletarianisation gives him a hatred of 'organisation.' The proletarianisation of the artisan took place in the late eighteenth century in England, and because the possibilities of revolution were more hopeless, his rebellion took the form of Ludditism – the smashing of the machines which expropriated them. The next great proletarianisation of the craftsmen was marked by the rise of the general labourers' unions in the face of the opposition of the craft unions, and the struggle then was a struggle between a developing proletariat and the capitalists, with the craft unions standing aside.

Thus the final crisis in England found the craftsman a man who, as the result of the long springtime of English capitalist development, occupied a privileged position in production. He formed the famous labour aristocracy who made it seem as if England, not content with a bourgeois aristocracy and a bourgeois monarchy, aimed also at a bourgeois proletariat. In the final crisis it soon became apparent that this favoured position was only the expression of the temporary supremacy of England in world capitalism and vanished with the growth of competition and tariffs. Unemployment, insecurity, wage-cuts and dismissals as the result of rationalisation, from 1929 to 1936, ravaged all ranks of the 'craft' and 'professional' elements of England just as, at a somewhat earlier date, they had those in Germany. So far, however, from proletarianisation in all cases producing an anarchic frame of mind in these types, it has an opposite effect in those who are 'key' men rooted in the heart of industry everywhere – in the tool-room of the factory, as supervisors, foremen, technicians, specialists, managers and consultants. In these positions they find that their skill is wasted, not by the organisation of men into factories, but because the progress of this organisation – its logical conclusion in an immensely increased human productivity – is defeated by the characteristic anarchy of capitalist production – the individual ownership and mutual competition of the various factories.

Hence their revolution against the system which is crippling them is not reactionary in content, like the artisan's, but genuinely progressive, in that it demands greater organisation – the extension of the organisation already obtaining in the factories to production as a whole.

But though progressive in content, it by no means follows that this demand will find an outcome in a progressive act. Even at this revolutionary stage the craftsman halts at two paths. One leads up to the bourgeoisie, with whom his responsible position and higher salary have always associated him – indeed the doctor, architect and artist, owing to the 'ideal' content of their work, have actually been a genuine part of the bourgeoisie. The other path leads downward to the proletariat, from whom his privileged position has always sundered him – for proletarianisation, because it has involved worsened living conditions, has been something to be avoided at all costs. Hence he has an ingrained repulsion from alliance with the proletariat. In the past he has measured his success and freedom by the distance he has climbed up from the proletariat to the bourgeoisie – the famous petty bourgeois snobbery and exclusiveness which is only the cold reflection of man's constant desire for freedom.

If he chooses the upward path, he chooses organisation imposed from above by the bourgeoisie – in other words, Fascism. Of course this organisation is a mere sham – it is a cloak for further rationalisation, and the consolidating of the power of the most reactionary section of the capitalist class. It results, not in the increased organisation of production but in greater anarchy and more bitter competition. Rationalisation is in fact irrationalisation. It leads to an increase in anarchy outside and inside – internally by a profound disturbance in economy resulting from the growth of armament and luxury industry at the expense of necessities and a general lowering of wages, and externally by an increase in tariffs and imperialism and a general drive towards war. The only real organisation consists in the counter-revolutionary regimentation of the proletariat and petty bourgeois classes and the smashing of working-class organisations.

But equally the craftsman may choose the downward path, and he is the more likely to do so as the development of the industrial crisis and the objective examples of Fascism abroad reveal the inevitability of this move. This path consists of allying himself with the proletariat and extending the organisation of production as a whole by liquidating those rights which stand in the way – individual ownership of the means of production. Since this right is the real power of existing society, this means the substitution of workers' power for capitalists' power. When he makes this choice, the craftsman, because of his key position in production, has privileged income (giving him more leisure and cultural opportunities), and his experience of responsibility, becomes a natural leader of the proletariat, instead of their most treacherous enemy, as he is when he is allied with the bourgeoisie.

It is for this reason that the last three years in England have been marked by the development of a revolutionary outlook among those very craft and bourgeois types – the 'labour aristocracy' – who formerly displayed all the reactionary qualities that made a craft union notorious in this country and made many of their spokesmen in Germany actual supporters of the Fascist régime. Anyone familiar with trade union affairs is aware that just as the craft unions and those industrial unions with a strong craft composition formerly opposed the general labourers' unions as being too militant and 'socialist', it is now the craft and semi-professional unions like the E.E.U., E.T.U., A.S.L.E. & F., N.A.U.S.W. & C. and N.U.C.[11] who at the Trades Union Congress and through their branches and Metropolitan Councils or District Committees press for militant action and are reproached by the general unions for being too extreme and communist. In the same way those craftsmen whose ideal theoretical content has given them a special position among the bourgeoisie itself – doctors, scientists, architects and teachers – are now moving Left and entering the Communist Party in considerable numbers, passing straight from Liberalism without an intermediate sojourn in the Labour Party.

The same final movement of the bourgeois illusion is reflected in the growth of the People's Front, where all the liberal elements, representing the craft content of modern society, put themselves under the leadership of the proletariat in a formal alliance limiting the scope of that leadership.

In English poetry this is reflected in the fact that English poets, without ever moving completely into *surréaliste* anarchy, change from a position near *surréalisme* into its opposite – a communist revolutionary position, such as that adopted by Auden, Lewis, Spender and Lehmann. How far this is genuinely communist and what level of art it represents, is a consideration which will be deferred . . . , for with this movement the bourgeois contradiction passes into its synthesis. It now starts to revolutionise, not merely its productive forces but its own categories, which now impossibly restrict those productive forces which its tension has generated. This movement is farther advanced in France, with Gide, Rolland, Malraux and Aragon wearing the uniform at which all once sneered.[12] Here it has only begun.

Notes

1. *New Verse* 25 (May 1937): 20–2. Cf. H. A. Mason's very different review, 'The Illusion of Cogency', *Scrutiny* 6.4 (March 1938): 429.
2. Then again, Louis MacNeice argued that Marx and Freud were 'the figure-heads of transition' for the age at large (see Sullivan, p. 71).
3. See Hynes's introduction to Caudwell, *Romance and Realism* (Princeton: Princeton University Press, 1970), p. 13.
4. The Transport and General Workers Union; the National Union of General and Municipal Workers.
5. The Amalgamated Society of Engineers.
6. Cf. Leavis (see above, pp. 20–1).
7. Cf. Empson (see below, p. 163).
8. Cf. Leavis (see above, p. 21) and Day Lewis (see below, p. 284).
9. Cf. Cornford (see above, p. 112).

10. 'There can be no progress – real, which is to say moral (progress) – except in the individual and by the actual individual.' Baudelaire discusses progress – which he calls 'that grand heresy of decrepitude' (*cette grande hérésie de la décrepitude*) at several points in his essays. See 'Notes nouvelles sur Edgar Poe', in *Oeuvres Completes*, ed. Claude Pichois (Paris: Gallimard, 1976), vol. 2, pp. 324–5, and 'Exposition Universelle-1855: Beaux-Arts,' *ibid.*, pp. 580–1. Thanks to Tom Orange and Colin Hutchens for their work on this material.

11. For example, the Electrical Trades Union, the Associated Society of Locomotive Engineers and Firemen, and the National Amalgamated Union of Shop Assistants, Warehousemen and Clerks (presumably, though Caudwell omits an 'A').

12. Louis Aragon joined the French Communist Party in 1927. A prominent member of the surrealist movement, he broke with the surrealists in 1931 – ironically the year in which their journal *La Révolution surréaliste* changed its name to *Le Surréalisme au service de la révolution,* in recognition of their new Marxist goals. By 1935, Aragon was one of the secretaries of the French section of the newly founded International Association of Writers for the Defence of Culture. One of the others was André Malraux, who had travelled the previous year to Berlin with Gide to work for the release of Dimitrov. Gide opened the Congress attended by Aragon in 1935, and like Romain Rolland, travelled to Russia in the mid-1930s.

17 Alick West *from Crisis and Criticism (1937)**

Valentine Cunningham remarks cuttingly (p. 214) that 'West's sharpest critical point' in *Crisis and Criticism* was his realization that the politically amorous bourgeois individual's 'desire to abandon individualism for a consciously social life', to 'feel, think and say "we", instead of "I",' runs aground on his or her confusion over who 'we' are: 'Bourgeoisie or workers?' Notwithstanding Frank Kermode's proper acknowledgement of *Crisis and Criticism* as one of 'the three major books of early English Marxist criticism' (p. 38), few readers today would not find both its premises and arguments on the whole somewhat cloudy. As they introduce West's work in their *Marxist Literary Theory* (1996), for example, Terry Eagleton and Drew Milne in fact minimize its 'theoretical contribution'; 'what remains of value in British Communist Party Literary Criticism is its materialist orientation and specific critical readings' (p. 103). It is important to grasp, however, that the cloudiness typical of West's entire critical enterprise was not a mere stylistic idiosyncrasy, but the inevitable outcome of what he was trying to do in intellectual terms – namely, to 'use Marx's work', as he puts it towards the end of the present extract, 'to give material meaning to the ideas of Shelley and Coleridge'. Whatever else good might come of it, pellucidity is perhaps not what could be expected of a project that seeks to reconcile the Kantian idealism of Coleridge with the Hegelianism of Marx.[1] An important factor in West's persistent desire to lay Marxist materialism upon an idealist foundation was the profound Christian faith in which he was raised. This, though disavowed by him as a matter of dogma before 1934 and his entry into the Communist Party of Great Britain, continued to shape his thinking throughout his life, as Elisabeth West has argued.[2] His work therefore invites comparison with that of Eric Gill, Frank Sheed and Christopher Dawson – although West's religious allegiances, when he still felt them or when he showed their influence, were to the nonconformist rather than the Catholic tradition.

At one time a teacher of Christopher Caudwell, West knew little more than his pupil about European Marxism. In fact, Arnold Kettle argues that the two men shared with others of their contemporaries – Fox, Day Lewis, Jack Lindsay and George Thompson, for example – 'a certain suspicion of the kind of "ideological" criticism found in the work of continental Marxists trained in the Hegelian tradition'. Instead they developed 'a strong consciousness of the progressive aspects of the English literary heritage, especially in the work of Shakespeare, Milton, Bunyan, the Romantic poets and the 19th-century novelists'.[3]

* Reprinted from Alick West, *Crisis and Criticism and Selected Literary Essays* (London: Lawrence and Wishart, 1975), pp. 75–80, 85–93 and 98–9.

In his autobiography, *One Man in His Time* (1969), West unequivocally placed socialism as theory and practice *below* 'Culture', which term he used in a manner synonymous with 'Art'. Rejecting once again the slogan, 'Culture is a weapon in the fight for socialism', he went on:

> I said that culture, as Caudwell had written of poetry in *Illusion and Reality*, heightens our consciousness of the world we want to win and our energy to win it. In this sense it was true that culture is a weapon in the fight for socialism. But the truth depended on recognition of the greater truth that socialism is a weapon in the fight for culture. For our final aim was not the establishment of a political and economic structure, but the heightening of human life. Without this recognition, the slogan became a perversion of the truth, since it degraded culture into a means to a political end.[4]

If this understanding of culture and its relation to politics seems very different from (because very much more conservative than) the attitudes expressed in the Writers' International *Statement of Aim* (see above, pp. 54–5), or the *Manifesto* of the Second International Congress of Writers (see above, pp. 107–8), it is at the same time far from the 'minority' views of F. R. and Q. D. Leavis. Indeed, disagreement with F. R. Leavis would provide the starting-point for West's later 'studies in conflict and unity', *The Mountain in the Sunlight* (1958).

The following extract from *Crisis and Criticism* is of particular interest because it amply demonstrates West's singular contribution to Marxist literary and cultural speculation in the 1930s – his attempt to rescue 'aesthetic feelings' from 'the bourgeois conception of aesthetic value'.

Language and Rhythm

That literature is a part of the movement of society, applies to all literature, good, bad and indifferent. But it does not follow from this that Marxist criticism only aims at discovering the economic and social forces at work in any piece of literature, while it ignores its aesthetic value. It aims at judging its aesthetic value in terms of its relation to the movement of society. The belief that Marxist criticism ignores aesthetic values, comes from the assumption that the idealistic conception of aesthetic value is the only true one. The belief sometimes expressed, whether in theory or practice, that Marxist criticism ought to ignore aesthetic value also comes from the same assumption – aesthetic value is bourgeois idealism, and therefore ought to be ignored.

The bourgeois conception of aesthetic value is idealistic, and therefore ought to be attacked. But aesthetic value is not an invention of the bourgeoisie; and even if it was, that would not necessarily be a reason for rejecting it. The attempt to suppress aesthetic experience seems due to the fact that those feelings of social solidarity which are awakened in aesthetic experience are still attached to bourgeois society, and a vague realisation of their incompatibility with consciously accepted Marxism leads to the demand for the suppression of aesthetics, in oneself and in everybody else, as the easiest solution of the conflict. This impoverishes Marxist criticism; and as the aesthetic feelings cannot be continually and completely suppressed, their separation from the consciously accepted Marxism only delivers them over to the bourgeois conception of aesthetic value.

Before dealing with the relation of the aesthetic value of literature to its social origin, it is helpful to consider why it is valuable to us that we have a language at all, and how its value is related to its social origin.[5]

Two main ideas in the researches into the origin and function of language bring this out well.

The first is the abandonment of the conception of language as being originally a means for the expression of thought, and as having developed out of intellectual processes. Instead language is now realised as inseparably connected with action, both in its purpose and its origin.

Ludwig Noiré, in his book on the origin of language,[6] says: 'Language is a product of an active, not of a passive process.' Noiré also shows that this active process is work, the common work of a particular society: 'Common activity directed to a common aim, the primeval work of our common ancestors were the sources from which language and rational life sprang.' The author also maintains that this relation of language to common activity is not only one of origin, but in the very fibre of the language itself. 'Originally,' he says, 'language describes the things of the objective world not as being forms, but as having been formed; not as active beings that exercise an effect, but as passive beings on whom an effect is exercised . . . The earliest meanings of verbal roots referred to human activity.' Objects are only isolated and only named in relation to common social activity, and the word denoting the object denotes the social activity exercised on it.

In addition to this insistence on the connection of language and common work, the theory has also been put forward that language is itself the specialisation of a particular element in the act of work – the pantomimic gestures of the tongue, as we see them, for example, in a child rolling its tongue to help its pen. This theory has been worked out by Sir R. Paget.[7] He maintains that such pantomimic gesture, accompanying activity, when vocalised and recognised by the hearer through his unconsciously reproducing the gestures, is the material of language.

This removal of language from the abstract sphere of thought and its expression to that of practical activity is the first characteristic of recent research. The second is the stress on the importance of language, not as a means of communication in response to the individual's need to put himself in touch with the consciousness of another individual, but for the organisation of society as a whole. In a book which approaches the question of language through the study of the function of animal cries, G. A. de Laguna[8] writes: 'It is to the great superiority of speech over animal cries as a means of *social control* that we must look for the chief cause of its evolutionary origin and development. The primary function of speech is the co-ordination of the behaviour of individual members of the social group . . . Its fundamental and primary value, the value that has led to its conservation and evolution, lies in its social function of associating individuals in a new and vastly more effective type of group organisation.'

The function of language in relation to the organisation of the group, and not only in relation to the activity of the group with the organisation taken for granted, is also recognised by Noiré. He writes: 'The phoneme is originally the expression, accompanying common activity, of heightened social feeling.'

The most graphic portrayal of language in this social function is given by the Russian philologist, N. Marr. He points out that in primitive languages there is no word for 'speak'. The word for 'speaking' in Grusinian literally means 'being Scythian ("Scythianising" is more accurate, as the suggestion of a distinction between "being" and "Scythian" is misleading) – Scythianising with the lips (or the face)'. That is, speaking is social existence in a particular mode.

In fact, language, according to Marr, is social existence become articulate. Its great achievement was that a vocal complex characteristic of a tribe because of their physiological type gained the sense of the name of the group totem, and then the name of the group. Thus it became possible for the members of the tribe to express together in sound the most mysterious of the pictures in their mind, their sense of their own social existence.

But Marr does not regard this social function of language as operating only in the isolated sphere of speaking. He also links it up directly with work. For it was in the process of work that this power to express the social existence of the group was most valuable. The repetition of the word roused all the latent reserves of social energy and fired to greater effort. In the apparently meaningless 'abstract' refrains of many primitive tribes is the real powerful meaning of the name unconsciously symbolising for them their own social existence. The reader is, however, warned against assuming that because language does in this literal sense express common social existence, it is therefore the expression of a society completely united in this common social existence. Common social existence is not social harmony. On the contrary, Marr points out that the differentiation of class within society also affects language from its very earliest stages, and that its exclusive use by a privileged class is one of the reasons of its supposed magical power.

Another sign of the weakening of the intellectualist view of language is the importance now accorded in its development to the hand. Marr states that human speech did not develop directly out of the technique of the production of sounds. The specialisation of sound production as speech required preliminary preparation, which was accomplished by the hand as the natural tool for pointing to things before they could be named. Evidence in language itself of the importance of the hand is the fact that in Japanese languages many dozens of words are formed from the root of the word for 'hand'. Noiré also holds that the hand, the tool of tools by which objects in the natural world were made distinct objects of human action, thereby made speech possible. Paget also quotes medical authority for the fact that the speech-centres of the brain develop out of the hand-gesture centres.

Beyond this concept-forming work of the hand, as one may call it, there opens yet another long history of the practical activity by which man developed the use of the hand to point with and to grasp.

Moving forward also in the growth of language, the specialisation of sound as the vehicle of speech is again the result of work. The use of tools on the one side refined the powers of distinguishing and grasping and thus enriched the basis of speech; on the other side, the hand was now so occupied that it was no longer available for speech purposes. 'It was the *continued* use of man's hands,' writes Paget, 'for craftsmanship, the chase, and the beginnings of art and agriculture, that drove him to find other methods of expressing his ideas – namely, by a specialised pantomime of the tongue and lips.'

I do not wish to give the impression of unanimous certainty on these questions, especially as I am not a competent judge of them. Marr, for example, is strongly opposed to such a standpoint as that of de Laguna's, that a study of animal cries gives a good ground for tackling the problem of human speech; he believes that human speech is radically different from animal cries. Others believe that Noiré overstresses the importance of work; and that both his and Marr's inferences from roots are arbitrary and unreliable. But I think that there would be general concurrence in the rejection of the intellectualist view and in the acceptance of the standpoint that language, instead of being a mere reflection of thought serving for communication by an individual consciousness, is an instrument of concerted social action.

Returning to the question why language in itself is valuable for us, we can say that it is valuable as a means whereby a social group stimulates and organises the energy of the group as a whole and the individuals as members of it, and facilitates the exercise of that energy by defining the objects of the natural world in terms of the group's activities in relation to them. It organises the group, and its particular activity, through its form and content. The form of speech, through which a statement made in one language differs from a statement of the same meaning made in another language, appeals to the individuals' common membership of the society, through whose past activity their speech has received its present form. The form has the value, through past activity, of stimulating those to whom it is addressed, because it is a call from a social group within which, as they know from past experience, a successful activity is possible. Through its content it directs and organises the stimulated energy in the particular activity of the moment, and thereby stimulates it further.

Attention may also be drawn to the similarity of function in the first rhythmical stylisation of language. In his book, *Arbeit und Rhythmus* [1909], Karl Bücher, starting from the fact that originally music and poetry always accompanied one another, finds the origin of their common characteristic of rhythm in their connection with work. Rhythm, and poetry and music together with it, developed out of the regularly repeated movements of the body in work (which, with this accompaniment of poetry and music, was very different from work under capitalism). Its function, according to Bücher, was twofold: to economise the energy expended by the individual body by making the movement and the pauses between them regular, and by co-ordinating the action of one individual with others. (The objection made to Bücher's theory that he concentrates too exclusively on work, and neglects sex, war, play and religion, does not invalidate his main position; it only extends the range of bodily activity which is rhythmically organised. And I think Bücher was quite right to put the stress on work, for the other activities either derive from work, or without work would never lead to rhythmical speech.)

In addition, rhythm has the same function as that of the repetition of the name of the tribe mentioned by Marr: by co-ordinating the movement of the individual with that of the rest of the group, by fixing a movement in which all can take part as one, rhythm not only saves energy, but also, like the word, calls up the latent reserves of social energy. It is essentially the same process as takes place even under capitalist production, when, as Marx says, co-operation awakens the forces of the species within the individual. Books of travel give graphic accounts of how natives, lying on the ground with minds and bodies wearied, would waken up at the sound of one of their favourite songs, begin to sing and dance, and then set to work again, 'as if the dance of Machielo', to quote one of these travellers, 'had communicated to them new courage and new vigour'.

Thus the rhythmical stylisation of language continues the functions of language itself. It is a means whereby a social group stimulates and organises the energy of the group as a whole and the individual members of it, and directs it to a particular activity. Here also there is a similar relation between form and content: the rhythmical form depends for its effect on the group's previous activity, without which rhythmical speech could not exist and could not stimulate, and appeals to the bodily memory of the previous activity; the content relates to the particular activity now to be undertaken.

Form

... [T]he value of literature always consists in its organising social energy in a particular activity.

We must now consider again the activity of the social organism, of whose movement literature is a part.

The basic activities of that organism are production and consumption. No absolute division can be made between them, since production consumes labour power and consumption produces it. There is, however, a general difference, which we must note. It requires more energy to produce food than to eat it, and as, further, every individual spends the first part of his life consuming without producing anything except himself, there is a greater readiness in him to consume what is there than to go and produce what is not needed at the moment. There is a corresponding difference in the general attitude associated with production and consumption. That associated with production is more valuable, because it participates more readily in the higher organisation required for production than for consumption.

It must also be noted that in production the particular activity to be undertaken is necessarily seen in terms of the group which is to perform it, of the wishes centring round it, and of the aim to be attained; while at the same time, if that aim is to be attained, the material objects on which the activity is exercised must be seen as they really are. To illustrate my meaning from primitive times, vegetation rites expressed the wishes about the grain, and noted its growth as if it were human; but the seed was planted in earth, not in rocks. Or to take an example from science: some scientist – unfortunately I forget where I read the incident – was half day-dreaming on top of a 'bus and saw in his mind's eye a group of girls advancing with linked hands, as in a children's game; observing more closely how their hands were linked, he suddenly realised that it solved a problem of molecular arrangement which he had long been struggling with. He saw his aim in human terms, but as it was in itself.

Through the work of production the world in itself is made into a world for us; and through this work we see the world as it is in itself and in terms of our aim of making it a world for us, a human world.

The basis of the value of literature is the relation of the writer to this productive activity.

Many people, being more ready to consume what others produce than to produce themselves, assume the existence both of society and the human world. They consume without thought the energy required to produce what they consume; the things are simply there. They assume that the world exists as it is, and are oblivious of the energy that has changed it into a world for us. The world – natural and social – simply exists, as you can see for yourself; there is nothing in that to make a song about.

The fact that they take for granted all the creative activity of society, and placidly believe that they are responsible for their own existence, colours, rather than dulls, their speech, and if they write, their style. They write on the same level as when they ask for a ticket on the Underground. 'Four, please,' utilises a previously established organisation, and the only contribution which the form of expression makes to the maintenance of the organisation is the possible effect of the 'please' on the man who gives them their ticket. When they write, they similarly assume the existence of the achieved organisation, that everything is simply there, that their own power to see it has been born with them or is just a part of their intelligence; and again their contribution to the continued existence of all they write about and write with, is not much more than 'please' – and an occasional 'thank you'. They live on what society has already produced. Because they merely consume, there is no bodily excitement of activity, which is the vigour of idiomatic style, in their so-called works.

The good writer does not take for granted. In some way, of which at present we know very little, he actively feels the productive energy of society and identifies himself with it. He realises, not necessarily consciously, but perhaps through the alternations of energy and fatigue, that neither the world nor our living in it are mere plain facts. They are the facts to make songs about. So far from the world being established and firm, we and it are founded, not on the void, but on human energy, by which we have produced ourselves and made the world in itself a world for us. If that energy stops, we and the human world also stop. The writer feels the living truth of the words that society is the wonder of our existence. Not only society, but everything that social energy has made real for us, is a wonder, the wonder of continual creation.

With this sense in his body of the productive energy that alone continues the existence of us and our world, the writer's language is quickened. His whole writing expresses that participation in social energy through which he feels the life of the world. Instead of language being merely a complicated and delicate machine for making use of everybody else's previous achievements, the writer uses it in such a way as to continue and develop its basic functions. Language was not invented in order that one individual might get what he wanted from others; it grew, as a form of social organisation. Literature as art continues that growth. It lives language; it carries on the social activity of which language in its very existence is the creation and creator.

Literature does in the large what idiom does in the small. Idiom is a kind of expression in which the content is vivid because the form conveys the feeling of the bodily movement in social activity related to it.[9] In literature, a much more general and complex content is vivid because the form conveys a bodily feeling of the social energy necessary to make that content real for us.

The ways in which it does this are so subtle, intricate and various that the attempt to give a general statement in a few pages must inevitably be dryly schematic; but the idea will hardly be intelligible without the attempt being made.

Literature conveys this feeling of social energy by expressing the conflicting phases in its organisation, and giving a symbolical form of achieved organisation.

In the first place, literature relates its content to the conflicts inherent in the organisation of any group. As the high proportion of abuse and exhortation in idiom indicates, one of the main tasks is to hold an organisation together and to continue its action. This does not happen without the expenditure of energy; and there is a tendency in every individual, developed in him by his early experiences as a consumer, to withold that energy and let other people do the work. As idiomatic expression alternates between abuse and encouragement, so literature works with a similar alternation in the allied moods. The content is shown in relation to succeeding or mingled feelings of activity or inertia, hope or fear, courage or despondency.

Literature also uses the alternating feelings of the individual towards society which accompany these moods. Just as it is the function of idiom to convey to the individual either that he is outside the pale and sunk to the level of animals, or – though far less rarely – that he is an honoured part of it, so literature expresses its content through alternating moods of feeling oneself a part of society, or being in rebellion against it or outcast from it. This latter distinction corresponds to two different causes why the general opinion of a society may expel an individual member – either because he only consumes and is below the general standard of social activity, or because he is above it, and produces in a new way. (The conflicts of class relations will be touched on later; the statements here correspond to the general conditions of production, not to the particular movement.)

One of the ways, then, in which literature makes its content living, is that it relates to these fundamental experiences in social organisation. But, as already said, the variations in method are numberless.

Literature also relates its content to the character of human work, which has to see the world as it is in itself, in order to be able to change it into a world for us. Just as idiom expresses a situation in terms of the body or of bodily movement, so literature, and especially poetry, through comparisons and images describes human and non-human in terms of one another, and thereby makes the non-human into an expression of the human. But at the same time, through accurately describing what is used for an image as it is in itself, it shows the non-human in its true character. Literature shows both the natural and social world in terms of the actual and desired relation to them and their objective reality. In the case of the social world, the process is especially complex; in a novel for example, the characters are made to behave in such a way that the general action shall symbolise the actual and desired relation to the social world, but they must also act according to objective standards of psychological truth.

In either case, the presentation of the world as our world and as itself awakens the feeling of social energy because it is a repetition of our own activity in making the world human through work.

Literature does not only show its content in terms of the conflicts inherent in organising a group and its particular activity. It also conveys the sense of power to achieve organisation and to use its energy. The very fact that a new content is integrated into the forms of language and literary expression created in the past, has an effect, because it suggests that the instruments of language and expression through which we have got thus far, will also enable us to meet this situation. But that is common in some degree both to literature and other printed matter. The effect of form in literature is partly due to the fact that it is contradictions and conflicts that it unites; the form is felt as form by contrast with what would break it. It is also partly due to the fact that words in literature have echoes of their other senses than the plain one of the obvious context. They have more of their social body, as it were; and this, together with the rich suggestion arising out of their greater significance, conveys a bodily feeling of the social weft of our lives. Finally, the coherence of the mutually modifying parts into one whole appeals to our experience of social existence, and gives the sensation of a more harmonised organism than the social organism actually is.

The earlier statement, that literature lives language, thus means that as language organises a group and its particular activity, so literature expresses its content in terms of the conflicts inherent in this organisation and of their reconciliation in the completed work.

The interpretation of literature in terms of our actual social experience only takes account of the general conditions of that experience. It neglects the movement described by Marx . . . from one form of social organisation to the next, and this movement is the essential character of the changing social organism. Nevertheless, it may be well to illustrate by an example what has been said up to the present. I take a well-known sonnet by Shakespeare:

> That time of year thou mayst in me behold
> When yellow leaves, or none, or few do hang
> Upon those boughs which shake against the cold,
> Bare ruin'd choirs, where late the sweet birds sang.
> In me thou seest the twilight of such day
> As after sunset fadeth in the west;
> Which by and by black night doth take away,
> Death's second self, that seals up all in rest.
> In me thou seest the glowing of such fire,
> That on the ashes of his youth doth lie,
> As the death-bed whereon it must expire,
> Consum'd with that which it was nourish'd by.
> This thou perceiv'st, which makes thy love more strong,
> To love that well which thou must leave ere long.

Since we have not yet considered the movement of society, the significance of the sonnet content cannot be discussed. What will be attempted is – not an interpretation of the sonnet – but to show how the above analysis helps us to appreciate how this particular form makes the realisation of the sonnet a moving experience.

Applying the general idea that literature makes its particular content living for us by conveying a bodily feeling of the social energy without which that content could either not exist at all, or could not be spoken about, we note in the first place, that the sense of transience throughout the sonnet is indirectly a stimulation of the energy that strives against the universal wasting by time. It awakens the fundamental experience that continual energy is required in the endless war against the forces of disintegration. Every form of life that our social organisation has created, falls into nothing unless it is continually renewed. That sense is strong here, because the poem shows not only nature in itself – autumn, twilight, and the fire – moving towards its annihilation; nature's decay is also that of man. It is this ceasing to exist of nature and man that indirectly, by contrast, arouses the energy which shall maintain the world.

This general feeling is conveyed in a manner similar to that noted by Mr Pearsall Smith in his remarks on the kinaesthetic perception through phrasal verbs.[10] In the first four lines, the few yellow leaves, so clearly seen and so near falling after the preceding 'none', evoke a physical sensation of the stillness of an autumn day, when the yellow leaves, that a breath would remove, are hanging on the boughs; and there is a muscular feeling of how a single touch would make them fall. Then there is an alternation in the manner of conveying transience through bodily perception similar to the fundamental contrast between organisation and disintegration, activity and passivity. In the first four lines, we wait, as it were, on transience; it is in the surrounding air, while the leaves hang motionless. In the next four lines, the mere passive expectancy has become active motion, the fading away of the light in the west; and the indefinable mental sensation as the attention goes from the leaves quite near to the distant horizon makes us take part in the movement to nothingness; and the impending act of 'black night', with its contrast to the yellow leaves, intensifies the effect of this change from waiting to movement. Then, with a similar effect in our sensation, the transience which had been far away in the sky, is concentrated in the glowing of the fire, which, in that it lies waiting on its death-bed but still glowing, unites the contrary impressions of passivity and activity in the preceding lines. Because of this form of expression, transience is not a mere idea, but a material, bodily feeling of those experiences that make it a significant reality for us.

Another tone in this is the alternation of feeling in the individual towards society according as he participates or not in its activity – the alternation between feeling himself a part of society and being isolated from it, which the precariousness of our individual and social existence makes a continual fear. The effect of this sonnet is not only due to its evoking the energy that fights against disintegration of organised life, but also the energy of the desire to remain a part of that life, not to follow the light into nothingness, not to be removed from living society.

At the same time, this alternation between energy and decay, between being a part of society and thrown into outer darkness, also expresses the alternation between the world as it is and the world as we make it, the world as the object of that organised energy which the first alternation awakens. The autumn, the twilight, the fire are made human in meaning; and yet the more human they are made, the more vivid is the sense of their own reality. The 'bare ruin'd choirs' are human; yet just for that very reason the phrase only intensifies the physical apprehension of the actual boughs 'which shake against the cold'. In the last image, the personification ('his youth') is most direct; yet the objective realisation of the glowing among the ashes is most actual. The world is human, and itself, with equal reality. That is the double character of the world as the object of human work. The manner in which the sonnet expresses its content, epitomises our social existence.

The last two lines resume the conflicts between energy and disintegration, activity and passivity, membership of and isolation from society; and between the world in itself and the human world.

> This thou perceiv'st, which makes thy love more strong,
> To love that well which thou must leave ere long.

The realisation of transience is a stimulus to love actively, instead of merely accepting; to be one with all the energy of life, before leaving it. And, taking up and reversing the line, 'Consum'd with that which it was nourish'd by', these last two lines transform the transience, which has been shown as a power that man cannot resist, into the source of human energy, which is now nourished by what consumes it.

Further, the ability to impose significant order on these conflicts stimulates still further the social energy which the expression of them has aroused, by making it feel its creative power.

We feel the content of the poem with sadness and delight, because its form awakens the life of our fundamental experience, our existence as members of a society organising itself to make a human world. For the moment we perceive as active social beings, not accepting life as given, but knowing that its continuance depends on us. For the poem does not merely take and use the existing words. 'This thou perceiv'st' is itself perception. By its expression through the fundamental conflicts inherent in it, the poem continues that social organisation which has made us able to perceive autumn and twilight, and able to love. The form conveys the content in such a way that we have a bodily feeling of the social life which alone has made the content real for us.

Before proceeding to the relation of literary value not merely to the general conditions of production and consumption, but to the social relations in which they are carried out, and to their change, I would like to remark on the relation of this standpoint to the kind of idea put forward by Hegel, that 'the object of art should be contemplated in itself, in its independent objectivity, which, though existing for the subject, does so only in a theoretical, intellectual way, not practically, and without any reference whatever to desire or will' (quoted in *Problems of Soviet Literature*, p. 197).

Though I agree with Bukharin that this is wrong,[11] I do not believe that it is utter nonsense, as he says. To take an example from the Underground again: if, instead of merely waiting for the train to come, as trains always do come, we look down the tunnel, feel the wind begin to blow out of it, then see the gleam from the approaching train, the sense of excitement may make us momentarily forget whether we are waiting for a Highgate or a Golder's Green train. In that sense, we are disinterested. The train is not a given object, by which we travel to Highgate, which we consume. We look at it without reference to our desire to get to a particular station. But it is untrue to say that it exists for us only in an intellectual way, without any reference whatever to desire or will. We see it with a sense of exhilaration that there should be any trains at all, with a feeling of the social energy that has created them. We do not want only to use trains, but to take part, in our field, in the activity that produces them. The element of truth in Hegel's idea is that in an aesthetic experience we do not desire as mere consumers; but we do desire as producers, and this desire, though not necessarily the only one, is dominant.

It will also be clearer now that the critical theories examined in previous chapters [of *Crisis and Criticism*] err, because, without a clear realisation of doing so, they consider the value of language only as a means of stimulating energy through the appeal to previous social experience within a particular society, and ignore its function and value as a means of organising that energy in the new activity of the moment. The position both of Mr Eliot and Dr Richards means that the function of poetry and literature is to stimulate the energy attached to the previous forms of social activity, and to divert attention from the question of what form of social activity is to be organised now. It is fundamentally conservative: its intention is that the emotion deriving from past social experience in a group supposedly as homogeneous as the character of a language appears to be, shall make the practical issues before society now seem a blasphemous question asked by the intellect that conceitedly claims to run man.

Similarly, surrealism, concentrating only on the fact that human work sees the world in terms of its desire to change it into a human world, and ignoring the work by which alone this change on the world as it is can be accomplished, arrives at the position that the mere act of seeing the world with the desire to change it will change it. It makes a mystical fusion between the function of a statement as a statement by somebody in a particular language, as an appeal to previous social experience, and the objective world which the statement is about. In its bearing on literary theory, surrealism also concentrates only on language as created by and appealing to previous social activity, and ignores its function and value in organising new activity.

Form and Content

. . . In [the] . . . unity of content and form, content is of prior importance, in that the writer's response to the tensions of social movement, which leads him to select a particular content, determines the energy of his vision. If his response is that he aligns himself with those forces which are most active in his time, he can feel and see life in the making; and that is the necessary condition for artistic form. If he puts himself on the side of the enemies, he either keeps the thought of their creative energy out of his mind or condemns it in the name of abstract principles, whose existence he assumes; in either case his vision and expression are deadened. It is these particular social decisions, expressed in the content, that determine the general social attitude resulting in richness or poverty of form; the general social attitude comes from previous particular decisions and actions, not the other way round. This, of course, does not mean that the particular decision represented by the content of Shakespeare's sonnet determines its sonnet form; but it modifies the previously existing sonnet form. And the form which Shakespeare finds ready to his hand is itself the result of an endless number of new contents slightly modifying the form in which previous contents had been embodied. In this sense, content, the particular action, determines form, the result of previous action.

Because literature, as content and form, expresses and is social change, it hastens it. Literature is therefore propaganda. But not all propaganda is literature. As already indicated, the propaganda which is not literature states only the objective and appeals only to energy as concentrated on that objective. The propaganda which is literature states the social forces against which action is to be directed as a necessary condition of the action; it states the action as their end and as their continuation. It awakens the energy attached to them, as well as that which has been liberated from them. It has the practical character of other propaganda, but more full and profound.

Though literature is propaganda, its value, as Marx and Engels insist, does not depend on its manifest programme. A work may talk revolution; but if it does not show revolution through society's creative movement, it is not fulfilling its function as literature; and the consequent abstractness of presentation in what claims to be a poem or novel, may repel from the aim it sets forth. Or a work may talk reaction; but if it conveys the sense of the social movement it condemns, the manifestly reactionary work is more valuable than the manifestly revolutionary.

Summarising the results of this analysis, the value of literature is socially determined, in the sense that form and content enable us to see with the energy of our basic experiences in the continuance of ourselves and our world through social activity. They direct the energy which is thus aroused to the change in the social organism in which the writer . . . participates.

The source of value in the work of literature is the social energy and activity which makes the writer's vision a continuation of the development of the power to see, his use of language a continuation of the development of the power to speak; and not merely the consumer's use of what society has already produced.

Our perception of that value is the stimulation in us of the same social energy and activity. The energy attached to our basic social experiences is available for the perception – which is an act, not a passive event – of the particular content. It comes alive for us, because for the moment we see, like the writer, with our full social being. The resulting sense of beauty makes us feel the power to create a human world.

The basis of this interpretation of the value of literature is, as already said, Marx's development of romanticism. It attempts to use Marx's work to give material meaning to the ideas of Shelley and Coleridge that a poem and a society are organic in the same way, that relations in society constitute beauty in art.

The relation of literature as art, distinguishable from other literary matter, to the social and economic development that determines all literary production, good, bad, and indifferent, is through the fact the economic basis is not an automatic machine, but living men and women, whose energy has to be organised. Good literature contributes to that organisation and to the changing of it; bad literature consumes its products, and debases them.

Notes

1. I am indebted to Matthew Trebb, whose explanation of this tension in West helped bring me back to *Crisis and Criticism* with greater patience and understanding.
2. See West's introduction to *Crisis and Criticism* (the 1975 edition used here), p. 5.
3. Preface to *Crisis and Criticism*, p. 3.
4. Quoted by Elisabeth West in her introduction, p. 8.
5. In his essay on 'Writing' (see above, pp. 37–9), Auden resorts to a similar justification for the language arts in times of political difficulty. Language is imagined as coming into being simultaneously with – and as a constructive influence towards – society. An important difference is that, for West, the importance of language is not 'as a means of communication in response to the individual's need to put himself in touch with the consciousness of another individual [very much Auden's view], but for the organisation of society as a whole'.
6. According to Grace Andrus de Laguna, whom West goes on to cite, Noiré's theory is not 'to be regarded as a serious scientific hypothesis' (p. 4; see n. 8 below).
7. Sir Richard Paget published *The Nature of Human Speech* in 1925 (Tract no. 22 of the Society for Pure English [Oxford: Clarendon Press]). His *Human Speech* appeared in 1930.
8. Grace Andrus de Laguna, *Speech: Its Function and Development* (New Haven: Yale University Press and London: Humphrey Milford/Oxford University Press, 1927).
9. West's chapter on idiom occurs between the sections marked here 'Language and Rhythm' and 'Form'. 'All good literature has richness and vigour in its style,' he writes, 'and one source of this is to a certain extent traceable – the use of idiomatic expression' (p. 81). He stresses – following Logan Pearsall Smith in *Words and Idioms* (London: Constable and Co., 1925) – that many idioms cluster around the human body, and that in another large group 'the idiomatic quality lies in the description of a content through conveying the bodily activity and effort of performing it'. 'The generalisation can therefore be made that idioms describe their content by conveying the bodily movement or sensation of performing it; and that this bodily movement or sensation is connected with all the various activities of a society or with the social relations among its members' (p. 82).
10. Discussed by West in his chapter on idiom, where we are given the following quotation from Pearsall Smith: phrasal verbs 'are formed from simple verbs which express the acts, motions, and attitudes of the body and its members; and these, combining with prepositions like "up," "down," "over," "off," etc. (which also express ideas of motion), have acquired, in addition to their literal meanings, an enormous number of idiomatic significations, by means of which the relations of things to each other, and a great variety of the actions, feelings, and thoughts involved in human intercourse, are translated, not into visual images, but into what psychologists call "kinaesthetic" images, that is to say, sensations of the muscular efforts which accompany the attitudes and motions of the body' (Smith, pp. 250–1). See *Crisis and Criticism*, p. 82.
11. In *Problems of Soviet Literature* (Zhdanov *et al.*), Bukharin quotes the passage from Hegel and comments: 'All this is utter nonsense. Take the art of ancient Greece. The comedies of Aristophanes are political journalism, but at the same time admirable works of art. There you will find the struggle of parties, definite political tendencies, ridicule of political opponents, etc.' (p. 197).

18   Ralph Fox   *from The Novel and the People (1937)**

After Ralph Fox died fighting in Spain at Christmas 1936, Harry Pollitt – long-time secretary of the Communist Party of Great Britain – recalled him in this way: 'Fox, in his combination of qualities, his devotion to the Communist Party and his intellectual ardour, was able to foreshadow the alliance between mental and manual worker in the fight against Fascism and war, the destroyers of culture.'[1] For Pollitt, that devotion was notable – even surprising – particularly because Fox's origins were middle-class. But the man's comparatively slender years (he was 36 when he died) make his intellectual contribution to the 'alliance' even more remarkable: as early as 1922 he was publishing on 'Social Changes as Seen in Literature', and on relations between 'Literature and Life',[2] and in 1927 the CPGB published his *Defence of Communism, in Reply to H. J. Laski*; the 1930s then saw the appearance of his biography, *Lenin* (1933; described by Sidney Webb as 'the most acceptable introduction to Soviet Communism for British inquirers'),[3] and several important studies in Marxism – including two volumes of *The Class Struggle in Britain in the Epoch of Imperialism* (1933), 'The Relation of Literature to Dialectical Materialism' (1934),[4] and *Communism and a Changing Civilisation* (1935). In 1934 he played a part in establishing the British section of the Writers' International and, with Montagu Slater, Edgell Rickword and Tom Wintringham, founded the influential *Left Review*.

As is obvious, Fox was not working in quite the same isolation as Christopher Caudwell, whose major work he did not know. Jeremy Hawthorn points out that while *The Novel and the People* in practice draws no more on contemporary Marxist criticism than does *Illusion and Reality*, Fox was familiar with such works as *Problems of Soviet Literature* (1934)[5] and R. D. Charques's *Contemporary Literature and Social Revolution* (1933). Yet to neither of these does he refer directly in the book, reacting instead 'against spokesmen of the cultural élite such as David Garnett, and draw[ing] his inspiration from the politics of the age: [Georgi] Dimitrov in Leipzig, the Popular Front in France'.[6] Hawthorn also cites an early Fox essay, 'Think Before Writing' (1929),[7] as evidence of the writer's commitment to avoiding what T. A. Jackson described as the 'two besetting sins of British Marxist writers – the substitution of a Party jargon for living English; and its concomitant: the substitution of fossilized and frozen concepts for real thinking'.[8] The following extract provides ample confirmation of Fox's hostility to the 'fossilized and frozen': Marx and Engels, when cited, testify to those factors which 'unevenly' and 'often unclearly' – but inevitably – complicate the relationship

* Reprinted from *The Novel and the People* (1937; London: Lawrence and Wishart, 1979), pp. 19–34.

between economic base and ideological superstructure. For Fox the novel, writes Hawthorn, 'is as much the product of the genuine knowledge of the world gained through the "praxis" of developing the productive forces, as it is the record of blindnesses and misperceptions resulting from the need to conceal the exploitation of man by man'.[9] Fox's emphasis on 'praxis' and his insistence that Marxism 'accepts nothing as fixed and immutable' perhaps together account for the very open tone of his work – a tone quite different from that of Caudwell, for whom the principal appeal of Marxism lay in its 'integrative' potential, its status as a totalizing system.

This essay makes no pretension to deal with the whole vast field of the relation between art and life. It has a more limited aim, to examine the present position of the English novel, to try to understand the crisis of ideas which has destroyed the foundation on which the novel seemed once to rest so securely, and to see what is its future.

At this point I might perhaps say that I do believe that the novel has a future, even though it has only a very shaky present. It is the great folk art of our civilisation, the successor to the epic and the *chanson de geste* of our ancestors, and it will continue to live. Life, however, means change; possibly, in art at least, not always a change for the better, but change nevertheless. It is the changes which must take place in the novel if it is to retain its vitality that are to be the subject of this book.

New arts have been born in the course of the history of man, like the cinema, for instance, but so far no art has completely died out. Man clings to every extension of his consciousness, to everything which enables him to heighten his sensitivity to the real world in which he lives. The novel is also a new art. True, its roots go back very far, to Trimalchio's Banquet, to Daphnis and Chloe, perhaps even further, to Herodotus. But the novel as an art in its own right, with its own rules, with its universal acceptance and appreciation, is a creature of our own civilisation, a creature, above all, of the printing press.

It is only a part of literature, that is true, but so in a sense, is the drama, and none would deny the drama its dignity as an art in its own right. The novel is not merely fictional prose, it is the prose of man's life, the first art to attempt to take the whole man and give him expression. Mr. E. M. Forster has pointed out that the great feature which distinguishes the novel from the other arts is that it has the power to make the secret life visible. It gives, therefore, a different view of reality from that given by poetry, or the drama, or the cinema, or painting, or music.

All these can express aspects of reality beyond the reach of the novel. But none of them can quite so satisfactorily express the full life of the individual man, woman or child. The why and wherefore of this I shall deal with elsewhere in this essay. Here I must be contented to state the fact and ask the reader to accept it for the moment.

Is there really such a crisis in the art of the novel that people must write books about it, cry shrilly to attract attention as you do when you see someone taking a direction you know must lead them into danger? Yes, most people professionally concerned are by now agreed that the English novel is in a sad state, that it has, in fact, lost direction and purpose. The novel, which above all depends on the fact that it is widely read, is rapidly becoming unreadable.

Of course, this does not imply a stay-in strike on the shelves of the tuppenny libraries. More novels are read to-day than ever before, but it is the unreadable which is read. Since paradox is not a meal for a hungry man, I will try to explain the position as I see it.

First, there is a crisis of quality. Certainly there were never so many writers producing excellent popular novels, those which tickle our immediate fancy, that we read with pleasure when the wireless is turned off (or even when it is turned on), or in the train, or at the seaside, read them once and never again, unless by sheer accident, having quite forgotten, till half-way through, that we had read them before. These novels, except very incidentally, do not, however, concern us here, for they do not deal with reality.

Naturally, their authors try to picture a real world, but the amount of reality achieved, unless by some accident of individual circumstance having nothing to do with the author, something in the reader and not in the book, is not sufficient to produce that violent shock which brings us, our emotions taut, our mind alert, into the country of those who see, and having seen through their eyes, we never forget the experience.

To-day the novel-reviewer ploughs week after weary week through dismal acres of printed pages only to shrink from the second-rate emotions and adolescent relationships in cynical disgust. Mr. Cyril Connolly, franker than most reviewers, tells us he often finds it all but impossible to read the books he reviews, while his amusing articles are generally, fortunately for us, much more concerned with Mr. Connolly than with that melancholy raw material which provides Mr. Connolly with his inadequate daily bread.

Strangely enough, the spate of bad books is not due to the increase in the reading public.[10] It is made possible by the way in which the tastes of the ever-growing public are being served by the publishers. The reader no longer gets what he likes, he has to like what he gets from the publishing colossus.[11]

These immense and highly rationalised concerns, often possessing their own printing and binding works, and usually also that essential condition of modern business, a healthy overdraft on the bank, are compelled to seek books to keep them going. They must have more and more books, preferably novels, for the author of a novel need not be paid as much as the author of non-fiction, his book can be more cheaply produced and is sure of a ready market in the libraries if it can be guaranteed free of all originality.

The publishers must have more and more titles on their lists as part of their competitive war with one another, they must print more books in order to keep their print shops busy, or, where they do not own their own print shops, to satisfy the printer who undertakes their business. What they print is not of great concern. It will be printed in the same type, on the same paper, bound in the same cloth, given the same dust jacket and sold to the same libraries, whether it be rubbish or a hidden masterpiece. In either case the publisher in his 'blurb' will acclaim it as a masterpiece, and most reviewers, having long ago abandoned the hopeless task of discrimination, will wearily accept the publisher's valuation at a greater or less discount, according to the mood of the moment or their personal relation to the publisher concerned.

The author himself has become a mere cipher in this great game of making publishing pay. When his books sell he is made into an important person, which gives him some independence, but he is still only a part of the game, transferred to the publicity side of the business. The commercial side will now treat him with some deference, but deference, properly handled, can also be made to pay.

Much could be said about the publicity aspect, about the various book of the month clubs, about back-scratching, about the art of managing the Press, about the 'services' of broadcasting to literature, but there would be little point in it, so far as the objects of this essay are concerned.

What we are interested in, as author and reader, is the fact that publishing is now an integral part of big business. It would be foolish to blame the publishers, who have been forced into the position by what our parents used to call 'the facts of life'. It is only necessary to note that the effect on literature, and particularly on the novel, has been deplorable. Quality has vanished from the aims of the book business and quantity has taken its place.

There is, however, an even more important crisis, a crisis of outlook among the novelists themselves. Despite the terrible flood of bad novels and poor work, there are good novelists, honest workmen, producing to-day. It is only a very short time since D. H. Lawrence died. James Joyce and E. M. Forster are still alive. Rebecca West, Aldous Huxley and half a dozen others are still seriously and conscientiously writing novels, with what degree of success we are not here concerned.

The difficulties facing the serious writer to-day are profound ones. A writer more than any other artist expresses his country. His novels are translated and read throughout the world. The England of yesterday was judged abroad by Wells, Kipling, Galsworthy and Conrad. The England of to-day is judged by Huxley, chiefly, and after him by a few younger writers whose works are just winning recognition in translation.

The novelist, therefore, has a special responsibility both to the present and the past of his country. What he inherits from the past is important, because it shows what are the sections of his country's cultural heritage which have meaning to-day. What he says of the present is important, because he is assumed to be expressing what is most vital in the spirit of his time. It may be objected that the novelist is not concerned with other people's attitude to his work. What he inherits, what he expresses, is strictly his own affair.

Even if it is his affair alone, he cannot, however, cut himself off from the outside world's reactions to his work. In a world where nationalism has run mad in its most egoistic and destructive forms, the attitude of a serious and important writer towards nationalism is an important one. To their infinite credit it can be said that every serious English writer of to-day understands this and that the majority of them are very seriously concerned about the problems involved.

Shall the writer renounce his country for a religion? Mr. Evelyn Waugh has done this, only to find that it lands him in the receptive lap of another country's nationalism. Apparently to-day Roman Catholicism implies support for fascist Italy, the most aggressive and egoistically brutal, after Germany, of all modern States. Shall he accept the logical consequences of D. H. Lawrence's blood and race cult? Then he may end by supporting Nazi culture with its arguments of the mediaeval torture chamber and its 'spiritual' glorification of war.

Mr. Waugh has written the life of Edmund Campion, the Jesuit martyr, and been crowned with the Hawthornden prize, one of the two distinctions it is possible for an English author to win.[12] But would Shakespeare or Marlowe have considered Campion a martyr? Or would they not have inclined to the view that his activities, at a time when England was fighting for national existence, fighting for the conditions which created our national culture, were best characterised by Shakespeare's reference to:

> the fools of time,
> Which die for goodness, who have liv'd for crime.

Clearly, the writer of to-day has to distinguish very sharply between what is truly national and what is merely nationalistic or anti-national. The past matters as much as the present. We must carry it with us on our march and therefore we are concerned that the burden should not weigh us down too heavily, that we should be able to choose from the past what is real enough to be of help, and abandon, for the time, what can only be a hindrance.

The crisis of outlook is concerned with philosophy, and therefore with form. Since the War the philosophical outlook of most European writers has been deeply influenced by that last of European liberals, Sigmund Freud.[13] Psycho-analysis, as developed by Freud, is the apotheosis of the individual, the extreme of intellectual anarchy. It has certainly affected the English novel in the last twenty years more than any other body of ideas. It has also brought it to a state of almost complete intellectual bankruptcy, even though some strikingly original work also owes much of its force to the revelation of the individual made possible by Freudian analysis.

The last point which troubles the mind of a writer to-day is what I will call the social question. Can a novelist remain indifferent to the problems of the world in which he lives? Can he shut his ears to the clamour of preparing war, his eyes to the state of his country, can he keep his mouth closed when he sees horror around him and life being denied daily in the name of a State pledged to maintain the sanctity of private greed?

More and more novelists are beginning to feel that eyes, ears and voice are, in fact, organs of sense, responsive to the stimulus of the human world, and not mere passive servants of a spiritual world supposed traditionally to be the domain of 'art'. They understand that they live in a time in which nothing less than the fate of humanity is being decided, and they deeply resent the suggestion that man's fate is not the concern of those whose traditional pride has always been their humanism.

They are aware that there are two important views as to the future of civilisation. One view believes that civilisation will continue to develop on the basis of private property, war and insane egotism expressed in the dictatorial nationalist state. The other view believes that humanity is fighting for a new series of values based on social property, which shall banish war, destroy nationalism, and replace it by the free growth of healthy nations co-operating with one another in a world civilisation.

Most writers, to a greater or less degree, incline to the second view. Some of them, more clear-sighted than others, feel that such a new civilisation will come largely as a result of the struggle now being led by the working-class and that the beginnings of that new civilisation are already apparent in the

Soviet Union. This has made them interested in Marxism, the outlook on life of the revolutionary section of the working-class and of the great Union of [Soviet] Socialist Republics with its 170 million inhabitants.

The view has hitherto prevailed that though the working-class movement and the Russian Revolution might be good in themselves, Marxism, because it is a 'materialist' philosophy, is a philosophy hostile to artistic expression. This view is generally put in the form of suggesting that Marxism 'binds the artist in chains of dogma'.

Perhaps that is no longer stated with quite the same conviction. People know more about Marxism to-day. But it prevails in general, and even among those who sympathise with Marxists there are many who still believe that such formulas as 'socialist realism' or 'revolutionary novel' are not to be accepted seriously save as political slogans.

It is the aim of this essay to show that the future of the English novel and therefore the solution to the problems which vex the English novelist lies precisely in Marxism with its artistic formula of a 'socialist realism' which shall unite and re-vitalise the forces of the left in literature.

Marxism is a materialist philosophy. It believes in the primacy of matter and that the world exists outside of us and independently of us. But Marxism also sees all matter as changing, as having a history, and accepts nothing as fixed and immutable. In the seventeenth century few English writers would have quarrelled with a materialist view of life, though their view of materialism would not have been the same as that of Marx and Engels. To Shakespeare, drawing his philosophical views from Rabelais and Montaigne, there would have appeared nothing outrageous in the Marxian view of life. For the greater part of the eighteenth century a materialist view of life would have been accepted without question by many of the greatest British writers.

It is not so to-day. It has not been so for more than a century. To-day the literary journalist protests that materialism and imagination cannot go to bed together. The result, they suggest, would not be creation, but simply an unholy row. It is a curiously perverted view, for it would appear to be the most natural thing in the world for the imaginative writer, and particularly the novelist, to adopt a materialist view of life.

'Being determines consciousness' is the Marxist definition of the ultimate relation between matter and spirit. Whether or not this is the actual view of the artist it must, in fact, be the basis of his creative work. For all imaginative creation is a reflection of the real world in which the creator lives. It is the result of his contact with that world and his love or hate for what he finds in that world.

It is the lights and colours, the forms and shapes, the breath of the winds, the scents of life, the physical beauty or the physical ugliness of animal life, including the lives of human beings, the acts, the thoughts, the dreams of actual men and women, including the creator himself, that form the stuff of art.

Milton demanded three things of poetry: that it be 'simple, sensuous and passionate'. Art that is not sensuous, that is not concerned with perception of the real world, with sensible objects, is not art at all – not even the shadow of art. The essence of the creative process is the struggle between the creator and external reality, the urgent demand to master and re-create that reality. 'But does not Marxism claim that works of art are merely a reflection of economic needs and economic processes?' it will be objected.

No, this is not the view of Marxism, though it is the view of a number of materialists of the nineteenth century of the positivist school whose views have nothing in common with Marxian, dialectical, materialism. Marx has clearly stated his ideas on the relationship between the spiritual processes of life, of which artistic creation is one, and the material basis of life, in the famous Preface to his *Critique of Political Economy*. Here is the passage:

'The mode of production of the material means of existence conditions the whole process of social, political and intellectual life. It is not the consciousness of men that determines their existence, but, on the contrary, their social existence that determines their consciousness. At a certain stage of their development, the material forces of production in society come in conflict with the existing relations of production, or – what is but a legal expression for the same thing – with the property relations within which they had been at work before. From forms of development of the forces of production these relations turn into their fetters. Then opens an epoch of social revolution. With the change of the economic foundation the entire immense superstructure is more or less rapidly transformed. In considering such revolutions the distinction should always be between the material revolution in the economic conditions of production which can be determined with the precision of natural science, and the juridical, political, religious, aesthetic, or philosophic – in short, ideological forms – in which men become conscious of this conflict and fight it out.'

Marx, then, certainly believed that the material mode of life in the end determined the intellectual. But he never for a moment considered that the connection between the two was a direct one, easily observed and mechanically developing. He would have laughed to scorn the idea that because capitalism replaces feudalism, therefore a 'capitalist' art immediately replaces 'feudal' art, and that all great artists must in consequence directly reflect the needs of the new capitalist class. Nor, as will appear later, did he consider that because the capitalist mode of production was a more progressive one than the feudal, capitalist art must therefore always stand on a higher level than feudal art, while feudal art in turn must stand above the art of the slave States of Greece and Rome, or the ancient Eastern monarchies. Such crude and vulgar views are foreign to the whole spirit of Marxism.

Changes in the material basis of society, Marx rightly urged, can be determined by the economic historian with the precision of natural science (which, of course, is not the same thing as saying that these changes are scientifically determined). But no such scientific measurement of the resulting changes in the social and spiritual superstructure of life is possible. The changes take place, men become conscious of them, they 'fight out' the conflict between old and new in their minds, but they do so unevenly, burdened by all kinds of past heritage, often unclearly, and always in such a way that it is not easy to trace the changes in men's minds.

It is true, for example, that the *Code Napoléon* is the legal expression of the social and economic changes wrought by the French Revolution. Yet the knowledge of this does not in itself explain the *Code Napoléon*. One must understand also the past history of France and the relation of classes in that country before the Revolution, one must understand the course of the Revolution itself and the changes in class relationships which the Revolution brought about, and finally, one must understand Napoleon's military dictatorship. Then only does the *Code* become comprehensible as the legal expression of the new bourgeois society and the French industrial revolution which began during the Napoleonic period. And law is perhaps the most responsive part of the ideal superstructure, it changes most easily in accordance with changes in the mode of production. But art is much farther from the basis, responds far less easily to the changes in it.

Engels in a letter to J. Bloch written in 1890 was quite emphatic about this point. 'According to the materialist conception of history,' he wrote, 'the determining element in history is *ultimately* the production and reproduction in real life. More than this neither Marx nor I have ever asserted. If therefore somebody twists this into the statement that the economic element is the *only* determining one, he transforms it into a meaningless, abstract and absurd phrase. The economic situation is the basis, but the various elements of the superstructure – political forms of the class struggle and its consequences, constitutions established by the victorious class after a successful battle, etc. – forms of law – and even the reflexes of all these actual struggles in the brains of the combatants: political, legal, philosophical theories, religious ideas and their further development into systems of dogma – also exercise their influence upon the course of the historical struggles and in many cases preponderate in determining their *form*. There is an interaction of all these elements, in which, amid all the endless *host* of accidents (i.e., of things and events whose inner connection is so remote or so impossible to prove that we regard it as absent and can neglect it), the economic movement finally asserts itself as necessary. Otherwise the application of the theory to any period of history one chose would be easier than the solution of a simple equation of the first degree.'

Marxism, therefore, while reserving the final and decisive factor in any change for economic causes, does not deny that 'ideal' factors can also influence the course of history and may even preponderate in determining the *form* which changes will take (but only the form). It is only a caricature of Marxism to suggest that it underestimates the importance of such a spiritual factor in human consciousness as artistic creation, or to make the absurd claim that Marx considered works of art to be the direct reflection of material and economic causes. He did not. He understood perfectly well that all religion, or philosophy, or tradition can play a great part in the creation of a work of art, even that any one of these or other 'ideal' factors may preponderate in determining the *form* of the work in question. Among all the elements which go to make a work of art it is, however, only the economic movement which asserts itself as *finally* necessary, for what Marx and Engels considered to be true of historical changes they also considered true of aesthetic creation.

It is often objected against Marxism that it denies the individual, who is merely the prey of abstract economic forces which drive him to his doom with the inevitability of a Greek fate. We will leave aside the question of whether or not the conception that man is driven by external fate to an inevitable end makes the creation of a work of art impossible. Perhaps Calvinism has never produced great art, but the idea of doom and fate has done so – in the Greek tragedies, in the works of Hardy, to mention only two instances. It is nevertheless possible that the objection, if it really represented the Marxian view, would be a valid one. At least this objection is prompted by the humanist tradition of the great art of the western world, and is therefore worthy of respect, even though it is based on a grave misunderstanding.

For Marxism does not deny the individual. It does not see only masses in the grip of inexorable economic forces. True, some Marxist literary works, particularly some 'proletarian' novels, have given innocent critics cause to believe that this is the case, but here perhaps the weakness has been in the novelists who have failed to rise to the greatness of their theme of man changing himself through the process of changing nature and creating new economic forces. Marxism places man in the centre of its philosophy, for while it claims that material forces may change man, it declares most emphatically that it is man who changes the material forces and that in the course of doing so he changes himself.

Man and his development is the centre of Marxist philosophy. How does man change? What are his relations with the external world? These are questions to which the founders of Marxism have sought and found answers. I do not wish here to outline Marxist philosophy, for that is done more capably elsewhere; but let us examine for a moment this question of man as an active historical agent, man at work and struggling with life, for this is the man who is at once artistic creator and the object of art. This is the way in which Engels explained the part of the individual in history:

'History makes itself in such a way that the final result always arises from conflicts between many individual wills, of which each again has been made what it is by a host of particular conditions of life. Thus there are innumerable intersecting forces, and infinite series of parallelograms of forces which give rise to one resultant – the historical event. This again may itself be viewed as the product of a power which, taken as a whole, works *unconsciously* and without volition. For what each individual wills is obstructed by everyone else, and what emerges is something which no one willed. Thus past history proceeds in the manner of a natural process and is also essentially subject to the same laws of movement. But from the fact that individual wills – of which each desires what he is impelled to by his physical constitution and external, in the last resort economic, circumstances (either his own personal circumstances or those of society in general) – do not attain what they want, but are merged into a collective mean, a common resultant, it must not be concluded that their value = 0. On the contrary, each contributes to the resultant and is to this degree involved in it.'

Here is not only a formula for the historian, but also for the novelist. For the one concern of the novelist is, or should be, this question of the individual will in its conflict with other wills on the battleground of life. It is the fate of man that his desires are never fulfilled, but it is also his glory, for in the effort to obtain their fulfilment, he changes, be it ever so little, in ever so limited a degree, life itself. Not $X = 0$ is the Marxist formula for the fate of man, but 'on the contrary, each contributes to the resultant and is to this degree involved in it'.

The conflict of wills, of desires and passions, is not, however, a conflict of abstract human beings, for Engels is careful to emphasise that man's desires and actions are conditioned by his physical constitution and, finally, by economic circumstances, either his personal circumstances or those of society in general. In his social history it is, in the last resort again, the class to which he belongs, the psychology of that class, with its contradictions and conflicts, which plays the determining part. So that each man has, as it were, a dual history, since he is at the same time a type, a man with social history, and an individual, a man with a personal history. The two, of course, even though they may be in glaring conflict, are also one, a unity, in so far as the latter is eventually conditioned by the former, though this does not and should not imply that in art the social type must dominate the individual personality. Falstaff, Don Quixote, Tom Jones, Julien Sorel, Monsieur de Charlus, are all types, but they are types in whom the social characteristics constantly reveal the individual, and in whom the personal hopes, hungers, loves, jealousies and ambitions in turn light up the social background.

The novelist cannot write his story of the individual fate unless he also has this steady vision of the whole. He must understand how his final result arises from the individual conflicts of his characters, he must in turn understand what are the manifold conditions of life which have made each of those individuals what she or he is. 'What emerges is something no one willed.' How exactly that sums up each great work of art, and how well it expresses the pattern of life itself, since behind the event that no one willed a pattern does exist. Marxism gives to the creative artist the key to reality when it shows him how to discern that pattern and the place which each individual occupies in it. At the same time it consciously gives to man his full value, and in this sense is the most humanist of all world outlooks.

Notes

1. 'Ralph Fox', in Lehmann *et al.*, p. 3.
2. *Plebs*, June 1922.
3. Lehmann *et al.*, p. 7.
4. In H. Levy *et al.*, *Aspects of Dialectical Materialism* (London: Watts and Co., 1934).
5. Speeches made at the 1934 Soviet Writers' Congress, including Gorki, Radek, Bukharin and Zhdanov. Reissued by Lawrence and Wishart, 1977.
6. Hawthorn, Preface to *The Novel and the People*, p. 13.
7. *Communist Review*, March 1929; reprinted in Lehmann *et al.*, pp. 217–21.
8. Quoted in Hawthorn, Preface to *The Novel and the People*, p. 14.
9. Preface, p. 17.
10. Compare with this F.R. Leavis's attitude to the reading public and to Arnold Bennett as reviewer in *Mass Civilisation and Minority Culture*, pp. 12–20. (See also above,

p. 21). An even more rebarbative approach to the same issue is to be found in 'Disintegration of the Reading Public', Chapter IV of the second part of Q. D. Leavis's *Fiction and the Reading Public*. (See also below, pp. 175–81.)

11. Cf. George Orwell on 1930s fiction, reviewing and publishing: 'In Defence of the Novel', *New English Weekly*, 12 and 19 November 1936; reprinted in *An Age Like This*, pp. 249–55.

12. Waugh began work on his biography of Edmund Campion in mid-1934. Martin Stannard argues that the work is evidence of Waugh's increased political awareness at the time. He wrote later that 'we are nearer to Campion than when I wrote of him. We have seen the church drawn underground in country after country . . . The haunted, trapped, murdered priest is our contemporary and Campion's voice sounds across the centuries as though he were walking at our elbow.' 'Though written after the Second World War,' comments Stannard, 'this describes equally well his contemporary approach' (pp. 385–6). The book appeared in September 1935, and in May the following year Waugh received word that the book was to be awarded the Hawthornden Prize – for 'a work of imaginative literature by a British author under forty-one' (see Stannard, p. 418).

13. The phrase is borrowed from Mr Day Lewis. [RF]

Valentine Cunningham (p. 141) notes that Empson's argument here – that 'Pastoral is the truly proletarian literature' – was a response 'to the 1934 Soviet Writers' Congress dicta about socialist realism'.[1] Empson's further claim, however, that even Alice in Wonderland 'does indeed stand for something that produces a feeling of solidarity between classes' Cunningham labels a 'cheeky dodge' on a 'tenuous theoretical basis'. It shows Empson, in his view, party to 'the Old Boys' school and university world' in which 'characters out of nursery stories and rhymes [get] . . . turned into touchstones of the imagination and of an attempted political analysis'. Interestingly, Geoffrey Grigson's contemporary review in *New Verse* no. 18 (December 1935) singled out the choice of Alice in Wonderland as a 'stroke of genius' (p. 18). The 'subtlety' of Empson's argument, wrote Grigson, 'illustrates in itself the attitude which it describes':

> Mr. Empson's essay on Proletarian Art is pastoral. Propaganda appears as Peace-in-terms-of-War (shock brigades on collective farms), and Pastoral is War-in-terms-of-Peace (contests between shepherds, amoebean dialogues). To identify the two is to impose a poetic armistice on all artists to whichever side of the class struggle they may belong. The middle-class intellectual who joins the communist party is joining the shepherds; and perhaps it will encourage him, when he thinks that, partaking in the squalor and bitterness of the de-classed life, he partakes in the laborious fight against the Earth (economic conditions, reality) from which pastoral poetry emerged at Ascra.

Exactly what is meant by – and what qualifies as – 'proletarian writing' was a topic much discussed throughout the decade, and in various forums. An ongoing debate on the topic is to be found, for example, in the pages of the *London Mercury* (March to May 1936) and, in response to this correspondence, a most interesting editorial on 'Worker's Writing' appeared in the *Left Review* 2 (1936–7): 417–18. Also of interest is a discussion on the BBC Home Service on 6 December 1940, between George Orwell and Desmond Hawkins, published in the *Listener* as 'What Is Proletarian Literature?'[2] H. A. Mason, reviewing *Some Versions of Pastoral* rather negatively for *Scrutiny*, declared nevertheless that Empson's essay on 'Proletarian Literature' spoke 'good sense on a topic which has exercised most of our contemporary critics and provoked much nonsense'.[3]

---

* Reprinted from *Some Versions of Pastoral* (1935; New York: New Directions, 1950), pp. 3–9 and 11–23.

It is hard for an Englishman to talk definitely about proletarian art, because in England it has never been a genre with settled principles, and such as there is of it, that I have seen, is bad. But it is important to try and decide what the term ought to mean; my suspicion, as I shall try to make clear, is that it is liable to a false limitation.

As for propaganda, some very good work has been that; most authors want their point of view to be convincing. Pope said that even the *Aeneid* was a 'political puff'; its dreamy, impersonal, universal melancholy was a calculated support for Augustus. And on the other hand proletarian literature need not be propaganda; *Carl and Anna* is simply a very good love-story; it counts as proletarian because no other social world (ideology) is brought in but that of the characters who are factory workers. Of course to decide on an author's purpose, conscious or unconscious, is very difficult. Good writing is not done unless there are serious forces at work; and it is not permanent unless it works for readers with opinions different from the author's. On the other hand the reason an English audience can enjoy Russian propagandist films is that the propaganda is too remote to be annoying: a Tory audience subjected to Tory propaganda of the same intensity would be extremely bored. Anyway it is agreed that there is some good work which a Marxist would call proletarian; the more pressing questions for him are whether some good work may be bourgeois and whether some may not be class-conscious at all.

Gray's *Elegy* is an odd case of poetry with latent political ideas:

> Full many a gem of purest ray serene
> The dark, unfathomed caves of ocean bear;
> Full many a flower is born to blush unseen
> And waste its sweetness on the desert air.

What this means, as the context makes clear, is that eighteenth-century England had no scholarship system or *carrière ouverte aux talents*. This is stated as pathetic, but the reader is put into a mood in which one would not try to alter it. (It is true that Gray's society, unlike a possible machine society, was necessarily based on manual labour, but it might have used a man of special ability wherever he was born.) By comparing the social arrangement to Nature he makes it seem inevitable, which it was not, and gives it a dignity which was undeserved. Furthermore, a gem does not mind being in a cave and a flower prefers not to be picked; we feel that the man is like the flower, as short-lived, natural, and valuable, and this tricks us into feeling that he is better off without opportunities. The sexual suggestion of *blush* brings in the Christian idea that virginity is good in itself, and so that any renunciation is good; this may trick us into feeling it is lucky for the poor man that society keeps him unspotted from the World. The tone of melancholy claims that the poet understands the considerations opposed to aristocracy, though he judges against them; the truism of the reflections in the churchyard, the universality and impersonality this gives to the style, claim as if by comparison that we ought to accept the injustice of society as we do the inevitability of death.

Many people, without being communists, have been irritated by the complacence in the massive calm of the poem, and this seems partly because they feel there is a cheat in the implied politics; the 'bourgeois' themselves do not like literature to have too much 'bourgeois ideology'.

And yet what is said is one of the permanent truths; it is only in degree that any improvement in society could prevent wastage of human powers; the waste even in a fortunate life, the isolation even of a life rich in intimacy, cannot but be felt deeply, and is the central feeling of tragedy. And anything of value must accept this because it must not prostitute itself; its strength is to be prepared to waste itself, if it does not get its opportunity. A statement of this is certainly non-political because it is true in any society, and yet nearly all the great poetic statements of it are in a way 'bourgeois', like this one; they suggest to many readers, though they do not say, that for the poor man things cannot be improved even in degree. This at least shows that the distinction the communists try to draw is a puzzling one; two people may get very different experiences from the same work of art without either being definitely wrong. One is told that the Russians now disapprove of tragedy, and that there was a performance of *Hamlet* in the Turk-Sib region which the audience decided spontaneously was a farce. They may well hold out against the melancholy of old Russia, and for them there may be dangerous implications in any tragedy, which other people do not see. I am sure at any rate that one could not estimate the amount of bourgeois ideology 'really in' the verse from Gray.

The same difficulty arises in the other direction. Proletarian literature usually has a suggestion of pastoral, a puzzling form which looks proletarian but isn't. I must worry the meaning of the term for a moment. One might define proletarian art as the propaganda of a factory-working class which feels its interests opposed to the factory owners'; this narrow sense is perhaps what is usually meant but not very interesting. You couldn't have proletarian literature in this sense in a successful socialist state. The wider sense of the term includes such folk-literature as is by the people, for the people, and about the people. But most fairy stories and ballads, though 'by' and 'for', are not 'about'; whereas pastoral though 'about' is not 'by' or 'for'. The Border ballads assume a society of fighting clans who are protected by their leaders since leaders can afford expensive weapons; the aristocrat has an obvious function for the people, and they are pleased to describe his grandeur and fine clothes. (This pleasure in him as an object of fantasy is the normal thing, but usually there are forces the other way.) They were class-conscious all right, but not conscious of class war. Pastoral is a queerer business, but I think permanent and not dependent on a system of class exploitation. Any socialist state with an intelligentsia at the capital that felt itself more cultivated than the farmers (which it would do; the arts are produced by overcrowding) could produce it; it is common in present-day Russian films, and a great part of their beauty (for instance the one called *The General Line* when it came to England).[4] My reason for dragging this old-fashioned form into the discussion is that I think good proletarian art is usually Covert Pastoral.

Before theorising about this I had best speak of some recent English artists. A book like Lionel Britton's *Hunger and Love*, one of the few ostensibly proletarian works of any energy that England has to show (I disliked it too much to finish it), is not at all pastoral; it is a passionate and feverish account of a man trying to break his way out of the proletariat into the intelligentsia, or rather the lower middle class into the upper. As such it may be good literature by sheer force, and useful propaganda if it is not out of date by the time it is written, but what the author wanted was the opportunity not to be proletarian; this is fine enough, but it doesn't make proletarian literature. On the other hand, nobody would take the pastoral of T. F. Powys for proletarian, though it really is about workers; his object in writing about country people is to get a simple enough material for his purpose, which one might sum up as a play with Christian imagery backed only by a Buddhist union of God and death. No doubt he would say that country people really feel this, and are wiser about it than the cultivated, and that he is their spokesman, but the characters are firmly artificial and kept at a great distance from the author. W. W. Jacobs makes the argument amusingly clear; it is not obvious why he is not a proletarian author, and it would annoy a communist very much to admit that he was. Probably no one would deny that he writes a version of pastoral. The truth that supports his formula is that such men as his characters keep their souls alive by ironical humour. A subtle mode of thought which among other things makes you willing to be ruled by your betters; and this makes the bourgeois feel safe in Wapping. D. H. Lawrence's refusal to write proletarian literature was an important choice, but he was a complicated person; to see the general reasons for it one had best take a simpler example. George Bissill the painter, who worked from childhood in the mines and did some excellent woodcuts of them, refused to work for the *New Leader* (which wanted political cartoons) because he had rather be a Pavement Artist than a Proletarian one. As a person he is obviously not 'bourgeois', unless being determined not to go back to the mines makes you that. Such a man dislikes proletarian art because he feels that it is like pastoral, and that that is either patronising or 'romantic'. The Englishman who seems to me nearest to a proletarian artist (of those I know anything about) is Grierson the film producer; *Drifters* gave very vividly the feeling of actually living on a herring trawler and (by the beauty of shapes of water and net and fish, and subtleties of timing and so forth) what I should call a pastoral feeling about the dignity of that form of labour.[5] It was very much under Russian influence. But herring fishermen are unlikely to see *Drifters*; for all its government-commercial claim to solid usefulness it is a 'high-brow' picture (that blasting word[6] shows an involuntary falsity in the thing); Grierson's influence, strong and healthy as it is, has something skimpy about it. Of course there are plenty of skilled workers in England who are proud of their skill, and you can find men of middle age working on farms who say they prefer the country to the town, but anything like what I am trying to call pastoral is a shock to the Englishman who meets it on the Continent. My only personal memory of this sort is of watching Spaniards tread out sherry grapes and squeeze out the skins afterwards, which involves dance steps with a complicated rhythm. I said what was obvious, that this was like a Russian Ballet, and to my alarm the remark was translated; any English worker would take it as an insult, probably a sexual one. They were mildly pleased at so obvious a point being recognised, and showed us the other dance step being used in a neighbouring district; both ways were pleasant in themselves and the efficient way to get the maximum juice. The point is not at all that they are living simple pretty lives by themselves; quite the contrary; some quality in their very own harsh lives made them feel at home with the rest of civilisation, not suspicious of it. This may well show the backwardness of the country; for that matter there were the same feelings in Russian for the Soviets to use if they could get at them. They seem able to bring off something like a pastoral feeling in Spain and Russia, but in an English artist, whatever his personal sincerity, it seems dogged by humbug, and has done now for a long time. This may well be a grave fault in the English social system, but it is not one an English artist can avoid by becoming a proletarian artist . . .

The essential trick of the old pastoral, which was felt to imply a beautiful relation between rich and poor, was to make simple people express strong feeling (felt as the most universal subject, something fundamentally true about everybody) in learned and fashionable language (so that you wrote about the best subject in the best way). From seeing the two sorts of people combined like this you thought better of both; the best parts of both were used. The effect was in some degree to combine in the reader or author the merits of the two sorts; he was made to mirror in himself more completely the effective elements of the society he lived in. This was not a process that you could explain in the course of writing pastoral; it was already shown by the clash between style and theme, and to make the clash work in the right way (not become funny) the writer must keep up a firm pretence that he was unconscious of it. Indeed the usual process for putting further meanings into the pastoral situation was to insist that the shepherds were rulers of sheep, and so compare them to politicians or bishops or what not; this piled the heroic convention into the pastoral one, since the hero was another symbol of his whole society. Such a pretence no doubt makes the characters unreal, but not the feelings expressed or even the situation described; the same pretence is often valuable in real life. I should say that it was over this fence that pastoral came down in England after the Restoration. The arts, even music, came to depend more than before on knowing about foreign culture, and Puritanism, suspicious of the arts, was only not strong among the aristocracy. A feeling gradually got about that anyone below the upper middles was making himself ridiculous, being above himself, if he showed any signs of keeping a sense of beauty at all, and this feeling was common to all classes. It takes a general belief as harsh and as unreal as this to make the polite pretence of pastoral seem necessarily absurd. Even so there was a successful school of mock-pastoral for so long as the upper and lower classes were consciously less Puritan than the middle. When that goes the pastoral tricks of thought take refuge in child-cult.

One strong help for the pastoral convention was the tradition, coming down from the origin of our romantic love-poetry in the troubadours, that its proper tone is one of humility, that the proper moments to dramatise in a love-affair are those when the lover is in despair. (Much theorising might be done in praise of this convention; some of it comes into Poe's absurd proof that melancholy is the most poetical of the tones. For one thing the mere fact that you don't altogether believe in the poet's expression of despair makes you feel that he has reserves of strength.) Granted this, the low man has only to shift his humility onto his love affairs to adopt the dignity of a courtly convention. There is a good example in *As You Like It*; we see Corin for a moment bewailing his hopeless love with an older shepherd, and then the gentry try to get food out of him.

CLOWN. Holla! you, clown!
ROSALIND. Peace, fool, he's not thy kinsman.
CORIN: Who calls?
CLOWN: Your betters, sir.
CORIN: Else they are very wretched.

Rosalind has heard the previous conversation, but no doubt she would understand this anyway; the shepherd is giving himself airs rather than being humble, but he has every right to it, and the court clown is silenced for the rest of the scene.

The convention was, of course, often absurdly artificial; the praise of simplicity usually went with extreme flattery of a patron (dignified as a symbol of the whole society, through the connection of pastoral with heroic), done so that the author could get some of the patron's luxuries; it allowed the flattery to be more extreme because it helped both author and patron to keep their self-respect. So it was much parodied, especially to make the poor man worthy but ridiculous, as often in Shakespeare; nor is this merely snobbish when in its full form. The simple man becomes a clumsy fool who yet has better 'sense' than his betters and can say things more fundamentally true; he is 'in contact with nature', which the complex man needs to be, so that Bottom is not afraid of the fairies; he is in contact with the mysterious forces of our own nature, so that the clown has the wit of the Unconscious; he can speak the truth because he has nothing to lose. Also the idea that he is in contact with nature, therefore 'one with the universe' like the Senecan man, brought in a suggestion of stoicism; this made the thing less unreal since the humorous poor man is more obviously stoical than profound. And there may be obscure feelings at work, which I am unable to list, like those about the earth-touching Buddha. Another use of the clown (itself a word for the simple countryman) should be mentioned here; the business of the macabre, where you make a clown out of death. Death in the Holbein Dance of Death, a skeleton still skinny, is often an elegant and charming small figure whose wasp waist gives him a certain mixed-sex quality, and though we are to think otherwise he conceives himself as poking fun; he is seen at his best when piping to an idiot clown and leading him on, presumably to some precipice, treating this great coy figure with so gay and sympathetic an admiration that the picture stays in one's mind chiefly as a love scene. It is a far cry from pastoral, but the clown has such feelings behind him among his sources of strength.

Thus both versions, straight and comic, are based on a double attitude of the artist to the worker, of the complex man to the simple one ('I am in one way better, in another not so good'), and this may well recognise a permanent truth about the aesthetic situation. To produce pure proletarian art the artist must be at one with the worker; this is impossible, not for political reasons, but because the artist never is at one with any public. The grandest attempt at escape from this is provided by Gertrude Stein, who claims to be a direct expression of the Zeitgeist (the present stage of the dialectic process) and therefore to need no other relation to a public of any kind. She has in fact a very definite relation to her public, and I should call her work a version of the child-cult, which is a version of pastoral; this does not by any means make it bad. The point is to this extent a merely philosophical one, that I am not concerned to deny any practical claim made for what is called proletarian literature so long as the artist has not been misled by its theory; I only call it a bogus concept. It may be that to produce any good art the artist must be somehow in contact with the worker, it may be that this is what is wrong with the arts in the West, it may be that Russia is soon going to produce a very good art, with all the vigour of a society which is a healthy and unified organism, but I am sure it will not be pure proletarian art and I think it will spoil itself if it tries to be.

It seems clear that the Worker, as used in proletarian propaganda, is a mythical cult-figure of the sort I have tried to describe. This is not peculiar to one party. As I write, the Government has just brought out a poster giving the numbers of men back at work, with a large photograph of a skilled worker using a chisel. He is a stringy but tough, vital but not over-strong, Cockney type, with a great deal of the genuine but odd refinement of the English lower middle class. This is very strong Tory propaganda; one feels it is fair to take him as a type of the English skilled worker, and it cuts out the communist feelings about the worker merely to look at him. To accept the picture is to feel that the skilled worker's interests are bound up with his place in the class system and the success of British foreign policy in finding markets. There is an unfortunate lack of a word here. To call such a picture a 'symbol', like a sign in mathematics, is to ignore the sources of its power; to call it a 'myth' is to make an offensive suggestion that the author is superior to common feelings. I do not mean to say that such pictures are nonsense because they are myths; the facts of the life of a nation, for instance the way public opinion swings round, are very strange indeed, and probably a half-magical idea is the quickest way to truth. People who consider that the Worker group of sentiments is misleading in contemporary politics tend to use the word 'romantic' as a missile; unless they merely mean 'false' this is quite off the point; what they ought to do is to produce a rival myth, like the poster. In calling it mythical I mean that complex feelings, involving all kinds of distant matters, are put into it as a symbol, with an implication 'this is the right worker to select and keep in mind as the type', and that among them is an obscure magical feeling 'while he is like this he is Natural and that will induce Nature to make us prosperous'. The point is not that myths ought not to be used but that their use in proletarian literature is not as simple as it looks.

The realistic sort of pastoral (the sort touched by mock-pastoral) also gives a natural expression for a sense of social injustice. So far as the person described is outside society because too poor for its benefits he is independent, as the artist claims to be, and can be a critic of society; so far as he is forced by this into crime he is the judge of the society that judges him. This is a source of irony both against him and against the society, and if he is a sympathetic criminal he can be made to suggest both Christ the scapegoat (so invoking Christian charity) and the sacrificial tragic hero, who was normally above society rather than below it, which is a further source of irony. Dostoevsky is always using these ideas; perhaps unhealthily, but as very strong propaganda. But I doubt whether they are allowed in pure proletarian literature; the communists do not approve of them, either as tragic or Christian, both because they glorify the independent man and because they could be used against any society, including a communist one.

I am trying here to deal with the popular, vague but somehow obvious, idea of proletarian literature, which is what is influential; there may be a secret and refined definition which disposes of what I have to say. What seems clear from the varying accounts of the position of authors in Russia is that no one definition is generally accepted. Sympathisers tell you there is an arrangement by which authors are expected to do journalistic jobs, writing up conditions in a distant chain of factories or what not, and in their private writing have only to avoid active sedition; this seems healthy if the Government would stick to it but not of much critical interest. Gorki, in his speech to the 1934 All-Union Congress of Soviet Writers,[7] made a wider use of the crucial formula of proletarian literature, 'socialist realism'.

> To invent means to extract from the totality of real existence its basic idea and to incarnate this in an image; thus we obtain realism. But if to the idea extracted from the real is added the desirable, the potential, and the image is supplemented by this, we obtain that romanticism which lies at the basis of myth and is highly useful in that it facilitates the arousing of a revolutionary attitude towards reality, an attitude of practically changing the world.

I hope that this use of the word 'myth' will show that my use of it is not a distortion. The idea of the wheel going on revolving, even if you add dialectical materialism by saying that this gives it progress along the ground, is one that a communist must not push too far – revolutionary proletarian literature, in intention at any rate, is obviously a product of transition; and the second sentence must be misunderstood as an appeal for lying propaganda. But the only real trouble about this as an account of proletarian literature is that it applies to any good literature whatever. When communists say that an author under modern capitalism feels cut off from most of the life of the country, and would not under communism, the remark has a great deal of truth, though he might only exchange a sense of isolation for a sense of the waste of his powers; it is certainly not so completely true as to make the verse from Gray pointless to a man living under communism. The way this sense of isolation has been avoided in the past is by the conventions of pastoral with which I am concerned. (Even Alice in Wonderland, though her convention corresponds to a failure in the normal tradition of pastoral, does indeed stand for something that produces a feeling of solidarity between classes.) When they say that a proletarian writer is the 'spokesman and representative of the proletariat' this is something like a definition; but once everybody is proletarian he is merely the representative of man; and in any case a representative is conscious that he is not the same as what he represents. When Radek[8] in his speech at the same congress appealed for the help of foreign writers in the production of a great proletarian literature of 'love to all oppressed, hate toward the exploiting class . . . Into this literature we will pour the soul of the proletariat, its passions and its love . . . ' his rhetoric is meant to shift from a political idea to a universal one. To say that the only way a present-day writer can produce good work is by devoting himself to political propaganda is of course another thing from defining proletarian literature, and in some cases true. But it seems fair to say that there is some doubt about the definition.

The poetic statements of human waste and limitation, whose function is to give strength to see life clearly and so to adopt a fuller attitude to it, usually bring in, or leave room for a reader to bring in, the whole set of pastoral ideas. For such crucial literary achievements are likely to attempt to reconcile some conflict between the parts of a society; literature is a social process, and also an attempt to reconcile the conflicts of an individual in whom those of society will be mirrored. (The belief that a man's ideas are wholly the product of his economic setting is of course as fatuous as the belief that they are wholly independent of it.) So 'fundamentally true' goes to 'true about people in all parts of society, even those you wouldn't expect', and this implies the tone of humility normal to pastoral. 'I now abandon my specialised feelings because I am trying to find better ones, so I must balance myself for the moment by imagining the feelings of a simple person. He may be in a better state than I am by luck, freshness, or divine grace; value is outside any scheme for the measurement of value because that too must be valued.' Various paradoxes may be thrown in here; 'I must imagine his way of feeling because the refined thing must be judged by the fundamental thing, because strength must be learnt in weakness and sociability in isolation, because the best manners are learnt in the simple life' (this last is the point of Spenser's paradox about 'courtly'; the Book of Courtesy takes the reader among Noble Savages). Now all these ideas are very well suited to a socialist society, and have been made to fit in very well with the dogma of the equality of man, but I do not see that they fit in with a rigid proletarian aesthetic. They assume that it is sometimes a good thing to stand apart from your society so far as you can. They assume that some people are more delicate and complex than others, and that if such people can keep this distinction from doing harm it is a good thing, though a small thing by comparison with our common humanity. Once you allow the arts to admit this you will get works of art which imply that the special man ought to be more specially treated, and that is not proletarian literature.

It is for reasons like these that the most valuable works of art so often have a political implication which can be pounced on and called bourgeois. They carry an implication about the society they were written for; the question is whether the same must not be true of any human society, even if it is much better than theirs. My own difficulty about proletarian literature is that when it comes off I find I am taking it as pastoral literature; I read into it, or find that the author has secretly put into it, these more subtle, more far-reaching, and I think more permanent, ideas.

It would be interesting to know how far the ideas of pastoral in this wide sense are universal, and I think that to attempt a rough world-view brings in another point about the communist aesthetic. With the partial exception of Alice they are all part of the normal European tradition, but they might seem dependent on that, especially as dependent on Christianity. In my account the ideas about the sacrificial hero as Dying God[9] are mixed up in the brew, and these, whose supreme form is Christianity, mainly belong to Europe and the Mediterranean. *The Golden Bough* makes a clear distinction between this hero and the Sincere Man as One with Nature, who is also sacrificial so far as national calamity proves that the emperor is not sincere, but refuses to try to separate them; it seems clear that they are at home respectively in the West and the East. On the other hand interest in the problems of the One and the Many, especially their social aspects, is ancient and obvious in the East, and many of the versions of pastoral come out of that. The idea of everything being included in the humble thing, with mystical respect for poor men, fools, and children, and a contrasting idea of everything being included in the ruling hero, were a main strand of Chinese thought by the third century B.C.; before Buddhism and not limited to Taoism. In China the feeling that everything is everything so nothing is worth doing, natural to this mode of thought, was balanced by the Confucian stress on the exact performance of local duties and ceremonies. One can make a list of European ideas with the same purpose, of making the immediate thing real, all of which stress the individual more or less directly and are denied in the East. God is a person; each separate individual is immortal, with the character he has acquired in this life; so one must continually worry about whether he is free; and he is born in sin so that he must make efforts; and because of this only a God, individual like the rest of us, is worthy to be sacrificed to God. These ideas were knocking about Europe before they were Christian, and the rejection of Christ may well be a less dangerous element in the communist position than the acceptance of Hegel. Gorki said in the early days of the soviets that the great danger for Russia is that she may 'go East', a pregnant remark even if the East itself is innoculated against this sort of philosophy. It may be said that men always go in droves, and that all versions of the claim to individualism are largely bogus; but that gives the reason why the prop of individualist theory is needed. Once you have said that everything is One it is obvious that literature is the same as propaganda; once you have said that no truth can be known beyond the immediate dialectical process of history it is obvious that all contemporary artists must prepare the same fashionplate. It is clear too that the One is limited in space as well as time, and the no less Hegelian Fascists are right in saying that all art is patriotic. And the dialectical process proceeds through conflicts, so we must be sure and have plenty of big wars. Of course to talk like this is to misunderstand the philosophy, but once the philosophy is made a public creed it is sure to be misunderstood in some such way. I do not mean to say that the philosophy is wrong; for that matter pastoral is worked from the same philosophical ideas as proletarian literature – the difference is that it brings in the absolute less prematurely. Nor am I trying to say anything about the politics and economics, only that they do not provide an aesthetic theory.

Notes

1. See A. I. Stetsky on the 'guiding line' of Socialist Realism (pp. 263ff.) and Karl Radek, 'James Joyce or Socialist Realism?' (pp. 150ff.), both published in the proceedings of the congress (Zhdanov *et al.*, *Problems of Soviet Literature*).
2. Reprinted in Orwell, *My Country Right or Left*, pp. 38–44. Useful recent studies of the subject include Tortosa and Ortega's collection of essays, Ashraf, Klaus, Worpole and Hawthorn.
3. *Scrutiny* 4.4 (March 1936): 431.
4. Eisenstein's *The General Line* was retitled *The Old and the New* (*Staroye i novoye*) on its release in 1929.
5. See below, p. 309.
6. See discussions of this term in the extracts by F. R. and Q. D. Leavis (pp. 21 and 174 respectively), Day Lewis (p. 284) and Auden (p. 39) included in this volume.
7. See Zhdanov *et al.*, pp. 27–69.
8. Zhdanov *et al.*, pp. 73–182.
9. Paul Alpers writes that in *Some Versions of Pastoral* Christ is 'the one hero who fully takes on the conflicts of other men and experiences them as his own' ('Empson on Pastoral', *New Literary History* 10 [1978]: 118). Heroism is a recurring theme in Empson's book.

20 Q. D. Leavis *from Fiction and the Reading Public (1932)*[*]

For the Leavises, 1932 was – as Ian MacKillop (p. 135) puts it – an *annus mirabilis*: F.R.L.'s *New Bearing in English Poetry* was published in February, and Q.D.L.'s *Fiction and the Reading Public* in April. In the closing pages of the latter, reflection on the 'terrifying' and apparently relentless erosion of minority culture leads to the following conclusion: 'If there is to be any hope, it must lie in conscious and directed effort. All that can be done, it must be realised, must take the form of resistance by an armed and conscious minority' (p. 270). The founding of *Scrutiny* – its first issue appeared in May – was intended to open up a new front in that campaign (see Mulhern, pp. 34–41).

What follows is an extract from *Fiction and the Reading Public*, Part II, Chapter IV: 'The Disintegration of the Reading Public', from a section entitled 'Levelling Down'. By this point in her study Q.D.L. has established – for her purposes, at least – that the early decades of this century have seen achieved a 'complete . . . revolution in the outlook of the reading public'. In the following pages she elaborates 'some at least of the contributory factors' (p. 190), indicating in the process the essential features of that revolution.

It is worth making two points here. First, by the 'new journalism' Q.D.L. refers, of course, to the work of the mass-circulation press, especially papers such as the *Daily Mail* (founded 1896), the *Daily Mirror* (founded 1903) and the *Daily Express* (controlled by Lord Beaverbrook since 1916). It was especially the founder of the *Mail* and the *Mirror*, Alfred Harmsworth (after 1905 Lord Northcliffe), who attracted the ire of the Leavises; 'What Northcliffe had done [with his papers],' writes Q. D. Leavis as she begins to consider the 'levelling down' of the reading public, 'was in fact to mobilise the people to outvote the minority, who had hitherto set the standard of taste without any serious challenge' (p. 185). For useful background, see Nicholas Rance, 'British Newspapers in the Early Twentieth Century', in Bloom, pp. 120–45.

Secondly, while this extract ends with a quotation from *Mass Civilisation and Minority Culture*, Q.D.L.'s elaboration of Leavisite doctrine differs from her husband's work in at least two significant ways. In the first place, she does not share his dislike of 'highbrow' as a critical term: whereas he views it cautiously as 'an ominous addition to the English language' (p. 25), she elaborates and then applies a full taxonomy of 'Highbrow', 'Middlebrow' and 'Lowbrow' (p. 45). Mulhern (p. 38) remarks that this 'trichotomy . . . was less an analytic discovery

[*] Reprinted from *Fiction and the Reading Public* (1932; London: Chatto and Windus, 1965), pp. 185–202.

than an evaluative representation of the literary field as seen through the optic of "culture", not the result of analysis but its unchallengeable presupposition' (p. 38). In the second place, where F.R.L. will use the word 'mass', Q.D.L. comes increasingly to choose the rather more disturbing term, 'herd'. In this she acknowledges a debt to W. Trotter's quasi-anthropological book *The Instincts of the Herd in Peace and War* (1916), so there is reason to grant the word more academic objectivity than would at first seem to be possible. On the other hand, John Carey (pp. 51 and 93) reminds us that in the Leavises – and generally in the British literary intelligentsia after 1880 – there is discernible a very real and visceral loathing of suburban, middle-class life.

Undoubtedly the new journalism played a major part, reinforcing the more gradual influence of the new bestseller, but a corresponding series of social changes, less evident because extending over a longer period, helped at least as much; without them the immediate success of the Northcliffes and Frankaus would have been impossible. The first is, of course, the more or less complete transformation of the upper and middle classes effected by the modern Public School system, which has replaced the famous 'eccentric' Englishman of the Augustan and Georgian ages by the 'simple but virile' type, imposing upon a nation whose governing class has been for several centuries noted as having pronounced (because highly developed) personalities and keen intellectual interests, an ideal whose key words are correctness and sport.[1] This ideal has had the effect of arresting the development of whole generations at adolescence; the first expressions of it in fiction are the novels of Thomas Hughes and the Kingsleys – there is nothing like their writings in the language before them, but a great deal after. Another social change of some cultural importance is that in the status, antecedents, and acquirements of the clergy; it used to be said for the Established Church that at least it put a scholar and a gentleman in every parish, a function which it has for some time ceased to fulfil. A parallel is provided by two other professions formerly open to the serious and disinterested – It is no longer possible for an intelligent man to make politics his career, like Balfour, or to earn by journalism a handsome living while preserving his self-respect, like 'Honest John' Morley. In addition, scientific interests have alienated a large proportion of the more intelligent of the community from culture. Altogether the character of the governing and professional classes has radically altered. The people with power no longer represent intellectual authority and culture.

Authority depends on the recognition of standards other than those of *l'homme moyen sensuel*, and after many centuries of unquestioning assent to authority the natural man has reasserted himself. We thus have a situation closely resembling that of the United States, marking a new phase in our history and one which, as it is likely to continue indefinitely, is perhaps worth dwelling upon. Most noticeable is the extension of business ethics and all that the word 'business' implies to fields of activity which had formerly non-commercial values, for since the business man is the average man, the 'worth while' measure must be applied all round. Journalists, advertising agents, editors of magazines, and popular authors were naturally the first to discover that it is more profitable to make use of man's suggestibility as a herd animal than to approach the reader as if he were what used to be called 'the thinking man'; fear of the herd, approval of the herd, the peace of mind that comes from conforming with the herd, are the strings they play upon and the ideals that inform their work. The practical effects of the triumph of the business ethos are – to the anthropologist, at least – exciting. For example, it has already been mentioned that the Press now depends on the advertiser – 'To-day the newspaper is, in its commercial aspect as a matter of pounds, shillings, and pence, a by-product of Advertising' (Thomas Russell, *Commercial Advertising*, 1919). It is to the interest of the advertiser that the public should be kept from any kind of alarm so that it will spend without hesitation, therefore the contents of newspaper and magazine must create confidence, preserve the *status quo*, reassure and divert attention from political and economic troubles. Hence the insistence . . . on cheerful stories, bright articles, happy endings, and the avoidance of any 'unpleasant' (*i.e.* disquieting) note. Reinforced by the average man's preference for a comfortable outlook, this has brought about a public sentiment overwhelmingly in favour of blind optimism. An inspection of the slogans displayed on Wayside Pulpits[2] (they represent one of the popular substitutes for religion and their success makes them a reliable index) reveals that they are largely devoted to denunciation of an attitude described as pessimistic, or easy assurances of everything turning out well if left alone. This is not without significance. The Wayside Pulpit posters are tags collected from such sources as newspaper headlines and articles, 'songs sung over the Wireless', etc., and they are representative of the mental stock-in-trade of the general public; such tags are expressive of an attitude, it must be noted, which is not based on personal experience. Yet they are what the man in the street now lives and shapes his life by; they rise irresistibly to the lips in an emergency, for instance. Contrast them with the local and national proverbs which till recently (*i.e.* till such standardising forces as the cinema, radio, large-circulation newspapers and magazines destroyed traditional culture and local differences) served as a rule-of-thumb for dealing with the major as well as the minor situations of life. [Plenty of samples may be found in *Adam Bede* and *The Mill on the Floss*, where the speech of the lower-middle classes is largely composed of traditional similes and dicta . . .][3] They are the growth of ages of individual experience (the experience, that is, of the shrewdest and most intelligent of the community) tested by generations of use and pooled to form a stock of social wisdom. And they suggest that the standardising forces just mentioned have destroyed something worth preserving, if only for utilitarian reasons.

The extent to which the attitude approved by the herd is fixed by such agencies for imposing conformity as the Public Schools, advertising and the Press, cannot be overestimated. It is more than difficult, it is next to impossible, for the ordinary uncritical man to resist when, whichever way he looks in the street, from poster and hoarding, and advertising in bus and tramcar, whichever paper or novel he picks up, whatever play or film he attends for amusement, the pressure of the herd is brought to bear on him. Not the least effective, and certainly the most subtle part of the campaign, is the use of the indubitable fact that it is pleasanter to be one of the herd, *i.e.* less wear and tear is involved in conforming than in standing out against mass sentiment; righteousness and goodwill are accordingly arrogated to the man who behaves like his fellows, the lowbrow, who accepts uncritically the restrictions imposed by the herd, while the highbrow,[4] who does not, is vilified as a 'superior' or arrogant person. This has a direct bearing on literature. Skim through the bound volumes of *Punch*, and it becomes evident that from baiting the merely rich, the vulgar, and the stupid, it now reserves its powers, and they are by no means negligible, for attacking nonconformity in manners and originality in ideas and art. There has recently grown up a whole *Punch* literature – *Punch* humour, *Punch* essays, even *Punch* fiction – and all markedly anti-highbrow. This becomes serious when one remembers that whereas a century ago there was a solid body of opinion behind the Reviews, which organised and expressed the attitude of the cultured minority – 'no genteel family *can* pretend to be without it,' Scott wrote of the *Edinburgh Review* – perhaps the only periodical every genteel family can now be counted on to take is *Punch*. Such a *volte-face* has innumerable indirect effects on the life of the nation.

It follows that in such a society the critic's office is not popular, criticism of any kind appearing to be disloyalty to the herd. The more subtle implications of literary criticism are equally distasteful, for since genuine criticism demands from the reader a real effort and continual readjustment, and above all asserts the standards of a severe taste, it is felt to be insulting to the natural man. Thus criticism has been – in general esteem at least –

replaced by belles-lettres (writing about writing); a comparison between the reception accorded to the collection of light essays so popular now (a representative one would include essays on writers with the status of Boswell and Lamb, Masefield, Coventry Patmore, Beddoes, Humbert Wolfe . . .), and of a book attempting a critical appraisal of serious writers or a discussion of fundamental critical problems, will put this point beyond dispute. It is not merely that the former is invariably reviewed too kindly, but that animus is betrayed against the latter . . . Herd values in art (what the natural man likes in books or pictures or tunes is literature or art or music) tend to be supported by denying distinctions. This is a fair example, though more subtle (and insidious) instances are commoner:

> Poor is the man (and the critic, too) whose spirit is so illiberal as to restrain him from being on good terms simultaneously with Job and Jacobs, Boccaccio and Francis of Assisi, Milton and Edgar Wallace, Donne and P. G. Wodehouse. (A. C. Ward, *Twentieth Century Literature*, 1928)[5]

Here one notices the accent of hearty good-fellowship employed to reinforce the suggestion that anyone who denies the P. G. Wodehouses and Edgar Wallaces a place in literature along with Milton and Donne is mean-spirited as well as arrogant. The same accent, the mark of a 'good mixer', is an essential part of the equipment of the writer who supplies periodicals and newspapers with a regular weekly essay. The stock facetiousness about highbrow art, novel and drama, and 'modern' poetry, that *Punch* popularised has now been taken over by weeklies with more serious pretensions. Rather more subtle manifestations of herd animus are to be found scattered throughout low- and middlebrow fiction . . . [Q.D.L. quotes illustrative passages from Hugh Walpole's *Hans Frost* and Warwick Deeping's *Sorrell and Son*.]

The chief difference appears to be that the middlebrow is anxious to get the best of both worlds while the lowbrow is concerned only to speak of the other with sufficient 'knowledgeableness' (as the advertising agents call it) to be able to deny its value. The quality of knowledgeableness is very noticeably present in the writings of three of the most successful and representative modern bestsellers, Kipling, Arnold Bennett, and Gilbert Frankau. Gilbert Frankau's would have to be the name to fill the last place in the list that includes Defoe . . . Richardson . . . Scott, Lytton, Dickens . . . Marie Corelli, Florence Barclay; Arnold Bennett's weekly articles in the *Evening Standard* exhibited in the most concentrated form the spirit of contemporary reviewing; while, as the *Publishers' Circular* says, 'Rudyard Kipling is the only author whose new poems are events to be cabled to every corner of the civilised globe'. It is significant that these three writers share the idiom and ideology of the copywriter, and that all three possess to perfection the 'note of authority and "knowledgeableness"': it is this which principally accounts for their success as purveyors of what the public wants. Gilbert Frankau's novels play upon the same appeals as the modern advertisement – his heroes are to be visualised as the faultlessly groomed strong silent men with the shaving-soap advertisement chins, their eyes are always narrowing to pin- or needle-points, great play is made with the words 'purposeful', 'vision', 'urge', 'personality', the business man self-dramatisation is the unvarying ideal ('calm with that peculiar frozen calmness which serves big men in big issues', 'a mind trained to deal instanter with the minds of its fellow-men'),[6] and so on. These, however, are only surface indications of the trend of this fiction. A suggestion was made [earlier in *Fiction and the Reading Public*] . . . that the twentieth-century bestseller is concerned with supporting herd prejudices, and in fact it will be found that this kind of writing caters for the Babbitt element of society. Marie Corelli, Hall Caine, Florence Barclay, Edna Lyall, start from the assumption that the reader, like the writer, is passionately in favour of the Christian ethic, the accepted social and moral code, family affection, altruism, and self-sacrifice. Their successor pulls another set of strings, the loyalties of the club, the regiment, and the Public School. So the idiom employed by Arnold Bennett and the Book Clubs is not critical, it merely sizes up a work by the business man's criterion – 'a big book', 'value for money', 'a worth-while experience', '*Rogue Herries* is a real full-time man's job in fiction' – the only criterion known to Mr. Frankau whose heroes are always aiming at 'the big things of life – money and power',[7] The body of a magazine is now carefully selected to endorse the 'message' of the advertisements, and it looks as though a general infection has taken place. It would be impossible to find a more complete illustration of what might be called the magazine outlook of modern fiction than Bennett's last novel, *Imperial Palace*. It is full of 'entrancing, perfect,' and 'fabulously expensive' women, millionaires, luxurious living, and bluff man-of-the-world horse-sense masquerading as psychology and insight . . .

Enough attention has perhaps been given to the effects of the overthrow of minority values, but a few stray threads must be drawn in before dismissing the subject. One is the high-level bestseller status achieved by Ernest Hemingway in this country, traceable to the acceptability of the formula in which he so ingeniously works. The glorification of the 'regular man', the figure set up by twentieth-century bestsellers, magazine writers, journalists, and advertisers in opposition to the highbrow, naturally prepared a sympathetic public for the simplification of existence achieved by the hero of *A Farewell to Arms* [1932] and expressed in the crude idiom of the he-man. More surprising is the fact that Hemingway has become something of a cult in highbrow circles, and this suggests how strong is the temptation to adopt an easy (because popular) attitude: in contemporary society man separates himself from the herd at his peril. Then there is the effect on publishing of the triumph of materialistic standards. In *The Commercial Side of Literature* Michael Joseph defends the bestseller on ground that without him the publisher would be unable to print literature:

> One publisher of my acquaintance said to me recently, 'I prefer to publish fiction of quality, what most people call "highbrow" novels, even if the margin of profit is very small, rather than concentrate on slush; but I must admit I couldn't afford the luxury of pleasing myself if it weren't for So-and-so and So-and-so' – and he named two very popular writers in his list – 'who pay my rent and salaries and overhead charges.'

This is well enough as a *faute de mieux* so long as the tradition that connects the publishing profession with literature survives, but there are signs that it is preparing to snap, and when that profession too becomes a trade contemporary literature stands an excellent chance of ceasing to exist for the public at large:

> Moreover, once the standards of publishing success became purely pecuniary ones, the author who merely brought honour or glory to the house would be dropped from the books: when Standard Books, Inc., took over half a dozen firms, they would naturally 'write off' such authors, and take good care that they did not appear again on the lists. I remember the ominous words of a capable advertising executive, one of the best in that unfortunate trade, when I discussed the publishing business with her a few years ago. 'If I consented to handle a publisher's advertising, I would do exactly what I do with other manufacturers. "How many lines do you produce?" Perhaps he will answer, thirty. I would say: "Cut them down to five and advertise them." That's the way to put books across.'

It has already become practically impossible to get a book reviewed unless it is advertised, and highbrow novels, which return little or no profit, cannot stand the enormous cost of advertising. We may well see a return to the primitive circulation of manuscripts among a select company.

A final point must be made to prevent misunderstanding. Throughout [the previous chapter of *Fiction and the Reading Public*] . . . numerous references were made to the formative force of society, while in [this chapter] . . . an apparently identical force described as the herd is alleged to have overthrown the work of the previous ages. 'Society' has to be interpreted in the eighteenth-century sense in which, like 'the world', it meant a select, cultured element of the community that set the standards of behaviour and judgement, in direct opposition to the common people. Thus the highest definition of man was that of a social animal: the gregarious instinct he shares with sheep and wolves. The ameliorating influence of associating with the well-bred and cultivated was universally acknowledged – it accounts for the horror of being confined in the country, away from 'the world', so noticeable in the literature of the Restoration and eighteenth century, until the Romantic poets discovered the superiority of solitary to social man. If one accepts the argument [made by F. R. Leavis in *Mass Civilisation and Minority Culture*] that 'In any period it is upon a very small minority that the discerning appreciation of art and literature depends: it is only a few who are capable of unprompted first-hand judgement . . . The accepted valuations are a kind of paper currency based upon a very small proportion of gold. To the state of such a currency the possibilities of fine living at any time bear a close relation', then it becomes evident that the individual has a better chance of obtaining access to the fullest (because finest) life in a community dominated by 'society' than in one protesting the superiority of the herd.

Notes

1. Q.D.L. provides an elaborate note here, quoting from Fremantle's *England in the Nineteenth Century* (1801–5, pp. 96–8): 'No country in the world had so well informed a middle class. Higher in the scale, the quintessence of intelligence was fully developed . . . ' (p. 313). Her observations on 'correctness and sport' invite connection and comparison with Sylvia Townsend Warner's views on 'Man's Moral Law' (see above, pp. 89–100).
2. About five thousand churches now exhibit Wayside Pulpit posters. *Vide* the *Advertising World*, December 1925, for an article by the Church Publicity Secretary on 'How the Wayside Pulpit Scheme was Organised': 'At the Church Advertising Section of the great World's Advertising Convention at Wembley, I had met leading Americans who ran big Church advertising movements in the States. Their enthusiasm was infectious, and their charts, diagrams and statistics, inspiring,' etc. *Vide* booklets published by the Church Publicity Section of the National Free Church Council, especially 'The Wayside Pulpit at Work', for evidence of the success of 'this result-bringing enterprise'. The same organisation issues a '*Free Churchman* inset' which helps to make 'a bright, homely, and thoroughly alive Church Magazine', for 'however well edited the local pages of a Church Magazine may be, if an inset is commonplace, narrow in outlook and lacking the bright

journalistic touch that the public is accustomed to in modern popular journals, the magazine will fail to "grip"' . . . The activities of the Church Publicity Department form a record of the influence of journalism on the modern Church . . . (pp. 315–16). [QDL]

3. Q.D.L.'s brackets.
4. For other uses of 'highbrow', see F. R. Leavis (p. 21), Day Lewis (p. 284), Auden (p. 39) and Empson (p. 165), in this volume.
5. 'Judex damnatur cum nocens absolvitur' was the motto of the *Edinburgh Review*. [QDL]
6. Quotations from Frankau's *Gerald Cranston's Lady*.
7. Again, a quotation from *Gerald Cranston's Lady*.

21   C. H. Sisson   *Charles Maurras and the Idea of the Patriot King (1937)**

After the abdication of Edward VIII in 1936 it was perhaps inevitable that the role of the monarchy would come to figure prominently in theorizing about Britain's broader cultural and political crisis – especially on the right. In C. H. Sisson, however, we have a highly considered, self-critical and informed apologist for monarchist government; at the time of writing these essays, Sisson was a civil servant with considerable experience in the practice of governing and a background of study in political science.

Lest his advocacy of Maurras as a model – and his denigration of morality and freedom as bases for political organization – prompt us to relegate him too hastily to the far right of the political spectrum, it would be as well to remember that others of his contemporaries went a good deal further. In October 1936, for example, Count Potocki of Montalk – a native of New Zealand claiming right to a Polish title – began publishing, from his London home and 'entirely by . . . [his] hand', *The Right Review*. At the head of the first editorial stood a quotation from 'H.R.H. the Count of Paris, heir to the throne of France': 'Only the King can be at the same time revolutionary and conservative.' 'The principal aims of this review,' wrote Potocki, 'are to voice the opinions and the works of the editor, to carry out a frontal attack against the noisy and misleading propaganda of the communists . . . and to harbour any Poets and other men of real genius whom the Editor can come across.' The full position of the review was stated thus:

> It is our aim to show that the Divine Right of Kings is the sanest and best form of government, being in the last resort the only fount of power and consequently of human life. We intend to prove that such government is ultimately beneficial to the whole human race including the lowest races of mankind. In this way we hope to provide the Right Wing with a living ideology. The reason why the Right Wing is so weak ideologically – which is almost as much as to say spiritually – is because it is such a very Left Wing Right Wing. (No. 1, October 1936, p. 1)

Between the first issue of the review and the second occurred the abdication, and this drew from Potocki a most remarkable specimen of vitriol: the monarchy had been betrayed by 'the governing clique', 'the money bags and their man Baldwin', and especially by 'the Archplotter of Canterbury and his minions': 'How

* Originally published in the *New English Weekly*, 22 July 1937. Reprinted from C. H. Sisson, *The Avoidance of Literature: Collected Essays*, ed. Michael Schmidt (Manchester: Carcanet, 1978), pp. 15–16.

revolting it is to see the English patting themselves on the back for their perfectly incredible lack of loyalty, lack of "guts", and lack even of those merely Public School virtues which forbid a Gentleman to kick a man (even though he be a King) when he is down' (No. 2, February 1937).

Since Potocki's political writings do not rise much above this level, no more of his words need be included here. Sisson's essays, by contrast, represent effectively a more serious, circumspect and considered attempt to clarify problems in British public life – from a personal perspective neither then nor now well-enough known or understood.

We have several political poets and too many publicists, yet scarcely any writer since Hulme has formulated a precise political idea. Inevitably, both poetry and political analyses are the worse for the lack of political doctrine. I believe that Charles Maurras[1] is almost the only writer capable of re-directing our political enquiries. He is not, by Englishmen, to be swallowed whole, but to be used. What is needed is a transposition of his ideas to fit our own place and prejudices. That difficult transposition is not attempted in this essay, which is simple experiment. I have taken a single idea of Maurras (an idea not peculiar to him no doubt) and placed it beside an idea of Bolingbroke;[2] the two are allowed to react in such a way as to expose a common contemporary English error.

Maurras finds in the identification of a king's interest with the public interest a chief guarantee of the efficacy of monarchy. While not without a good word for personal qualities which his taste disposes him to admire, he aims at showing the value of the monarchy independently of the value of the monarch.

Bolingbroke is concerned with a 'rare phenomenon', a patriot king, but there are fortunately passages in his essay which are susceptible of commoner application. He claims at the start that his method is sceptical, yet he is soon engaged in discussing 'duties' in a manner which is not sceptical. His intention, however, is coherent. '"Salus reip. suprema lex esto" is a fundamental law: and sure I am, the safety of a commonwealth is ill provided for, if the liberty be given up.' Liberty is justified because it contributes to the safety of the state. Similarly, we read:

> I speak not here of people, if any such there are, who have been savage or stupid enough to submit to tyranny by original contract; nor of those nations on whom tyranny has stolen as it were imperceptibly, or had been imposed by violence, and settled by prescription. But I speak of people who have

been wise and happy enough to establish, and to preserve, free constitutions
of government, as the people of this island have done. To these, therefore,
I say, that their kings are under the most sacred obligations . . .

The king must be moral because the people has a mind to be free. The
constitution is such, Bolingbroke says elsewhere, that 'no king who is not a
patriot can govern with sufficient strength'. The need for morals arises from
the nature of the constitution. The famous English talent for humbug is not
all stupidity; it corresponds to the facts of our situation.

Maurras, despite his comparative unconcern for rights and wrongs, does
not represent a contrary point of view. The government he wishes to realize
is decentralized; the monarchy is therefore not unlimited. In national affairs,
however, the king exercises a power which he may delegate but which he
shares with no one. The English constitution provides for a division of power
in national as well as local affairs; the business of the king is merely to prevent
the disintegration of the central authority. The difference between the theories
of Bolingbroke and Maurras, therefore, arises out of the difference of function
of the English and French monarchies; it is accidental. In essence, Bolingbroke
and Maurras aim at the same thing – the utilization of the king to secure the
unity and coherence of the nation.

The morals of Bolingbroke are forced into their place in an empirical
system. They are in no sense the starting point of his political theory. In this,
Bolingbroke is at one with Maurras, who, at every point more consistent,
declares himself an atheist.

If we are content to identify, as for this purpose we may, the 'justice' and
'injustice' of the Pinks with the 'absolute standards' of the Oxford Group and
the 'development of consciousness' of the Artists' International Congress,[3] it
will be clear that this relegation of morals, or sentiments, to a position of
dependence in politics, is in conflict with the assumptions of a wide section
of political writers in this country.[4] While Bolingbroke, attempting to justify
the position of the king deductively, was taking notice of the habits of his
countrymen to such an extent that his method was in fact empirical groping,
most contemporary writers, while claiming to adhere more or less to scientific
schools of political thought, deduce their politics from their ethical and
sentimental prejudices. An English interpretation of the ideas of Maurras
would make their fault evident, and might rid us of those humane philosophies
which provoke violence by demanding excessive change.

Prejudice as an Aid to Government *(1938)**

In the fourth and fifth books of *De l'Esprit des Lois*, Montesquieu defines three springs of government and describes the education which favours each. Honour is the spring of monarchical government, fear of despotism and virtue of democracy. The 'principle' of a government is what makes it work. The government does not, however, entirely stand on its own legs; and appropriate education is required for the production of suitable citizens and subjects.

No European state now belongs wholly to one or the other of Montesquieu's three types of government. England, for example, is a democracy pervaded by snobbery which is in part a decadent left-over from a monarchical caste system and by a little tyranny more lately introduced. Democracy is, of Montesquieu's three, apparently the chief ingredient of England as it is of all modern European states. (All are at least governments in which the people appears to have some voice.) We should therefore examine more closely the virtue which makes democracy work.

This virtue is, Montesquieu insists, a 'vertu politique' and has nothing to do with morals. In a later book, he illustrates this by telling us that the avarice of the Chinese is a 'vertu', whereas the honesty of the Spaniard is bad for the prosperity of the state. These examples, however, prove nothing about the nature of 'vertu politique'; they merely show that a moral virtue may cause the state to disintegrate, and a vice may hold it together. 'Vertu politique' is more closely defined in the fourth book, and there it is not successfully distinguished from moral virtue. As one might expect, if many are to govern they must be possessed of honest manners, uprightness and forbearance. Otherwise the government will disintegrate or be transformed either into a monarchy or a despotism by the vice of one man or of a group.

The 'sentiment de l'éducation' which, according to Montesquieu, is appropriate to democracy, is the honesty learned from the manners of one's parents. Englishmen, with their long democratic tradition, should obviously be instinct with this honesty. As everyone knows, however, the young do not imitate their parents; rather, perhaps, the old prefer to be like their children rather than to be models for them; the family, except as a breeding-ground, is disappearing. There are few opportunities of exercising virtue in public life. The citizen drops his paper in the ballot-box with a cross against the name of one of two or three distasteful candidates. This action may help the state to cohere; the mere repetition of it produces a sense of uneasiness; it is not, however, 'virtuous,' or in itself even 'politically virtuous' and it has little to

---

* Originally published in the *New English Weekly*, 7 April 1938. Reprinted from *The Avoidance of Literature*, pp. 17–19.

do with democracy. There is virtue in the air, however, in England, of the sort that the League of Nations was built on. We may examine it more closely.

The first thing to notice is that the citizen does not do anything with it politically. He carries it about with him and he can produce it like a driving licence. It does, however, enable him to react in a certain way, or rather, it is a label which tells one how he will react. If it is useless to him, therefore, it may still be of use to someone else and it is in fact useful to the man who makes him react – the advertiser with something to sell, or the politician. The passive sense of what is right does therefore help to hold the state together. It is, however, a mechanical sentiment and by no means an active quality.

The political thoughts which drift in most minds in England are 'Is it right?' and 'It's not fair'. That these should be the most popular thoughts is due partly to our tradition of democracy and partly to our liking for religion of a certain brand. It is clear, however, that the function in the state of passive virtue is precisely the same as that of the passive sense of national honour which is exploited by the leaders of Germany. Hitler has said that the German soul has two or three strings, and one can count on getting a certain response by plucking them. An English statesman might say the same of the English soul. The notes would be different, that is all.

The modern governor uses in an unprecedented fashion the sentiments of his subjects as an instrument of propaganda. The typical modern state is in fact run by propaganda. Wherever the nominal government is, the power will lie with whoever controls opinion and a government which offends public opinion will go under. Most governments, of course, once established, take care that they shall more than anyone else control opinion.

The sentiments appealed to usually are of some nobility. In England they are moral and sporting canons;[5] everywhere they are meant to dispose people to be disinterested. Hitler has written in *Mein Kampf* an interesting chapter on propaganda. He says: 'All propaganda must appeal to the people and must be put at the intellectual level of the most limited of the minds it is directed to . . . The capacity of the mass of men is very limited, their understanding small, but their forgetfulness great.' The second sentence at once recalls Machiavelli – 'It is to be asserted in general of men, that they are ungrateful, fickle, false, cowards, covetous . . . ' Hitler is speaking of peaceful persuasion; the fact that he is an unpleasant Nazi should not blind us to that. His words might be used by any politician or man with muffins to sell. Machiavelli recommended the utmost violence. If he were our contemporary he would change nothing in his view of man; he would, however, no doubt see that a subject who can be clubbed into obedience by propaganda is not in need of rougher treatment. One may, by friendly words, give a despotically-governed people the illusion that it is free. The nobility of the sentiments the new despot governs by, makes it hard for people to understand his tyranny. Blows have this advantage, that even the stupidest do not think them signs of good intentions.

from **Order and Anarchy (1939)***

Order and Anarchy did not, in Sisson's view 'deserve to be called an enquiry into political principles', but it was 'a demonstration made in favour' of an enquiry into political principles. 'In it,' he wrote, 'certain questions are asked which, if they were truly answered, would make ease of mind more attainable, and all its inhumanity is there. I am aware that there are persons of good sense who believe that one should immerse oneself as fully as possible in the torments of the age, and who will therefore be out of sympathy with the motives of the essay. The motive of the essay is not, however, its subject, and the humane reader will not be shocked by an account of the virtues of the serene life. He may, I hope, be induced to consider by what gentle roads one may come upon fanaticism.' In particular, the essay as a whole 'concerns the state of the free person' (p. 84), and it proceeds through an examination of various topics: 'The Relationships Between Person and State', 'The Mind as a Force in Public Affairs', and 'The Method Appropriate to Intellectual Liberty', for example.

Propaganda

We are little concerned, in this essay, with the effects of physical violence on the free person, but much with the manipulation of sentiments. The latter method of exercising force supplements the method of physical violence and government is complete only when both methods are used. As literacy has spread, the manipulation of sentiments has taken a larger part in government, and it may be said to have replaced some physical violence.

All propaganda has this characteristic, that it tends to make of one opinion those to whom it is directed. The opinion is not necessarily that of the person who is responsible for the propaganda, but it may be assumed to be an opinion which he desires for good reason that people should hold. Propaganda unites the people in such a manner that they are more useful to the propagandist.

---

* Originally published in *Purpose*, September–December 1939. Reprinted from the longer version in *The Avoidance of Literature*, pp. 87–8 ('Propaganda') and 92–3 ('Literature and Intellectual Liberty').

It is only people influenced by propaganda who are united by it, and propaganda diffused by people of opposed interests is likely to form hostile groups. Propaganda in favour of a race and propaganda in favour of a class have the same effect in this: they unite some people only to divide them more sharply from others. It may be said, I think, that *ceteris paribus*, the more propaganda there is in any group the less physical violence there is, but propaganda tends to intensify the feeling of difference of one group from another and therefore causes more hostility and probably more violence between them.

It follows from what has been said of the unifying effect of propaganda that liberal propaganda, which none the less claims to exist, is a contradiction in terms. The propaganda invites one to abandon one's individuality, and propaganda pretending to be in favour of individualism really serves some other cause. It forms a compact mass of minds which tends, when it moves, to move as a whole. Even if the propaganda which united the mass was not consciously directed, its effect is to form a mass which may with ease be directed. The mass may, moreover, be directed by persons whose sympathies are not at all with those (supposing, what is not difficult, a case in which they exist) who originated the propaganda because they believed in it. The great efficacy of liberal and individualist propaganda lies in the fact that it denies it is propaganda. The innocent individualist, by helping a work of propaganda, produces a work which is the opposite of this intentions. With great enthusiasm and good will he plays into the enemy's hands.

The battle of the individualist in politics must in the nature of the case always be lost, and in the nature of our case the battle must today be more than ever completely lost. That may of course not be a reason for declining to fight it, but the matter of this section should provide reasons for not fighting it with the enemy's weapons.

Literature and Intellectual Liberty

It is not my intention to attempt, in a section of a brief essay, to propound a new theory of art, nor have I one to propound. But because any conception of intellectual liberty which is of any interest must allow for the free production of works of literature, and because I was stimulated to write this essay partly by a feeling of dissatisfaction with the verse of certain of my immediate seniors, it may be well to make a few observations on the relations of literature and government. I should perhaps add that these remarks are not made in the belief that political criticism can replace literary criticism, but in the belief that the two are complementary. The uneasiness one feels in reading faulty political verse is due to literary faults, but political criticism may be able to account, in part, for the manner in which the faults arise. And this may be of use to the common cause which literary and political criticism serve.

The political critic would have nothing to say about the verse of Mr. Herbert Read (although he would no doubt have something to say about Mr. Read's recent theorizings).[6] The faults of the verse, which give most of it, interesting though it is, too low a degree of tension for poetry and make it fall without impact on the mind, are faults which can be explained satisfactorily without going beyond the limits of literary criticism. Mr. Auden's work is different: its method, no less than its subject matter, invited one to examine its author's political position.

The position of Mr. Auden is well known. Expensively taught, and then an expensive teacher. He professes socialism. I am not sure that a purely proletarian communist movement could exist, and I am aware that there are theories which justify the position of the bourgeois instigator of revolution, but I do not understand the virtue of a socialism whose vital parts are bourgeois. It looks extremely like the usual politician's game of liberating the people for the politician's advantage.

In this essay it is not the virtues and vices of Mr. Auden's socialism as such which concern us, but the effect which the contradictory position he stands in has on his writing. Because he is a communist,[7] Mr. Auden must appear to oppose the bourgeoisie, and because he is a bourgeois he cannot do so by having the sentiments of a proletarian. Every writer in a manner opposes his class when he sets his original perceptions beside the popular and sentimental productions which embody the prejudices of his class. This opposition would not, however, suffice for Mr. Auden and his friends, because it would not be a political opposition. For a political opposition it is necessary to pit one body of prejudices against another, and because the prejudices of the working class are not his to use, Mr. Auden had to make an artificial opposition. This is the function of the group of friends whose names appear often on the poems and dedications. They form a band which fights a harmless and often imaginary battle against our rulers. The prejudices of the group are a variety of the prejudices of the bourgeois proper, and they are in fact part of the sentimental means by which we are governed. It will scarcely be denied that Mr. Auden's best work is that in which these prejudices have least part, and in which he merely records his perceptions. The bad part of his work is the sentimental and political part.

This distinction between public sentiments and private perceptions appears to me to be fundamentally the same as the distinction between good writing and bad. If this in fact is so, it may be said that bad writing is writing which expresses the politically manoeuvrable sentiments and is therefore part of the system of force which is government. Good writing alone may be described as independent of government, and one has intellectual liberty just so far as one has the capacity to distinguish between valid work and invalid.

Notes

1. Maurras was leader of the Action Française movement, founded in 1899. In 1937 he published *Mes idées politiques*, summarizing the position he had been developing since *L'Enquête sur la monarchie* (1900). During 1940–44 he served in effect as theorist to the Vichy regime, receiving a life sentence for collaboration at the end of hostilities. See Lewis on Maurras, pp. 201–2.
2. Henry St John, 1st Viscount Bolingbroke (1678–1751), published *The Idea of a Patriot King* in 1739. Bolingbroke's political theory focused on the theme of corruption, defined by him as the absence of civic virtue. See I. Kramnick, 'Bolingbroke', in Miller *et al.*, pp. 44–5.
3. Presumably, the Artists' International Association, founded in 1933, with a consciously Marxist agenda. The Association's definition of aims appeared in *International Literature* in April 1934; an exhibition on 'The Social Theme' – featuring, among other figures, Eric Gill – was mounted in 1934. See Harrison, pp. 251–2, and Morris and Radford, *The Story of the AIA, passim.*
4. Cf. Mitchison on the moral basis of politics below, pp. 235–9. See also Riding's demurrer at Mitchison's view of morals below, pp. 245–6.
5. Cf. Warner above, pp. 92–5.
6. Read's *Art and Society* appeared in 1937.
7. In fact, Auden was by this time no longer linked to the party. In his biography of the poet, Carpenter says that it was during the latter part of 1932 that Auden 'seriously contemplated becoming a Communist – or even believed that he already was one' (p. 152). That autumn, however, he wrote to Rupert Doone: 'No. I am a bourgeois. I shall not join the C.P.' (Carpenter, p. 153). By 1939 Auden judged his earlier interest in Communism quite harshly.

22 Evelyn Waugh *from **Robbery under Law:***
The Mexican Object-Lesson (1939)*

In early 1938 the wealthy Pearson family, which had lost a considerable sum of money through the Mexican Government's recent nationalization of foreign oil companies, offered to pay Waugh's way to Mexico if he would undertake to write a book exposing the injustice of that appropriation. Carpenter (1989) notes that Waugh accepted a large cash payment for the project, plus an expense account of £800, yet nowhere in *Robbery under Law* does he mention this backing by the Pearsons (p. 323). 'This is a political book,' he declares in the very first sentence of his introduction, and a little later: 'its aim, roughly, is to examine a single problem; why it is that last summer a small and almost friendless republic jubilantly recalled its Minister from London,¹ and, more important, why people in England thought about this event as they did; why, for instance, patriotic feeling burst into indignation whenever a freight ship – British only in name, trading in defiance of official advice – was sunk in Spanish waters, and remained indifferent when a rich and essential British industry was openly stolen in time of peace.² If one could understand that problem one would come very near to understanding all the problems that vex us today, for it has at its origin the universal, deliberately fostered anarchy of public relations and private opinions that is rapidly making the world uninhabitable.' The substance of the book, he summarized, was 'notes on anarchy' (p. 3). Two extracts are included here: Waugh's political creed as stated at the end of his introduction, and his postscript in which 'The Object' and 'The Lesson' for European culture are pointed.

I was a Conservative when I went to Mexico and . . . everything I saw there strengthened my opinions. I believe that man is, by nature, an exile and will never be self-sufficient or complete on this earth; that his chances of happiness and virtue, here, remain more or less constant through the centuries and, generally speaking, are not much affected by the political and economic conditions in which he lives; that the balance of good and ill tends to revert to a norm; that sudden changes of physical condition are usually ill, and are advocated by the wrong people for the wrong reasons; that the intellectual communists of today have personal, irrelevant grounds for their antagonism to society, which they are trying to exploit. I believe in government; that men cannot live together without rules but that these should be kept at the bare minimum of safety; that there is no form of government ordained from

* Reprinted from *Robbery under Law: The Mexican Object-Lesson* (London: Chapman and Hall, 1939), pp. 16–18 and 273–9.

God as being better than any other; that the anarchic elements in society are so strong that it is a whole-time task to keep the peace. I believe that inequalities of wealth and position are inevitable and that it is therefore meaningless to discuss the advantages of their elimination; that men naturally arrange themselves in a system of classes; that such a system is necessary for any form of co-operative work, more particularly the work of keeping a nation together. I believe in nationality; not in terms of race or of divine commissions for world conquest, but simply this: mankind inevitably organises itself into communities according to its geographical distribution; these communities by sharing a common history develop common char-acteristics and inspire a local loyalty; the individual family develops most happily and fully when it accepts these natural limits. I do not think that British prosperity must necessarily be inimical to anyone else, but if, on occasions, it is, I want Britain to prosper and not her rivals. I believe that war and conquest are inevitable; that is how history has been made and that is how it will develop. I believe that Art is a natural function of man; it so happens that most of the greatest art has appeared under systems of political tyranny, but I do not think it has a connection with any particular system, least of all with representative government, as nowadays in England, America and France it seems popular to believe; artists have always spent some of their spare time in flattering the governments under whom they live, so it is natural that, at the moment, English, American and French artists should be volubly democratic.

Having read this brief summary of the political opinions I took with me to Mexico, the reader who finds it unsympathetic may send the book back to her library and apply for something more soothing. Heaven knows, she will find plenty there.

* * * * * *

We are justly suspicious of people who see the world in terms of a single problem in which they have a personal interest and specialised knowledge. We saw too many of them in the post-Versailles period, people who espoused the cause of neglected minorities or became obsessed by cartographical slips. Their foibles seemed innocent enough, but the result of them has been a series of incongruous alliances which has aggravated every political situation. Thus Catholic anti-semites in France have found themselves defying the Pope and pleading the cause of semitic Arabs against Christian rule, liberal Parlia-mentarians found themselves identifying the autocratic–imperialist rule of the Amharas with the cause of Democracy, champions of Basque nationalism were allied with international communism. Such are the confusions that arise through a piecemeal view of politics. At the beginning of this book I suggested that the present condition of Mexico had a world-wide significance. In subsequent chapters I have tried to sketch the conditions. So what? Why should any ordinary American, still less a European, be interested?

First there is Mexico's geographical position, lying across the continent of North America separating the United States from the Panama Canal and sharing with her an immense, arbitrarily defined frontier which has been the scene, on both sides of it, of a long succession of bloody outrages. Internal disorder in Mexico has always constituted, and will always constitute, a lively physical danger to the United States citizens living near the border. Hundreds of men are still living who followed Villa in his raids into the United States.

Secondly there is her financial position. She bears debts of the New and Old world which she will never be able to pay. She is feverishly augmenting them by confiscations. She has great mineral wealth, notably in petroleum, for which the world has a use and which it *will* use one way or another.

Thirdly there is her political condition. For a generation there has been anarchy which has made it clear to herself and to outside observers that she has not the aptitude for the particular kind of individualist representative government which, it was assumed, would afford an eventual solution to her troubles. To President Wilson her only problem was to elect good men; at this time there seemed only two kinds of government, one of which was discredited in 1918; there was democracy, as it was understood in France, England and the United States – government by rich men competing against one another for popular favour – and hereditary monarchy. Since then two forms of proletarian rule have appeared, Nazism and Communism. Mexico is at present enjoying an uneasy compromise between the two. Her adoption of either, or the outbreak of a civil war between them, would be an acute embarrassment to the United States.

Nor does the danger remain local. The Monroe doctrine[3] is being challenged by Germany all over South America. Its peaceful acceptance in the first place by Europe was due to two main considerations. Communications across the Atlantic made a campaign there intolerably expensive and precarious, and, at the end of the last century, Europe was too busy parcelling up Africa to think about South and Central America. Since then an American army has fought in France. South America has become accessible as a battle-ground while at every point the German–Japanese alliance threatens vital American interests. An anti-Cáardenas coup, which his policy increasingly provokes, might well result in Mexico joining the anti-Comintern pact. She is exactly the kind of country where Nazi methods of government and industrial organisation might be expected to bring substantial results. Germany and Japan know this; so do the United States; so do a few Mexicans.

It is in small countries, not in large ones, that world wars start; particularly in heterogeneous states like Mexico.

But, the reader may object, when there are so many causes for alarm, everywhere, what is the good of multiplying them with purely hypothetical dangers? Because the ordinary news services of paper and wireless bulletins have not the time to keep the public informed of anything beyond day to day news. When a crisis is announced we hastily turn to our atlases and look out the new danger spot. We feel that these sudden explosions of international enmity, first in one part of the world, then another, are as wantonly strewn about the map as the bombs of the I.R.A. We have not the time to watch them as historical events in a series of cause and effect. If we have not heard of the problem before, we see it as unimportant; the result of some purely irresponsible and malicious agency. The truth is that, at this moment, when the papers are full of other things, Mexico is as dangerous to us as any part of the world.

And secondly, there is the simple cautionary tale of the origin and consequences of Mexico's decadence. Every state has something to learn from that. We were most of us brought up on the historical theory of recurrent waves of civilisation which lasted a few centuries, built massive cities and tombs and were literally buried in the sands; an ebbing and flowing tide, city-desert, city-desert, [*sic*] to which, presumably, our own culture would one day be subject, but at a date so distant that it need no more be considered in practical calculation than the Last Judgement. We were educated in the assumption that things would not only remain satisfactory without our effort but would with the very minimum of exertion on our part become unrecognisably better. The elimination of physical pain and privation was assumed not only by buoyant characters like Mr. H. G. Wells but by Mr. Aldous Huxley, who limited his apprehensions to pointing out that a life without pain and privation might be compensatingly dreary. Even at the time of writing when tempers are gloomier, the air is one of nervous vexation that progress should be checked by malicious intervention; progress is still regarded as normal, decay as abnormal. The history of Mexico runs clean against these assumptions. We see in it the story of a people whom no great external disaster has overwhelmed. Things have gone wrong with them, as they went right with us, as though by a natural process. There is no distress of theirs to which we might not be equally subject.

Some try to comfort themselves by supposing that the difference of races put Mexico at an initial disadvantage, but, in fact, it is difficult to find any stage at which this was decisive. The white Spaniards interbred freely with the Indians and the prestige and advantages attaching to white blood were little, if at all, more than those attaching to noble and gentle blood in contemporary Europe. As purely heraldic standards of eminence began to decline in Europe, so did those of racial purity in Spanish America. For the last hundred years Mexican leaders of all opinions have been white, Indian and mixed without distinction. Americans and British who see the colour question as vital to Mexico are arguing in terms of their own country and colonies.

Nor has there been any lack of what are generally spoken of as 'enlightened ideas'. Almost every unhappy figure, from Iturbide[4] to Cárdenas, who has appeared as a leader of the country, has spoken in the phrases of contemporary advanced thought. The country has known, in form at least, Napoleonic–masonic monarchy, liberal–representative democracy, German-enlightened–constitutional monarchy, international–individualist–capitalism, socialism, dictatorship of the proletariat, and, it seems probable, will shortly develop a species of Hitlerism. There is no question of Mexico decaying, as have other civilisations, by reason of a rigid system that has proved itself inadequate to changing needs. Every marked step in her decline, in fact, has corresponded with an experiment towards 'the Left'.

The reasons for her decline have been primarily moral; the majority of her rulers have not been men of goodwill and their aims have been purely material; if one starts by assuming that the only real good of which man is capable is the enjoyment of consumable goods – and that has been the assumption of the 'Left' for a hundred years – it is a very easy step – logically an inevitable step – to accumulate the goods exclusively for oneself. Altruism does not flourish long without religion. The rulers of Mexico have almost all started by denying the primary hypothesis of just government.

Secondly, in the political sphere, there has been no true conservatism in Mexico. There have been rival politicians appealing to the interests of rival groups.

A conservative is not merely an obstructionist who wishes to resist the introduction of novelties; nor is he, as was assumed by most nineteenth century parliamentarians, a brake to frivolous experiment. He has positive work to do, whose value is particularly emphasised by the plight of Mexico.

Civilisation has no force of its own beyond what is given it from within. It is under constant assault and it takes most of the energies of civilised man to keep going at all. There are criminal ideas and a criminal class in every nation and the first action of every revolution, figuratively and literally, is to open the prisons. Barbarism is never finally defeated; given propitious circumstances, men and women who seem quite orderly, will commit every conceivable atrocity. The danger does not come merely from habitual hooligans; we are all potential recruits for anarchy. Unremitting effort is needed to keep men living together in peace; there is only a margin of energy left over for experiment however beneficent. Once the prisons of the mind have been opened, the orgy is on. There is no more agreeable position than that of dissident within a stable society. Theirs are all the solid advantages of other people's creation and preservation, and all the fun of detecting hypocrisies and inconsistencies. There are times when dissidents are not only enviable but valuable. The work of preserving society is sometimes onerous, sometimes almost effortless. The more elaborate the society, the more vulnerable it is to attack, and the more complete its collapse in case of defeat. At a time like the present it is notably precarious. If it falls we shall see not merely the dissolution of a few joint-stock corporations, but of the spiritual and material achievements of our history. There is nothing, except ourselves, to stop our own countries becoming like Mexico. That is the moral, for us, of her decay.

Notes

1. In 1938, the increasingly severe economic–nationalist legislation of the Mexican National Revolutionary Government under General Lázaro Cárdenas gave rise to a crisis involving foreign (especially British and American) oil companies. A sweeping Appropriation Law of 1936 had empowered the Government to seize property not only for public necessity but also for 'public and social welfare'. When foreign companies refused to comply with a court order increasing the wages and benefits of their workers, Cárdenas on 18 March seized the property of the seventeen companies involved. After heated communication between the two powers, Mexico broke off relations with Britain.
2. Here Waugh contrasts public indifference to the 'theft' (i.e. nationalization) of British oil interests in Mexico with the outrage expressed when British freighters – carrying supplies to Republican Spain in defiance of government policy – were sunk off the Spanish coast. The comparison, presumably, demonstrates for Waugh (a) the illogical consequences of embracing a Leftist perspective, and (b) the broad (essentially unthinking) acceptance of that perspective in the population at large. Wyndham Lewis looked at the latter phenomenon, and with a similar incredulity, in his *Left Wings over Europe*.

3. 'The Monroe Doctrine': the policy, declared by United States President James Monroe on 2 December 1823, that regarded the Old and New Worlds as fundamentally distinct political spheres, and pledged the United States never to interfere either in a European war or in the internal affairs of a European nation.
4. Agustín de Iturbide, Mexican revolutionist and Emperor of Mexico, 1822–3. He was executed by firing squad in 1824.

23 Wyndham Lewis *from **Detachment and the Fictionist** (1934)**

This piece dates from the end of the year in which Lewis published *Men Without Art*, 'his most original and incisive critical work', according to Jeffrey Meyers (p. 224). Lewis's critique of T. S. Eliot in that book (in particular of Eliot's advocacy of 'a maximum of *depersonalization*' [p. 72]), is continued here, as to a lesser extent is his consideration of 'Mr. I. A. Richards's theory of *pseudo-statement* or *pseudo-belief*.'[1] SueEllen Campbell notes that for Lewis 'Eliot's kind of impartiality is both impossible and undesirable. As the exaggeration that characterizes the enemy [persona he adopted][2] illustrates, for Lewis all principles began from personality' (p. 53). As he was to remark years later, 'the whole virtue of accurate observation is that it is a *person* observing',[3] from which Campbell infers that for Lewis 'intelligent and ethical criticism actually *depends* on our partiality' (p. 54). In the essay which follows he develops the rather paradoxical argument that the more personal is a writer, the more 'detached'. Though strange, such ideas were by no means exclusive to the political right; a version of the same thing is to be found in many avowed Marxist writers, in whom passionate commitment to the cause is invariably read as a link to what is objectively 'true'.

That the handling of the material of art or of science – of *fact*, in other words – does 'detach' a man from his personality (composed as the latter is of race, class, period and the rest) is obvious; and the more he abandons himself to this objective material the better the artist, or man of science, he is, that goes without saying. Bias is *not*, clearly, the ideal. But it is after all something to do with the business; for a god would not be particularly interested in 'discovery' at all; there would be nothing to discover; there would be no incentive to all this mechanical application; if you were not mortal, if you were not in the dark, you would not be so spurred. As a *game* it must be regarded, no more, all that we do – a rather maniacal one, passionately engaged in; not a game, or a *sport*, in the traditional English sense at all.[4] The Japanese artist who described himself as an old man mad about drawing, was making use of the *mot juste* all right when he said *mad*. We are, in fact, like the schoolchild of Newton, picking up pebbles upon the boundless ocean of Truth, or however it was he put it.

So in dramatic writing, and a great deal of fiction is that, sides have to be taken; but do not be ashamed of that. Whichever cause you adopt – the red

* Reprinted from *English Review* 59 (November 1934): 570–3.

cause of Moscow and materialism, or the Fascist cause of nationalist idealism, or whatever other cause it may be – it is a game purely and simply (nothing that would be recognized as 'a game' certainly by the cricketer or fox-hunter, but yet not anything able to change reality by a pin's point – something very contingent, indeed, even at its utmost expansion). The only important thing is to be on the side to which you belong, if you understand me. There is no right side or wrong side. That is nonsense. *Sub specie aeternitatis* both sides are equally right. But what *is* unalterable is that there is a right and a wrong side *for you*. There is such a thing as being offside! (to make use of a term from the playing-field for things that the sportsman would regard as in a different category altogether to sport—for things that unquestionably are *not* cricket).

But as a fiction writer, and in handling the contemporary scene, and dramatizing it in your novels, you cannot afford to treat contemporary society as though it were *dead* – as you would waves, rocks and clouds. Essentially, of course, it is that; but not *for you*. In order to get the maximum of drama out of it you must 'in the destructive element immerse', allow it to bring into play your personality – you must encourage it to force that into its proper camp (however much your personality may vociferate, as it is forcibly conducted thither, that it is as *impersonal* as possible, and a good deal more)! You must separate yourself from all the people who would force you into the camp to which you do *not* belong – as a matter of social discipline. You must not be afraid to say, 'In this, I am a partisan!' It would be very silly and girlish of you to object to that.

Further, you will find that the more you use your personality in this deliberate fashion, the less notice you will take of it – the less it will interfere with you. It is the people who try to disguise their personalities (like a certain well-known poet, I need not name him here), with whom the personality becomes a morbid parasite of great power, a skeleton in the cupboard and, in short, an old man of the sea – like petticoat government by a technically inferior better-half! There is really absolutely nothing to fear on that score. Do not be intimidated, whatever you do, into never uttering a Yes or a No by the propaganda of the *nuance* – the prevarication – the half-light – the *pseudo*-statement and the *pseudo*-truth – those barren lands of fashionable literary criticism.

Enter into the spirit of the game – such, under correction, is what I recommend; enter fully into the spirit of the side-taking and it will become *a game* for you (in the sense indicated above) – a game in which there is only one rule: namely, that you *must* place yourself on the side to which you belong – and *not* romantically masquerade as a black if you are white (as

D. H. Lawrence did). You will find you will achieve more true 'detachment' that way than by playing at Mr. Fair-Play, and doing as much harm as you can to the people to whom you do belong – as the Anglo-Saxon has been doing for so long, in his cold frenzies at suicidal liberalism, and burning sympathy for every race except his own.

If it is, as has been said, the sign that you are by nature a philosopher, if you are inclined to doubt the reality of the world, it is equally the sign that you are an artist if you recognize that the struggles you engage in are a game, in which *vous jouez votre personalité*. You play at being yourself – and so you *are* yourself; it is quite unnecessary to play at being anybody else to be completely the artist. If you cannot be 'detached' with *yourself*, there is nothing you can be detached with! And if you are so endowed as to wish to turn from the human scene to the less subjective material of nature, you will not find that playing Number One, of the First Person Singular, has cramped your style in a mode where that character is not wanted.

from *The Hitler Cult* (1939)*

Lewis's *Hitler* was published in 1931.[5] Setting out 'the oneness of "Hitlerism" and of Hitler', the book presented both the movement and the man as essentially peaceful. Even on the 'vexed question of the "antisemitic" policy of his party' Lewis was sanguine: 'I believe Hitler himself – once he had obtained power – would show increasing moderation and tolerance' (p. 48). His view of Hitler as a man of peace was based upon a distinction he perceived between nationalism of the German sort and other forms of European nationalism. In a passage which invites comparison with C. H. Sisson's piece on 'Charles Maurras and the Idea of the Patriot King' (see above, pp. 183–5), he writes that

> the militancy of the Hitlerist will be misunderstood if it is identified in any way with that of the Action Francaise.[6] Self-conscious Gallic nationalism today is a very frail thing indeed. A handful of Catholic royalists – that is the Action Francaise movement. It is true that recently it has shown a tendency to grow in sympathy with Hitlerism. But it is still a Paris political fad, rather than a National Movement.
>
> The nationalism of Adolf Hitler is, it must always be remembered, national-*socialism*. It is the militancy of an armed peasant, not the

* Reprinted from *The Hitler Cult* (1939; New York: Gordon Press, 1972), pp. 37–41 and 47–53.

> aristocratic militancy of a dispossessed aristocratic class; or that of a
> royalist intellectual, of aristocratic disposition, like Charles Maurras. (p. 45)

Maurras and Leon Daudet he accused of 'dogmatic anti-Germanism' in the post-1918 period, and similarly argued that 'Monsieur Coty, the founder of *L'Ami du Peuple*' suffered from an automatic phobia against the traditional enemy across the Rhine'. Such national phobias, he argued, would lead eventually to the 'Balkanization' of Europe. Hitler in his view was '*not* a "Nationalist" of the "Balkanizing" order' (p. 46), and for that reason Lewis was interested in the Nazi movement.

In October 1937 Lewis travelled with his wife to Berlin 'to find out', as she wrote, 'how things were under Hitler. And the result was *The Hitler Cult* and *The Jews, Are They Human?*' (quoted in Meyers, p. 242). Lewis's views underwent a dramatic transformation.[8] In *The Hitler Cult* the *Führer* has become a 'Jingo God' and Hitlerism 'a jingo creed' (p. ix). Although Lewis declared in his foreword that 'it was not on account of Herr Hitler's beautiful eyes, or of the cute little face of Dr Goebbels, that I adopted "neutrality",' his abandonment of the latter in 1937–9 nevertheless manifested itself in a remarkable critique of Hitler's physical appearance. I have chosen to include this discussion because it shows Lewis engaging in an analysis of cultural codes not unlike the sort of thing we see in Holtby's essay on *Cavalcade* (see below, pp. 337–41), and Mass-Observation's account of the Lambeth Walk (see below, pp. 289–300). Here, and in 'Hitler as a Fairy-Tale', Lewis grasps the extent to which 'Adolf Hitler' was less a person – as Lewis had insisted in the 1931 study – than a construction of culture and ideology. This was a point elaborated with great brilliance in Katherine Burdekin's too-little-known novel appearing in the very year of Lewis's disillusionment, *Swastika Night*.[9]

Herr Hitler's Personal Appearance

The *Führer* must be taken to pieces. This engine for producing mass-emotion is very interesting indeed. And in nothing is it so interesting as in what it offers *the eye*. For this is, after all, a talking-box to be *seen* as well as to be *heard*. The cut of a soap-boxer's coat, or the colour of his hair, is as important as the timbre of his voice.

There are warlike persons who, perhaps with the intuition of the quarrelsome in recognising another of their kind, spotted Hitler at once as a potential Tamerlane.[10] There are some people, too, who go about looking for

Tamerlanes. But heavens! what a flair a man must have to detect Tamerlane beneath that platitudinous exterior – that plebeian protégé of the Junker Papen, with the humble cut of whose German sports-jacket, and with whose disarming toothbrush moustache, we are all now so familiar. Still, I confess that in one respect I was badly taken in, in 1930. What more than anything else caused my judgement to trip was that unusual trinity of celibacy, teetotalism, and anti-nicotine.

I was cowed at the thought of such superiority to alcohol, such a contempt for tobacco, such sublime indifference to the sex-urge. Yet that there was something sinister about this pointed abstinence was elementary. I should at once have been on my guard at the spectacle of more than two major inhumanities.

As it was, I allowed my suspicions to be lulled. This could not be a dangerous man – he was a crude puppet; and when he had served his turn he would be knocked on the head and popped back into his box, by his tough and wily junker masters – as came very near to happening in June 1934.[11]

I gazed at Herr Hitler with complete equanimity. No one had anything to fear from so commonplace an agitator: who would probably do his stuff; clean up a social mess beyond the Rhine; put the French jingoes and armament crooks in their places, and save Europe from war – *not* bring back that boring phantom, which is what has happened.

The argument from his abstinence was unsound. But what two things are more inseparable than alcohol and war? My experience as a soldier had established that fact firmly in my mind. And then there was no *meat* either. Somehow milk and watercress do not seem to rhyme with blood and iron.

Every fool knows, however, that the non-smoker and non-drinker is the most dangerous of all amorists. Here was a man who was a strict abstainer from *women* too. It was really a clear case of something very unpleasant indeed. But there was that little anchoritic shack in the Bavarian Alps. I pictured this harmless little patriot sitting in his log-cabin and concocting his simple-hearted speeches. And then one day I saw a photograph of a gigantic spa. Containing (so I read with dismay) forty bedrooms: a vegetarian spa, it is true, but a different place from the humble shack of Nazi propaganda.

Last of all, I heard of the traffic in interviews: that an interview with Herr Hitler costs three thousand pounds for five minutes. Herr Hitler had become an industry. And as to the Nazi bonze, strutting about in the neighbourhood of the shrine, he is not an attractive type.

When three years ago I informed an English admirer of Herr Hitler that I was going to Germany he wrote me to say that it had been arranged that I should see the *Führer*. That, however, I had no desire to do, and I told him so. I passed through Germany *en touriste*, as I have always done, except for a few contacts with literary people and casually met officials. I have never seen Herr Hitler except in the distance, but the masses of photographs that accompany the propagation of this cult inform one, with a thoroughness that leaves nothing to the imagination, as to his personal appearance. He has been taken from every conceivable angle, and dished up in every possible mood, from playful buffoonery to savage admonition. And a more prosaic person it would be difficult to find.

Of all the accounts I have read of Hitler I consider that a woman's is the most useful. It is to be found in my friend Martha Dodd's book . . . She knows Nazi Germany 'like her pocket', and has an excellent eye in her head. The following is her description of the *Führer*:

> We went to the Kaiserhof, and met the young Polish singer, Jan Kiepura . . . Hitler came in with several men . . . He sat unostentatiously at the table next to us . . . Putzi [Hanfstängl] left me for a moment, leaned over the Leader's ear, and returned in a great state of nervous agitation. He had consented to be introduced to me. I went over and remained standing as he stood up and took my hand. He kissed it very politely, and murmured a few words . . . I went back to the adjoining table with Putzi and stayed for some time . . . receiving curious, embarrassed stares from time to time from the Leader.
>
> This first glance left me with a picture of a weak, soft face, with pouches under the eyes, full lips, and very little bony facial structure. The moustache didn't seem as ridiculous as it appeared in pictures . . . As has often been said, Hitler's eyes were startling and unforgettable – they seemed pale blue in colour, were intense, unwavering, hypnotic. Certainly his eyes were his only distinctive feature . . . This particular afternoon he was excessively gentle and modest in his manner. Unobtrusive, communicative, informal, he had a certain quiet charm, almost a tenderness of speech and glance. He talked soberly to Kiepura, and seemed very interested and absorbed in meeting both of us. The curious embarrassment he showed in meeting me, his somewhat apologetic, nervous manner, my father tells me – and other diplomats as well – are always present when he meets the diplomatic corps *en masse*. This self-consciousness has created in him a shyness and distaste for meeting people above him in station or wealth. As time went on, Hitler's face and bearing changed noticeably – he began to look and walk more and more like Mussolini. But this peculiar shy strain of character has to this day remained.[12]

Not very like Tamerlane, is it? There may really be some excuse for not detecting at once the calamitous vanity and thirst for power concealed beneath so much modesty and mildness – such exemplary commonplace. I was not the only person who was deceived. The Junkers who put Hitler where he is obviously held much the same view that I did of this deceptive person. Today I have a higher, and not a lower, opinion of Herr Hitler than formerly, though I regret that in my rather contemptuous tolerance of him I overlooked the danger latent in so much harmlessness.

Hitler is not in the same category, of course, as the cured and beautifully dressed Borgian dandies of the Renaissance, about whom Machiavelli instructs us. But he has a feminine strain. He has the 'shyness' and the 'gentleness' (cf. Miss Dodd's account above), if he has not the Borgian sleekness and seductive grace.

> The young Baglionis, Vitellis, and Orsinis grouped round Signorellis preaching Antichrist at Orvieto are the veriest assemblage of harmless dandies, pretty and insipid; he can scarcely believe that these mild and beardless striplings, like girls of sixteen, are the terrible Umbrian brigands, *condottieri* – Gianpaolos Simonettis, Vitallezzis and Astorres.

I quote from *Euphorion*.[13]

Hitler, when he became *Reichskanzler*, was a stocky, middle-aged ex-soldier, uncouthly South German, and so it might seem far-fetched to compare him with 'colourful' robber-princes of Machiavelli's Italy. Yet these mild externals, in the case of Herr Hitler, are the stumbling-block, just as they were for the lady quoted in the last paragraph. Such 'harmless dandies' ferocious political bravoes! Impossible!

But Adolf was far more deceptive even than that. Great elegance is always vaguely suspect in the Anglo-Saxon eye. Whereas the homeliness which the personality of Herr Hitler exudes is a very different matter. Why, in his way, Hitler is as disarming as Mr. Chamberlain.

In this age of 'Unknown Soldiers', or of 'cosy', commonplace, Mr. Everyman-statesmen, it is with the Stanley Baldwins we should be on our guard, rather than with the 'brilliant' and spectacular Churchills. The latter are innocuous in comparison. Most of the really gigantic harm (of the Ottawa Agreement[14] type) is done by the quiet and disarmingly 'stupid' person. And it is done quietly at a conference to which the public pays no attention at all. With these dangerous (given-the-opportunity-catastrophic) nobodies Herr Hitler is to be classed. A 'peculiar shy strain' is still his stock-in-trade – even in these days of unchallengeable power, when he has become afflicted with a 'fatal Napoleonic strut'.

All the same, and making full allowance for the snags to be met with in these dangerous shallows of democratic technique – where the insipidity of the protective colouring becomes more and more pathetic – I do not believe . . . that Herr Hitler will be such a handful as Napoleon. I still cannot think of Herr Hitler as anything more than two-dimensional. This is not an *iron* Chancellor. He *is* a softer variety of Chancellor to that. I no longer regard him as papier mâché, that is all . . .

Hitler as a Fairy-Tale

Hitler is not quite real, that is probably the main thing to be remembered about him. This brown-coated man, Herr Adolf Hitler, is a fairy-tale. This is not a real man that we read about in the newspapers, or in *The House that Hitler Built.*[15] Even his name is like a name on a nursery rhyme – *Hitler*; it is somehow painted and wooden. His power belongs to the realm of folk-lore and fable. Embalmed in the breast of the peasant are the beliefs of the poets and saints. Hitler is a peasant. He is a peasant with a 'soul'; the embodiment of 'Ye Olde Germanie', as archaic as a Christmas card – as one of those Christmas cards that he once made a living by painting.

If you sit in the beer-cellar of the *Rathaus* in a German town, encased in dark oak panelling, stiff with all the archaic accessories of such places, the Gothic characters of its advertisements cutting you off from the Latin West, you are taken back into the spacious countryside of Albrecht Dürer. The battlements of buff-green cities; the raftered farms with their precipitous roofs; the village musicians going up to an untidy bluff from which they can look down into the village street, to sweeten the evening air with the strumming of their rustic instruments; the twentieth century is left behind, you are back amongst the *Zeitgenossen* of Dürer or of Altdorfer . . .

If the past is everywhere in the great cities – *wished* there as a factor in dreams of very modern dominion, in oppressive fake-antique – it is more omnipresent in the provinces. In Berlin it was consciously retained, in *Weinstube* or *Biersalon*, until the Jews built the Kurfürstendamm – a typically Jewish misdemeanour, in the eyes of Hitler, the Lutyens-manqué of Germany.[16] Even the jokes the German makes are Gothic jokes, sly, hearty, and animal, assimilable by the gargantuan mind of the cowherd as much as by the *Chef de Protocol.*

When you enter a *souk* at Fez you walk headlong into the Past. Nothing has changed: quite authentically you are invading another dimension. In Germany it is quite different from that; you are never far from factories. This is not *really* the world of Luther or Altdorfer. But like a mirage, artificially induced, there, nevertheless, blended with the new, is everywhere the *Mittelaltertum*. The Gothic past still lives: it is not only tolerated sentimentally, but it is energetically preserved, upon equal terms with the present.

In the midst of all this fustian, and half-fustian, Hitler is the real thing – or to be more precise, *almost* the real thing. Hitler did not 'put the clock back', as Mr. Edgar Mowrer said he did. For him it had stood still: it had never moved, or scarcely at all. He is an emanation of the old many-schlossed, spiky, and bosky landscapes, the feudal valleys of the Oesterreich. Passionately he has desired to remain a part of that old dream. In the midst of the petrol-age that was very irrational. Hitler is nothing if not irrational.

In *Faust* we meet with 'the spirit which wills the evil and does the good'. There is, throughout life, its counterpart: namely the spirit which wills good and does the evil. Whether or not Hitler wills the good according to the humanitarian canon – and he has given way to vindictive passions which nowhere could be regarded as very edifying – certainly he is of the 'good-man', or *bonhomme*, type, the standard peasant. He is what Nietzsche described as an 'agriculturist of the spirit'.

Evil spirits, Nietzsche points out ('evil' according to the agriculturist morality) have been those who awakened the spirit of contradiction – the delight in the new, in the adventurous and untried. To the agriculturist mind all that is anathema – to the peasant mind.

> The new [to quote from Nietzsche] is under all circumstances the *evil*, as that which wants . . . to uproot the old boundary-stones, and undermine the old pieties. Only the Old is the Good! The good . . . go to the roots of the old thoughts and bear fruit with them – the agriculturists of the spirit.

Good, in the sense of unsubversive, the enemy of the New, Herr Hitler is. As well as in social origin, likewise in mind and in the quality of his morality, he is the agriculturist. The Soil (about which you hear so much in Nazi tracts), just as it is – the men who live upon it, just as they are – constitutes *the good*. This transcends all more universal moralities. It becomes a mystical absolute, in this emotional philosophy.

As a sort of consequence of this, other people's soil, the earth of alien peoples, is not exactly evil, but yet not *good*, in the way German soil is. It is not quite 'the gaud earth'. For there cannot be two goddesses, or two measures of goodness. To be foreign, to the Hellene, was to be 'barbarian'. To be foreign to Herr Hitler is to be a barbarian, too. But it takes with it a further handicap. What is foreign is wanting in *goodness* (since Herr Hitler is not an artist, like the Greek, but a moralist instead). And it is an easy step from that (especially if the foreigner displays a lack of appreciation of the German goodness) to being downright *bad*.

This man in his agony of peasant nostalgia would make use of machinery of the Machine Age to defend his sacrosanct past from our machines. He would make himself proficient in the arts of the civilisation he hates, so as to have weapons terrible enough to defend his *heimat*, which is threatened by that civilisation.

That is the situation. In France, when somebody forecloses and gendarmes have come to arrest a defaulting farmer, one has often heard of the enraged peasant barricading himself in his house, with his sons or brothers beside him. The officers of the law have been peppered with buckshot; a siege has ensued. That is what Hitler is like. Only Hitler has howitzers and tanks. Great armies must go to fetch *that* defaulter.

Yet, it is quite certain that Hitler would, without compunction, massacre every one who irreverently invaded his archaic wonderland. 'Let us alone!' how often has he not cried – when compelled to pay attention to some importunate demand made on him by the Western politicians. 'Lass' uns doch allein!'

Yet obviously this non-interference he demands is today an impossibility. For his dreamland, however idyllic, bristles with engines of destruction, as I have said, just as modern and unsuitable as could be found in the unromantic backgrounds of any of his 'pluto-democratic' enemies.

We have our dreams, too. That is another thing not to be ignored. Paris, Manhattan – even *Berlin Westen*, in his own native land, which the Jews built with their customary optimism.

The fact of the matter is, as regards this quarrel between Herr Hitler and ourselves, we do not belong to that particular *conte de fée*, nor do we want to belong to it. We do not recognise its importance. Yes, it is all right, we agree; in its time and place. In a World Fair we might drop into ye Olde Bavarian *Gasthaus* to have a *Seidel*. But all this is on a par with Celtic Twilights, with Ossian, Tibetan Monasteries, *The Moon and Sixpence* – 'Noa Noa': a thing that cannot be reconstituted and that certainly is not worth massacring millions of people to bring back.

One or two of us, here and there, can understand the passionate regret of this misguided peasant for the dream that was handed down to him, and which he all too faithfully and naively has received. The Yeatses, Singes [sic], and the rest of them – even Mr. James Joyce, I suppose – would see the point of it. But it is a madman, merely, who could suppose that it can be defended with phosgene[17] and with bombs.

But *defence*, of course, involves and entails a remaining upon your own native territory. And where that 'goodness' of Hitler's passes over into evil is that this good German earth does not end abruptly at the frontiers of the Reich. This mysterious excellence that pertains to the soil of the fatherland gives the fatherland a kind of prescriptive right over all *neighbouring* soil: since, as we have just seen, to be foreign is to be less good; and to wish to deny – in your unworthy egotism – to the more good access to what is less good, may easily become exceedingly evil, and worthy of condign punishment. And so it is that it comes about that this benevolent *Führer* (as he seems to regard himself) is apt, in the eyes of other people, to be the personification of evil.

The Australian economist-journalist, Mr. Stephen Roberts, asserted that 'Hitlerism cannot achieve its aims without war; its ideology is that of war'. Its aims postulate 'the complete disappearance of six nations and the mutilation of several others'. That obviously could not be effected without war. The conclusion of Mr. Roberts has proved to be a perfectly sound one. For the *soil* business acts both ways. All Germany's neighbours have 'soils' as well. And whether it is stupid – or even wicked – to do so or otherwise, they will automatically defend them. So that fairy-book vocable, 'Hitler,' spells *war*.

But it spells unsuccessful war for Germany, because this peasant-dream runs counter to many other peasant-dreams – not to speak of all the very solid realities it affronts. This soil-imperialism is less promising, on the face of it, than any other kind of imperialism – say financial imperialism – because it is so undisguised, and so perfectly calculated to stir up the maximum of mystical resistance.

Notes

1. Treated in detail in *Men Without Art*, pp. 85ff.
2. On the enemy persona, see Meyers, pp. 55–7.
3. *Rude Assignment: A Narrative of My Career Up-to-date* (London: Hutchinson, 1950), p. 70.
4. Here cf. Warner on sport as a model for moral action above, pp. 92–4.
5. Quotations are from the Gordon Press reprint (New York, 1972).
6. French extreme-right political movement founded by Charles Maurras in 1899, distinctive for the monarchist, anti-Semitic and Catholic colouring of its policies.

Lewis's anticipation of a growing sympathy between the Action Française and Nazism was borne out during the Second World War (still eight years away as he was writing), when the movement collaborated with occupying Nazi forces. It was outlawed by the French Government immediately after the war.

7. Nationalist and pro-fascist mass-circulation paper founded by François Coty, perfume manufacturer and newspaper publisher – notably, of *Le Figaro*.

8. For a full discussion of this, see Bridson, pp. 209–29.

9. Published originally under the pseudonym 'Murray Constantine'. The book has been reissued with an introduction by Daphne Patai (New York: Feminist Press, 1985). See Daphne Patai, 'Imagining Reality: The Utopian Fiction of Katharine Burdekin', in Ingram and Patai, pp. 226–43.

10. Timur, renowned conqueror born in 1336 at Kesh, south of Samarkand.

11. In June 1934 Hitler reached a dead-end in attempts to control his ally, the radical revolutionary Ernst Röhm. When Röhm was executed, Hitler's position was strengthened with the military and leaders of industry.

12. Martha Dodd, *My Years in Germany* (London: Gollancz, 1939). The book was published in the United States as *Through Embassy Eyes* (New York: Harcourt, Brace and Co., 1939). The passage quoted appears on pp. 64–5 of that edition.

13. Euphorion of Chalcis. I have been unable to trace Lewis's exact source.

14. The Ottawa agreements (1932) established a number of policies, based on the principle of imperial preference, governing trade between Britain and the Commonwealth.

15. By Stephen H. Roberts (New York and London: Harper Brothers, 1938).

16. Lewis is referring, presumably, to Sir Edwin Landseer Lutyens (1869–1944), British architect better known for his designs in the traditional, indigenous idiom than for his originality. John Summerson writes that his death brought to a close 'the last epoch of the great country house as the seed-bed of British architectural genius, as well as the last in which British imperialism would be celebrated in the arts' ('Architecture' in Ford, p. 231). Lewis associates him with British imperial nostalgia, as he does Hitler with German nationalist nostalgia.

17. Carbonyl chloride, poisonous gas used in the First World War.

24 Stephen Spender *Writers and Manifestos (1935)**

An expanded and modified version of this piece – a response to the plethora of declarations and 'statements of aim' issued by writers and artists in the first half of the decade – was included by Spender later in 1935 in his first major critical work, *The Destructive Element*. His declared aim in that book was 'to show that, apart from all questions of tendency, there is, in our modern literature, a consistent tradition of writing that has a political–moral subject' (p. 278). In its compounding with 'moral', 'political' in that sentence undergoes a peculiar attenuation of meaning, something also suggested by Spender's assertion that the 'political–moral subject' exists 'apart from all questions of tendency', or partisanship. In *The Destructive Element* he writes in defence of writers who are, 'in the widest sense, political' (p. 190), which is to say writers who seek 'to discover a system of values that are not purely subjective and individualistic, but objective and social; real in the world of a society *outside* the artist in the same way Nature is real' (p. 223). Crucial to the argument, though – and typical of Spender at this stage of his development – is the idea that notwithstanding the writer's commitment to a system of values, their specific 'tendency' is of 'no literary interest . . . because art does not illustrate a point of view, it does not illustrate at all, it presents its subject in a new form' (p. 279). At this point Spender had not yet joined the Communist Party (he would do that in 1937 after a visit to Spain), but his reluctance to concede to notions of art as a political instrument endured through even that brief period of more intense commitment. In *World Within World* (1951) he writes that 'the speeches of those who tried to connect writing with political tasks always left me uneasy'. Finally, no political programme could or should govern the individual expression of the artist, because 'no "historic correctness" . . . achieves good independently and in spite of the moral qualities of those who support the cause' (p. 252).

'We can no longer permit life to be shaped by a personified ideal, we must serve with all our faculties some actual thing,' Mr. Yeats has written in a recent preface.[1] This seems to me true. The 'actual thing' is the true moral or widely political subject that must be realized by contemporary literature, if that literature is itself to be moral and serious. Any other art will tend to become a 'personified ideal'. The weakness of Lawrence is in this tendency. He wrote about a kind of life which was serious and real: but whereas he meant to write about people, about the life around him, he tended,

* Reprinted from *Left Review* 1.5 (February 1935): 145–50.

as he went on, only to write about himself. For in his search for values he invented a way of life that did not betray those values: but, most unfortunately, it was only possible to himself. It was the outcome of a personal struggle: and the result dangerously bordered on the 'personified ideal'.

It seems then that the position of writers who are endeavouring to serve some 'actual thing' – that is, who are endeavouring to write about it – is worth considering. Mr. Day Lewis has said:

> Yet living here
> As one between two massing powers I live
> When neutrality cannot save
> Nor occupation cheer.
> None such shall be left alive:
> The innocent wing is soon shot down,
> And private stars fade in the blood-red dawn
> Where two worlds strive.
>
> The red advance of life
> Contracts pride, calls out the common blood,
> Beats song into a single blade,
> Makes a depth-charge of grief.
>
> Move then with new desires;
> For where we used to build and love
> Is no man's land, and only ghosts can live
> Between two fires.[2]

This poem asserts that two worlds exist and are fighting: the striving worlds are obviously intended to represent the class war, or at all events the rivalry between revolution and reaction. This contest is so important that neutrality is impossible. 'The innocent wing is soon shot down.' The poet is evidently on the side of 'The red advance of life' because he believes that 'only ghosts can live/Between two fires'.

The poem then is not only about communism, it also has a propagandist element: it argues, and some of the argument is, to say the least, controversial. For example, the simplification of issues might seem to some people premature, if not grotesque. But this does not really affect the real claim of the poem to value. The implicit assertion of the poem is that it is about realities: that the struggle between two worlds is *real* – as real as the descriptions of environment in novels – that the material of the poem is life.

If I am right in saying that the struggle of communism or socialism against the anti-social forces of the whole world exists, I think that the reader, in judging left-wing literature, must not judge it in the same way as he argues against communism. It is not a question of whether he thinks the premises are false, but of whether the premises are about realities, in the sense that there are political and moral realities which are more enduring than the external world of literary realism. What he should ask is: Does this communist approach lead to a greater and more fundamental understanding of the struggle affecting our whole life today?

Now one of the chief aims of communism as a political creed is that it is materialist. The materialist conception of history, the theory of surplus value, the idea of crystallized labour: all these are solids, they are material subject matter and yet move in the world of ideas. The writer who grasps anything of Marxist theory, feels that he is moving in a world of reality, and in a purposive world, not merely a world of obstructive and oppressive *things*.

Lastly, it is well to remember that perhaps the most fundamental of all ideas illustrated by drama and poetry, in all history, is the idea of justice.[3] We live in an age in which we have become conscious of great social injustice, of the oppression of one class by another, of nationalities by other nations. Communism, or socialism in its completed form, offers a just world. A world in which wealth is more equally distributed, and the grotesque accumulating of wealth by individuals is dispersed: in which nations have no interest in destroying each other in the manner of modern war, because the system of competitive trade controlled by internecine and opposed capitalist interests is abolished.

These aims are so broad and so just that no amount of abuse and sneering can affect the people who hold them. It is no use telling me that I am a bourgeois intellectual, that I know nothing, or next to nothing of the proletariat, etc.[4] All that and a lot more may be true. The point is that if I desire social justice I am not primarily concerned with myself, I am concerned with bringing into being a world quite external to my own interests; in the same way as when one writes a poem, one is allowing the poem to have its own, impersonal, objective being, one is not shoving oneself into it.

The socialist artist is concerned with realizing in his work the ideas of a classless society: that is to say, applying those ideas to the life around him, and giving them their reality. He is concerned with a change of heart.[5]

He is not primarily concerned with ways and means, and he is not paralysed by the argument that the economic system is rigid. The economic system was made for man, and not man for the economic system, so that if man changes, that is to say, if he has a new and strong conception of justice, the economic system will also change.

It also follows that the writer is primarily interested in man, and not in systems, not even in a good economic system. Systems are rigid, and they must always be forced externally, by external criticism, to change. In that sense art, because it insists on human values, is a criticism of life.

Good architecture is a criticism of slums. Good painting is a criticism of the pictures we have, the clothes we wear, all the appearances with which we surround ourselves. Good poetry is a criticism of language: of the way in which we express ourselves, the direction of our thoughts, the words we hand down to our children. Our industrial civilization has proved almost impervious to that criticism of life which we find in architecture, painting, music and poetry. Art has been resisted, and the artists have been driven to form cliques with a private language and private jokes. But no system can afford to be without the criticism of art. The whole point of artists adopting a revolutionary position, is that their interests may become social and not anti-social, and that their criticism may help to shape a new society.

When one considers the position of artists in a socialist state, it is well therefore to remember that the art which has 'roots in the masses', must be free to tell the truth and criticize life. Lenin said, 'Art belongs to the people. It ought to extend with very deep roots into the very thick of the broad toiling masses. It ought to be intelligible to these masses and loved by them. And it ought to unify the feeling, thought and will of these masses, elevate them. It ought to arouse and develop artists among them.'

A democratic art has always been popular with certain writers, who have appealed in their work from a small set of fellow artists to the people (the classic example is the appeal to the taste of *Das Volk* in *Meistersingers*). The point of such an appeal is that by widening his audience, the artist also widens and deepens his subject matter: he draws strength from deeper roots. The writer who is starving because he cannot reach any audience but a small clique, and who finds the whole literature, painting and music of his time a prey to the same cliqueiness, will suspect that there is something wrong with our sectarian literature. Now whatever may be the faults of Russian writers to-day, they do at least reach a wide audience, and they do succeed in writing about matters which passionately concern the people. In order to awaken this wide interest they do not play down to their audience, in the fashion of our popular modern writers, and the English press.

Nevertheless, Russian literature suffers, or has until recently suffered, from its own sectarianism. This consisted in the establishment of what amounted to a monopoly of publishing and criticism by a small group of writers who formed an organization called RAPP (Russian Association of Proletarian Writers). The business of this Union, and its various companion organizations, was to insist on the proletarianization of art, and to persecute artists who were not correct in their party ideology. Mr. Max Eastman has written a book called *Artists in Uniform*,[6] which is an extremely prejudiced account of the activities of RAPP: he is clearly carrying on a personal vendetta against the editors of the American periodical, *New Masses*, which he finds to be subservient to Moscow. He is also a Trotskyist, and a violent critic of the Stalin dictatorship. He draws attention to RAPP's many blunders, but he does not admit that several writers have been exceptionally well treated. For example, he ignores the case of Nekrassov,[7] and he is so anxious to prove that RAPP has destroyed all literary talent in Russia that the name of Gladkov does not occur in his book. In spite, though, of defects of over-statement, the indictment he draws up is alarming, and, in some ways, almost overwhelming. There are many examples of persecution by RAPP. The suicides of Yessenin, Maiakovsky, and several other poets, may have been inevitable, since their faulty 'individualism' perhaps made it, in any case, impossible for them to adapt themselves to the revolution. Far more serious is the case of Zamyatin, whose novel *We* was not published in the Soviet [Union], but a copy of which was pirated in a Prague émigré magazine: this misfortune was used as a frame-up against Zamyatin, and he was compelled to live in exile. Romanov, who is well known in England for his novel, *Three Pairs of Silk Stockings*, was so unfortunate as to receive a favourable review in the London *New Statesman*, in which the reviewer remarked that it was a mystery that Romanov's books should be allowed to appear in Soviet Russia. The mystery did not cease, but Romanov was compelled to recant publicly. Another writer, Pilnyak, on being charged with counter-revolutionary tendencies, managed to make an art of humiliating himself and begging for Marxist instruction: he has become one of the most prosperous writers in the Soviet Union.

Since RAPP no longer exists, Mr. Eastman's remarks may now seem irrelevant, because I do not suppose that even the Soviet Government would now defend RAPP's actions. But he holds that matters are now little if at all better, and that RAPP was only liquidated because its destructive function was completely performed. The next few years will show whether or not this accusation is just: but meanwhile Mr. Eastman's charges should be read and considered. It is not enough to dismiss him as a counter-revolutionary, if what he says is true.

The following principles were dictated to the Kharkov Congress, a meeting of communist writers gathered from every part of the world,[8] by Auerbach, a young representative of the political bureaucracy:

1. *Art is a class weapon.*
2. Artists are to abandon 'individualism' and the fear of strict discipline as petty bourgeois attitudes.
3. Artistic creation is to be systemized, organized, 'collectivized', and carried out according to the plans of the central staff like any other soldierly work.
4. This is to be done under the 'careful and yet firm guidance of the Communist Party'.
5. Artists and writers of the rest of the world are to learn how to make proletarian art by studying the experience of the Soviet Union.
6. 'Every proletarian artist must be a dialectical materialist. The method of creative art is the method of dialectical materialism.'
7. 'Proletarian literature is not necessarily created by the proletariat – it can also be created by writers from the petty bourgeoisie', and one of the chief duties of the proletarian writer is to help these non-proletarian writers to 'overcome their petty bourgeois character and accept the viewpoint of the proletariat'.

It is evident that the aim of this manifesto is to convert art into an instrument that can be used for party purposes. It is not the business of the artist to observe, but to conform. He must not be a two-edged instrument which might turn against the party. It is his business to go where he is sent, and to observe what he is told.

There is not the least doubt that a great many communists look on art purely as a party instrument. To take a small instance, I read in a proposed manifesto sent by Alec Brown to the third number of *Left Review,*[9] that 'during the initial period of our magazine [it is] most important to carry on rigorous criticism of all highbrowism, intellectualism, abstract rationalism, and similar dilettantism'. And to whom do these abusive, ill-defined terms apply, one must ask? The answer is only too simple: to everyone who is not one of US.

It may be argued that there is a severe censorship now in almost every country outside Russia, and that even in England there will soon be no great freedom of speech. But there is a great difference between even the most stupefying and severe censorship and the attempt to regard art as a mere instrument in the hands of a party. The difference is that censorship cuts or bans books which are already written: but the principles laid down in this manifesto order the manner in which they should be written; what books should be about, and what attitude the writer should adopt to his material. No censorship has ever gone so far as this. This instrumentalization encourages, too, a school of critics whose business simply is to apply the canon. To attack writers because they are bourgeois, because their novels, if they are about life as they know it, are not proletarian, or, if they are about the working classes, because they are not militant. One need only read the American magazine *New Masses* to discover plenty of such criticism.

Against this, one must set some statements by Russian writers, which are published in *Literature of the Peoples of the U.S.S.R.,* vols. 7–8.[10] Some of the declarations here seem admirable and honest. For instance, A. Selivenovsky, in an essay on 'The Poetry of Socialism', says: 'To become an artist of socialism means, if you come from the intelligentsia, that not only must you be convinced that the ideas of socialism are correct, but that you must alter your previously-formed poetic style. It means that you must overcome and discard many of your former ideas about life; you must change your way of looking at the world. But this alteration does not imply, of course, that the subject-matter, imagery, and style of the poet of socialism is made to lose all individuality, is reduced to complete uniformity. That is far from the case. The fact is that it is socialism that ensures the all-round development and growth of the human individual.'

This seems excellent. Good, too, is V. Kaverin's essay on literature and science, in which he pleads for a more scientific subject-matter in modern literature. C. Zelinsky is narrower: 'Criticism acquires a function of a principally intellectual–educational order: to struggle against the heritage of capitalism in consciousness by exposing it in art.' He has hard, almost sinister things to say of Voronsky, a figure of the recent past: 'Voronsky based his conception of art on the work of Tolstoy and Proust, writers in whose work direct observation is most prominent. In such a system of views, however, the very core of the Marxian conception of literature, its very heart, class activity, was lost. It was not by chance, therefore, that Voronsky proved to be allied with Trotskyism.'

Even officially, the position of literature in communist society seems then to be extremely controversial. All I want to emphasize here is that if one is on the side of the greatest possible degree of freedom, if one insists that one should write as one chooses and about what one wishes, one is not a traitor to the cause of world socialism. No system is in itself a complete solution of world problems. If there is to be any sort of freedom and improvement, one has got to push and sometimes even fight the systems of one's own choice. Unless artists insist on their right to criticize, even to be 'human-itarian' (a despised term), communism will become a frozen epoch, another ice age.

Lastly, the view of Lenin was not at all that of a bureaucrat. Polonsky in his 'Outline of the Literary Movement of the Revolutionary Epoch'[11] relates how he pencilled comments on an article of Pletnev, 'On the ideological front', which was printed in *Pravda,* in the autumn of 1922. '"The creation of a new proletarian class front is the fundamental goal of the Protecult," wrote Pletnev. "Ha, Ha!" wrote Lenin in the margin. There are many other comments such as "humm!" and "What a mess!", surviving in that margin. In two places he writes "Bunk".'

The Left Wing Orthodoxy (1938)*

This essay was included in a double number of New Verse which bore the general title, *Commitments.* In his editorial note, Geoffrey Grigson rather ambivalently affirmed that 'the aesthetic attitude is now decidedly out of place, [and so] it is obvious that poems are not the only things to be expected from poets'. For that reason 'several contributors were asked to commit themselves on the relationship, more or less, between those who are not poets and those who are'. 'This number of New Verse marks one particular thing: the end of poetic isolation' (p. 2). Besides the piece by Spender, the issue contained much else of interest to students of the period: Auden's 'The Sportsmen: A Parable', Kenneth Allott's *obiter dicta*, 'Several Things', 'Past and Present: the Business of a Poet' by Louis Prokosch, and an open letter from Herbert Read to the BBC, encouraging that institution's new director to assist in getting 'ink out of the body poetic' and returning poetry to the medium of the spoken word.

Near the end of the issue came Charles Madge's outrageous, premature obituary for T. S. Eliot: 'though neither spiritually nor physically dead, . . . his relation to the world of letters and to the public was such that the *obituary* was in fact a proper form in which to discuss him.' 'Only in this age, when the accent is on the *decline* of a social system, the royal poet may be expected to appear as a dead king, or King of the Dead' (p. 18). Evidently the spur for this essay – and for Grigson who appears to have suggested the idea to Madge – was Eliot's much-discussed 1928 religious conversion and his description of himself in *For Lancelot Andrewes* as 'Classicist in literature, royalist in politics, and anglo-catholic

* Reprinted from New Verse 31–2 (Autumn 1938): 12–16.

in religion.'[12] In a similar vein and also in this issue, *New Verse* pronounced Laura Riding 'a most peculiar dead poet': 'She is dead because she is a neutral, living in a kind of Nowhere, in between things, like a bead which has slipped down between boards.' Her poems are 'ghost poems excessively tenuous (and tedious), and *as poems* they are worthless, a paradoxical series in language which is only neat'. Riding herself is 'the Queen-bore among all poets writing at present'. A vintage *New Verse* review.

Precisely which of Wyndham Lewis's writings provoked this reply from Spender is unclear, but his most extended critique of left-wing opinion up to this time was *Left Wings over Europe* (London: Jonathan Cape, 1936).

When Mr. Wyndham Lewis writes of the Left Wing orthodoxy of contemporary writers and intellectuals, none of them – except perhaps those who call themselves non-political even when they are taking part in protests against Fascism – should quarrel with the description. As the Queen's Hall meeting addressed by famous writers showed, most well-known British writers are now aware that the whole tradition which they represent is being challenged, that writers corresponding to them in Germany and Italy are forced into exile or prison or dulled acquiescence, that most of the famous living writers in Spain are on the Black List of those who will be shot when Franco wins. Apart from the direct threat to freedom of expression, the writer is forced to realise that the liberal assumptions of progress and freedom which form the so respectable background of most bourgeois literature today, are being challenged by the violent and destructive methods of power politics. He must submit to this challenge, reconsider the moral assumptions that flow so easily into his writing, or come out with a new set of values.

To put it bluntly, the orthodoxy which unites the writers of the Left should be a new realism, a new realisation of the structure of society today, the relation of society to the individual, an examination of the assumptions on which democratic societies rest. In society itself this realisation of changing values is compulsory, no one who may have to take part in or be the victim of war, can escape it. In what is essentially a revolutionary period, the task of the imaginative writer, whether he is a poet or a novelist, is tremendous: it is to realise by every means at his disposal the nature of what is happening, and clarify this realisation for his audience.

There is no more difficult problem to discuss than that of the nature of a writer's contact with reality. This is largely a personal matter. Some writers, like Balzac, acquire their knowledge by methodological inquiry, statistics and the direct methods of Mass Observers.[13] Others, like Tolstoy or Dostoievsky, or, in a different way, Goethe, from the violence of emotional experiences into which they are plunged by their own restless and avid temperaments. Others, like Flaubert, by shutting themselves into a room, and re-inventing, as it were, for their own satisfaction, society. Very introspective writers, like Kafka, or say, Eliot, who seem completely isolated, yet through the exploitation of their own unhappiness, arrive at remarkable comments on society: the neurotic is after all only a social symptom, and if he analyses his own neurosis profoundly enough, he arrives at roots which are growing into the life of his time.

I think that today there is a very real distrust amongst the younger writers, of the validity not only of their own experiences, but of the experiences which they may have derived from the comparatively narrow environment of their upbringing. This explains the attractions of a movement like Mass Observation, it also explains the purely literary motives which may have played a part in making several writers of different nations join the International brigade . . . André Malraux plunges into the life of action in order to create for himself an environment of violence and movement from which words may spring – the search for inspiration.

All this activity is probably a good thing, but when the necessity to break away from the known to the unknown (the bourgeoisie to the proletariat) becomes assumed as an obligation, it results often in frustration and the curious kind of isolated dilettantism which impresses one if one looks over, say, several numbers of *Left Review*.

In the discussions on Literature of the members of the Writers' Association for Intellectual Liberty, the competitiveness and the snobbery of the writers as to who is most closely in contact with the working classes (who have become synonymous with Reality), amount to burlesque. These meetings are like meetings of a group of characters in a play by Chekhov, all of whom yearn to go to a Moscow which they will never reach, Moscow here being some industrial area where there are plenty of workers. At the last meeting which I attended (a discussion between Mr. Goronwy Rees and Mr. Day Lewis) there was very lively play put up by Mr. John Brophy, who rather unsportingly attacked a speaker for not having carried sacks about at any period of his career, as Mr. Brophy himself had done. Unfortunately for Mr. Brophy, the speaker was able to trump this card, by proving that he had sprung from the working classes and would at this moment be a miner but for the extenuating circumstance (perhaps to be regretted after all!) of a scholarship at Oxford. Mr. Brophy then played his Ace: he had brought a Worker to the meeting with him, who, it was assumed (if silence means consent), thoroughly approved of everything Mr. Brophy had said. At this moment, another Worker, who had slipped in unawares (a *real* worker with a *real* accent) got up and said that anyhow the workers didn't want a proletarian literature; what they wanted to read about was the love affairs of the upper classes. Confusion.

Most meetings of English Left Wing writers tend to degenerate into this kind of thing.

If we agree with [Louis] Aragon, that the orthodoxy of the Left consists in a reconsideration of the position of the writer in relation to the world, a new realism, is there nothing to discuss in the task of re-stating values and interpreting the world to the world, except an inverted social snobbery?

Actually, there is quite a lot to discuss. To begin with, we have to ask, is the writer's way out of his present comparative isolation in society to be found, as some communist writers and critics seem to assume, in the proletarian-isation of all literature? If it were simply a matter of the poet or novelist who goes over to the working class, producing work that is as imbued in the life of the masses as, say, the chapter in *Capital* called 'The Working Day', or an epic of the class struggle in Spain, one could only say that here was a subject which for moral profundity, heroic magnificence, seriousness, made all other subjects seem either reflections of trivial fashions of the day or of a purely personal interest.

Unfortunately, however, what is far too liable to happen is that the writer, overwhelmed by his new subject and environment, finds that he is disqualified by the weight of his past environment, for which he has now lost all respect, from writing: e.g., Edgell Rickword.[14] Poets are the most sensitive registers of this reaction; they join the communist party, they deliberately cut themselves off from the roots of their own sensibility, which derive from a life they have come to despise, and then they either stop writing or they produce stuff in which new and undigested material is imposed on a medium which was adapted to quite different material. The result is something effete, disappointing to the writer and to his comrades. The poetry of Randall Swingler provides an example of this process. Educated at Winchester and New College, sensitive, perhaps deeply impressed at a decisive stage in his development by some such aesthetic experience as reading the *Testament of Beauty*,[15] Swingler now writes poems which in delicate tracework show all these influences, except for their grimly class-conscious subject-matter: the effect is of an agricultural instrument wrapped up in lace.

Whilst one should not withold a certain admiration for the idealism of writers who make such sacrifices, one should insist that here a real difficulty has arisen, and a difficulty that involves the discussion of books and poems and criticism, not the economic situation of the writer, the writer's relations with the workers, and the various other topics which are all really an escape from the problem provided by the poems themselves. Of course, there are many reasons why writers should be communists today, but the essential thing both from the writer's own point of view and from that of the communist party is to see that in becoming communists writers do not indulge in a tendency to commit literary suicide.

The solution lies in refraining from pressing writers to write about experiences and ways of life and even ideas which they are incapable of absorbing; and equally to insist that they do write truthfully about the life which interests them and which they know about, applying to it all the theoretical knowledge which enables them to have a profounder understanding of it.

But 'Left Wing Orthodoxy' is a phrase which unfortunately at the moment does not mean a new realism so much as respectability coupled with a certain amount of log-rolling. From a tactical point of view, there is a great deal to be said for the Left becoming respectable, for the writers' meetings being adorned by the golden features of Sir Hugh Walpole, for Cecil Day Lewis being on the Council of the Book Society, for W. H. Auden going to Buckingham Palace to receive the King's Medal. It is really simply a question of whether in the process of absorption the Left absorbs the representatives of the ruling classes, or whether they absorb the Left. Undoubtedly, from the point of view of the 'older generation' these successes which Day Lewis and Auden probably regard as tactics, are part of a process by which the English writer who has a good heart at the age of twenty and is therefore a socialist, develops a good brain at forty and becomes a conservative. Past experience goes to show that the English ruling classes are cleverer than any other at absorbing their opponents by a process of tolerance, invitations, and sharing out places corresponding to that of a Public School Prefect. If Mr. Day Lewis is given a job on the Book Society, it is because he can be relied on not to shock the taste of Book Society readers, in spite of his Bolshie principles; and even though he may exercise his influence to get *Letters from Iceland* chosen as Book of the Month, that is partly because that particular book is considered harmless, and is the price of Mr. Day Lewis becoming the most respectable of the younger critics, writing in a style and developing an attitude adapted to the quotations printed on publishers' advertisements.

I don't blame Mr. Day Lewis for his job on the Book Society or Mr. Auden for his Gold Medal. Literary life is largely a contemporary racket, and if one goes in for it, I suppose one can't be squeamish. All the same, it's worth pointing out that Left Wing writers are subject to just the same kind of temptation as the late Mr. Ramsay MacDonald, visiting Buckingham Palace, or Trade Union Leaders.

Another danger of Left Wing Orthodoxy is the extent to which belonging to the Left is becoming a career. If you want to have reviews taken by all but one of the weekly periodicals, if you want to have a book chosen by the Left Book Club, if you want to be looked at by the older generation of critics as a little Pink (just like they were in their youth), you had better be dressed in suitable opinions, and, when the time comes, you can always gracefully backslide into religion or the camp of National Labour.

All these things are inevitable, but they ought to be recognised. I admire Randall Swingler for his fervour, Edgell Rickword for his comparative silence. I am rather alarmed at my own success, more alarmed perhaps at Day Lewis's growing respectability, and I rather wish that Auden had decided against that Medal. Yet it is not the opinions, the successes, the acts themselves that matter; it is their effect on the poems, novels and criticism of those who hold opinions, succeed and act. To be practical as a writer interested in writing is only to judge these things in their relation to work.

It is worth noting that when French writers meet, they discuss books, when English writers meet they discuss opinions and make vague gestures towards revealing their autobiographies. At the meeting of international writers held in Paris in June, André Chamson pleaded for a kind of writing which was the fruit of silence and maturity, not a missile thrown at an objective: Aragon once again went into public penance for his surrealist days, and demanded that writers should be realists. In the meetings of the English Writers, I have scarcely ever heard the name of a book mentioned, certainly not a book or a theory of literature seriously discussed in the sense that Chamson was discussing, by implication, André Malraux's *L'Espoir*, and Aragon the books of the surrealist writers.

The position can be stated thus: the writers of the Left stand on the verge of an orthodoxy which is really fundamental, because it is capable of extension into a unified and truthful picture of the contemporary world. The creative imagination must apply the socialist view of contemporary society in two ways: firstly, by showing that in every instance the socialist analysis of the problems of the individual in his relation to society gives us a profounder picture of a given situation than any other, for a non-political view would arrive at the same conclusion which implied a challenge to the whole capitalist society; secondly, by pressing so deeply and widely into the reality of the present that it begins to yield an extended view of the socialist society of the future.

This struggle suggests a critical approach to the problems of contemporary literature, and a basis on which one can discuss several achievements. We are able to discuss the success of writers who share our orthodoxy, in their interpretations of reality. We are able to attack most contemporary bourgeois literature by claiming that it is superficial in its portraiture of life and society, that it shows no understanding of the structure of the environment which it is describing, that it is a reflection of the fashions and prejudices spread by the newspapers, cinemas and wireless.

On the other hand, it is essential to judge work by its achievement and not by the opinions of the writer. Where we recognise that a writer has given a true picture, we should relate it to our own picture, thus making use of the best creative writing and criticism of our time. The failure to do this explains the insularity and dilettantism of a great deal of Left Wing literature. What is required is a critical study by Left Wing writers of the achievements of non-political writers who have had a very realistic view of their time. The royalist Balzac, the liberal and social snob Henry James, the mystic Rilke, all have an extremely penetrating view of capitalist society and arrive at conclusions which are devastating to it.

Why then does the Association of Writers for Intellectual Liberty, in its literary (as apart from its practical) discussions, make no joint study of the methods of Balzac or any other great realist? Why is there no attempt to hammer out a critical approach to literature? Why is there no discussion (without sneers) of the value which the criticism of I. A. Richards[16] and T. S. Eliot might be to us? Why is no attitude taken up towards surrealism? Why when a book life *Poetry and Anarchism* [1938], by Herbert Read, is published, is it not discussed by the writers? If the writers have an Association, must they always prove to themselves that they are too practical to relate their orthodox view of the world to books, though they must always be relating their lives to their political activity and contacts with workers?

To realise the truth of any contemporary situation which is related to the background of society, becomes daily harder. We live in a world over whole areas of which people's private feelings – their taste, their love, their desire to propagate, what they wear, etc. – are faked for them by State Propaganda. In our own industrialised society, values and feelings are not so much faked as – like food – adulterated. The attitude of a 'leader' in the *Daily Express* stating that no serious situation which might lead to war exists in Europe today, is extended to every sphere of life. The serious is made trivial either by the outright assertion that it does not exist, or else by a process of inflating it to a point where it no longer seems serious. The trivial, the isolated, the unimportant right and 'freedom', are, on the other hand, made portentously serious. This applies, from our earliest education, as much to private as to public affairs. Literature is one of the few strongholds where it is still possible to retain a sense of values and apply those values to the world. It is worth remembering that in such a world, truth is a land mine deeply tunnelled under every position and wherever it is struck, there is an explosion. Not the least disconcerting, but comforting, feature of today is to discover that in the matter of the Spanish War nearly every serious writer, whatever his opinions, is passionately on our side. We should insist on reality and the achievement; the opinions will come afterwards.

Notes

1. From Yeats's introduction to *The Words upon the Window Pane* (Dublin: Cuala Press, 1934). Reprinted in *The Variorum Edition of the Plays of W. B. Yeats*, ed. Russell K. Alspach (London: Macmillan, 1966), p. 957.
2. 'The Conflict' (1933), in *The Complete Poems of C. Day Lewis* (London: Sinclair-Stevenson, 1992), pp. 183–4.
3. Cf. the contrasting attitude to 'justice' in Sisson (see above p. 185) and also his 'Remarks on a Letter of Junius' (*New English Weekly,* 16 December 1937): 'Junius objected to justice and conscience as legal criteria because when the judge becomes "human" and swayed by prejudice his power is unlimited and there is no freedom. In place of justice, therefore, Junius wished, in the English fashion, to put precedent. One might say that he opposed to the state of fantasy the state of fact. He wished to limit the public exhibition of virtue, in order that people might escape from the tyrannical consciences and appetites of others. His task remains to be done again. Without a clear conception of the State liberty is not attainable' (reprinted in *The Avoidance of Literature: Collected Essays*, ed. Michael Schmidt [Manchester: Carcanet, 1978], p. 17).
4. This is almost certainly a response to John Cornford's trenchant – probably hurtful – attack on Spender in an article written at Cambridge in late 1933. In 'Left?' Cornford attacked Spender and others for perpetuating a bourgeois 'contradiction between art and life, between the life of the artist and the life of society'. Spender he singled out for writing 'poetry of revolution as a literary fashion': 'No wonder Spender is the pet of the bourgeois-liberal critics. If this is the revolution, then there is no need to fear such an idealist romantic affair! But this is not the revolution. This is only the intelligentsia playing at revolution.' Earlier in the essay he explains D. H. Lawrence's failure to affect the working class by drawing attention to the fact that Lawrence 'was divorced from industry and never participated in a single struggle of his class'. Presumably Spender's faults

were in Cornford's view also linked to his 'divorce' by birth from the proletariat. See 'Left?', in *Understand the Weapon, Understand the Wound: Selected Writings of John Cornford*, ed. Jonathan Galassi [Manchester: Carcanet New Press, 1976], pp. 57–62).

5. Cf. Auden's poem, 'Sir, no man's enemy, forgiving all' of 1929, printed as the final poem in *Poems* (London: Faber and Faber, 1930), which petitions its addressee (God?) on ways to redeem humanity and society. The famous ending runs: 'Harrow the house of the dead; look shining at/New Styles of architecture, a change of heart.' The poem was omitted from collected editions after 1950, but is reprinted in *The English Auden*, p. 36.
6. Max Eastman, *Artists in Uniform* (New York: A. A. Knopf, 1934).
7. For information on Nekrassov and the various other Soviet writers named here, see Max Hayward, *Writers in Russia* (New York: Harcourt Brace Jovanovich, 1983), and also Gleb Struve, *Russian Literature under Lenin and Stalin 1917–1953* (Norman: University of Oklahoma Press, 1971.
8. Second International Conference of Revolutionary Writers, Kharkov, 1931.
9. Brown's letter in response to the 'Statement of Aim' of the Writers' International (British Section) is included in this volume (see pp. 56–8).
10. *VOKS Illustrated Almanac*, 7–8 (1934), published by the Soviet Union Society for Cultural Relations with Foreign Countries (VOKS) and the International Commission of the Organizational Committee of the Union of Soviet Writers.
11. Polonsky's article forms an appendix to Max Eastman's book, pp. 217–52. [SS]
12. *For Lancelot Andrewes: Essays on Style and Order* (1928; London: Faber and Gwyer, 1929), p. ix.
13. See below, pp. 289–300.
14. Rickword was a communist writer and editor of the *Left Review.* In 1935, Cunningham notes, 'Rickword went after [Spender's] *The Destructive Element* like a badly brought up guard dog – it was sincere, but also unclear, liberal, empiricist, naïve, and misconceived' (p. 34).
15. Robert Bridges's 'Poem in Four Books,' dedicated to the King, and first published in 1930.
16. There is considerable discussion of I. A. Richards in West's *Crisis and Criticism* (especially Ch. 6).

25   Naomi Mitchison   *from The Home and a Changing Civilisation (1934)**

This book was part of *The Twentieth Century Library*, a series on topical subjects, published by John Lane and the Bodley Head, and edited by V. K. Krishna Menon. Among other works in the series were: *Art* (Eric Gill), *Women* (Winifred Holtby), *Communism* (Ralph Fox), *The Black Races* (J. H. Driberg), *The Jews* (Norman Bentwich) and *Broadcasting* (Raymond W. Postgate).

Jill Benton tells us that Mitchison dictated *The Home* 'in a white heat. She was angry. Her words, seething near the surface of her thinking, came quickly' (p. 96). What had brought her to this state was the difficulty of placing her latest book – *We Have Been Warned*, a political novel about the Labour Party – with a publisher. One problem was the work's frank treatment of assertive female sexuality and sexual talk, principally the reason Jonathan Cape declined to publish it. When Mitchison offered the work to Victor Gollancz, that difficulty was compounded by his belief that his 'efficiency as a publisher of Socialist books would be seriously damaged' by association with it. As Benton notes, Gollancz was acutely sensitive to the dynamics of socialist politics in Britain at the time: 'In no quarter of Labourite socialism were men accepting Naomi's socialist–feminist tenet that women had a right to possess their own bodies, and to share their bodies with whoever and as many as they might choose or, for that matter, not to share with anyone . . . Women's problems and varieties of feminism, perhaps because they would have been divisive, were the last issues to be considered by those striving to save their vision of a better, more equal world' (p. 95). It was while waiting for a solution to the problems with her novel – and with a powerful sense of the issues at stake in that process – that Mitchison turned to write her history and analysis of the concept of home.

At present the feminists are depressed. They won what looked like great victories, but the world is still the same. Can it be that their difficulty is that they have tried to change the home without altering its fundamental characteristics? Are they not perhaps afraid of facing what a real change means?

So far, then, we have not been able to discover any acceptable solution for this basic difficulty of the twentieth century: the changing and most unsatisfactory home. Some solutions which are put forward are definitely retrogressive, others fail to tackle the roots of the matter. No doubt those who

* Reprinted from *The Home and a Changing Civilisation* (London: John Lane/Bodley Head, 1934), pp. 139–51.

think their own solution is the one and only right one, will accuse me of falsifying them, and no doubt I am biased (like everyone else, only one does not count it when the other person is biased one's own way). This is a short book on an enormous subject; all I have hoped to do is to put forward the most interesting and cogent facts and criticisms and, if possible, remedies. But so far none of these remedies and solutions seem very impressive, though that may be my fault for not being impressed.

So now, I suppose, I must try to make out my own solution. Obviously I have got to start with the inner content of the home, the group, and with the first group, the couple. I have to produce a theory of how men and women can live happily together. It is not much good trying to patch things; one can put right plain injustices and install labour-saving and temper-saving devices, but that is not really any use, and the whole thing is very urgent. Nor is it much use going Lawrencing about the country, talking about BLOOD; the man himself could do it, but there seems to be something wrong with all his followers. Ideas like his can be put across once by a genius, but the next time they have to be modified; the difficulty is that most of the diadochoi[1] stick to the text as closely as a good communist sticks to Marx. It is possible that they are all men in Lawrence's own kind of position: ill, fretted, full of grievances – mostly very real – bothered by transference from one social class to another, and most unwilling to face political realities. But some of them certainly try to make one suppose they are normal in their relations both with women and with politics. It is not convincing. They are mostly afraid of society and they all hate women as Lawrence did (though he tries all the same to help them, just as one might try to help sick people, the very sight of whom makes one shudder). It must be fairly obvious that Lawrence could never really stand the idea of a woman enjoying herself sexually (I wish I could use plain, honest English words about all this). He had the idea that if she did she was in some way taking from the man, triumphing over him, stealing some of those queer qualities which he had to describe by symbols, because he was never sure what they were. When he tries to describe a woman enjoying herself, there is always a certain amount of hate about it; and also it is all blurred and goes off into mists and fireworks, as in *Lady Chatterley's Lover*. He neither knows what it is like, nor wants to know; he refuses to imagine it. Perhaps no man can imagine accurately what a woman feels like, both locally and generally, but he might imagine, if he took trouble, a great deal better than Lawrence did. But his imagination was blocked by hate, and the fear which started it. And it is this hate which is making most of the trouble. Why cannot we get rid of it? Cannot we all just be kind?

If we are unable to be kind and fearless, what is it that is stopping us? That is the hare I have been chasing all through; it is ownership. That is why, in this book, I have constantly written as though men were an enemy: as they have been. And as they need not be. None of us want to be enemies if we are given a chance and disentangled from the things which are hurting us. But it is not quite simple; nothing is, especially after it has been talked about and written about and legislated about and above all lived about, for some thousands of years. What angered Lawrence and made him hate us, was that he wanted to go on owning – and when a woman was enjoying herself she was an equal, she was not owned. All of his book, *Fantasia of the Unconscious*, is really about men owning women, men being leaders and masters; he could not get away from it. And the converse of that was that he was terribly afraid of being owned: a man being owned by a woman seemed to him monstrous and horrible, a sin against the Holy Ghost. And so it is, but what he did not realise is that there are two sorts (at least) of ownership which he had never disentangled from one another. And this is, I think, the one really important thing I have to say.

There are at present two ways of conduct for all of us, over almost everything, and half our troubles are that we do not distinguish them, or that we get into terrible muddles when they run counter to one another. For instance, it seems to me that *personally* one must be a complete pacifist, completely gentle and willing to turn the other cheek indefinitely, but *socially*, at present, one must not only be willing to fight for certain things, but also one must prepare the fight (and what one is fighting for is the possibility of a remote time when personal pacifism will be a good enough guide to social conduct). This conflict is extremely painful and difficult, for there is a border-line of action, when one cannot be intellectually sure whether one is acting personally or socially; for many of us it is perhaps the main conflict of the present day.

Again, with possession. Socially, possession is a terrible evil, leading to every kind of hatred, cruelty, insecurity and despair. But personally it is all right. It is the necessary assuagement of our inherited instincts from the social apes. Everybody minds being owned economically, even when they acquiesce; nobody minds being owned in love. (Or, more accurately, everybody wants to be owned in love.) But when the two things are mixed there is the devil to pay, and Lawrence had them hopelessly mixed, partly perhaps because he had been socially and economically owned as a boy, the son of a miner. For that matter, we have all got them a bit mixed, and that is why the devil is in our sexual relationships. For either women do not want to be owned socially and have got it so mixed up that they will not be owned personally (especially as being owned personally is dreadfully apt to involve being owned socially) even though it hurts them not to be – those are the intelligent women. Or else they really do not want to be owned, but because they like being owned personally, they acquiesce in being owned socially and either try to get round it by grabbing back in some way – being actually owners themselves – or else by pretending to be very proud of it and trying to be as much owned as possible. And these are often intelligent too, and sometimes happier. Or else they just are owned both ways, and do not think about it much, particularly if they are in the class of society which is anyway owned altogether, men and women and children, by the others. There are all sorts of possibilities. But the unhappiest ones of all are the women who are owned socially but are not owned personally; their only chance is fantasy making, usually religion.

It is the same with the men, only perhaps even more complicated. Either they do not want to be owned socially and have got it mixed up so that they will not be owned personally (and this is only too often because women do not understand that personal owning is not social owning too, but try to make it social as well, as I think the women Lawrence knew must have done): and these are often the best sort of men. Or they do not want to be owned socially, and are not, but insist that the converse of not being owned is owning, and try to own other people – or, usually, one other person: not only personally, but socially as well. Or they are both owned and owning, both socially and personally, or in any combination of the two. As a matter of fact, over this matter of owning and being owned, and wanting and not wanting, actively and passively, personally and socially, there are a very large number of possible permutations and combinations (not supposing that anyone *wants* to be owned socially, but allowing that one class of person acquiesces in it). So no wonder people are in a muddle. But some of these combinations are rare, perhaps even perversions, and some of them are certainly unhappy-making. It seems to me that there is only one really happy-making combination out of the lot, which applies to both men and women.

The happy-making combination is one of the simplest ones. Here, both man and woman are not owned socially (and do not want to be), and do not own socially (and do not want to) but they are owned personally by one another (and want to be) and they do own one another personally (and want to). That is to say, there are no real conflicts, and the only possible source of conflict is that the overlap between personal and social may not be completely obvious. Yet it is much clearer here than, for instance, in the earlier example about pacifism . . .

Once we can split up these two aspects of ownership, all sorts of things get simplified, among them, immediately and obviously, a lot of the difficulties which 'conscious' and intelligent people have in their love affairs. They cannot go into them whole-heartedly; they are constantly stopped by considerations of pride, especially the woman. You see, Lawrence, and Ethel M. Dell, and all the low-brows, *croyants et pratiquants*, are right: physically, the maximum fun and heightening of consciousness, toppling over the edge of known feelings into hyperaesthesia that directly affects the mind, is to be had when the woman is overwhelmed and 'possessed' by the man. But this very rarely comes off and when it does it is often followed by a reaction and feeling of guilt. Why? Because this 'possession' has become mixed up with another kind of possession: the very word makes one react against it. One's historical mind gets at one, pointing out that one is the 'weaker sex', for this reason oppressed and exploited, and one mixes that up with what ought to be the very pleasant feeling of being gripped by muscles of a different strength and texture to one's own, and, hating the one, one's hatred is transferred to the other. One wants, passionately, *not* to be the weaker, and this is understandable considering the history of the last several thousand years, but why on earth should one bother? Men are weaker than elephants and less able to do lots of things: but elephants do not oppress them. Again, one cannot help realising how much of man's traditional courtship is really a crafty way of getting round one so that one should forget that he is really the master, the patriarch, and so, even when the courtship is now done without any economic content at all, one may still find it annoying. And all these irrational angers and reactions are below the surface of consciousness, so one never knows when they are not going to jump out at one.

Then again, the guilt feeling, the depression. This is largely the same thing. The *'omne animal triste'* tag is incorrect observation. Sleepy, perhaps, but not *tristis*. If a relationship is purely personal there should be no sadness; the sexual feelings which have been centred entirely on the object and which are discharged with the sexual act, have no doubt been reduced suddenly and violently, but that is no reason for sadness; there are plenty of other feelings which they may have masked, to take their place. But what may happen is that the woman, reacting against possession, may sadden the man, and a socially sensitive man may react directly, feeling that he has been doing something too like the owning which he himself hates.

All this is largely a matter of words and the ideas connected with them; unfortunately they have been used one-sidedly. But the deepest kind of owning is both ways. One tries to keep off the phrase 'being in love' because it has no clear meaning, yet perhaps the most essential and satisfactory thing about it is the identification of two people with one another, entirely a plus process, where, as Freud says: 'the ego has enriched itself with the properties of the object.' The difference between this kind of possession and ordinary social and economic possession is that here nothing is taken away although something is added. Yet in ordinary romantic phraseology we can only think of it as a swap: 'My true love hath my heart and I have his.' Nation of shop-keepers that we are!

Then again, we are up against the old point of view that a man's 'possession' of a woman should be violent. Why? Because it is taken for granted that no one likes to be possessed, to have something *taken from them*: so it must be by violence (this again is connected with the old patriarchal overvaluation of virginity for commercial purposes, a purely male valuation which generations of men have wished upon women until they, too, come to over-value it just as much or worse). A certain amount of violence is all to the good; it quickens the circulation and makes one more alive. Yet complete 'possession' may be as gentle as you like, and yet give the same feeling.

But, with all this, the thing does not work properly. The well-known phenomenon of the difference of timing in women, especially conscious women, is probably due to the same complex, the same holding back from being owned. I should very much like to know whether it would happen in a society where social and economic owning did not happen.

Thus far, from the woman's side. Her 'possession' of the man is a deeper thing, parallelled by the biological difference in her structure. Physically, it may be rather frightening to a man at first, because he has scarcely expected it, he is apt to think that he alone is the active one, and resents any muscular action by the woman, as Lawrence and others seem to have. But surely all this is just fear of being got at, triumphed over, 'used' – exploited? It cor-responds to something in the mind. Day Lewis, a sensitive modern, who certainly hates the idea of social ownership, speaks to the loved woman in his poem, forbidding her to own him, terrified of her trying to:

> Content you. Be at home
> In me. There's but one room
> Of all the house you may never
> Share, deny or enter.

But is not this the same muddle? Nobody who thinks for themselves *can* be entirely owned or understood or in general apprehended by anyone else, however loved and loving. But thought or feeling or cerebral activity of any kind has ultimately to be in some way made clear and shared. It will not be shared quite as it first turned up, of course; one does not oneself perhaps know that (say) the sight of a distant mountain under the sunset moved one to a dissertation on economics or a poem about a baby. But when it is shaped it is and should be shared: because we are apes and not gorillas. But because it is shared it is not taken away from one. It is not owned.

Am I making clear what kind of thing this personal ownership is? After all, one is several kinds of being. One is the social being, part of the community, with social relationships, and, as this, one is not really an 'I' at all – one is not *whole*, any more than a single bee taken from a hive is, biologically speaking, a true bee at all. The community goes on and is, if not really eternal, sufficiently so for one's need for immortality; that is the biological side of things. And then one is a personal being, and that includes one's mortal body, tossed about by hormones or emotions or whatever, and all one's apeish longing for a closer contact than the social ones and a good deal of one's Freudian ego, which really takes one very little further than any other definitions, though it is helpful for moderns who dislike the other definitions. That is, perhaps, the physiological or the physiological–psychological side of things. This part of one is not completely lonely nor does it die completely with one's own death, for it is mixed with a lot of things and people and especially perhaps with the family group. And also one is an intellectual being, and here one is and should be alone, except in so far as one can translate one's thoughts into something personal or social. Perhaps some people are never this at all, or very little; perhaps it is a fairly new thing in human development, since, say, the last five thousand years or so, and we are still unused to it and bothered by it. We feel it is unnatural to be alone, and we either want to be owned here too – to share – or else we realise we cannot be and we are bothered (like Day Lewis) at the thought that other people might want to own or share. But it is all right, he need not really bother, one cannot be owned there. The stoics understood that. All that other people can do is to worry one and stop one from getting into this category of existence. Personal ownership, lovely and necessary as it is, does not touch one here, though the moment one begins to shape and translate whatever one has brought out of one's loneliness it touches at once and may be of infinite help . . .

All this could be expanded indefinitely into the realms of psychology, medicine, law, and so on. But I am only going for a moment to touch on some of the concomitants and meanings of personal ownership. It cannot, I think, for a moment mean exclusive ownership either way: that is entirely an economic idea, to do with ownership of children from the man's point of view, and provision of food and shelter from the woman's. Jealousy is no more 'natural' than patriarchy; it has been talked about as though it were a personal thing, but that only shows how easily we are taken in. The more identification, which is perhaps the mental core of personal possession, there is about a love relationship, the less jealousy there can be, for whatever the object does and is and feels, the possessor and identifier can follow it. The purely sexual libido is pretty easily satisfied (people who find one another at all attractive should not inhibit one another – but that is perhaps another story); it is the other components of 'love' which make jealousy. This personal possession is not, like other possessions, bounded by ordinary time and space; it seems possible to have an overlapping relationship between several people. That horrible thing, sexual contempt, is almost always the result of a reaction from being owned, and should never occur when that is smoothed out. Resentment, too, is usually though not always entangled with the idea of ownership. Sexual resentment is one of the most interrupting of all emotions, and seems to come almost always from men or women trying to own someone more than personally – and the someone refusing to be owned.

And now I am going to try to indicate the kind of home which this implies. For the group grows its home, much as a snail grows its shell. This we have seen in the past.

The first thing is that there must be no social ownership, no patriarchy. How is that to be done? I am not going to say that the U.S.S.R. is the perfect state – it is not – but so far, it has come nearer than anywhere else to realising this ideal. Perhaps we can do no better; no harm in trying, anyhow. But personally, I cannot see how it is going to be done without some form of equalitarian society.

When social ownership has been done away with, then you can have people owning one another, to their hearts' and bodies' content, in friendship and in love. They can make as close a home as they like; they can be happily and unwaveringly monogamous all their lives. If a woman is physically capable of standing it, as some women are, she can have a baby a year, and, so long as the social contract is not broken, so long as this does not put her under anyone's social and economic ownership, and so long as there is room in the world for that much more population, there is nothing against it. It seems likely that most women who have gone so far as to have one or two children, would like to have one or two more, if the situation allowed of it. Pregnancy is one of the most complete – and if taken properly one of the most satisfying – forms of being personally possessed. But at present in most countries women react against it because it means in practice that they are immediately put into a state of being economically possessed when they become pregnant. They react against it consciously by using contraceptives, or, when contraceptives are forbidden by state paternalism or too expensive, by having abortions; and there is a case for saying that much of the sickness and malaise of pregnancy is psychical and caused by unconscious reaction against it. I do not know how much real evidence there is about this, but when I was in Russia I did observe that a large proportion of the female population were obviously pregnant, but they were going about their jobs and looking well and happy, as few pregnant women do in this country. It would be interesting to get statistics on the health of pregnant women in (*a*) a socialist state, (*b*) a Protestant capitalist state, and (*c*) a Catholic capitalist state. It seems possible that the extra value put on to the idea of motherhood in Catholic countries may to some extent counteract the economic facts. But so far, women's health and happiness have not been thought sufficiently interesting for this type of statistics to be collected.

Here, then, is the basic family group of the good home. In this home, which could be as large as they liked and as the state of the world could afford, a couple could have personal possessions, that is to say things which are not used for owning other people; they could have furniture, decorations, pictures, beautiful and comfortable clothes: I see no reason why they should not have diamond tiaras and ropes of pearls – it would be a pity to throw all the pearls in the world back into the sea, and if they are not worn they lose their gloss and beauty (unlike Mr. Woolworth's pearls[2] which will, I believe, keep indefinitely). Yet I doubt if they would want very elaborate homes, because they would both be thinking so much of other things, of the much more interesting and complicated workings of an un-owning, un-patriarchal society, of personal relationships, of the things they would be making or doing which would be the material basis of their economic freedom. However, I leave the degree of elaborateness to the future.

The Moral Idea and the Political Vision (1938)*

The book from which this extract comes was written by Mitchison in direct response to events in the public world after 1935. The revolutionary cause, the peace movement – both appeared to her to be losing their momentum. Benton observes that when Mitchison chose to affiliate herself with Mass-Observation 'she was putting the final nail in the coffin of her relationship with Gerald Heard

---

*Reprinted from *The Moral Basis of Politics* (London: Constable and Co., 1938), pp. 25–31.

[whose essay on the new pacifism is included in this volume, pp. 101–6, and] whose theory of inevitable social progress was harshly criticsed by Tom Harrisson' (pp. 108–9). Heard left England for the United States in 1937, and Mitchison later wrote of his mystical pacifism: 'it is certainly easier to practice deep meditation and the crossing of psychological barriers for someone who does not have a husband and children and a house and a number of practical commitments.'³ Disillusionment of this sort, laid upon the death in 1936 of her beloved father, J. S. Haldane, brought her to take up again the treatise on morals and politics which she had begun in 1935. It appeared in 1938 and signalled a change in the direction of her life: she would henceforth live mostly away from London, distinct from the movements with which she had been aligned in the first half of the decade.

Political conflict exists. In certain countries it is heavily suppressed, but even there it exists in people's minds. Why is it? Why is the government of any country and, further, of the whole world (that is to say, how groups of people are to be related to one another and to their material environment) not as simple and as little to be thought of ordinarily as the main drainage system of a large town? Why is it, instead of being this, a matter of conflict?

We are going to try and find out.

In general political conflict arises from the differences between two main kinds of thought and action. One kind wants things to stay as they are on the whole; the alterations it seeks are for the perfecting of already existing institutions with their attendant modes of thought and action (such as empire, church, and private ownership of property); it believes these institutions are capable of perfection and capable of producing a happy and prosperous society. In general those who hold these beliefs are also materially interested in the continuance of existing institutions, or else suppose themselves to be; but this material interest is not in itself necessarily their conscious motive for support of these institutions, and we are only deluding ourselves when we say it is. There are plenty of Conservative and Imperialist 'idealists' who are ready to make the utmost sacrifice for their vision of institutions. And equally there are millions of genuine Conservative voters in this country who are not materially interested in existing institutions.

Here, then, roughly, is one side. The other kind of thought wants things to be altered, not towards any perfecting of existing institutions, but towards their complete abolition and supersession by something different in kind. It believes that unless this is done there can be no general happiness or prosperity. In general, those who hold these beliefs have either no material interest in upholding existing institutions (that is, no obvious and immediate personal interest – though a Labour Lancashire cotton operator may be interested in the survival of the British Empire, taken as a single institution), or else, if they are materially interested, they are in some way incommoded by existing institutions. In this latter category, however, are a good many who, on economic and social balance, are a good deal more interested than incommoded. The large majority of people who hold this kind of belief are not only not materially interested in the continuation of existing institutions, but are actually oppressed by them (that is, as a class, forced to be iller, hungrier, uglier, more frightened, more insecure, more easily hurt and more unhappy than the people who are interested in the continuance of the present system). But I am going to contend that the political action which they take because of their beliefs is not necessarily caused by their lack of material interest in existing conditions and institutions, nor yet by their material interest in the overthrow of such institutions.

This is the basis of political conflict. These two main sets of people have different and mutually exclusive visions of the good.[4] The question of *why* the two sets have made two different moral judgements is historical, and is plainly and directly correlated with their interests. People are conditioned by their material interests in the most obvious and simple way; if they can satisfy their instincts and appetites under one kind of institution and cannot see how they can do so under another (very often they do not even go so far as to consider this), they make a moral – and usually a religious – idea imperative to support them. They do not do this deliberately, or very rarely and only quite lately in human history; they just do it as simply as a dog barks or a bird flies away. Nor have we, until recently, known enough about ourselves to question our mythologies and moralities.

It may seem artificial to claim that, in politics, there are two distinct processes going on in people's minds: first the material interests making an idea or vision of morality, and then the idea or vision making action. But I believe that this is of great practical importance. It leaves the chink through which a change can come – sometimes, at least, the change which is called catharsis or conversion . . .[5]

I hope this idea is quite plain. In case it is not, let me give one or two schematic examples. Here is the first. The poor man oppressed by the rich has a direct and obvious interest in taking away the rich man's money and redistributing it amongst himself and his friends. He may, if circumstances allow of it, act immediately from this interest. Nothing will stop him but physical and moral force, and he may use the redistributed money to oppress, in his turn. But he may, after considering his oppression and its causes, form a moral idea about equality of money-power and about people not oppressing one another. If he acts on that, he is liable to behave differently with the money when he gets it, and also, he can be approached, not by way of force, but by way of discussion, intellectual, religious or emotional appeal, etc.; he may be persuaded that his moral idea or vision is correct, and he may choose to modify it in this or that way (or even abandon it altogether). This method of approach through moral ideas is specifically human.

Here is the second example. One nation may decide that it is in its interest to conquer another nation and take its land and enslave its inhabitants, as the Athenians decided to do with Melos. If the conquerors are completely cynical (cynical, from *kuon*, a dog, *i.e.* not human!) and only consider their immediate material interests, they cannot be appealed to or persuaded in any way to alter the course of their action, as the Melians found when they tried to argue with the Athenian envoys on moral grounds, but found there were none which the Athenians admitted. But few modern states have quite the fifth-century effrontery;[6] most of them are nominally Christian; they have to make themselves up a moral vision adequate to sanction their action. And it is on this moral vision that they can be 'got at' and have the course of their actions changed, if it can be proved that the moral idea is incorrect, and if this proof can be brought home with a sufficient intellectual and emotional charge. This does not always work, as we may have noticed lately when Italy's action in conquering Abyssinia was attacked on the moral plane by the spokesmen of other nations.[7] It seems possible that this moral disapproval might have worked had those who made the moral attack *really* believed that the Fascist vision was incorrect (but their own immediate imperialist predecessors had seen the same kind of moral vision and they had been brought up to honour it) and particularly if they had been able to express their views to the people of Italy themselves. Actually, the moral disapproval was mainly unsuccessful, but has had the curious effect of leaving those who disapproved of the Italian moral vision feeling guilt and ashamed of themselves. We have not had enough practice in these rather difficult large-scale human relationships yet. But occasionally the incorrectness of a moral vision is demonstrated afterwards, too late to alter the immediate action at least. This happened after the Boer War.

Now to go back to why people hold their vision or beliefs: I know well that this first statement is not all that is to be said about the two sides. I am aware, for instance, that fear and impatience lead to violence, and that violence, to be effective nowadays, has to be expensive. The people who believe in conserving existing institutions have a great deal more money than the others: and can, and do, pay for effective violence. If one is in the position to pay for violence, one is apt to believe in order, discipline and the sanction of force. It is quite possible that one believes in this because it is part of one's idea of the good life (as it may be in some visions of the Good); but it certainly encourages this belief if one feels that it can be put into practice. Most of those who have heard the 'call to order'[8] and acted in accordance with their beliefs, throughout the ages, have certainly had mixed motives.

Notes

1. Greek for 'descendants' or 'successors'.
2. See above, p. 19.
3. *You May Well Ask: A Memoir 1920–1940* (London: Victor Gollancz, 1979), p. 116. Quoted and discussed in Benton, p. 108.
4. I use the word vision, not with any mystical significance, but because it is the handiest word. What I mean by it and how much it is unconscious will, I believe, appear during the course of the chapter. I do not believe anything is to be gained by trying to decide whether and how much we are all determined by our unconsciousnesses. [NM]
5. Mitchison enlarges upon these terms in Chapter III: 'Violence and Conversion'. By conversion or catharsis she means 'the change of heart, the sudden thing which is the alternative to hatred-made-active as violence' (p. 108).
6. The Melian dialogue never, of course, really took place. It was invented by Thucydides to exemplify the kind of thing which was happening. No doubt there was a discussion between Melians and Athenians, but not as clear-cut as Thucydides made it. [NM]
7. Here it might be interesting to consider – in the light of Mitchison's argument – Evelyn Waugh's approach to the Abyssinian question in *Waugh in Abyssinia* (1936; reprinted Harmondsworth: Penguin, 1986).
8. The 'call to order' was heard throughout Europe in the inter-war years, especially in the period before 1930. One of its most striking results is the revival, in European art, of classical motifs and practices. On neoclassicism in figures like Picasso, Léger and de Chirico, see Cowling and Mundy *passim*, but especially p. 11. The apotheosis of this trend was, of course, the frigid neoclassicism of art in the Third Reich (on which, see Adam's study of the subject, and Deane, *At Home in Time*, pp. 7–17). Obviously Fascism itself was evidence of a widespread preoccupation with order. One more benign, but not unrelated, domestic British answer to the call was Sheed and Ward's *Essays in Order* series (see below, pp. 345–55), as was the journal *Order* out of which the series grew. *Order* was founded and edited in 1928–9 by T. F. Burns, Harman Grisewood and René Hague. See discussion of the journal in relation to the Catholic group, which included Christopher Dawson, Eric Gill and David Jones, in Elizabeth Ward, *David Jones: Mythmaker* (Manchester: Manchester University Press, 1983), pp. 43–5.

26 Stevie Smith *from a letter to Naomi Mitchison (1937)**

Smith and Mitchison became friends in the 1930s, and the relationship is fondly recalled by the latter in her memoir, *You May Well Ask* (pp. 153–9).[1] Whatever drew them together, it was not agreement on political issues. Barbera and McBrien observe, 'Stevie, conservative in her sympathies (if indeed someone so non-political can be characterized in standard terms), complained to Denis Johnston, "I like Naomi but of course we are poles apart as far as World Problems goes, but if she thinks she's going to rope me into the Haldane–Communismus gang she is mistaken"' (p. 106). Even so, after the success of her *Novel on Yellow Paper* in 1936, Smith's circle did broaden to include many intellectual radicals, some 'Reds' (as Mitchison bluntly described them) as well as others of a different political colour.[2] Recalling her own letter which provoked the following response, Mitchison recalled, '1937 was a year when various things were going not too well and I was becoming more and more aware of the possibilities of fascism or war';[3] it was the period in which she took up work again on *The Moral Basis of Politics* (see above p. 235).

No. I don't think we can pass the buck to forces of evil or to anything but our own humanity. We are bloody fools – but then, we are hardly out of the egg shell yet. I think we want to keep a tight hand – each of us on our own thoughts. I think at the present moment you are in a state of mind that hungers for the disasters it fears. If there are these forces of evil, you see, you are siding with them, in allowing your thoughts to panic. You mind is your own province – the only thing that is. Yes, this brings up another point. There is a sort of hubris in this world-worrying. For if you have achieved peace in your own mind, when the worst happens (if it does) you will have reserves of strength to meet it. And if you have not achieved peace in your own mind, how can you expect the world to do any better. You are the world & so am I – & at the moment the world is a great deal too articulate! (You will agree!!) And worries too much – & so on. My God – the hungry generations – ours appears to be famished. If you knew the letters I still get. The ones from the women – all so hungry & worrying. Hungry for a nostrum, a Saviour, a Leader, anything but to face up to themselves & a suspension of belief. They are so unhappy too you know. (I am thinking of one particular letter. I'd send it to you but I had my bag pinched the other day & the damned thing in it.) It is sad for them. It is like a baby cutting its teeth – & fighting against it all the

* Reprinted from *Me Again*, ed. Jack Barbera and William McBrien (London: Virago, 1981), pp. 257–8.

time: 'Oh what is to happen to me now, oh these teeth. The future is nothing but one large tooth, or is there no Saviour to save me from my tooth?' Yes, our times are difficult but our weapon is not argument I think but silence & a sort of self-interest, observation & documentation (I was going to say 'not for publication' but I am hardly in a position to say that!).

Mosaic (1939)*

'Mosaic' was Smith's monthly column in a short-lived Newnes and Pearson magazine, *Eve's Journal*. It was *Novel on Yellow Paper* which had brought her to the attention of the editor, Christine Jope-Slade. Her chosen mode in the column was diaristic: 'Some small incident served as a slender plot on which Stevie draped her views about quotidian concerns or depicted unusual characters' (Barbera and McBrien, p. 124). Here the incident is Chamberlain's conference with Hitler at Munich in September 1938. An interesting comparison might be drawn between this short essay and Louis MacNeice's *Autumn Journal*, which covers the same period.

Friendship and the revolt from friendship is the stuff of life. I am so grateful to my darling friends, to all my darling friends, but for the moment adieu. When I get home my noble aunt is reading the papers. At the time I was writing this the number of people reading the papers was more than usual. To keep out or not to keep out of war, that was at that time the question. Now, perhaps we are already again at war, perhaps not. My aunt is a staunch Tory, and equally staunchly she is regarding Germany as the ultimate enemy. Unlike many of the people who live in my own high-class suburb, she is well read in the political game. Tonight is the night of the announcement of the flight of the Premier. Flight into darkness, say some, echoing the beautiful title Schnitzler chose for his suicide novel. I am listening at the house of a friend, an old mamma, she is really the church friend of my aunt, or the church sweet enemy, since my aunt carries on her church work in a fury of disagreement with the other ladies. Mrs A., we will call her, has a radio, which my aunt and I have not. My aunt does not like 'the noise'. Mrs A.'s radio announces the flight. On this great day of stress Mrs. A has not seen a paper. She has been too busy. So I say: 'The news looks serious. Japan is coming in with Germany. That will be not so hot for Australia.'

---

* Originally published in *Eve's Journal* (March 1939). Reprinted from *Me Again*, pp. 105–7.

Mrs A. pants rather; she is making a wool rug and the colours must be matched nicely. She pants: 'Oh, yes, Australia! Mr A. has bought a new car.' So now the great news comes through that the Premier is flying to Berchtesgaden. 'So that is the best news I've heard today.' 'What is?' says Mrs A. 'That the Premier is flying to Berchtesgaden.' 'Oh,' Mrs A. says. 'Oh.' Then she says: 'Mr Parker was just in. He said: "Why are we interfering in Czecho-Slovakia?"' I am rather intrigued by this piece. Bottle Green, I guess, is calling all suburbs. Now, I hurry to say to you that I am not high hatting the suburbs; suburbs are very O.K. in many ways. I use the term spiritually, not geographically. I am thinking of the people who say: 'Where the hell is Czecho-Slovakia?' These people often don't live in suburbs at all; suburbs (it is unfortunate for suburbs) is a term of abuse, and these people earn abuse. Their forefathers, I guess they said: 'Where the hell is Waterloo?' 'Where the hell is Trafalgar?' But they would have known what the hell all right if Napoleon had invaded England. So they will know what the hell all right if Germany goes on her *Drang nach Kolonien*, like hell they will, like hell. So Mrs A. has two sons just down from Oxford, just the right age. I said, *just the right age*. So Mrs A. says now something so sad to make the angels weep, and so ridiculous. Alas, that human beings have the special privilege to be so often at the same time ridiculous and sad. So what does Mrs A. say? 'Whatever happens my boys will not be involved – because we have all signed the Peace Pledge.'[4] Oh, sad echoing of fiendish laughter! Oh, the hollow laughter that goes echoing round the halls of hell upon these words. 'We have signed the Peace Pledge.' And already upon my eyes there is darkness and a great wind blowing over dead battlefields, and the stench of death without honour, and the ridiculous sad cry: We never knew. 'Oh, now I must go!' I say. 'Yes, you have heard the news,' says Mrs A. with a meaning note. Oh yes, I suppose I am very rude, to hear the news and go.

I think of the old man flying to Berchtesgaden with his umbrella, this famous son of a famous Joe. Later the American papers said: *The mountain has gone to Mahommet.* They said: *An incomparably dramatic moment.* They begin later to hint that one can pay too high a price for insecure peace. America? Their own cruel Civil War was fought on this issue only. To deny to the Confederate Government the right to secede. America is a signatory of the Versailles Treaty. Will she with men and money defend the Czechs against partition, against Germany, against Hungary? Where does America stand? And England? Is it not better that three-and-a-half million German Czechs should secede than that Europe and the world should be at war? Is it not expedient that one country die? One country? How many others? Where will it end? The Germans are very good road builders. When I was in Germany we did eighty miles per hour upon those magnificent surfaces . . . After all, what is Czecho-Slovakia? The frivolous, pompous questions and answers, the irrelevant comments fly backwards and forwards; they are like dead leaves before wind that is blowing up storm-strong. This is a record of dead leaves. A friend of mine says: 'I know of two Austrian Nazis who helped their Jewish friend to escape. Yes, he was forced to scrub the pavements of Vienna, but he laughed while he did it; he took it in the right spirit. Some old Jews begged not to be made to do it; they were forced to. They did not laugh; you see they did not take it in the right spirit.' I think, and think. My friend says: 'You see I do not see people as nations; I see them as men and women.' Ah, the honey-sweet falseness of that vision. Men are good and evil, and women, too; some must die. They are not good and evil in essence, but in the sum of their actions they are good and evil, and on that plane only to be judged, to live or die. This is the scope of human judgement, and human judgement within this scope must upon occasion act. And so with nations. If there is no possibility of two opposed ideologies existing side by side, then the choice must be made, even the choice of war. And 'my boys' who will not be involved because 'we have signed the Peace Pledge'? Ah, bitterest choice of all! For when war has broken out there is no existence of a private peace; you fight for your country or, refusing to fight, you yet fight, and directly for the enemy. That is perhaps the ultimate most horrible demand of war; the State must have your conscience. War does not initiate a moratorium upon the Sermon on the Mount. The thoughts and actions, the jealousy and greed that led to war, our own most favourite imperfection, so long ago began it first. The phrase itself, attractively coined by Lord B[5] – in the course of the last upheaval, upon scrutiny, is empty of sense. 'Stuff and nonsense,' says my aunt. Stuff and nonsense is a song of high explosives. How many wars has she seen, this dear aunt? The Franco-Prussian – well, almost – (no, the lady is not so old), the Boer War, Egyptian, Burmese, African and Chinese affrays and annexations. For a peace-loving people we are somewhat frustrated in our affections. So you won't fight? 'Czecho-Slovakia,' says Germany, this anachronistic sad monster, begotten by falsehood upon weakness, this savage mystic, this unutterable bore, Germany. Already in the lazy English people there is a feeling of exasperation running so easily to hatred. Germany might be a menace and we should not care (where *is* Czecho-Slovakia?) – but a bore, ah, that is something.

Notes

1. See above, p. 239 n.3. Mitchison in fact reprints this letter, pp. 155–6.
2. Here see Barbera and McBrien, pp. 106–7.
3. *You May Well Ask*, p. 155.
4. The Peace Pledge Union was founded in 1934 by a group including Arthur Ponsonby, Donald Soper and Bertrand Russell. In the same year David Cecil launched the Peace Ballot, which by June 1935 showed that while 6.8 million people supported the use of force against aggressors, 2.4 million opposed military sanctions – even in defence. There was massive support for the League of Nations and other related issues: disarmament, prohibition of private arms sales, and non-military measures. See Thorpe, *Britain in the Era of the Two World Wars 1914–45*, p. 178. Also Annan, pp. 191–2, and Chapter 13 *passim*: 'The Obsession with Munich', which bears directly on 'Mosaic'.
5. Lord Beaverbrook, the Canadian financier who had emigrated to England and become a Member of Parliament in 1910, and then Conservative Party Leader in 1911. By 1916 he had acquired a majority interest in the London *Daily Express*. During the 1930s he exercised considerable influence as one of the 'press lords' and as leader of the United Empire Party.

27 Laura Riding *from The World and Ourselves (1938)**

'The troubles of the world', wrote Riding in her foreword, 'are not insoluble. They will not be solved, however, by economic, political or diplomatic means; nor will they be solved by religious faith' (p. ix). In *The World and Ourselves* she laid out a number of recommendations based broadly on the conviction that the 'outside' world of public affairs – typically, in her view, a male world – might be transformed by the entry into it of 'the "inside" people', 'in the wide use of the word, female', those who 'serve the amenities of private life, and all the inner realities of the mind' (p. 16). In a move typical of the survey-taking and mass-observing 1930s, Riding decided first to test her 'personal sense of world troubles' (p. x) by conducting a survey, and accordingly sent out about four hundred copies of a letter. In this she set up her key distinction between the 'remote, outer traffic' of public and international affairs and the life and values to be found *'inside the houses'* (p. 15); the latter, she presumed all would agree, are the more 'important'. Among the specific questions to which her correspondents were invited to reply were the following: 'What shall we [the inside people] do?'; 'Can we rehumanize . . . [those "outside"] by thrusting ourselves into the outer employments?'; 'Can we make them [the "fretful, blundering Napoleons"] stop? For that, surely, is the only remedy?' (pp. 17–18).

As might well be imagined, this perspective – reminiscent as it is of the nineteenth-century cult of true womanhood – attracted somewhat trenchant responses from feminists on the left. Naomi Mitchison, for example, described the distinction between inner and outer worlds – and their equation with the female and the male – as 'archaistic': 'It ceased to be valid at about the time it became cheaper to buy jam than to make it oneself' (p. 73). Furthermore,

> When you say that 'political employments . . . are intrinsically commonplace and blank' I just feel that you don't begin to know about them. After all, politics is dealing with people and groups of people in relation to one another and their material environment, and what is wrong with that as a living occupation? The moral basis of politics goes down to our deepest roots; politics means danger and beauty, conversion and rebirth. It also means lots of small ordinary things – more dust-bins and bathrooms for people who haven't got them, more leisure and more education for people who need them desperately and at the same time it means dealing with old so-and-so's pension and young what's-his-name's affiliation order. (p. 74)

---

* Reprinted from *The World and Ourselves* (London: Chatto and Windus, 1938), pp. 389–94 and 415–20.

Responding to this criticism, Riding took issue with Mitchison's assumption that politics has a 'moral basis': 'Politics do not spring from moral instincts, but are motivated by convenience; attempts to inform them with personal morality must always be extra-political' (p. 77). On this, see the Mitchison essay in this volume (pp. 235–9).

The following extracts are drawn from the conclusion to *The World and Ourselves*, a body of recommendations compiled in response to the replies Riding received to her initial letter. While the first section, 'Women as Hostesses', invites comparison with Naomi Mitchison's commentary on the home, the second on 'The Responsibilities of Writers' proceeds from an assumption fundamental to W. H. Auden's 'Writing' essay as well: 'the terms of contact [with others] which the writer stabilizes for his writing he arrives at by practice of contact in his life.'

Women as Hostesses in the Outside World, Rather Than Job-holders

Formerly, I have said, the sexual sympathies of women were adapted to the male need of forgetting the stress of the present; in sex women exercised on men a sympathetic provocation toward the future. Now, I have said, the sexual sympathies of women should be employed in helping men to shift the emphasis not from present to future, but from past to present. For what was then the future has come to be increasingly contained in our present; the nightmare – and sex is the language of nightmare – used to be the present, is now the past. The nightmare elements in contemporary life are haunting reminiscences. But we treat them as contemporaneously real – thus futurizing the sanities of the present. It is my belief that sex is playing the part in contemporary life of recreating old nightmares, and breeding futuristic fancies in which to escape from them. Sex itself has grown unreal, in not having adapted its mechanism to a level of life in which the balance of power is with mind rather than with body. And in growing unreal, it has lost its saving character of sympathy, and been reduced to a meaning of animal desperation that falls below the sex-conception of primitive humanity. The so-called 'sane', realistic modern conception of sex, as exemplified in the most advanced books on the subject, reduces sex to a beautiful science of copulation – in which any animal, except perhaps the horse, could give us better instruction.

The realities of sex have ceased to be those of copulation. In their minds, at least, people have stopped doing it: they do it in anonymous dissociation from themselves. But people remain, nevertheless, sexually differentiated beings. It is in the nature of the male – I do not mean his physical nature, but his nature in the full, universal sense – to resort to the female when he finds consciousness unendurable. It is in the power of the female to supply him with oblivion in the animal sense of sex, or with a new lease of consciousness in the mature sense of sex. And mature sex is practised by the co-habitation of presences, not by the co-habitation of bodies.

In spite of the infiltration of women into the job-world of men, there is very little actual intermixture of male and female presence there. Men largely work with men; and even where men and women are associated in work, there is a rule of 'impersonality', of exclusion of all but work interest, which is good in that it is directed against the admission of animal sex into working life, but disadvantageous in that it excludes the interaction of mature sexual sympathies. However, the outside job on which men and women work together is generally not of a kind to admit of much personal interaction – not even of the sympathetic interaction of sexual presence, which is a relatively negative form of personal contact.

The insistence that women should have jobs in the outside world is based on an artificial principle of sexual equality – artificial because the notion of practical equality disregards the significant differences between men and women. A relation based on a principle of mere equality is no relation. The job is one problem: whether women should be admitted into a certain kind of job can only be properly determined from the point of view of the job, by an estimation of whether women could introduce excellences into it that men could not. The relations between men and women is an altogether separate problem, to be dealt with by a sensitive adjustment of their differences which does not deny their differences. A principle of mere equality makes their differences meaningless, and when applied to the problem of jobs introduces just so much meaninglessness into the job's own quality: the relations between men and women are reduced in significance, and the significance of the job itself is reduced.

I am here not interested in the job, but in men and women in the world of jobs. The job-world is still largely a world of men. How should women move in that world, as it is – not as job-holders, but as women? If they moved in it more actively as job-holders, they would still not be moving in it more actively as women. And this is what I am interested in: for in it lies a way in which they may exercise their mature sexual sympathies, healing the violences of past struggle that haunt the daily present.

In the outside world men associate largely with men. They lunch together, drink together, assemble in all-male clubs. In the exclusive association of men with men there is instantly recognizable the lack of a quality which in informal language might be called a lack of social charm. They can work up in common the harsh brilliance of heroism, or the shabby flicker of all-male humour; but the brotherhood of man, in the exclusive sense of the term, is a dramatic pretence. It is not really comfortable—its ease is the slouching ease of undress. Nor really inspiring – its energies are all energies of strain. This changes, however, when the presence of women is added – except when, as in the business world, the women assume the male business manner and behave like just so many more men.

Men should not be left alone with themselves. Long alone with themselves, they breed either violences or fatuities. And then, when each goes home to the particular woman of his life, his sexual approach is in terms of seeking oblivion in her from outside unpleasantness. If he came home to her from a world into the texture of which the presences of women had been richly interwoven, his immediate consciousness would not lie upon him heavy with old nightmares; he would approach the particular woman of his life in the sense of hoping to achieve through her a happy intensification of conscious-ness – not in the sense of forgetting to-day and being propelled into to-morrow. Indeed, if the daily action of men were generally qualified by the female accent, their contact with their particular women would lose its physically sexual emphasis; the particular relation would cease to have the effect of a privacy that shut out, in its sexual narrowness, the rest of the world and the reality of others.

Women should be widely present in the outside world, not as job-holders necessarily, but as women. If in every factory, every shop, every office, a legitimate place were made for women as responsible for the domestic and social graces, we should soon see to how many jobs women could profitably devote themselves from the exclusive point of view of the job. There is no concern of the outside world in which there is not room for, not a necessity for, the administration of the social graces. Not only offices and factories, but even streets, especially streets; even underground trains and platforms, especially underground trains and platforms.

A conventional feeling exists against the employment of women in the rougher jobs, which has a real basis in sensitive instinct. The cliché about 'the refining influence of women' is only foolish and irritating when it is used as an axiom to prove that the influence of women should not be admitted into the physically urgent problems of life. To civilize the atmosphere in which the rougher jobs are done is to reduce them to their proper degree of urgency. Let women not do the rougher jobs, let men take over, take back, all the rougher jobs that women have assumed in the practice of artificial equality. The only real meaning that sexual equality has is in the necessity of the equal *presence* of women in the world of men.

This, in fact, is what civilization is: the penetration, into the rough physical exterior of life, of feminine and feminized sensibilities – the domestication of the material world. In the interior is the more intimate and personal drama of relations between the female and male forces of existence – the drama of mental reconciliation. But in order that this shall have a meaning of literal immediacy, the outside world must be the immediately relevant setting. And it cannot be that except through the introduction of female inflections into its temper. The mere holding of outside jobs by women will not accomplish this; the danger of emphasizing the right of women to the outside job is that it comes to be regarded as an adequate substitute for the work of reconciliation which men and women have to do on the plane of the mind, and which is the true end of conscious existence. The importance of the outside job is confined to the importance of means. It matters less that women should take an active part in the production of the means of civilization than that they should exert their presences to prevent the concern with means from reviving the pains of early material struggle, when to struggle seemed itself an end.

It better suits the character and functions of women to be the hostesses of outside activities than to be job-holders in them; or, rather, the proper jobs for them there are the hostess jobs, and that outside job in which they can least exercise hostess-presence is the one that is least suitable for them to hold.

I intend this as a practical recommendation: if women can succeed in forcing themselves into traditionally male jobs which are often characteristically male ones, and in creating male jobs for themselves, how much more easily could they create jobs for themselves which had an obvious appropriateness to their character? No equalitarian or sociological argument should be necessary to persuade people of this point. It should be recognizable, in its simplicity, by the simplest faculties of judgement – appealing as it does to emotional accuracy, not to the rational accuracy of opinion.

No more is needed than that women and men with a simple emotional sense of the distinctions between women and men resolve to act toward one another in the outside world by these distinctions. This would be a resolve of mutual employment of one another: for as men need to resort to the mature sexual sympathies of women, so women need to resort to men for the mature expression of their sexuality. One might draw up a plan of jobs based on the value of women as female presences rather than as job-holders, and in a commercially plausible way. But the issue depends on emotional recognition of the values involved: any such plan would follow spontaneously from an acceptance by women of this different view of themselves as agents in the outside world.

The Responsibilities of Writers

What we have to consider here is, really, economy of contact – though it might at first seem that a rule by which the conception of friendship was enlarged was anything but economy of contact. But if we admit that the contact which it is possible to establish between author and reader on a page is the best kind of contact – a direct contact of mind, purified of physical distraction and conversational irrelevancy – economy of contact and wide extent of contact are not incompatible terms. By economy of contact I mean the best kind of contact, and that kind only, with the greatest possible number of people.

Much of the ordinary contact between people in modern life is idle contact; is not intimacy but a relaxation from the strain of the compelled, as against the chosen, associations. The leisure association is thus frequently no more than that which makes the least demands – instead of being, as it should, the one that makes demands of a kind to use the best part of us. The feeling of not being used to the best possible effect in their work drives people to associations in which they are used, use themselves, to no effect at all: these, at least, in having no pretence of fruitfulness, bring no sense of frustration. The negative pleasure of idle association influences in turn the unsatisfactory working association; it becomes the object in that to use oneself as little as possible. The tendency in modern life is for both working and leisure time to be perfunctory in emphasis. Instead of constructive economy of contact, people practise a self-protective avoidance of contact.

In an age where, in most of the physical activities of life, the element of personal contact is eliminated, there should at last be a chance to enjoy personal contact on a real basis: on a mental basis. But who is to assume the responsibility of formulating such contact and giving the good example? I think it is the writer's special responsibility: mental contact is the realm over which the writer presides. When the presidency is not conscientiously fulfilled, it is not surprising that people in general seek the easiest instead of the best kind of contact.

It is the writer's responsibility to be the good example. He is the specialist in mental contact. And his opportunities are not only those of the printed page. Those are, we might say, the perfect opportunities: entirely safeguarded against the intrusion of impurities or irrelevancies of contact. But a writer also lives; he must risk all the chances of human contact in all the uneven circumstances of life. The more conscientious he is in trying to maintain, in his life, the best kind of contact with the greatest number of people, the more equivalence there will be between the temper of his life and the temper of his work – and in this the more actual his work will be. A writer should, indeed, make as little distinction as possible between his life and his work. In his work there will be either the designed contact with people, or none at all; while in his life there will be some contacts which exceed in potentiality those provided for on the printed page, and some which are below what he would wish. But it is only in life that he can test the possibilities. And it is only by testing the possibilities that he can stabilize the measure of certainty that he must employ in his work if it is to be true work.

The writer must maintain in his life, as nearly as he can, the temper of his work. Any discrepancy between standards of life and standards of work inevitably shows in the work: it is not possible to pretend in writing. One can even say that the kind of life a writer chooses to lead determines the kind of work he will do. Either a writer must imitate in his life the high standards he sets himself in his work, or he will in his work imitate the low standards of his life. When standards are high they are standards of work – whether the person is a writer or not, whether or not he records his standards in anything that can be conventionally called a work at all. To work is to contribute – in however small or unobvious a way – to the orderly integration of the permanent and fundamental elements of life. There are many stages in this general work of integration; and everyone may be said to be engaged in some part of it, if he has any claim to the title 'good person' at all. The writer must be held to be engaged in the final stage of this work, by his choice of those means of integration which are both the most precise and of the most comprehensive reference – the means of words: the writer, in choosing to be a writer at all, is undertaking to be the best kind of person that it is possible to be.

It is the writer's responsibility to be the good example. His work is to make life into consciousness of existence: so that we may be that which truly is, and only that. His own life, therefore, must be lived with a motive of study – study of himself and others, himself in relation to others, and others in relation to others: that we can expect in no other kind of person to the degree of persistence and purity that we can in him. He must not only be at work all the time: his time is properly longer and fuller than the time of others – for he must be presumed to be more arduously a conscious being than others.

The writer must conceive it his privileged obligation to use himself to the best effect all the time, and to use others to their best effect and to encourage them so to use themselves. He must not conceive the relations which he establishes with people on the printed page as ending there. He must be ready to serve as a constant source of encouragement for the conscious experience which he demonstrates in his writing to be possible; to treat tirelessly with people as they approach him in terms of his writing.

The terms of contact which the writer stabilizes for his writing he arrives at by the practice of contact in his life – that kind of contact, that aspect of mental contact, for which he is peculiarly equipped. By economy of contact he must develop the habit of concentrated contact. The problem of how to manage practically (in quantity) the variety of contacts that his responsibility implies will be solved in his maintenance of contact on the level on which his work is cast. The more strictly he limits contact with people that is not on this level, the more ungrudgingly he can give himself to the kind of contact that is.

This is a recommendation for friendship on a large scale, communication on a large scale. It applies, for example, to the problem of this book: how to communicate effectively with its appropriate public. I shall feel that people will have begun to work upon the subject of this book when they write letters about it to one another. Once again, the solution to the problem of association seems to me to be in letters. Letters establish a distance of communication; but, on the other hand, they eliminate many of the irrelevancies of close contact and can thus be instruments of intimate communication on the subject on which they are written. I would even say that the more conscientious a writer is, the more are his readers his working associates; their letters to him will be less letters than contributory work.

Writers should be, in their lives and in their work, centres of communication, of mental contact; and so regard themselves. I have throughout, here, described the writer as 'he'. This is always an inconvenient pronoun when used to mean 'anyone of that kind', if 'of that kind' does not mean, exclusively, 'of male kind'. It is the more inconvenient as the classification is more discriminating; and peculiarly inconvenient when the personal qualifications intended in the pronoun differ strongly from the common male characteristics. People of writing kind may, indeed, be said to be as females among people of other kinds, in the sense that it is their function to preside over the interior realities of existence. I do not wish to dwell on this point – on which much more might be said in the context of the special functions of writers as they are men, or women. Nor am I interested in inventing the convenient pronoun that would avoid this sort of ambiguity. It is important to keep the personal reference of the pronoun or pronominal adjective: better occasional ambiguity than the mechanical impersonality of the more inflected languages (*l'écrivain et son travail*), in which gender lies arbitrarily in the activity itself. The only real solution would be to cease to talk of writers as a race of vague number within the vague race of persons, and to talk of them by name alone. Here, for example, I am being not quite direct, in not saying who I think the true writers are and what I conceive to be the special function of each as a centre of communication and mental contact: hence the evasive 'he'. I should be saying that I think 'you' and 'you' and 'you' ought to be doing this and this and this. I am not, in fact, making the best possible use of myself in this respect as a centre of communication, not speaking fully as 'I'. The evasiveness, however, is only in my moderating my personal insistence on the nature of our responsibilities toward the possibility of common insistence: in my suiting my exhortation to the somewhat ambiguous evidence. But the function of writing is itself not an ambiguous one – the nature of our responsibilities should be clear enough. The difficulties of fulfilling them are great; but they become conquerable as we allow our work to take the difficult course, as we make them difficulties *within* our work.

If we act as centres of contact, then the boundary-line of our work is a movable, a living, one. Each writer is then extracting from 'his' special field of communication the very best there is in it; and not only extracting it, but preserving it. And as among writers themselves there is a co-operative centrality of communication, so will the entire world become a field of communication from which a very best can be extracted – and not otherwise.

We are each – each writer, each wide-working mind – a force of redemption. We are redeemers of everything that can be redeemed finally – that can co-exist without paradox, conflict or change. It can be dangerous, I know, to use the inspirational tone; but only when it leads one to say more than can be immediately substantiated. The madly self-conscious perversities in which many writers to-day spend themselves reveal, indeed, the poundings of their writer's conscience: the accents of wilful irresponsibility tell a guilt of responsibilities avoided. There might be a danger, in reminding writers of their responsibilities, of inspiring a vanity of writing in those without a real power of it. But I think my definition of these is severe enough, if acted on, to reduce rather than increase the number of writers. Or the danger might be, to be mocked – for speaking of writing, which seems to be adaptable to every journalistic degradation, with a quasi-religious fervour. But this is a danger which it is good to run: in order to learn the unabashed posture of demanding and being the best when others seem to be content with less.

The fervour of such a demand and intention of the best is not, however, quasi-religious. Religion consists of emotions, supported by just enough philosophy to act as a bridge between emotion and emotion. The fervour of writing is a height of mind, not a feeling; a constancy, not a fluctuation. Religion consists only of the emotions of people; there is no suprapersonal incorruptible element, as in an act of words. There is God, it might be said; but God, it might be said, is only the desire for good emotions. In an act of words there is the incorruptible element of truth; and in any abuse of truth the loyalty of words is with truth – what has been ill-written is brought in its own words to instantaneous judgement by what they have falsified or concealed.

Life in its most acute state of explicitness consists of acts of words. And it is the writer's function to be as the incorruptible element of this. In writing, more so than in any other activity, people can employ a best of themselves that is also a force in existence for the best; their work can be, with more identicality of work and self than in any other activity, what they are. They are the less writers as they are the less speaking concentrations of what is best. If writers can be moved to a courage of all that they are, the full doing of their good will mount in the practice of being of it. For the practice of themselves is a practice with others; truly to be a writer is to forswear the soothing negations of solitude, and the self-flattering affirmations of individualism. In the realm of behaviour the moral end is the good self; in the realm of language, the moral end is the good company. The writer is properly the discoverer and preserver of the world's good company.

28 Willa Muir *Women in Scotland (1937)*[*]

This essay appeared in an issue of the *Left Review* devoted in large measure to 'Scottish problems,' as the editorial called them:

> Scotland has for many years played a leading part in the Labour movement. Recently, the question of how far Scotland has a claim to political autonomy has been debated, and the inspirations of Scottish Nationalism and of Scottish Socialism have been to some extent in rivalry. It is of the first importance that any movements in defence of regional or national cultures should develop in a progressive rather than in a reactionary sense. We have therefore devoted a large part of this number to a discussion of Scottish problems, in the hope of throwing some light on the question how far an independent cultural tradition can be used in the fight against Imperialism, and how far the concept of Nationalism is today purely romantic. (p. 729)

At the time of writing this, Willa Muir (1890–1970) had moved with her husband, Edwin Muir, to Scotland, and was living in St Andrews – the city where she had studied as a university student in the first decade of the century. She found St Andrews conservative and oppressive, and would take her family to live in Edinburgh in 1942. But during the decade of the 1930s circumstances led Willa Muir to consider the place of women in small-town Scottish life, and to explore this theme in several books: it is central to her first novel, *Imagined Corners* (1931), for example, and also to her last, *Mrs Ritchie* (1933). The ground had been laid out in her earlier study, *Women: An Inquiry*, published by the Woolfs at their Hogarth Press in 1925. While accepting biological difference between men and women, Muir was especially concerned with social assumptions about sex and gender.[1]

Scotland, taken by and large, is, I suppose, a Socialist country. Yet it is difficult to speak of women's movements in Scotland, since most Scottish working-class women – and men, too – are dominated by the belief that outside the home men should have all 'the say'. In Scotland, again taking it by and large, woman's place is still considered to be the actual home. A Scotswoman at a mixed public meeting or on a mixed committee feels that it is not her 'place' to let her voice be heard, and she will not risk speaking up unless she has something very urgent to say. In consequence, the ordinary women of Scotland, petty bourgeois and proletarian alike, in the rural districts

[*] Reprinted from *Left Review* 2 (1936–7): 768–70.

and in the industrial towns, are untrained in public life, almost unrepresented, relatively unorganised and largely inarticulate outside the home. Even in purely feminine movements, such as the Women's Rural Institutes and Women's Citizen Associations, the ordinary working women let themselves be run by 'the country'. In other organisations they let themselves be run by their own menfolk, or by the Kirk, except when it comes to staging a bazaar or a social function. Ordinary Scotswomen, politically speaking, are as difficult to tempt into the open as the occupants of a Hindu zenana. The ratio of men to women contributors in this Scottish number of the *Left Review* is a fair reflection of what happens in Scottish public life.

Inside the home, of course, the tables are apt to be turned. A Scotswoman who is too timid to utter a word in public may tongue-lash her family in private with great efficiency. Inside the home she may have plenty of 'say', since her husband and her children are entirely dependent on her services. A Scotswoman at home can be a formidable figure; she is essentially a mother rather than a wife and comrade; she provides meals, darned socks and other comforts to the whole family, and from her point of view a husband is often enough only a more exacting child among the other children. It would be a mistake to assume that the 'missis' is a cypher merely because she keeps silent or goes off to wash the clothes whenever the menfolk argue about politics or religion. Her authority is rather a different kind of authority from her husband's; his is the concentrated authority of an individual, hers is the more diffuse, pervasive, atmospheric authority of an environment. And like other atmospheric conditions it can cause profound electrical disturbances.

This is an old pattern of domestic life. The mother as environment for her family is, so to speak, the basic diagram of womanhood. It is a pattern that survives from a world immeasurably older than our monetary civilisation in which we are caught up today, and you would recognise it, with local variations, in many parts of the world at different stages of history. It sounds a reasonable enough partnership: the man, as an individual, emerging from the home circle to dominate the alien world outside; the woman, as an environment, dominating the home circle. But it remains a reasonable partnership only when there is a fair balance between the prestige and rights of the partners, and the progress of our economic system has destroyed that balance. Today, at the present stage of capitalistic development, the circle of environmental authority within which a mother stands has both shrunk in area and dwindled in relative importance. Artificially created environments such as the State, the Big Business Monopoly, the factory, have encroached upon it and are steadily encroaching upon it.

These rival environments have economic status, while a mother has none. They interfere with and determine the education, the scale and nutrition, the medical treatment, the employment, the leisure recreations and personal loyalties of a woman's children. Unlike other mothers, the human mother cannot go out nowadays and forage independently for her youngsters' needs; she is hedged in by the bars of our monetary civilisation as if she were in a zoo; she must 'make do' with what she happens to get. The greater environment, the State, also has to 'make do', in theory, with what it can get from individual tax-payers, but it possesses compulsive powers and can control the amount of its levies. A mother has similar responsibilities on a smaller scale but no comparable rights. In theory, the father of the family is the conduit-pipe through which money flows into the house; in theory, the mother gets all she needs and administers it to the family, remaining outside the competitive economic market, preserving among the money values of the world an intact island of simple human values. It is a pretty theory. It has survived for so long simply because a woman nursing her own babies does not behave like a Milk Marketing Board. But in fact, in the world of today, the non-economic environmental services of women are horribly exploited. The monetary system by this time has encroached upon every corner of the home, and the simple human nucleus that makes a mother's world has shrunk almost to a pin-point. Her elemental needs, food, clothing and shelter for her children, are all prescribed by outside economic agencies over which she has no control.

The husband, of course, is equally a victim of economic circumstances, but his place is not considered to be exclusively the home; he has a certain economic status, he is in direct communication with the outside world, he is active politically and can make his voice heard in public. That is what makes the position of working-class women in Scotland so ambiguous today; they are confined to the home, and the home is shrinking visibly around them. They are still living by a tradition which modern economic life is hammering to pieces.

And the results? A startlingly high maternal mortality rate, a high infant death-rate, a general increase of unfitness, a rapid fall of the population. These are all signs showing not only the effects of economic depression but the profound, if inarticulate, discouragement of the women.

What is to be done about it? You can, of course, assume that in a new state of society private home environments will vanish completely. A mother would then rank as an individual, as a paid breeding-machine; she could park her children in State crèches, schools and institutes, and exercise her maternal gifts in administering the food, clothing and housing of a nation rather than a family. This system might possibly introduce more hygienic human beings than come out of the industrial slums where over-driven mothers are trying to cope with family life on the Means Test,[2] but nobody really believes it is humanly possible. The alternative policy is to create a right balance between the home environment and the outside world. That means a fifty-fifty partnership between men and their wives. It means that a mother should become also a political comrade, with an economic status of her own and a 'say' in public affairs. I suggest that Scotsmen accustom themselves to this idea, and do their utmost to enlarge the environmental circle within which their women are cramped. With a right balance between environment and individual, the family could be a solid basis for national life. A nation made up of such families would survive the disappearance of any State. Moreover, such a national ideal would appeal to the discouraged women of Scotland. Scotland as a nation has been for so long a 'puir auld mither' that Scottish mothers are likely to have a fellow-feeling for her. And if this fellow-feeling is not to be exploited by monopoly capital behind a barrage of Nationalist slogans, it must be used now as a means of enlightening Scotswomen. For they need to be shown where they stand, and I suspect that they are waiting for a lead.

Scotsmen, co-opt your women!

Notes

1. I am indebted to Beth Dickson's very helpful note on Willa Muir in *British Women Writers: A Critical Reference Guide*, ed. Janet Todd (New York: Continuum, 1989), pp. 487–9.
2. 'System introduced in 1931 for recipients of transitional benefit. All household income was taken into account in determining the level of benefit a person should receive. It applied the stigma of the Poor Law in all but name to many unemployed people, and was often administered in a petty way. The test, abolished during the Second World War, came to be seen as the embodiment of a perceived penny-pinching and unsympathetic National government' (Thorpe [1994], p. 177).

29 Philippa Polson *Feminists and the Woman Question (1935)**

The 'official occasion' referred to below was the Silver Jubilee of George V. Winifred Holtby's article, to which Polson replies, carried the descriptive title 'King George V Jubilee Celebrations', and appeared in *Time and Tide* (4 May 1935).[1] For a broader context to Polson's argument, see Jane Lewis, 'In Search of a Real Equality: Women Between the Wars', in Gloversmith, pp. 208–39. The criticisms made here of Holtby's bourgeois blinkers could be brought to bear with corrosive effect on Woolf's argument on behalf of 'the daughters of educated men' in *Three Guineas* (see below, pp. 264–71).

This year there has been official occasion for widespread balancing of national, social and personal accounts. The authorized version of the result advertised a preponderance of assets and called for festivity and bunting; the unauthorized version showed a heavy deficit and called for protestation. We protest. But it is interesting to find that a mouthpiece of one of the most vigorous protesting movements England has ever known – the feminist movement – should line herself up with the cheering section.

'Now I was reared,' Winifred Holtby has written in justification of her refusal to protest against the events of the past twenty-five years, 'conscientiously as a protestant, and I have spent a good part of my thirty-six years protesting ever since. But on this occasion I refused. I looked back on the past twenty-five years and decided that these were, on the whole, the most propitious that women in this country have ever known.'

This commonplace on the part of one of the accepted champions of women seems both dangerous and fallacious. Perhaps even a cursory examination of the position during these 'propitious' years will reveal the falsity of Miss Holtby's view.

First we must go back a bit. In 1882 the Married Women's Property Act was passed. This, as its name suggests, was an act which affected primarily – almost exclusively – the propertied classes, and it is significant that its champions were the kernel of what, in 1903, became the Women's Social and Political Union.[2] From 1903 until the outbreak of the Great War (when, as one might expect, the majority of its adherents went over to support the government's war policy) the W.S.P.U. was, in all its admirable and determined struggle, only demanding the enfranchisement of women *householders*.

* Reprinted from *Left Review* 1.12 (September 1935): 500–2.

At its zenith the suffrage movement represented a very considerable following and was supported by quite astronomically large funds, but by the very nature of the reforms it advocated it could only touch superficially the problems of the mass of English women. Even in its heyday, the suffrage movement drew its support almost exclusively from the bourgeois and petty-bourgeois classes, and even in its most revolutionary activities it was the women of the ruling class agitating for rights as members of their class, although their political non-existence forced them to extra-legal methods.

This struggle was characterized by an exceptional determination and devotion to principle; by the fillip it gave to the self-determination of women as human beings it undoubtedly did much to open up educational and professional venues to women of the ruling class. But the family as an economic unit remained unassailed and the double exploitation of working women continued unchanged.

It was the economic conditions of the Great War which finally opened the doors of all sorts and conditions of employment to upper class women and afforded to some of the women of the working class the opportunity of earning a wage that gave them a real, if temporary, independence of men.

It is popularly supposed that the war paved the way of women into industry. As regards the women of the upper classes this is no doubt true. But working women have been earning their bread (and the bread of their unemployed husbands, fathers, brothers) in mills and factories for a hundred years and more.

Allen Hutt, in his *Condition of the Working Class*,[3] puts side by side the words of a worker in 1844, quoted by Engels, and those of an unemployed worker in 1932: '1844: "There is work enough for women folks and children hereabouts, but none for men." 1934: "Seems as though it's only women and girls can get jobs these days."' The growing presence of working class women in industry marks no emancipation. Their exploitation within industry, both as workers and as women workers, remains unchanged.

The war-time boom was only a temporary phase during which employers, eager to find the hands to feed the fires of their exceedingly profitable war-time activities, dropped their habitual wail about feminine disability as an excuse for low wages, and welcomed the women as men.

The publicity which those four years afforded feminine labour threw into startling relief the nature of the peacetime exploitation of women.

'The opinion of the Factory Department,' says the preface to a report of the Home Office on the substitution of Women for Men in non-munition factories, 'is recorded that the substitution (of women for men in industry during the war) has proved successful in a great majority of cases; that women have shown capacity to take up many of the more skilled processes hitherto reserved for men and to carry them out completely and well, and have displayed unexpected readiness for work which at first sight seemed wholly unsuitable for them.' Consider also the illuminating statement made in 1919 by the report of the War Cabinet Committee on Women in Industry, to the effect that 'Similar evidence was given by the federation of Master Printers. In a number of cases where women were paid less than men, their output was so much more, that the employers gave it as a reason for not paying them equally, that their output might then fall as low as the men's.'

When they need and are willing to pay for women's labour the Cabinet Committee are eager to expose the old bogey that the children will pay for mother's independence; in the same report they say, 'poverty or an insanitary environment may have an even more injurious effect than the mother's absence. This is borne out by the low infant mortality rates in 1916 and 1917, years during which a continually increasing number of married women was being employed.'

This equality of capability, so eagerly averred in the days of war crisis, when labour of all sorts is at a premium, is, of course, strenuously denied in peacetime when the boot is on the other leg. When labour is no longer at a premium, the female labourer is hired, more often than not to do the work of a man, upon a strict understanding that her nature renders her quite incapable, that she is only playing at wage earning and a woman's real career is marriage. This is fine for the hirer.

Every day sees the tightening of the bonds of women. Where it is essential that female labour shall be kept at an apprentice level of pay (i.e. in teaching, nursing, civil service and office work) more and more employers refuse to countenance a wedding ring and none that I have ever heard of will offer any facilities for child bearing. Yet the proportion of female employment is steadily increasing. In other fields, wherever possible, cheap female labour is being substituted for male labour and a capitalist crisis which throws men out of work only speeds up this substitution. 'Seems as though it's only women and girls can get jobs these days.'

As revealed by the Ministry of Labour inquiry into the average earning of men and women, a woman's wage is never anything like as much as a man's and never is it a living wage even for a single person.

The following comparative figures will make this difference very clear.

AVERAGE WEEKLY EARNINGS, OCTOBER 24, 1931[4]

Industry	Males		Females	
	s.	d.	s.	d.
Engineering	52	6	27	7
Sheet metal	53	5	26	2
Tailoring	61	1	29	3
Dressmaking	57	6	28	9

Primarily, however, it seems, Winifred Holtby is not concerned with the working woman – in all conscience she couldn't be. Later in the same article she rejoices to have seen 'a woman Cabinet Minister walking through the lobby of the House of Commons; I have seen a woman architect chosen to design the Shakespeare Memorial Theatre; I have seen my own mother applauded by a county council when she was elected as its first woman alderman; I have myself been heckled as an agitator at Marble Arch, demanding the vote in the Equal Franchise Campaign of 1927 and 1928; and I have been enfranchised. I have voted.' No doubt in a middle class environment all these are real steps forward, but what earthly good have these individual achievements been to the great mass of women whose only hope of liberation is to throw off the yoke of their economic thraldom?

'To the great majority of women,' says August Bebel in the introduction to his admirable analysis of the woman question, 'it also remains a matter of indifference whether a few thousand members of their sex, belonging to the more favoured classes of society, obtain higher learning and enter some learned profession, or hold public office. The general condition of the sex is not altered thereby.'[5]

But is there full emancipation even for the women of the favoured class, to whom the achievements, so applauded by Miss Holtby, are open? Are not even they faced with the choice that, as a general rule, implies that marriage is a full time job, and that if a woman's wish is to obtain the fulfilment of her personal – sexual, if you like – life in marriage and children, then all her pretence at emancipation must go by the board?

'Part of a wife and mother's job is to be a sort of psychological shock-absorber, to comfort and help the weak-hearted,' writes F. E. Baily in his negation of the question CAN A WOMAN SERVE TWO MASTERS?[6]

If part of the price a woman has to pay for the privilege of being the receptacle of a man's sexual attentions is this function of buffer, then without a doubt, this slavery to one master is a full time job. But why this conception of service? Why, if woman is emancipated and the theoretical equal of man, must she serve the man with whom she sleeps? The answer is obvious.

She is fettered, by the level of wages for women, to an economic unit, the family. Within that unit she is dependent on her husband. Even when the husband is out of work and the wife is working, capitalism enforces a different form of this dependence; the wife depends on her husband's getting work in order to lift the family from intolerable misery. Because of this series of social relationships that we call capitalism, the relationship of marriage cannot be free from the 'shock-absorber' element, or from other inequalities.

When the woman worker takes her place beside her fellows of the other sex in the real productive work of the classless society, then, and then only shall we be able to speak of her emancipation, and judge her equality. And the years that bring this change we may well call propitious.

Notes

1. It is reprinted in *The Testament of a Generation: The Journalism of Vera Brittain and Winifred Holtby*, ed. Berry and Bishop, pp. 89–93.
2. The WSPU was formed in 1903 by Mrs Emmeline Pankhurst and became the principal organization in the campaign for women's suffrage. By 1905 it had developed the tactics for which the early women's movement became famous – tactics which provoked and transgressed civic authority. See Pearce and Stewart, pp. 207–8.
3. Hutt's *The Condition of the Working Class in Britain* (London: Martin Lawrence, 1933) was a landmark piece of political analysis in the early 1930s. His *Post-War History of the British Working Class* was published by Gollancz in 1937.
4. Joan Beauchamp, 'Women in Industry', *Daily Worker*. [PP]
5. *Die Frau und der Socialismus*, translated by Daniel de Leon as *Woman under Socialism* (New York: Labor News Press, 1904), p. 4.
6. *Woman's Home Journal*. [PP]

30 Virginia Woolf *from Three Guineas (1938)**

Three Guineas originated in Woolf's speech to the London branch of the National Society for Women's Service in 1931. Material from the speech was subsequently used by her in the polemical sections of her 'novel-essay', *The Pargiters*.¹ The novelistic parts of that work were then separated out to become *The Years* (1937), and in *Three Guineas* (1938) the polemical elements were developed and refined. The premise underlying the book is that its author is responding to an enquiry from a male correspondent: 'How in your opinion are we to prevent war?' (p. 153). The question, writes back Woolf, is one over which 'it is particularly difficult to avoid misunderstanding', but it is worth attempting an answer because the circumstances are so singular: 'since when before has an educated man asked a woman how in her opinion war can be prevented?' The question of women's influence in such affairs is a vexed one; 'it seems as if our influence must stop short at the surface,' Woolf argues, 'we to whom many doors are still locked, or at best ajar, we who have neither capital nor force behind us' (p. 181). The central difficulty that emerges is that 'the daughters of educated men' in Britain, about 1938, have more in common with subject peoples elsewhere in the world than with the male establishment in their own country. To oppose Fascism and dictatorship, from a woman's point of view, is to wage a battle not only abroad but at home as well – a battle, in fact, against the very parties who seek women's assistance in avoiding war. The man who in 1937 votes to prevent women becoming members of Cambridge University, and Adolf Hitler, who declares 'the woman's world is her family, her husband, her children, and her home': 'Are they not both saying the same thing?' (p. 229).

   As Woolf's argument develops towards the following passage, she points out that British men, faced with the threat of Fascist dictatorship, 'are feeling in your own persons what your mothers felt when they were shut out, when they were shut up, because you are Jews, because you are democrats, because of race, because of religion . . . The whole iniquity of dictatorship, whether in Oxford or Cambridge, in Whitehall or Downing Street, against Jews or against women, in England, or in Germany, in Italy or in Spain is now apparent to you. But now we are fighting together' (p. 304). That does not, however, mean that women can or should become members of a patriarchal society: 'It is from our difference . . . that our help can come' (p. 306).

---

* Reprinted from *Three Guineas* (London: Hogarth Press, 1938), pp. 192–206.

B ut this, you will say, if it means anything, can only mean that you, the daughters of educated men, who have promised us your positive help, refuse to join our society in order that you may make another of your own. And what sort of society do you propose to found outside ours, but in co-operation with it, so that we may both work together for our common ends? That is a question which you have every right to ask, and which we must try to answer in order to justify our refusal to sign the form you send. Let us then draw rapidly in outline the kind of society which the daughters of educated men might found and join outside your society but in co-operation with its ends. In the first place, this new society, you will be relieved to learn, would have no honorary treasurer, for it would need no funds. It would have no office, no committee, no secretary; it would call no meetings; it would hold no conferences. If name it must have, it could be called the Outsiders' Society. That is not a resonant name, but it has the advantage that it squares with facts – the facts of history, of law, of biography; even, it may be, with the still hidden facts of our still unknown psychology. It would consist of educated men's daughters working in their own class – how indeed can they work in any other?[2] – and by their own methods for liberty, equality and peace. Their first duty, to which they would bind themselves not by oath, for oaths and ceremonies have no part in a society which must be anonymous and elastic before everything would be not to fight with arms. This is easy for them to observe, for in fact, as the papers inform us, 'the Army Council have no intention of opening recruiting for any women's corps'. The country ensures it. Next they would refuse in the event of war to make munitions or nurse the wounded. Since in the last war both these activities were mainly discharged by the daughters of working men, the pressure upon them here too would be slight, though probably disagreeable. On the other hand the next duty to which they would pledge themselves is one of considerable difficulty, and calls not only for courage and initiative, but for the special knowledge of the educated man's daughter. It is, briefly, not to incite their brothers to fight, or to dissuade them, but to maintain an attitude of complete indifference. But the attitude expressed by the word 'indifference' is so complex and of such importance that it needs even here further definition. Indifference in the first place must be given a firm footing upon fact. As it is a fact that she cannot understand what instinct compels him, what glory, what interest, what manly satisfaction fighting provides for him – 'without war there could be no outlet for the manly qualities which fighting develops' – as fighting thus is a sex characteristic which she cannot share, so is it an instinct which she cannot judge. The outsider therefore must leave him free to deal with this instinct by himself, because liberty of opinion must be respected, especially when it is based upon an instinct which is as foreign to her as centuries of tradition and education can make it. This is a fundamental and instinctive distinction upon which indifference may be based. But the outsider will make it her duty not merely to base her indifference upon instinct, but upon reason. When he says, as history proves that he has said, and may say again, 'I am fighting to protect our country' and thus seeks to rouse her patriotic emotion, she will ask herself, 'What does "our country" mean to me an outsider?' To decide this she will analyse the meaning of patriotism in her own case. She will inform herself of the position of her sex and her class in the past. She will inform herself of the amount of land, wealth and property in the possession of her own sex and class in the present – how much of 'England' in fact belongs to her. From the same sources she will inform herself of the legal protection which the law has given her in the past and now gives her. And if he adds that he is fighting to protect her body, she will reflect upon the degree of physical protection that she now enjoys when the words 'Air Raid Precaution' are written on blank walls. And if he says that he is fighting to protect England from foreign rule, she will reflect that for her there are no 'foreigners', since by law she becomes a foreigner if she marries a foreigner. And she will do her best to make this a fact, not by forced fraternity, but by human sympathy. All these facts will convince her reason (to put it in a nutshell) that her sex and class has very little to thank England for in the past; not much to thank England for in the present; while the security of her person in the future is highly dubious. But probably she will have imbibed, even from the governess, some romantic notion that Englishmen, those fathers and grandfathers whom she sees marching in the picture of history, are 'superior' to the men of other countries. This she will consider it her duty to check by comparing French historians with English; German with French; the testimony of the ruled – the Indians or the Irish, say – with the claims made by their rulers. Still some 'patriotic' emotion, some ingrained belief in the intellectual superiority of her own country over other countries may remain. Then she will compare English painting with French painting; English music with German music; English literature with Greek literature, for translations abound. When all these comparisons have been faithfully made by the use of reason, the outsider will find herself in possession of very good reasons for her indifference. She will find that she has no good reason to ask her brother to fight on her behalf to protect 'our' country. '"Our country",' she will say, 'throughout the greater part of its history has treated me as a slave; it has denied me education or any share in its possessions. "Our" country still ceases to be mine if I marry a foreigner. "Our" country denies me the means of protecting myself, forces me to pay others a very large sum annually to protect me, and is so little able, even so, to protect me that Air Raid precautions are written on the wall. Therefore, if you insist upon fighting to protect me, or "our" country, let it be understood, soberly and rationally between us, that you are fighting to gratify a sex instinct which I cannot share; to procure benefits which I have not shared and probably will not share; but not to gratify my instincts, or to protect either myself or my country. For,' the outsider will say, 'in fact, as a woman, I have no country. As a woman my country is the whole world.' And if, when reason has had its say, still some obstinate emotion remains, some love of England dropped into a child's ears by the cawing of rooks in an elm tree, by the splash of waves on a beach, or by English voices murmuring nursery rhymes, this drop of pure, if irrational, emotion she will make serve her to give England first what she desires of peace and freedom for the whole world.

Such then will be the nature of her 'indifference' and from this indifference certain actions must follow. She will bind herself to take no share in patriotic demonstrations; to assent to no form of national self-praise; to make no part of any claque or audience that encourages war; to absent herself from military displays, tournaments, tattoos, prize-givings and all such ceremonies as encourage the desire to impose 'our' civilisation or 'our' dominion upon other people. The psychology of private life, moreover, warrants the belief that this use of indifference by the daughters of educated men would help materially to prevent war. For psychology would seem to show that it is far harder for human beings to take action when other people are indifferent and allow them complete freedom of action, than when their emotions are made the centre of excited emotion. The small boy struts and trumpets outside the window: implore him to stop; he goes on: say nothing; he stops. That the daughters of educated men then should give their brothers neither the white feather of cowardice nor the red feather of courage, but no feather at all; that they should shut the bright eyes that rain influence, or let those eyes look elsewhere when war is discussed – that is the duty to which outsiders will train themselves for peace before the threat of death inevitably makes reason powerless.

Such then are some of the methods by which the society, the anonymous and secret Society of Outsiders would help you, Sir, to prevent war and to ensure freedom. Whatever value you may attach to them you will agree that they are duties which your own sex would find it more difficult to carry out than ours; and duties moreover which are specially appropriate to the daughters of educated men. For they would need some acquaintance with the psychology of educated men, and the minds of educated men are more highly trained and their words subtler than those of working men. There are other duties, of course . . . But at the risk of some repetition let us roughly and rapidly repeat them, so that they may form a basis for a society of outsiders to take its stand upon. First, they would bind themselves to earn their own livings. The importance of this as a method of ending war is obvious; sufficient stress has already been laid upon the superior cogency of an opinion based upon economic independence over an opinion based upon no income at all or upon a spiritual right to an income to make further proof unnecessary. It follows that an outsider must make it her business to press for a living wage in all the professions now open to her sex; further that she must create new professions in which she can earn the right to an independent opinion. Therefore she must bind herself to press for a money wage for the unpaid worker in her own class – the daughters and sisters of educated men who, as biographies have shown us, are now paid on the truck system, with food, lodging and a pittance of £40 a year. But above all she must press for a wage to be paid by the State legally to the mothers of educated men. The importance of this to our common fight is immeasurable; for it is the most effective way in which we can ensure that the large and very honourable class of married women shall have a mind and a will of their own, with which, if his mind and will are good in her eyes, to support her husband, if bad to resist him, in any case to cease to be 'his woman' and to be herself. You will agree, Sir, without any aspersion upon the lady who bears your name, that to depend upon her for your income would effect a most subtle and undesirable change in your psychology. Apart from that, this measure is of such importance directly to yourselves, in your own fight for liberty and equality and peace, that if any condition were to be attached to the guinea [to be donated to you for your society] it would be this: that you should provide a wage to be paid by the State to those whose profession is marriage and motherhood. Consider, even at the risk of a digression, what effect this would have upon the birth-rate, in the very class where the birth-rate is falling, in the very class where births are desirable – the educated class. Just as the increase in the pay of soldiers has resulted, the papers say, in additional recruits to the force of arm-bearers, so the same inducement would serve to recruit the child-bearing force, which we can hardly deny to be as necessary and as honourable, but which, because of its poverty, and its hardships, is now failing to attract recruits. That method might succeed where the one in use at present – abuse and ridicule – has failed. But the point which, at the risk of further digression, the outsiders would press upon you is one that vitally concerns your own lives as educated men and the honour and vigour of your professions. For if your wife were paid for her work, the work of bearing and bringing up children, a real wage, a money wage, so that it became an attractive profession instead of being as it is now an unpaid profession, an unpensioned profession, and therefore a precarious and dishonoured profession, your own slavery would be lightened. No longer need you go to the office at nine-thirty and stay there till six. Work could be equally distributed. Patients could be sent to the patientless. Briefs to the briefless. Articles could be left unwritten. Culture would thus be stimulated. You could see the fruit trees flower in the spring. You could share the prime of life with your children. And after that prime was over no longer need you be thrown from the machine onto the scrap heap without any life left or interests surviving to parade the environs of Bath or Cheltenham in the care of some unfortunate slave. No longer would you be the Saturday caller, the albatross on the neck of society, the sympathy addict, the deflated work slave calling for replenishment; or, as Herr Hitler puts it, the hero requiring recreation, or, as Signor Mussolini puts it, the wounded warrior requiring female dependants to bandage his wounds. If the state paid your wife a living wage for her work which, sacred though it is, can scarcely be called more sacred than that of the clergyman, yet as his work is paid without derogation so may hers be – if this step which is even more essential to your freedom than to hers were taken the old mill in which the professional man now grinds out his round, often so wearily, with so little pleasure to himself or profit to his profession, would be broken; the opportunity of freedom would be yours; the most degrading of all servitudes, the intellectual servitude, would be ended; the half-man might become whole. But since three hundred millions or so have to be spent upon the arms-bearers, such expenditure is obviously, to use a convenient word supplied by the politicians, 'impracticable' and it is time to return to more feasible projects.

The outsiders then would bind themselves not only to earn their own livings, but to earn them so expertly that their refusal to earn them would be a matter of concern to the work master. They would bind themselves to obtain full knowledge of professional practices, and to reveal any instance of tyranny or abuse in their professions. And they would bind themselves not to continue to make money in any profession, but to cease all competition and to practise their profession experimentally, in the interests of research and for the love of the work itself, when they had earned enough to live upon. Also they would bind themselves to remain outside any profession hostile to freedom, such as the making or the improvement of the weapons of war. And they would bind themselves to refuse to take office or honour from any society which, while professing to respect liberty, restricts it, like the universities of Oxford and

Cambridge. And they would consider it their duty to investigate the claims of all public societies to which, like the Church and the universities, they are forced to contribute as taxpayers as carefully and fearlessly as they would investigate the claims of private societies to which they contribute voluntarily. They would make it their business to scrutinise the endowments of the schools and universities and the objects upon which that money is spent. As with the educational, so with the religious profession. By reading the New Testament in the first place and next those divines and historians whose works are all easily accessible to the daughters of educated men, they would make it their business to have some knowledge of the Christian religion and its history. Further they would inform themselves of the practice of that religion by attending Church services, by analysing the spiritual and intellectual value of sermons; by criticising the opinions of men whose profession is religion as freely as they would criticise the opinions of any other body of men. Thus they would be creative in their activities, not merely critical. By criticising education they would help to create a civilised society which protects culture and intellectual liberty. By criticising religion they would attempt to free the religious spirit from its present servitude and would help, if need be, to create a new religion based it might well be upon the New Testament, but, it might well be, very different from the religion now erected upon that basis. And in all this, and in much more than we have time to particularise, they would be helped, you would agree, by their position as outsiders, that freedom from unreal loyalties, that freedom from interested motives which are at present assured them by the State.

It would be easy to define in greater number and more exactly the duties of those who belong to the Society of Outsiders, but not profitable. Elasticity is essential; and some degree of secrecy, as will be shown later, is at present even more essential. But the description thus loosely and imperfectly given is enough to show you, Sir, that the Society of Outsiders has the same ends as your society – freedom, equality, peace; but that it seeks to achieve them by the means that a different sex, a different tradition, a different education, and the different values which result from those differences have placed within our reach.

Notes

1. See *The Pargiters*, ed. Mitchell A. Leaska (New York: New York Public Library and Readex Books, 1977), which includes the text of Woolf's speech, pp. xxvii–xxxxiv.

2. In the nineteenth century much valuable work was done for the working class by educated men's daughters in the only way that was open to them. But now that some of them at least have received an expensive education, it is arguable that they can work much more effectively by remaining in their own class and using the methods of that class to improve a class which stands much in need of improvement. If on the other hand the educated (as so often happens) renounce the very qualities which education should have bought – reason, tolerance, knowledge – and play at belonging to the working class and adopting its cause, they merely expose that cause to the ridicule of the educated class, and do nothing to improve their own. But the number of books written by the educated about the working class would seem to show that the glamour of the working class and the emotional relief afforded by adopting its cause, are today as irresistible to the middle class as the glamour of the aristocracy was twenty years ago (see *A la recherche du temps perdu*). Meanwhile it would be interesting to know what the true-born working man or woman thinks of the playboys and playgirls of the educated class who adopt the working class cause without sacrificing middle class capital, or sharing working class experience. 'The average housewife,' according to Mrs. Murphy, Home Service Director of the British Commercial Gas Association, 'washed an acre of dirty dishes, a mile of glass and three miles of clothes and scrubbed five miles of floor yearly' (*Daily Telegraph*, 29 September 1937). For a more detailed account of working class life, see *Life as We Have Known It*, by Co-operative working women, edited by Margaret Llewelyn Davies. *The Life of Joseph Wright* also gives a remarkable account of working-class life at first hand and not through pro-proletarian spectacles. [VW]

31 J. V. Delahaye *The People's Front (1936)**

After 1935 European Communism sought to stem the tide of Fascism by the formation of a 'popular front' – a movement that would bring together Communists, socialists and centrists united in resistance to a common enemy. Popular front governments were elected in Spain and France, but the idea did not win a strong following in Britain. When he wrote this, Jim Delahaye was secretary to the British People's Front Propaganda Committee. The latter had been founded by former Communist J. T. Murphy, who had first proposed the formation of a British Popular Front organization at a 1936 meeting of the Socialist League, of which he was then secretary. The aim of the League at that time was to establish a *'United* Front' against Fascism, and Murphy's proposal was not welcomed; the group opposed the idea of a 'Popular' Front because it could not envisage an alliance with any groups or individuals who were not socialist. Murphy regarded the League's exclusivity as self-defeating, and by June 1936 he had split from the group to found the People's Front Propaganda Committee – which, as the following extract makes clear, was prepared to welcome members of all political types, including 'democratic conservatives' as well as radicals. Delahaye had stood for election as a Labour candidate in the general elections of 1931 and 1935, but in fact the People's Front movement was never able to secure significant support in the Labour Party, and the Propaganda Committee was doomed as a result. By October 1937 it was no more, and Murphy, Delahaye and some other members had gone on to form a 'National Progressive Council'. Within the Labour Party, Stafford Cripps began to campaign for a People's Front in April 1938, but by then the party executive had hardened its stand against the movement and Cripps was expelled on 25 January 1939. For a full account, see Blaazer, *The Popular Front and the Progressive Tradition: Socialists, Liberals, and the Quest for Unity 1884–1939*, especially Chapter 7, and also John Coombes, 'British Intellectuals and the Popular Front', in Gloversmith, pp. 101–41.

A British People's Front has become the most urgent necessity alike for the people of Britain and the peoples of Europe. A propaganda committee is already at work. We are proceeding on the following assumptions:

(1) The people of Britain, the nation, are the ordinary men and women who in their millions earn their living by hand and brain. They have common needs for the maintenance of peace, the preservation of personal liberty, and the defence of their economic security.

---

* Reprinted from *Left Review* 2.13 (October 1936): 668–9.

(2) Unless the people themselves and in united strength make known their demands and their determination to achieve them, the present state of danger and indecision may continue for years.

(3) Failing such action the next general election may result in a political stalemate. Such a state of affairs and the continuance of dissension amongst democratic parties is the opportunity for reaction.

(4) A Government that would be really active in the pursuit of world co-operation and social reconstruction must have behind it the enthusiasm and goodwill of the politically active majority of people throughout the country. Then only can a Government really be made to implement its election promises.

(5) **Politics is much more than a matter of a General Election taking place every five years: Politics is life itself.** Every issue, whether in foreign affairs, the treatment of the unemployed, the health of the child, or the preservation of freedom, is a matter of common concern, a matter of politics. Liberty and peace must be defended wherever attacked.

There is now ample evidence in the Press and at political meetings that ordinary men and women throughout the country are willing in face of the common danger to work together. A People's Front is a movement of the British people in accordance with their historic traditions. Sectarianism and the reluctance of certain leaders to risk any threat to their authority are the only obstacles which confront us.

It is imperative, however, that the Labour Party, representing more than eight millions of the progressive electorate, should take the initiative in calling for the active co-operation of all men and women of goodwill.

Here, too, there is evidence enough that the democratic conservative, the radical, the active member of a peace society, and many others outside the Labour Party would welcome such a lead. Unfortunately, it is still necessary in some cases to point out that such initiative on the part of the Labour Party would enhance its reputation and strength. Finally, the maintenance of peace, the abolition of the degrading insecurity that hangs over us all, the upholding of the values of civilised life and the preservation of individual liberty are more than matters of party politics. They are matters of the deepest and most universal concern. Therefore, if the British People's Front is to succeed, the **co-operation of the scientist and artist, the writer, dramatist and philosopher is urgently needed**. Though the movement and desire for unity springs from the people themselves, in the work of education, information and persuasion their help is essential.

32 Arthur L. Horner *The Arts, Science and Literature as Allies of the Working Class (1936)**

Horner was at this time president of the South Wales Miners' Federation. This letter to the *Left Review* was printed in that journal alongside a number of other pieces on the subject of the People's Front. These included the short note by Jim Delahaye and the essay by C. Day Lewis, both included in this volume (see above, pp. 272–3, and below, pp. 276–80, respectively). Horner's phrase, 'a United People's Front', is somewhat problematic, conflating as it does two groups which, in practical terms, were rivals during the thirties. Blaazer remarks that

> the Popular Front campaign differed from the United Front campaign in tone, content, and context. The United Front campaign was largely concerned with British politics. Even when its supporters spoke of fascism they frequently understood it as a problem presented by British capitalism. The Popular Front campaign, by contrast, was concerned almost exclusively with foreign policy. The United Front, for the Labour left at least, had its basis in ideological considerations. Allies were to be sought among socialists who shared their theoretical perspective on the nature of capitalism and fascism. The Popular Front was largely ethical. Its supporters were united in their desire to stop the evil of fascism by removing from power in Britain a government which appeared to encourage it. (p. 173)

Despite his talk of a *People's* Front, it would seem Horner's sense of the movement was more in line with the United perspective.

To *The Left Review.*

Dear Comrades,

I can assure you that the South Wales miners welcome every effort which aims to bring allies to the side of the working class in its struggle against Capitalism. For too long have Arts, Science and Literature been used to impede and make more difficult the efforts of the workers to free themselves from the stranglehold of a contracting and sabotaging system of society.

Only the working class can unleash the tremendous potential productive forces. Only the success of the working class can enable science to have free

---

* Reprinted from *Left Review* 2.13 (October 1936): 670.

play for the initiative of its exponents. Art and Literature, these can be our allies in the great struggle to defeat reaction and to secure freedom.

The old tendency to regard the working class as sufficient in itself, being able to do everything with its own 'pure hands', must be thrown overboard. Recent history has taught that capitalism in its resort to fascism is suppressing large sections of the people as well as the wage-earning class. This common suppression gives us the basis for a united struggle against the common enemy. Such a movement should take the form of a United People's Front to achieve the objects desired by all those who suffer under the present order of society.

In the name of the South Wales miners, I welcome your journal as an addition to the armoury of the exploited, an instrument which can do effective work in the urgent and imperative fight against fascism.

Yours fraternally,

Arthur L. Horner

33 C. Day Lewis *English Writers and a People's Front (1936)**

Cecil Day Lewis must soon have regretted asking the question, in a 1934 sonnet, 'why do we all, seeing a communist, feel small?'[1] Wyndham Lewis's derisive references to the line in his novel, *The Revenge for Love* (1937), and the blustery retort of Roy Campbell ('who never felt this reverence for vermin')[2]: these responses, however excessive in their own way, might have been expected to have a chastening effect on his ingenuous if somewhat naive leftism. However, Sean Day-Lewis writes that his father's Communism, 'as well as a religious quality, . . . had an element of romance; he took a romanticized view of the British worker which could not survive too much contact; and a romanticized view of the enemy, the forces of reaction, as "a sort of composite caricature" taking in the Government, the Church, the Press, the Law and other branches of what is now identified as the Establishment' (pp. 61–2). For such a sensibility, of course, the idea of a People's Front would have been immediately appealing, drawing – as the movement was intended to do – very clear lines between opposing forces, and blurring factional divisions within each side. On its negative side – as those in the *United* Front perceived – the movement encouraged a politics based largely on 'composite caricature', and readers will possibly see in Day Lewis's expository style the remarkable clarity that he bought by his habit of oversimplifying in this way the political alternatives. Perhaps it is therefore correct to view the substance of these pieces as a peculiar kind of amorous bourgeois 'romance' rather than as politics; if so, the usual view taken of Day Lewis – as the one member of the Auden 'group' capable of truly involving himself in practical politics – needs to be reconsidered. This is especially so since the writings reprinted here represent quite accurately the short period in the 1930s when his political activities and interests were arguably at their most intense: he joined the Communist Party late in 1936, but in the summer of 1938 'withdrew from politics in favour of poetry' (Day-Lewis, p. 62). In the second piece which follows we can see that the justification for that withdrawal was already clear in Day Lewis's mind as early as 1935. It is possible, he tells us, for the 'true, original' artist to be 'so wholly concentrated on his work that he is often oblivious of economic conditions'; and yet at the same time – just by virtue of his being 'true and original', and probably *because* of his obliviousness and isolation – his art may end up being 'of value to the revolutionary'. In asserting that 'poetry is a recreation' he is suggesting its necessary and fundamental independence from what Spender called political 'tendency' (see above, p. 211),

---

* Reprinted from *Left Review* 2.13 (October 1936): 671–4.

but like Spender and other writers of a similar background, he would argue that the exercise of this very freedom can be the writer's most useful contribution to social re-creation. In some important respects Day Lewis was himself still – and always – subject to the very same neo-Romantic conception of Art, with its sanctity and separateness from the mundane world, that he suggested would prevent British writers entering enthusiastically into the People's Front.

In considering how writers may be drawn into the People's Front, and what part they can play, there is one vital point to be borne in mind: that is, the tradition of individualism and political indifference which the English writer inherits. Partly as a result of the considerable measure of freedom – freedom of life and freedom of expression – which he has enjoyed for the last 150 years, partly owing to the emphasis laid by the Romantic Revival on the writer as someone 'above the battle', as the high-priest of rites not to be shared by the vulgar, the English writer is bound by a strong belief in 'artistic detachment' and personal liberty. 'After all,' he says to himself, 'did not Shelley call poets the "unacknowledged legislators" of the world? That sounds good enough to me. Why concern myself with all this sordid business of practical politics when I am the real legislator, the prophet of the holy spirit of man?'[3] Moreover, English writers do not inherit the habit of organisation. We have literary cliques, of course: but 'schools' of literary thought, in the sense of bodies of writers closely organised for discussion and criticism and the interchange of ideas, have been unknown in recent years. The English writer really does like to think of himself as a sort of inspired amateur; he does not, as a general rule, look upon himself as a craftsman – as a person who has a trained gift for writing just in the same way as a metalworker has professional skill at working in metal. In consequence, our writers have been slow to organise professionally, let alone politically. Organisation – there is no use denying it – is still repugnant to them, because it seems to conflict with their 'amateur status' and their idea of artistic liberty.

I have myself encountered this repugnance again and again. Not long ago, for instance, I supported a motion that the Society of Authors (numerically the strongest literary association in this country) should apply for affiliation to the T.U.C. At this meeting, apart from the antics of peevish buffoons such as St. John Ervine, there was a body of perfectly honest opinion firmly entrenched on the idea that any form of political association is either unnecessary or positively dangerous for the individual writer. It is a hopeful sign, from our point of view, that this opinion is much more prevalent among the older generation than the younger.

This, then, is the main obstacle to be surmounted in the effort to draw writers into a People's Front. Few English authors of repute are reactionary; many, though, are indifferent – and indifferent, so to speak, on principle. Our point of approach to such authors must be the Liberty of the Writer. We should point out that, whereas in Germany, where writers were to a great extent politically unorganised, freedom of speech does not exist, in France – through the participation of intellectuals in the Popular Front – freedom of speech has been preserved. We must impress upon them the anti-cultural trend of Fascism ('whenever I hear the word culture, I reach for my gun'), the burning of books, the persecution of liberal writers. But it is far more important (and difficult) to convince the neutral English intellectual that this anti-cultural trend is not a mere isolated national phenomenon – not 'something that could never happen in *this* country'. The burning of the books was a fire that can easily leap the banks of the Rhine, and we must be prepared to repel it.

The exiled German writers are astounded by the political apathy of their English colleagues today. 'Do you mean to say, after all that's happened to us, you still haven't learnt your lesson?' one of them exclaimed to us recently. But it is a fact; we haven't. The first task of those who aim at drawing writers into a People's Front must be to break down this indifference; to show that, if English writers are not willing to forgo some of their cherished 'independence', they will inevitably lose every stitch of the liberty that at present they stand up in. Democracy is everywhere threatened. If the house of democracy falls, the fire of art – so nobly fed by the great line of English writers – will be extinguished with it.

But we must go farther than that. We must point out the positive and specific advantages which participation in the United Front would bring to the individual writer. He needs peace to write in: well, he must be prepared to work for that peace; and the most effective anti-war organisation in which he can work is a People's Front. He needs not only peace but a wide and intelligent public. A People's Front should indirectly increase the social effectiveness of writing, by putting into power a progressive government which will pay greater attention to education. In the early days of capitalism, when it was a revolutionary force breaking the grip of feudal aristocracy and offering the individual at least some hope of 'making good', the desire of the working classes and bourgeoisie for education was very powerful. Today, under monopoly capitalism, wide masses of the people have little incentive to 'improve their minds': they feel that it holds out no hope of a state wherein the trained mind, the sensitive imagination may have free scope for development. Today, because it is hopelessly at odds with the social order,

Art for the great majority must inevitably be merely an escape from the oppression of that order. There is little point – even if there were much possibility – in improving one's mind when one's mind seems to be cut off from action by adverse social conditions: small wonder, then, if many of the workers and middle classes remain contented with the cultural dregs which capitalism offers them. Under monopoly capitalism, the revolutionary worker alone has a powerful incentive to self-education.

Both the incentive to education and greater facilities for it will be provided by a progressive government. This – and an economic policy not obsessed by armament-building nor controlled by the needs of profit-makers – must lead, as it has led in Soviet Russia, to an enormous increase in the demand for books and in a raising of the cultural level of the country as a whole.

It is clearly to the advantage of writers that they should be able to wield directly a certain political influence. Organisations of authors, *as such*, with no political connections, cannot even now support adequately the interests of their members, and against Fascism they would be powerless. It is generally admitted, for instance, that the present Law of Libel bears very hard on writers. But such associations as the Authors' Society have been unable to do more than defend their members in particular cases: whereas it is clearly desirable that the law itself should be altered. Authors would be in a very much better position to achieve this aim if they were part of an organisation which could exercise more direct parliamentary power.

We have only to read the sections of the proclamation of the French Popular Front dealing with Broadcasting and the Press to see that in these departments too the English writer would benefit by the formation of a People's Front in this country. The man who writes for his living, whether he be poet, novelist, playwright, or journalist, is a man with more immediate power to tell the truth – and more temptation not to tell it – than any other. We may fairly say, I think, that under a reactionary government, under a social system which can only prolong its life by concealing its own defects, the writer has small hope of either finding the truth or of being allowed to tell it when it is found. Morally, therefore, the writer should be bound to align himself with a political movement that at least will strive to preserve the democratic rights of free speech and at most will succeed in bringing nearer a society adequate to the cultural needs of its members.

But the writer will not join in a People's Front just for what he is going to get out of it. To participate in a popular organisation, he must draw nearer to the life of the people: and this is what many English writers, as a result of their tradition of artistic detachment, are unwilling to do. The social function of art, so thoroughly understood and so fully accepted by the great Greek writers of the fifth century, is rejected – tacitly or openly – by numbers of English writers today. We cannot too often or too strongly reaffirm it. This article is not the place for arguing the question. But we can safely assert that, as literature draws its nourishment from the life of the people and as its ideology is deeply affected by the social conditions of its age, so it is in the interest of the writer to establish connection with this life and to fight for conditions more favourable to his art. As a member of the People's Front, he will not only be playing the most effective possible part in the struggle to defend culture; he will also be brought into contact with a diversity of men and women, a variety of opinion, aspiration and experience which cannot fail to enrich his own work. This does not mean that he will be either a parasite on the popular organisation or a mere attached correspondent of it. He will give his special powers and outlook to the movement; and he will receive from it the sense of community which alone can enable him to re-establish the social function of his art.

What steps should be taken now? It is doubtful whether we have in this country any revolutionary writers with the prestige of Romain Rolland and Henri Barbusse, whose appeal for the anti-Fascist conference at Amsterdam in 1932 had such enormous effect on French intellectuals. But we have a section of the International Association of Writers for the Defence of Culture;[4] and there are bodies such as For Intellectual Liberty and the Civil Liberties organisation, whose aims are in general agreement. I believe that more vigorous efforts should be made to win all reputable writers into the former organisation; and I believe that the time is now ripe for it to approach all kindred bodies, the T.U.C., and the political parties which claim to stand for democracy, and urge the necessity of a People's Front. A lead has already been given by the Communist Party in the country. Let the Association of Writers answer this lead and make a declaration of their own willingness to assist in the formation of a People's Front broadly based on the principles of democratic liberty, anti-Fascism, and peace. The ground must be carefully gone over. The programme of a People's Front must be such as to ensure the maximum inclusiveness of membership; at the same time it must be definite enough to direct the policy of the organisation over any given emergency. Writers can play a valuable part in the drawing-up of this programme and in the publicising of it. Let us act now, before it is too late, throwing off our parochialism and political apathy in the interest of the civilisation we have helped to build and can help to save.

Revolutionaries and Poetry (1935)*

The questions are often asked – 'What should be the attitude of Communists to poetry?' and 'Is poetry of any value to the revolutionary?' The answer to the first question obviously depends upon the answer to the second: the latter is being asked today, not only by workers in the revolutionary movement but by some of the poets themselves. 'Poetry today,' these poets are inclined to feel, 'has no real contact with the masses': it therefore has no social value, and we believe that – unless it has social as well as artistic value – it is not justified. With two million unemployed in the country and war growing daily more imminent, surely we are wasting our time singing away to ourselves in a corner. 'We would be much better employed doing something practical.' Now this feeling, though understandable, is a sentimental one. The writing of poetry is for some people their natural activity. We do not expect those who are good at hewing coal or ploughing or carrying out scientific research to cease from these activities when they become aware of world crisis and the necessity for revolution. Here, perhaps, the ordinary man will interrupt, 'But these are practical, necessary activities: the writing of poetry is a private affair, a kind of personal luxury.' This argument, though it is a common one, seems to me sentimental and unhistoric.

In the first place, until about fifty years ago, poetry was accepted as the finest medium through which human feelings can be expressed. Even when its influence and appeal were dwindling, it was held in respect. For centuries before this poetry represented the clearest insight into reality possible to mankind, and the poet was honoured as spokesman of his social group: he expressed what they were feeling both as a group and as individuals. The historic value of poetry to the revolutionary would be obvious thus, even if it had not been underlined by Marx and Lenin. It gives us the clearest impression of the feelings and aspirations of large groups of people in the past. It discloses for us emotionally, as science does intellectually, the hidden links in nature. Also, while psychology helps us towards the understanding of our own motives, poetry enables us to feel them more keenly and get them in perspective.

'That is all very well,' the revolutionary might argue; 'I admit the historic value of poetry, and I am prepared to believe that in the past the poet has been a mouthpiece of society and rightly honoured as such. But today his function has become obsolete. No one reads poetry; and therefore, even if the poet has the right ideas, he cannot get them across. Anyway, he seems to spend most

---

* Reprinted from Left Review 1.10 (July 1935): 397–402.

of his time at present writing stuff I cannot make head or tail of: it doesn't look as if he wanted to be the mouthpiece of anything more than his own complexes.' Let me take the last point first. When poetry is obscure now, it is largely the result of its unpopularity. Until fifty years ago, reading verse was a widespread mental recreation: Shakespeare, for instance, got his poetry across under the guise of entertainment. But the recent growth of newspapers, magazines, cheap fiction, cinemas, radio, etc., has taken the entertainment value out of poetry. Most people prefer watching Greta Garbo to reading Tennyson. The poet realises that he is no longer popular: accordingly, he has no incentive to gild his poetry with the stuff of entertainment: he is deprived of that feeling of writing for a wide audience which understood his language; and therefore he begins to write for the tiny circle of people with whom he is in contact, and his poetry sounds to outsiders – what in fact it is – the private language of personal friends. More recently, however, some poets have become dissatisfied with this limited audience and field of expression: they feel strongly the need to communicate with a wider circle: consequently they are trying to simplify their way of saying things, in the hope that this will bring poetry back into popular favour. We shall see, though, that such efforts on the part of individual poets cannot get very far without a revolutionary change in society. Many artists today, indeed, are beginning to realise that the full exercise of their powers is only possible under a classless society.

In the meantime, let me take the other argument of the ordinary revolutionary. 'Even if the poet has the right ideas, he cannot get them across'! This I believe to be demonstrably untrue. During the War, Siegfried Sassoon published a volume of poems called *Counter-Attack*: these poems expressed in satire his violent revulsion from all that the war meant. They were a personal expression, as all good poetry is, but they had a considerable influence amongst those numerous intellectuals who had been swept into the War on a tide of Rupert Brooke feeling: I know of several, indeed, whose disillusionment was crystallised by these poems and who became conscious revolutionaries from the moment of reading them. Another point is that a great deal of propaganda can be got across in verse which otherwise would be suppressed. If Sassoon had written his *Counter-Attack* in prose it is highly probable that the book would have been banned and himself imprisoned. But the authorities today are inclined to look upon poetry as something that has no bearing on real life, and consequently to overlook what may be contained in it. Again, during the past few years a number of young poets have been expressing their sympathies with Communism in their verse. This has had a very noticeable effect on certain sections of the middle classes, particularly on the students.

I know personally over a dozen young men who date their first interest in Marxism from the reading of this kind of poetry: it made them aware of a movement of feeling and action which before they had been blind to or had realised only as something academic, theoretical, unconnected with their own lives. I have had letters from many other intellectuals and not a few workers, both here and in America, which have made it quite clear that this revolutionary poetry has had a real earthquake effect on them – shaken up their ideas and altered the whole map of reality for them. It's a long step, of course, from reading poetry to becoming an active revolutionary: but poetry has in many cases been a first step.

Granted, then, that poetry can be of use to him, and is therefore something worth criticising, on what should the Communist base his criticism? I should like to make the following suggestions towards a Marxist critical position. First, we must guard against that form of literary sentimentality which would accept any piece of verse evidently written from a revolutionary standpoint and reject everything written from any other angle. The first qualification of a poem is that it should be a good poem – technically good, I mean. A badly-designed, badly-constructed house is not excused by the fact that it was built by a class-conscious architect and workmen. Equally, a poem may have been written by a reactionary bourgeois and yet be a very good poem and of value to the revolutionary; *The Waste Land* is such a one. Any good poem, simply because every good poem is a statement of the poet's feelings, is bound to be of value: it gives us insight into the state of mind of a larger or smaller group of people. Secondly, we must not expect a revolutionary poet to write about nothing but the revolution: he will, presumably, fall in love, admire natural scenery and the movement of machines, suffer personal despairs and exaltations; and he must write about all these. Thirdly, even when he is writing directly from a revolutionary stimulus, we must not expect the result to be the same as our slogans and our pamphlets: we must not look for *direct* propaganda. A poem appeals to the mass through the individual: a slogan, a political speech appeals to the individual through the mass. Poetry is of its nature more personal than 'straight' propaganda: the latter is the heavy artillery, the former is the hand-to-hand fighting. A good poem enters deep into the stronghold of our emotions: if it is written by a good revolutionary, it is bound to have a revolutionary effect on our motions and therefore to be essentially – though not formally – propaganda. Lastly, what we must ask of our own poets is this: not that they should litter the surface of their poems with red symbols, with hammers and sickles (though these will appear correctly enough in their place); nor with slogans and catchwords (poetry is taking a man aside and talking to him: we do not use slogans and catchwords then; the place for them is the demonstration and the political meeting): nor even that they should be always writing about the class-struggle: what we *have* the right to ask them is that they should thoroughly assimilate Marxism through theory and practical activity; if they have done this, and only if they have done this, will their poetry be revolutionary – blood, flesh, and bone. Otherwise, it will remain the old, unregenerate, soft-centred bourgeois, masquerading in a red tie, getting a cheap sensation.

Our attitude, then, towards those poets who declare themselves revolutionaries should be one of friendly but severe criticism. There are not so many of them that we can afford to alienate these by contemptuous references to their bourgeois origin, by charges of 'highbrow-ism',[5] by approaching them in an atmosphere of personal suspicion. It is their work that our criticism must concentrate on. We must make sure that it is technically good – that it is not imitative, sentimental, insincere, or banal. The poet *is* his poem: the poem is the expression of his real self; and a just criticism of his poem is the only necessary criticism of the poet. At the same time we need to realise that most poets – most artists of any sort – are likely to be 'fellow-travellers'. The artist is more nearly self-contained than any other type of man except the lunatic. The true, original artist is so wholly concentrated on his work that he is often oblivious of economic conditions – his own and those of other people equally: hunger and squalor do actually mean little to him *as an artist;* they do not affect his work to the same degree that they affect the working lives of others. He therefore may have as little incentive to revolutionary activity as the millionaire capitalist. On the other hand he does feel the need to communicate; and it is there that we may make contact with him and enlist his sympathy.

I have said above that 'many artists today . . . are beginning to realise that the full exercise of their powers is only possible under a classless society'. They wish their work to be understood and appreciated by a great number and diversity of people, not to be the preserve of a few dilettantes. They see that the present system of society divided into watertight compartments cuts off not only their work but themselves from contact with the masses. They feel that Art which is not rooted in the life of the people must be grievously impoverished and reduced soon to the status of a hot-house plant or a laboratory specimen. Because they need to re-establish contact with the masses, they are impatient of a system which prevents this. If they think on a bit further, they will see the force of the point made by Spender in his recent book *The Destructive Element*:[6] he says there, the reason why Hitler has been able to stamp out the literary culture of Germany so easily, by getting rid of writers and artists who refused to accept National Socialism, is that this culture had no roots in the life of the masses. Had they had these roots, individual writers might have been exterminated but their culture, their tradition must have remained. This seems to me a very important point, and one that is bound, if properly understood, to bring the 'fellow-travellers' into more active sympathy with the revolutionary movement.

If poetry is to survive as a means of communication, it must become necessary again to people. Necessary, not in the way that bread is necessary, but in the way that an annual holiday in the country is necessary to town-workers: as a refreshment of the emotional life. This may sound to modern ears an extravagant claim. But consider. Poetry is a recreation. It is, first, a perpetual re-creation of language: the poet must have an unusually sensitive ear for words; he listens to the idiom of his age and heightens it into a poetical language. He is the scientist of words; his experiments with them depend for their success on a hair's-breadth accuracy: he is perpetually seeking new combinations of them, as a scientist seeks new chemical combinations. In a period such as the present, when language suffers from exhaustion and from the feverish delirium of the yellow press, this function of the poet is of particular importance. But poetry is more than a recreation, a refreshment of language. It is also a refreshment of the emotional life. What is the instinct which drives people out into the country as often as their economic conditions permit it? We may talk contemptuously about 'escape' and 'nostalgia'. But such words simply shatter themselves on the hard fact. There can be no doubt that it is the instinct to get back to one's roots. For millions of years man lived on and by the land: we are still exiles in the city. The urge that drives us into the country is the desire to return for refreshment to the springs of human life. Well now, it is the same thing with poetry. Poetry was for centuries bound up with the economics of primitive life. The successful hunt, the terror of natural phenomena – earthquake, hurricane, eclipse, the hopes and fears for the harvest, the horror of barren winter and the delight in spring's fertility – all these were expressed by primitive man rhythmically, in dancing and poetry. They were a release of emotion; and that release meant, like the bursting of a thunder-cloud, refreshment in the end. Poetry was a necessary activity of primitive life. We still find the most vivid, poetical use of language amongst peasants. Now these emotions, based on the fear of cold and hunger, are as keen today as they were ten thousand years ago: they have grown a little more complex though the increased complexity of economic conditions: but their sources are the same. Poetry was one of the chief instruments through which primitive man, by expressing his emotions, gained strength to fight against the economic conditions which gave rise to those emotions. It is bound up therefore with our emotional life, and there seems no reason to suppose that it is less necessary to us than it was to our early ancestors.

But there is one important distinction. Most of us today live in towns and it is likely that the civilisation of the future will be more and more an urban one. Now just as the rise of nineteenth-century capitalism produced the proletariat, a new class of workers which must finally supersede its creator, so the new economic environment of town-civilisation must throw up a new class of poets to express the changed emotional conditions. The stage is set for the entrance of the proletarian poet. It is true that bourgeois poets of recent years have drawn their material more and more from town life. But they have been writing from *outside* this life: they are not, and cannot be, the voice out of the heart of the machine. Their verse has expressed, more often than not, a horror of, a desire to escape from, the realities of this new form of life. Even when they are sympathetic towards it and aware of its potentialities, the system of society prevents them from making more than surface contact with it. On the other hand, there is as yet practically no proletarian poetry in England: while in America, though many proletarians are now writing in verse, little first-rate poetry has been produced by them.

What are the difficulties for the proletarian poet? First, he has to make use of an alien tradition. The tradition of poetry for the last hundred years has been developed by a dominating class, the bourgeois. Until the domination of that class is ended, the writer has to make the best of its tradition. A tradition cannot be created independently of the social framework. Not even when the socialist revolution has taken place can we expect the immediate appearance of a new way of writing: a new tradition does not arrive by virgin birth – it must be worked painfully out of the body of the old. His second difficulty is that tradition in poetry affects the material no less than the material affects the technique. The worker poet at present has to write in a tradition not built for the material he wishes to put into it. What are these new things he wants to bring into poetry? Indignation at the conditions under which he is compelled to live; the feeling of solidarity with his own class and the conviction that he must be a spokesman of that class; the whole range of material data, altered values, and changed emotional stresses which his environment offers him. But, because tradition in poetry affects the material, he has much greater difficulty than the sympathetic bourgeois poet, although the latter feels these things far less strongly and directly, in putting them into the medium of verse. He has to work in an alien tradition – to put new wine into old bottles. His third problem is this. It has been in the interests of capitalism to keep the workers inarticulate. Art, because it speaks directly to the emotions, has always been potentially a revolutionary force. Thus capitalism, as it has given the workers the leavings of its economic production, has tended also to offer them the dregs of its artistic production. As the structure of capitalism has crumbled and the revolutionary situation grown more acute, an ever-increasing flood of false art has been turned upon the workers – the gutter-press newspapers, dope-fiction, sentimental and unreal films. The effect of this has been to weaken the workers' responses to the emotional effect of genuine art. Inoculated with false literature, they find it more difficult to catch the infection of vital and revolutionary literature. In consequence, the worker poet will find himself, like the bourgeois poet today, influencing at first only a few of his fellows.

But he has no reason to despair. If his work is true poetry, it will do more than a hundred Boards of Education and culture-fanatics to re-establish art as a vital force; and, if he is a real revolutionary, it will be a revolutionary force too. Let him not think of poetry as a mystery whose secret is held only by the educated bourgeois. If the writing of poetry is his natural activity (and he will soon find that out), all he needs is an English dictionary and a thorough soaking in the English poets. After that, it is a matter of compelling an alien tradition into his own service, just as the U.S.S.R. pressed the industrial technique of capitalist Europe into the service of Socialism. He has a magnificent opportunity before him. He stands inside the workers: he can see at first hand and feel immediately a world which has been to literature so far Terra Incognita. To speak of the workers and for the workers he does not need, as bourgeois poets do, to learn a new tongue: he has only to make poetry of what is his native language.

> . . . Sirs, you are that world
> Shall make a new world and be all the world.

Notes

1. *Left Review* (November 1934).
2. Quoted and discussed with wit by Cunningham, p. 160.
3. For an example of this view, see Laura Riding and Harry Kemp's *The Left Heresy in Literature and Life* (London: Methuen, 1939). In a chapter called 'Who Are the Workers?' Riding and Kemp reject the familiar leftist argument that writers should justify themselves by engaging in class politics. That demand, they argue, is nonsensical because the 'class' division of greatest significance is the one between artists and the rest of humanity: 'The necessity for class-consciousness? Very well, then, let us be class-conscious – ourselves, the true working class: those who are

professionally pledged to the work of truth. We, doing the primary labour by which reality becomes livable and knowable, are the abused class. The writer who turns Communist, in search of a class, transfers to a hypothetic class the outrages that he suffers for being a writer. For the intrinsic distinctions between people are those of consciousness, not of action' (p. 249).

4. See above, pp. 54 and 107.
5. See above, p. 182 n.4.
6. See above, p. 211.

34 Mass-Observation *from Britain by Mass-Observation (1939)**

Tom Harrisson and Charles Madge wrote and arranged this study, originally published in the topical series of Penguin Specials, conceived by Allen Lane as a means of informing readers about the events and issues to which ordinary lives were increasingly subject in the late 1930s. One hundred thousand copies are reported to have been sold in ten days. The origins of Mass-Observation are discussed obliquely in the extract which follows, but for a more full account see Angus Calder's introduction to the new edition of *Britain* used here: Madge and Harrisson teamed up early in 1937, the former a Fleet Street reporter 'fascinated by the newspaper medium — its astrologers and vox pops, its shock-horror headlines and strange human interest tales', the latter a self-proclaimed 'anthropologist' and author of a best-selling study of Malekulan cannibalism, *Savage Civilisation* (1937) (pp. x–xi). By the time of their meeting, Harrisson was already engaged in an 'anthropological' study of workers in a Lancashire cotton town, and Madge had already announced in the *New Statesman and Nation* (2 January 1937) that a group had been formed to approach British culture through anthropology – an aim reminiscent of Leavis, though finally very different in its valuation of popular culture. The group, which had been meeting occasionally since 1935 at the home of Madge and Kathleen Raine, appears at times to have included David Gascoyne (see above, p. 64) and documentary film-makers Stuart Legg and Humphrey Jennings. For an account of the relationship of Mass-Observation to the growth of documentary film (and to Jennings in particular), see Hodgkinson and Sheratsky, especially Chapter 4. The role of photography in the movement is discussed in detail in Jeremy Mulford's introduction to *Worktown People: Photographs from Northern England 1937–38* by Humphrey Spender.

New Verse no. 24 (February–March 1937) carried an important essay entitled 'Poetic Description and Mass-Observation', which not only clarified the relationship of the movement to literature, but also laid out some fundamental assumptions:

> Mass-observation is a technique for obtaining objective statements about human behaviour. The primary *use* of these statements is to the other observers: an interchange of observations being the foundation of social consciousness. The statements are useful also to scientists who can each utilize them in his own way. The number of scientific interpretations of a

* Reprinted from *Britain by Mass-Observation* (1939; London: Century Hutchinson, 1986), pp. 7–12, 140–3, 145–6, 156–8, 173–4 and 182–3.

given body of material is only limited by the number of scientific interpreters. Poetically, the statements are also useful. They produce a poetry which is not, as at present, restricted to a handful of esoteric performers. The immediate effect of Mass-Observation is to de-value considerably the status of the 'poet'. It makes the term 'poet' apply, not to his performance, but to his profession, like 'footballer'. (p. 3)

New Verse no. 25 (May 1937) included one of the oddest fruits of Mass-Observation – Charles Madge's 'Oxford Collective Poem' (p. 16). Clearly the editor was sympathetic to the aims and methods of Mass-Observation, but it would be a mistake to infer that the notoriously irascible Geoffrey Grigson was any less critical on this subject than on any other. When Harrisson published, in *Light and Dark* 2.3 (February 1938), an essay criticizing poets for their failure to support Mass-Observation, Grigson sharply rebuked him for his 'dotty and emotive language', 'his wild unreason and his unfounded attacks'. 'In your article,' ran Grigson's review, 'there is very little science or true knowledge, and your method is altogether unscientific in a way that discredits Mass-Observation' ('Science and Mass-Observation: Poets and Poor Tom,' *New Verse* 28 [January 1938]: pp. 15–16).

In *The Long Week-End*, their 'Social History of Great Britain, 1918–1939', Robert Graves and Alan Hodge suggest that although Harrisson and Madge were able to make their movement well-known by 'good publicity work', to know of Mass-Observation was not necessarily to approve it. They tell us that the movement received 'unfavourable notice' in the press, the *Sunday Times* describing it as 'Mass Eavesdropping', and the *Spectator* criticizing observers as 'Busybodies of the Left'. 'Despite the support of the zoologist Julian Huxley, and the qualified approval of the anthropologist Malinowski, the greater part of the press ridiculed Mass-Observation's claim to be a science. As the *Spectator* declared: "Scientifically they're about as valuable as a chimpanzee tea-party at the zoo"' (Graves and Hodge, pp. 402–3). See also Cunningham, Chapter 10.

'While Europe was tensely watching the crisis over Czechoslovakia, Herr Hitler, accompanied by eight of his generals, paid a surprise visit to the French frontier to-day.'

That is the way the newspapers talk about the world. These actual words were splashed across the *Star* on August 29, 1938. They are typical. But what can they mean? Europe is a continent, so it can't very well watch anything. Nor can the people in it watch a crisis in the literal sense. What is implied is that millions of people are on tenterhooks to know what is happening on the

German border, in Foreign Offices and at Cabinet Meetings. It is naturally difficult for people to get to know the facts about these things, because secrecy is essential when bluff and counter-bluff are the order of the day. This is a democratic country, so we are supposed to have some idea of what is going on. For this we depend on wireless and newspaper presentation of news. But can we believe what we read and hear? People want inside information, they want to get behind the news. This is impossible for the vast majority, so they have to accept what the newspapers say, or else stop bothering.

Of course, that is assuming that Britain, and the rest of Europe, really were at that time 'tensely watching'. But were they? How many more were more tensely watching the racing news and daily horoscope? That is another kind of fact we shall not know without trying to find out.

One thing we can be fairly sure of, namely that most readers of this book want to know these facts, and all other relevant facts which will help them to play their full part in the world – unless they paid their sixpence by mistake or without thinking. Fact is urgent – we are cogs in a vast and complicated machine that is going to blow us all to smithereens. In any case, life is short, and if we are at all interested in this world (instead of, or as well as, the next world) we had better hurry up and learn where we stand. We must have knowledge, at least sufficient for us to come to personal decisions.

There is an alternative view of things (not often openly expressed, more often implied or unconscious) according to which there can only be a handful of people who know the facts, it being their job to control the destinies of millions of other people. For these millions it is necessary only to sleep, eat, work, reproduce, and, if they have time to spare, amuse themselves. The question then arises: Do these millions, under the present order of things, have enough sleep, enough to eat, enough work, do they reproduce themselves enough, and do they get the amusements that they need and want? The most optimistic spokesman of this view of things could not maintain that this was the case.[1] It is by no means seditious to state the reverse. The most conservatively-minded would admit that we suffer in England from malnutrition, unemployment, a falling birth-rate and a 'leisure problem.' This being so, if the Handful-who-know can't do anything about it, there comes a point when the Man and Woman in the Street start uneasily wondering if there is anything they can do to help themselves. It is the function of the 615 members of our democratic parliament to voice the wishes, feelings, wants, needs, hopes, opinions, grouses, aspirations and criticisms of 45,000,000 people. But this democratic system has broken down in other countries, and may break down in our own, because the 45,000,000 do not feel sufficiently strongly that they are able to speak through Parliament. So they give it up as a bad job and resign themselves to being voiceless or get annoyed with the whole system. At least there is evidence pointing that way, as we shall see.

It is because of this situation – the urgency of fact, the voicelessness of everyman and the smallness of the group which controls fact-getting and fact-distributing – that this book came to be written. Other Penguin Specials have dealt with questions of international politics and the danger of war. This book aims to give the other side of the picture – to give both ear and voice to what the millions are feeling and doing under the shadow of these terrific events. Only by understanding this side can we, as individuals, hope to decide what *we* can do and, if there is anything we can do, then how to do it.

To understand, we must first have facts, and to get the facts a new kind of organisation is needed, or rather a new attitude towards getting facts and publishing them. There has been much talk about the social relations of science, the need for extending the Science of Ourselves and for studying the everyday lives and feelings of ordinary people, as well as the customs of primitive people and the feelings of neurotics. In America, much survey work has been done by the Universities, so that 'sociology' is rapidly becoming more than a name for a science not yet born. That very large numbers of Americans want factual knowledge about *people* is indicated by the success of papers like *Life* and *Time*, circulations of which have quickly soared past the million mark, and by documentary films like *March of Time*, *The River*,[2] as well as the great new drive of Worker Theatres and Federal Art Project.[3]

There are numerous reasons why the Man in the Street feels he is kept in the dark. Books are expensive to buy and not always available in libraries. The language they are written in is often difficult to understand. Often, too, there just isn't time or energy left at the end of a hard-working day for going back to school, as it were, and being lectured by some writer who obviously moves in a world of ideas quite different from one's own.

Some writers of popular science books have done the job very well, but unfortunately there is often as much distorting in the reporting of scientific discovery as in other kinds of news. It is the 'story', not the fact, that most newspapers or magazines aim at presenting. People like stories, and it is a natural and human tendency. Yet there is much evidence that a growing number of people want less stories and more facts. They want the facts, and they want them in a form that suits the times we live in.

The huge success of the Penguin and Pelican series is a proof of this. The 250,000 who read a Penguin Special are a drop in the ocean of possible readers, but they represent a big move in the right direction at a time when 'an important book can sell no more than 200 copies'.[4]

Out of the ordinary Man's bewilderment and desire for fact has grown also a new organisation called Mass-Observation. This consists at present of 1,500 amateur Observers, ordinary people who have volunteered to help in the making of factual surveys. Anyone can be an Observer, no special training is needed. In the two years of its existence M-O has been exploring new techniques for observing and analysing the ordinary. Through M-O you can already listen-in to the movements of popular habit and opinion. The receiving set is there, and every month makes it more effective. There is a staff of full-time skilled observers centred on London, Worktown and Blackpool . . .

The idea of Mass-Observation has definitely broken through. The newspapers with the biggest circulations already assume that their readers have heard of it. Moreover, since Mass-Observation started, similar ideas have been much in the air, partly because of M-O's example, and partly because M-O itself did no more than crystallise an already existing tendency. It is not a sect, and to be useful it must collaborate with all others who are working in the same field. And most needed of all forms of collaboration is collaboration with the Man in the Street.

Much lip-service is paid to the Man in the Street – politicians and newspapers claim to represent him, scientists and artists want to interest him in their work. Much of what they say is sincere, but it must remain ineffective while the Man in the Street has no medium through which he can express with equal publicity what *he* thinks of *them*.

The present position of the Intellectual Few is a relic of the times when the mass of the population consisted of serfs who could neither read nor write. Then a few people at the top could easily impose their beliefs and rule on the multitude. But the whole tendency of history has been away from this state of things. If only because industry requires an army of technicians and semi-technicians, universal education became a social necessity. Everyone can read and write now. Yet even so in many ways there is as much intellectual serfdom as ever. When there are social reforms, they are imposed on the mass from above. Not 'what they want' but 'what's good for them'. And the people who decide what is good for the millions are themselves a tiny group, with different habits of mind, ways of life, from those of the millions they are catering for. It is the same in art, religion, science and politics. The people who happened to start Mass-Observation – one a poet and newspaper reporter, the other an ornithologist and explorer, both aged 25 – had an inkling of the hiatus between the millions and their leaders; two years' observation has confirmed it beyond doubt.

The gap between science and everyman is particularly noticeable, and now one of the main problems of the survival of our civilisation. The gap is most striking in the field of human sciences. Despite numerous professorships, endowments and fellowships in Social Science, Sociology, Political Science, etc., the social relations of ordinary life and the scientific principles underlying politics have remained matters of argument, conjecture and monstrous generalisation, from which no potent research drive has emerged anywhere outside America. In this country, some good statistical work and some excellent administrative sociological reports on areas have been done. But nothing on normal behaviour, and nothing which has approached the formulation of fundamental laws in social relations and human behaviour – though the work of a South African, Dr. O. Oeser, of St. Andrew's University, Scotland, marks a distinct advance in the direction of Social Psychology. One main reason for this is the extra-specially special sort of life led by university people who have a monopoly of scientific funds. But the blindness and lack of general sense shown by most scientists is inherent in their whole approach. Anthropologists, who have spent years and travelled all over the world to study remote tribes, have contributed literally nothing to the anthropology of ourselves.

Doing the Lambeth Walk

In the fifth chapter of *Britain*, Mass-Observation turns its attention to a specific aspect of popular culture in the late 1930s – the Lambeth Walk, first 'a song that half the world started singing in 1938', and then 'a dance that was half a walk . . . [that] caught on as no new dance has done for years' (p. 139).

W hat is it, and how did it originate? When we have answered these questions, we shall be better able to answer the basic question: what was the reason for its wide appeal?

The song was part of a musical show, 'Me and My Girl', which started its very successful run at the Victoria Palace at Christmas-time, 1937. Lupino Lane, comedian, took the part of Bill Snibson, native of Lambeth (Cockney area, south of the river), who inherits an earldom but cannot unlearn his cockney ways. At a grand dinner party he starts *'doin' the Lambeth Walk'* with such effect that duchesses and all join in with him and his Lambeth pals . . .

While he sings [Douglas Furber's words of the famous song: *'Any time you're Lambeth way . . .'*], Lupino Lane walks up and down the stage with a swagger and roll of the shoulders which represents the typical cockney walk. When the show had already been running for some months, Mr. C. L. Heimann, managing director of the Locarno Dance Halls (and therefore one of the cultural directors of the country), saw Lupino do his walk, and was sufficiently impressed to get his ace dancing instructress, Miss Adele England, to elaborate the walk into a dance. Starting from the Locarno Dance Hall, Streatham, the dance-version of the Lambeth Walk swept the country.

Thus, baldly, the story. Clearly the Lambeth Walk, as now established, owes its origin to several sets of people:

1. The cockneys of Lambeth and elsewhere whose walk Lane imitated.

2. Lane – and with him Noel Gay who wrote the tune and Douglas Furber who wrote the words of the song.

3. Mr. Heimann and Miss England who invented and put over the dance.

To these we should add, as formative factors:

4. The BBC and the newspapers which gave the Lambeth Walk publicity.

5. The mass of people, without whose enthusiasm the Lambeth Walk would have been stillborn, and who in many cases used it in their own way and added their own spontaneous variations.

Of these five factors, 2, 3 and 4 represent the Few who cater for the Many – in this case successfully. Factors 1 and 5 represent the influence of the Many. The cockney world of Lambeth – its humour, its singing and dancing, the way it walks – is a mass product with a special local character. But this character is strong enough to appeal to a much wider mass of people as soon as it is made known on a wide scale.

'Lambeth you've never seen' say the words of the song, and thus emphasise the basic argument of this book – the ignorance of one section of society about how other sections live and what they say and think. 'Why don't you make your way there?' asks the song, and that is just the question which this book sets out to ask. Why not? If the song had been a rumba and the words had been 'Cuba you've never seen', there would be reasons of distance to explain why only a few people have seen Cuba or know what it is like. But Lambeth is not so far away, and there is the equivalent of Lambeth round every corner. Tyrolean or Hungarian songs and dances can be, and are, exploited by tourist agencies: as a result of the picture they suggest, people do make their way to Hungary and the Tyrol. But to invite people to go to Lambeth is a new kind of tourism.[5] Blackpool, Southend and Margate have followed suit and produced a Blackpool Walk and a Southend Walk and a Margate Walk, but these too are good publicity for holiday centres, they don't ask you to go to a place where 'The skies ain't blue and the grass ain't green'. None of them have caught on fully.

Lambeth Walk is a working-class shopping street, just off the arterial Lambeth Road and the Kennington Road with tributaries of Lollard Street, Jaxon Street, Old Paradise Street, much condemned housing; street market; a cinema also used as a chapel. It continues into Tyers Street, flanked on both sides by huge blocks of working-class flats. The people who live in these flats have mainly come from other parts of London and this is changing the character of the district. There are many factors which are tending to destroy the native cockney culture, but you don't have to look far to find it still vigorously existing . . .

A spontaneous talent for dancing and song is a Lambeth tradition, having its connection with music-hall tradition but also having a life of its own. It has many features in common with primitive dancing. Men dress up as women or pretend to be animals. Beer plays its part, but observation showed that those who take part may be *half* drunk, but are certainly not whole drunk. It certainly is true of Lambethians having a bit of fun that:

> 'Everything's free and easy,
> Do as you darn well pleasey . . .'

On August Bank Holiday night, an observer was asked along to one of the parties. It was the end of the holiday, most of them had 'been to Hampstead and got all boozed up'. On the Sunday there had been a big wedding party which some of them attended and at which the bride had broken her arm. Most would have to be starting work at 6 or 7 next morning. After closing time the whole party proceeded from the ___ ___ to a house nearby, carrying crates of beer, each holding four quart-bottles. Already at the ___ ___ they had started swaying into the dance, and on the pavement outside two of the women were dancing with linked arms.

The party was held in an upstairs sitting-room, about 14 by 12 feet, with a piano, two settees and chairs round the wall, and an elegant blue-tiled fireplace – the tiles came unstuck later in the evening. Men and women were there in equal numbers, and including one or two who came in and went out, there were 24 all told – and 28 quart bottles of beer. The party lasted from 11.30 to 1.30 a.m. Four performers took turns at the piano; they all played by ear, and they all played very well. Three others took turns with the accordion. Dances alternated with songs – there were solos by a woman, a young man, and an old man of 83. He was the best singer and his age didn't in the least prevent him from having a good time with the rest. His songs included 'Up Goes the Price of Meat, Ta Ra Ra' and 'My Bradshaw Guide'. All joined in the choruses of these and others, such as 'Lily of Laguna', 'The Lambeth Walk', and 'What Does it Feel Like to be Poor?'. The songs they enjoyed most were the ones that were nearest to their own lives, with economics well to the fore. (But the people who go to the Dorchester don't listen to songs about dividends.)

The first time the observer's glass was filled he emptied it. Then he noticed that the others after taking a swig from theirs, handed it on. Perhaps on the same analogy, when one man's nice-looking wife came in half-way through, another man, friend of the first, gave her a good kiss. It was all free and easy and went with a terrific swing, but order was kept and there were certain rules, like keeping silence during the solos. Mostly the women asked the men to dance. Everyone danced, old, middle-aged and young . . .

Something of this kind of background is conveyed by Lupino Lane's creation, Bill Snibson. Bill first appeared in 'Twenty to One', [a] musical show at the Coliseum. In this show he already had his characteristic 'Lambeth' walk, but it didn't play the same important part. In 'Me and My Girl' he becomes a Lord, but can't fit in with the smart people at Hareford Hall. He has lessons in deportment from the Duchess. She tells him: 'Don't wear your hat in the house'; 'You must aspirate your aitches'; and 'You must alter your walk'. The last is too much for Bill Snibson who protests (in the rhyming slang): 'You'll never alter my ball of chalk.' A letter arrives from Lambeth, marked private, which says:

> 'We have a lovely home now but it's near the soapworks and I'm sorry to say there's a horrid smell from Bob Martin.
> PS. We thank you for your invite which we can none of us accept because we're not your class.'

But Sally and the other Lambethians arrive all the same to the grand dinner party in the evening. Their behaviour shocks the upstage people, but when Bill starts to do his walk and sing his song, there is a terrific effect of social breakdown, everyone joins in and shouts 'Oi!' and the Duchess finally goes to dinner on Bill's arm, wearing his bowler on her head. (This was what happened when observers saw the show, but there is no 'book' and the gags change from one performance to another.)

The point of the show is essentially the contrast between the *natural* behaviour of the Lambethians and the affectation of the upper class. In a difficultly academic book of criticism called *Some Versions of Pastoral*,

William Empson[6] has pointed out how important this sort of contrast has been in literature, and it is worth quoting what he has to say at this stage, because it is this contrast which gives its basic appeal to the 'Lambeth Walk' song and dance. 'The essential trick of the old pastoral, which was felt to imply a beautiful relation between rich and poor, was to make simple people express strong feelings . . . It was much parodied, especially to make the poor man worthy but ridiculous, as often in Shakespeare; nor is this merely snobbish when in its full form. The simple man becomes a clumsy fool who has yet better "sense" than his betters and can say things more fundamentally true; he is "in contact with nature", which the complex man needs to be, so that Bottom is not afraid of the fairies; he is in contact with the mysterious forces of our own nature, so that the clown has the wit of the Unconscious; he can speak the truth because he has nothing to lose.' In Shakespeare, the final laugh is usually at the poor man, even when he is made a sympathetic character. Shakespeare's audience was composed of both rich and poor, and he had to please both, but it was more important to please the rich. In the show at the Victoria Palace the situation is rather different – there are plenty of West End people in the audience, but the laugh is really on them. There is an amazing scene in which Lane comes on in his full peer's robes and coronet and pokes unmistakable and uproarious fun at the solemnity of the Coronation; he even at one point lies on the floor wrapped in his robes, with his coronet on his stomach, in such a way as to suggest a comparison with the Lying in State of dead royalty. To some extent the reverse happens, and fun is made of the working-class girl who is given a five-pound note and doesn't know what it is. But the point comes out quite clearly that the working-class characters are 'nearer to nature' than the upper-class ones: George Graves, who takes the part of a whisky-drinking but benevolent member of the aristocracy, says to Sally the Lambeth girl: 'I like you and I like your Bill. You're two little simple children of nature.' Later he says to Bill: 'Your modesty, your simplicity, proves you one of nature's gentlemen.' But Lambeth, where 'The skies ain't blue and the grass ain't green', is a far cry from 'nature' in the ordinary sense. It is the cockney character which is more 'natural' than the upper-class character. Observers' reports show, as we shall see, that people who like the Lambeth Walk like it because it is natural; those who dislike it think it is 'common'. An observer's mother was one of many who lodged protests against 2 a.m. Lambeth Walk parties in Hill Street, Mayfair . . .

A big proportion of observers mentioned as an outstanding feature of the dance that it includes gesture, speech and action, and is therefore more like acting or impersonation than other dances. When you do the Lambeth Walk, you pretend to be a Lambethian. If you don't want to do that, there is no point in the dance, as appears from the following story:

> 'A German dental student who is a beautiful dancer said that he did not care to do it, it was a senseless dance. I explained that it was supposed to represent a couple of costers out together, he said: "But I do not wish to be these people – do you?"'

One thing which the huge popularity of the Lambeth Walk indicates quite definitely is a very widespread 'wish to be these people', though of course that wish is not a simple or straightforward one, and includes elements of make-believe and ballyhoo. The upper classes wish to masquerade as Lambethians; sixteenth century lords and ladies played, in pastoral make-believe, as shepherds and shepherdesses. The middle classes wish to be Lambethians because it temporarily lets them off a code of manners which they usually feel bound to keep up. The working classes wish to be Lambethians because Lambethians *are* like themselves, plus a reputation for racy wit and musical talent – partly they represent that part of the working class which knows how to have a good time.

All this quite reverses the more usual cultural current which flows from the upper class *down* to the working class. Shopgirls dancing foxtrots and rumbas are impersonating debutantes. With the Lambeth Walk the impersonation is the other way about. The 'conventions' which the Lambeth Walk breaks down are the means by which one class apes another which is better off. That sort of 'conventionality' goes pretty deep in the working class itself, and is one aspect of the each-for-his-own-self, individualist pattern which dominates the whole of 1938 England. As a symptom of changing social attitudes, the Lambeth Walk points the other way from Football Pools and Daily Horoscope. . .

That this mass-dancing accepts and glorifies the Lambeth Walk is significant of the nature of its social appeal, and makes it much more than a piece of middle-class romanticism about working-class conditions. It proves that if you give the masses something which connects on with their own lives and streets, at the same time breaking down the conventions of shyness and stranger-feeling, they will take to it with far more spontaneous feeling than they have ever shown for the paradise-drug of the American dance-tune. The dream-sex of the dance lyric points away from social feeling and activity and towards a world of personal superstition and magic (see the analysis of the dance by Tom Harrisson, *New Writing*, Winter 1938). It is no more about reality than Hitler's speeches are. Ballroom dancers sleep-walk to its strains with the same surrender of personal decision as that of uniformed Nazis. These Lambeth Walkers are happy because they find they are free to express *themselves* without the hypnosis of a jazz-moon or a Führer.

Notes

1. This passage bears a striking resemblance to Oswald Mosley's discussion of liberty (see above, p. 33).
2. *The March of Time* was a series of short subject films, the first of which was released on 1 February 1935 at the Capitol Theatre on Broadway. It was the idea of Louis de Rochemont, director of short subjects for Fox Movietone News, to transpose the *March of Time* radio programme into film. Robert T. Elson writes: '*The March of Time* combined news, documentary, and a dramatic presentation in a new form of compelling journalism . . . The achievement . . . was not so much its technique as its introduction into cinema of subjects of current controversy and significance.' A year from its first release, the estimated monthly audience for *The March of Time* was 15,000,000. See Elson in Jacobs, pp. 104–11. *The River*, directed by Pare Lorentz, was released in 1937.
3. Presumably, the Workers' Laboratory Theatre, one of a number of theatrical collectives active in the United States during the 1930s. Others were the League of Workers' Theatres, the Theatre Union and the Theatre of Action. See Scharine, pp. 22–3. On the Federal Art Project, see *The Federal Art Project: American Prints from the 1930s* (Ann Arbor: University of Michigan Museum of Art, 1985).
4. Thanks to a large order from Woolworth's (on which subject, see Leavis above, p. 19), Allen Lane launched his Penguin Books successfully in 1935. For details, see Feather, pp. 206–13, and Morpurgo *passim*. George Orwell, who Morpurgo notes might have been expected 'to welcome a series which was intended to offer the joys of book-collecting to the masses' (p. 101), was – like many reviewers – ambivalent. See his review of Penguin Books, *New English Weekly*, 5 March 1936 (reprinted in *An Age Like This*, pp. 165–7).
5. It would be worth comparing this form of inter-class 'tourism' with, for example, Orwell's *Road to Wigan Pier* or *Homage to Catalonia*. Paul Fussell's *Abroad* makes the case for the centrality of travel and tourism in cultural productions of the inter-war years. It was Samuel Hynes who suggested in *The Auden Generation* that 'travel books simply act out, in the real world, the basic trope of the generation' (p. 229). For a useful discussion of this in relation to Rebecca West's *Black Lamb, Grey Falcon*, see Montefiore, pp. 182–3.
6. See above, p. 165.

35 John Grierson *First Principles of Documentary (1932–3)**

John Grierson founded a film unit at the Empire Marketing Board in 1928, and in the following year released his first film, *Drifters*, a documentary about workers in the North Sea herring fishery. When Eisenstein's *The Battleship Potemkin* (up till then banned by the British Board of Film Censors and the London County Council) was shown by the Film Society for the first time in London in 1929,[1] *Drifters* was included in the programme. 'Looking back,' writes James Beveridge, 'one can imagine the impact – or to be more precise, the shock – of two such films with their harsh percussive styles set against the context of contemporary commercial feature films of 1929, sugary fantasies from a world of pure escapism' (p. 43). Grierson was to direct only one more film, in 1934, but it was through his work at the EMB, where he nurtured the talents of many others – including Paul Rotha, Basil Wright, Stuart Legg and Edgar Anstey – that he shaped the nature and goals of British documentary film-making. After overseeing over a hundred productions at the EMB, he moved the unit in 1933 to the GPO, and it was under the aegis of the Post Office that he produced some of the best-known works of the period, notably *Night Mail* (1936), on which he collaborated with W. H. Auden and Benjamin Britten.

Grierson firmly believed that film could and should be used for propaganda, but his politics – though left of centre – were somewhat unorthodox. Bert Hogenkamp describes his position as that of 'a decidedly non-Marxist young radical with a strong belief in the educational potential of film, even to the point of maintaining that the crisis of capitalism could be overcome by better educating the people regarding their civic responsibility'.[2] As a student and for some time afterwards, Grierson felt sympathetic to the aims of the Independent Labour Party (founded in 1893)[3]; but Rex Walford writes that 'he believed in the humanism of the Independent Labour Party movement, but not in its single-class identification. He felt that mankind (in Britain, in the 1930s) was entering upon a new kind of society, neither capitalist nor socialist, but one in which central planning might be achieved without loss of individual initiative' (quoted in Beveridge, pp. 98–9).

It has often been remarked that despite his leftward leanings, Grierson's programme of documentary film-making was almost entirely supported by agencies and individuals on the right; it would be a rare viewer today who would not be puzzled to notice that *Drifters*, with its heroic presentation of workers'

---

* Originally published in *Cinema Quarterly* 1.2 (Winter 1932): 67–72 and 1.3 (Spring 1933): 135–9. The two instalments, plus another from 1934, were edited together by Forsyth Hardy for inclusion in his *Grierson on Documentary* (London: Collins, 1946; reprinted New York: Praeger, 1966), pp. 78–89. The text here is Hardy's version, omitting material from the third instalment: pp. 78–86.

collective effort, carried the imprimatur of the office charged with selling British products to the Empire. Warner suggests that it was the absence from Grierson's work of doctrinaire socialism that made possible his close relation to the conservative establishment. Furthermore, while Labour during those years showed little interest in exploiting the mass media, the Conservatives 'had utilized the radio effectively as an instrument of national communication, and had paid considerable attention to graphic design in poster advertising and sloganeering on behalf of government programs' (Warner, in Beveridge, p. 99).

For more on the documentary movement, see Hardy, *John Grierson: A Documentary Biography*, pp. 57–71, and Paul Rotha's *Documentary Film*, published in 1935 with a preface by Grierson.

Documentary is a clumsy description, but let it stand. The French who first used the term only meant travelogue. It gave them a solid high-sounding excuse for the shimmying (and otherwise discursive) exoticisms of the Vieux Colombier. Meanwhile documentary has gone on its way. From shimmying exoticisms it has gone on to include dramatic films like *Moana*, *Earth*, and *Turksib*.[4] In time it will include other kinds as different in form and intention from *Moana*, as *Moana* was from *Voyage au Congo*.

So far we have regarded all films made from natural material as coming within that category. The use of natural material has been regarded as the vital distinction. Where the camera shot on the spot (whether it shot newsreel items or magazine items or discursive 'interests' or dramatised 'interests' or educational films or scientific films proper or *Changs* or *Rangos*) in that fact was documentary. This array of species is, of course, quite unmanageable in criticism, and we shall have to do something about it. They all represent different qualities of observation, and, of course, very different powers and ambitions at the stage of organising material. I propose, therefore, after a brief word on the lower categories, to use the documentary description exclusively of the higher.

The peacetime newsreel is just a speedy snip-snap of some utterly unimportant ceremony. Its skill is in the speed with which the babblings of a politician (gazing sternly into the camera) are transferred to fifty million relatively unwilling ears in a couple of days or so. The magazine items (one a week) have adopted the original 'Tit-Bits' manner of observation. The skill they represent is a purely journalistic skill. They describe novelties novelly. With their money-making eye (their almost only eye) glued like the newsreels to vast and speedy audiences, they avoid on the one hand the consideration of solid material, and escape, on the other, the solid consideration of any material.

Within these limits they are often brilliantly done. But ten in a row would bore
the average human to death. Their reaching out for the flippant or popular touch
is so completely far-reaching that it dislocates something. Possibly taste;
possibly common sense. You may take your choice at those little theatres where
you are invited to gad around the world in fifty minutes. It takes only that long –
in these days of great invention – to see almost everything.

'Interests' proper improve mightily with every week, though heaven knows
why. The market (particularly the British market) is stacked against them.
With two-feature documentaries the rule, there is neither space for the short
and the Disney *and* the magazine, nor money left to pay for the short. But by
good grace, some of the renters throw in the short with the feature. This
considerable branch of cinematic illumination tends, therefore, to be the gift
that goes with the pound of tea; and like all gestures of the grocery mind it is
not very liable to cost much. Whence my wonder at improving qualities.
Consider, however, the very frequent beauty and very great skill of exposition
in such Ufa[5] shorts as *Turbulent Timber*, in the sports shorts from Metro-
Goldwyn-Mayer, in the *Secrets of Nature* shorts of Bruce Woolfe, and the
Fitzpatrick travel talks. Together they have brought the popular lecture to a
pitch undreamed of, and even impossible in the days of magic lanterns. In this
little we progress.

These films, of course, would not like to be called lecture films, but this,
for all their disguises, is what they are. They do not dramatise, they do not
even dramatise an episode: they describe, and even expose, but in any aesthetic
sense, only rarely reveal. Herein is their formal limit, and it is unlikely that
they will make any considerable contribution to the fuller art of documentary.
How indeed can they? Their silent form is cut to the commentary, and shots
are arranged arbitrarily to point the gags or conclusions. This is not a matter
of complaint, for the lecture film must have increasing value in entertainment,
education and propaganda. But it is as well to establish the formal limits of
the species.

This indeed is a particularly important limit to record, for beyond the
newsmen and the magazine men and the lecturers (comic or interesting or
exciting or only rhetorical) one begins to wander into the world of documentary proper, into the only world in which documentary can hope to achieve the
ordinary virtues of an art. Here we pass from the plain or fancy descriptions
of natural material, to arrangements, rearrangements, and creative shapings
of it.

First principles. (1) We believe that the cinema's capacity for getting
around, for observing and selecting from life itself, can be exploited in a

new and vital art form. The studio films largely ignore this possibility of opening up the screen on the real world. They photograph acted stories against artificial backgrounds. Documentary would photograph the living scene and the original story. (2) We believe that the original (or native) actor, and the original (or native) scene, are better guides to a screen interpretation of the modern world. They give cinema a greater fund of material. They give it power over a million and one images. They give it power of interpretation over more complex and astonishing happenings in the real world than the studio mind can conjure up or the studio mechanician recreate. (3) We believe that the materials and the stories thus taken from the raw can be finer (more real in the philosophic sense) than the acted article. Spontaneous gesture has a special value on the screen. Cinema has a sensational capacity for enhancing the movement which tradition has formed or time worn smooth. Its arbitrary rectangle specially reveals movement; it gives it maximum pattern in space and time. Add to this that documentary can achieve an intimacy of knowledge and effect impossible to the shim-sham mechanics of the studio, and the lily-fingered interpretations of the metropolitan actor.

I do not mean in this minor manifesto of beliefs to suggest that the studios cannot in their own manner produce works of art to astonish the world. There is nothing (except the Woolworth intentions of the people who run them)[6] to prevent the studios going really high in the manner of theatre or the manner of the fairy tale. My separate claim for documentary is simply that in its use of the living article, there is *also* an opportunity to perform creative work. I mean, too, that the choice of the documentary medium is as gravely distinct a choice as the choice of poetry instead of fiction. Dealing with different material, it is, or should be, dealing with it to different aesthetic issues from those of the studio. I make this distinction to the point of asserting that the young director cannot, in nature, go documentary and go studio both.

In an earlier reference to [Robert] Flaherty,[7] I have indicated how one great exponent walked away from the studio: how he came to grips with the essential story of the Eskimos, then with the Samoans, then latterly with the people of the Aran Islands: and at what point the documentary director in him diverged from the studio intention of Hollywood. The main point of the story was this. Hollywood wanted to impose a ready-made dramatic shape on the raw material. It wanted Flaherty, in complete injustice to the living drama on the spot, to build his Samoans into a rubber-stamp drama of sharks and bathing belles. It failed in the case of *Moana* [1926]; it succeeded (through Van Dyke)[8] in the case of *White Shadows of the South Seas* [1928], and (through Murnau)[9] in the case of *Tabu* [1933]. In the last examples it was at the expense of Flaherty, who severed his association with both.

With Flaherty it became an absolute principle that the story must be taken from the location, and that it should be (what he considers) the essential story of the location. His drama, therefore, is a drama of days and nights, of the round of the year's seasons, of the fundamental fights which give his people sustenance, or make their community life possible, or build up the dignity of the tribe.

Such an interpretation of subject-matter reflects, of course, Flaherty's particular philosophy of things. A succeeding documentary exponent is in no way obliged to chase off to the ends of the earth in search of old-time simplicity, and the ancient dignities of man against the sky. Indeed, if I may for the moment represent the opposition, I hope the Neo-Rousseauism implicit in Flaherty's work dies with his own exceptional self. Theory of naturals apart, it represents an escapism, a wan and distant eye, which tends in lesser hands to sentimentalism. However it be shot through with vigour of Lawrentian poetry, it must always fail to develop a form adequate to the more immediate material of the modern world. For it is not only the fool that has his eyes on the ends of the earth. It is sometimes the poet: sometimes even the great poet, as Cabell[10] in his *Beyond Life* will brightly inform you. This, however, is the very poet who on every classic theory of society from Plato to Trotsky would be removed bodily from the Republic. Loving every Time but his own, and every Life but his own, he avoids coming to grips with the creative job in so far as it concerns society. In the business of ordering most present chaos, he does not use his powers.

Question of theory and practice apart, Flaherty illustrates better than anyone the first principles of documentary. (1) It must master its material on the spot, and come in intimacy to ordering it. Flaherty digs himself in for a year, or two maybe. He lives with his people till the story is told 'out of himself'. (2) It must follow him in his distinction between description and drama. I think we shall find that there are other forms of drama or, more accurately, other forms of film, than the one he chooses; but it is important to make the primary distinction between a method which describes only the surface values of a subject, and the method which more explosively reveals the reality of it. You photograph the natural life, but you also, by your juxtaposition of detail, create an interpretation of it.

This final creative intention established, several methods are possible. You may, like Flaherty, go for a story form, passing in the ancient manner from the individual to the environment transcended or not transcended, to the consequent honours of heroism. Or you may not be so interested in the individual. You may think that the individual life is no longer capable of cross-sectioning reality. You may believe that its particular belly-aches are of no consequence in a world which complex and impersonal forces command, and conclude that the individual as a self-sufficient dramatic figure is outmoded. When Flaherty tells you that it is a devilish noble thing to fight for food in a wilderness, you may, with some justice, observe that you are more concerned with the problem of people fighting for food in the midst of plenty. When he draws your attention to the fact that Nanook's spear is grave in its upheld angle, and finely rigid in its down-pointing bravery, you may, with some justice, observe that no spear, held however bravely by the individual, will master the crazy walrus of international finance. Indeed you may feel that in individualism is a yahoo tradition largely responsible for our present anarchy, and deny at once both the hero of decent heroics (Flaherty) and the hero of indecent ones (studio). In this case, you will feel that you want your drama in terms of some cross-section of reality which will reveal the essentially co-operative or mass nature of society: leaving the individual to find his honours in the swoop of creative social forces. In other words, you are liable to abandon the story form, and seek, like the modern exponent of poetry and painting and prose, a matter and method more satisfactory to the mind and spirit of the time.

Berlin or the Symphony of a City [1926][11] initiated the more modern fashion of finding documentary material on one's doorstep:[12] in events which have no novelty of the unknown, or romance of noble savage on exotic landscape, to recommend them. It represented, slimly, the return from romance to reality.

Berlin was variously reported as made by [Walter] Ruttmann, or begun by Ruttmann and finished by [Karl] Freund: certainly it was begun by Ruttmann. In smooth and finely tempo'd visuals, a train swung through suburban mornings into Berlin. Wheels, rails, details of engines, telegraph wires, landscapes and other simple images flowed along in procession, with similar abstracts passing occasionally in and out of the general movement. There followed a sequence of such movements which, in their total effect, created very imposingly the story of a Berlin day. The day began with a processional of workers, the factories got under way, the streets filled: the city's afternoon became a hurly-burly of tangled pedestrians and street cars. There was respite for food: a various respite with contrast of rich and poor. The city started work again, and a shower of rain in the afternoon became a considerable event. The city stopped work and, in further more hectic processional of pubs and cabarets and dancing legs and illuminated sky-signs, finished its day.

In so far as the film was principally concerned with movements and the building of separate images into movements, Ruttmann was justified in calling it a symphony. It meant a break away from the story borrowed from literature, and from the play borrowed from the stage. In *Berlin* cinema swung along according to its own more natural powers: creating dramatic effect from the tempo'd accumulation of its single observations. [Alberto] Cavalcanti's *Rien que les Heures* [1926] and [Fernand] Léger's *Ballet Mécanique* [1924] came before *Berlin*, each with a similar attempt to combine images in an emotionally satisfactory sequence of movements. They were too scrappy and had not mastered the art of cutting sufficiently well to create both the sense of 'march' necessary to the genre. The symphony of Berlin City was both larger in its movements and larger in its vision.

There was one criticism of *Berlin* which, out of appreciation for a fine film and a new and arresting form, the critics failed to make; and time has not justified the omission. For all its ado of workmen and factories and swirl and swing of a great city, Berlin created nothing. Or rather if it created something, it was that shower of rain in the afternoon. The people of the city got up splendidly, they tumbled through their five million hoops impressively, they turned in; and no other issue of God or man emerged than that sudden besmattering spilling of wet on people and pavements.

I urge the criticism because *Berlin* still excites the mind of the young, and the symphony form is still their most popular persuasion. In fifty scenarios presented by the tyros, forty-five are symphonies of Edinburgh or of Ecclefechan or of Paris or of Prague. Day breaks – the people come to work – the factories start – the street cars rattle – lunch hour and the streets again – sport if it is Saturday afternoon – certainly evening and the local dance hall. And so, nothing having happened and nothing positively said about anything, to bed; though Edinburgh is the capital of a country and Ecclefechan, by some power inside itself, was the birthplace of Carlyle, in some ways one of the greatest exponents of this documentary idea.

The little daily doings, however finely symphonised, are not enough. One must pile up beyond doing or process to creation itself, before one hits the higher reaches of art. In this distinction, creation indicates not the making of things but the making of virtues.

And there's the rub for tyros. Critical appreciation of movement they can build easily from their power to observe, and power to observe they can build from their own good taste, but the real job only begins as they apply ends to their observation and their movements. The artist need not posit the ends – for that is the work of the critic – but the ends must be there, informing his description and giving finality (beyond space and time) to the slice of life he has chosen. For that larger effect there must be power of poetry or of prophecy. Failing either or both in the highest degree, there must be at least the sociological sense implicit in poetry and prophecy.

The best of tyros know this. They believe that beauty will come in good time to inhabit the statement which is honest and lucid and deeply felt and which fulfils the best ends of citizenship. They are sensible enough to conceive of art as the by-product of a job of work done. The opposite effort to capture the by-product first (the self-conscious pursuit of beauty, the pursuit of art for art's sake to the exclusion of jobs of work and other pedestrian beginnings), was always a reflection of selfish wealth, selfish leisure and aesthetic decadence.

This sense of social responsibility makes our realist documentary a troubled and difficult art, and particularly in a time like ours. The job of romantic documentary is easy in comparison: easy in the sense that the noble savage is already a figure of romance and the seasons of the year have already been articulated in poetry. Their essential virtues have already been declared and can more easily be declared again, and no one will deny them. But realist documentary, with its streets and cities and slums and markets and exchanges and factories, has given itself the job of making poetry where no poet has gone before it, and where no ends, sufficient for the purposes of art, are easily observed. It requires not only taste but also inspiration, which is to say a very laborious, deep-seeing, deep-sympathising creative effort indeed.

The symphonists have found a way of building such matters of common reality into very pleasant sequences. By uses of tempo and rhythm, and by the large-scale integration of single effects, they capture the eye and impress the mind in the same way as a tattoo or a military parade might do. But by their concentration on mass and movement, they tend to avoid the larger creative job. What more attractive (for a man of visual taste) than to swing wheels and pistons about in ding-dong description of a machine, when he has little to say about the man who tends it, and still less to say about the tin-pan product it spills? And what more comfortable if, in one's heart, there is avoidance of the issue of underpaid labour and meaningless production? For this reason I hold the symphony tradition of cinema for a danger and *Berlin* for the most dangerous of all film models to follow.

Unfortunately, the fashion is with such avoidance as *Berlin* represents. The highbrows bless the symphony for its good looks and, being sheltered rich little souls for the most part, absolve it gladly from further intention. Other factors combine to obscure one's judgement regarding it. The post-1918 generation, in which all cinema intelligence resides, is apt to veil a particularly violent sense of disillusionment, and a very natural first reaction of impotence, in any smart manner of avoidance which comes to hand. The pursuit of fine form which this genre certainly represents is the safest of asylums.

The objection remains, however. The rebellion from the who-gets-who tradition of commercial cinema to the tradition of pure form in cinema is no great shakes as a rebellion. Dadaism, expressionism, symphonics, are all in the same category. They present new beauties and new shapes; they fail to present new persuasions.

The imagist or more definitely poetic approach might have taken our consideration of documentary a step further, but no great imagist film has arrived to give character to the advance. By imagism I mean the telling of a story or illumination of theme by images, as poetry is story or theme told by images: I mean the addition of poetic reference to the 'mass' or 'march' of the symphonic form.

Drifters was one simple contribution in that direction, but only a simple one. Its subject belonged in part to Flaherty's world, for it had something of the noble savage and certainly a great deal of the elements of nature to play with. It did, however, use steam and smoke and did, in a sense, marshal the effects of modern industry. Looking back on the film now, I would not stress the tempo effects which it built (for both *Berlin* and *Potemkin* came before it), nor even the rhythmic effects (though I believe they outdid the technical example of *Potemkin* in that direction). What seemed possible of development in the film was the integration of imagery with the movement. The ship at sea, the men casting, the men hauling, were not only seen as functionaries doing something. They were seen as functionaries in half a hundred different ways, and each tended to add something to the illumination as well as the description of them. In other words the shots were massed together, not only for description and tempo but for commentary on it. One felt impressed by the tough continuing upstanding labour involved, and the feeling shaped the images, determined the background and supplied the extra details which gave colour to the whole. I do not urge the example of *Drifters*, but in theory at least the example is there. If the high bravery of upstanding labour came through the film, as I hope it did, it was made not by the story itself, but by the imagery attendant on it. I put the point, not in praise of the method but in simple analysis of the method.

Notes

1. On the difficulties surrounding the screening of *Battleship Potemkin*, see Hogenkamp, *Deadly Parallels*, pp. 28–30.
2. 'Film and the Workers' Movement in Britain 1929–39', *Sight and Sound* 45.2 (1976): 72. Cited in Armes, p. 128.
3. On the ILP, its founding and its goals, see Pearce and Stewart, pp. 246–50.
4. *Moana*, directed by Robert Flaherty (1926); *Earth*, directed by Alexander Dovzhenko (1930); *Turksib*, directed by Victor Turin (English version shown by Grierson in London, 6 March 1930).
5. Universum Film Aktien Gesellschaft, German film production combine founded in 1917. See Klaus Kreimeier, *The Ufa Story*, trans. Robert and Rita Kimber (New York: Hill and Wang, 1996).
6. Cf. F. R. Leavis's allusion to Woolworth's, and to the problems of mass production and standardization, in *Mass Civilisation and Minority Culture*, p. 7. See above, p. 19, and also Naomi Mitchison, p. 235.
7. Grierson, 'Flaherty', *Cinema Quarterly* 1.1 (Autumn 1932): 12–17.
8. W. S. (Woody) Van Dyke took over the direction of *White Shadows* from Flaherty.
9. Flaherty and F. W. Murnau formed a partnership in 1929. *Tabu* was their only completed work together.
10. James Branch Cabell (1879–1958). The full title of the work Grierson refers to is *Beyond Life; dizain des demiurges* (1927).
11. Grierson omits 'Big' from the title, which in the original German of Ruttmann's film is *Berlin—Die Symphonie einer Grosstadt*.
12. Mass-Observation was also to be part of this fashion – not surprisingly, given that two associates of Grierson – Stuart Legg and Humphrey Jennings – played a part in its formation. See above, p. 289. *Mass-Observation at the Movies*, ed. Richards and Sheridan, collects a wealth of interesting material on cinema and cinema-going.

By 1937 Jameson had published over twenty-five books, had managed for over ten years the British branch of Alfred Knopf the American publisher, and was shortly to be elected president of the International PEN, English Centre. She had, in other words, a good deal more experience in the world of writing and publishing than many others who were quicker to write about it. She had already published two critical studies – one on *Modern Drama in Europe* (1920) and another on *The Georgian Novel and Mr. Robinson* (1929) – and as she wrote this piece she was planning *The Novel in Contemporary Life*, which appeared in 1938. Vera Brittain's diary of the 1930s records Jameson's presence in the chair at a debate between Amabel Williams-Ellis and Ellis Roberts on 'That Modern Fiction is out of touch with everyday life,'[1] and Jameson herself lived in close contact with the everyday – both as a nearly destitute single parent after her divorce in 1924 and as a campaigner for justice and civil liberty. She was one of the founding sponsors of Canon Dick Sheppard's Peace Pledge Union at its launch on 22 May 1936, but when Germany annexed the Sudetenland in 1938 and then invaded Czechoslovakia in 1939, she resigned from the PPU, convinced that Hitler could only be resisted by force.[2] What shows in this essay very clearly is Jameson's characteristic combination of a profound social awareness and clear-sighted practicality. Her introductory note, which she appended to the essay for publication in *Civil Journey* (1939) and which I include for its self-deprecating wit, provides a telling contrast to the earnest self-inflation which was rather the norm in 'personal' public notes of this type during the period. The issue of *Fact* in question is, interestingly, the very one in which Arthur Calder-Marshall portentously labelled the 1930s a 'time of transition'[3]

> This essay was written for Fact, *for an issue called 'Writing in Revolt'. It was a singularly inapt title – foolish, too: writers may revolt, though surely not in a vacuum, but writing? Neither the theory nor the examples offered could have been labelled revolutionary in any proper sense of that bundle-word. This essay is as mild, orthodox and one-sided as the annual conference of the Conservative Party, and much more so than any Mother's Meeting. But then a Mother's Meeting, in Yorkshire at any rate, could give points in revolutionary outlook to any nest of singing rebels in Bloomsbury or elsewhere.*

---

* Originally published in *Fact* 4 (July 1937). Reprinted from Jameson, *Civil Journey* (London: Cassell, 1939), pp. 261–74.

I believe we should do well to give up talking about proletarian literature and talk about socialist literature instead – and mean by it writing concerned with the lives of men and women in a world which is changing and being changed. A socialist must be immediately concerned with this change; he must be struggling continually to understand it. His writing must reflect his experience of it and his understanding of his experience. And since the change is world wide, and is taking place on innumerable levels at once and all the time, the difficulty of attempting to write anything on the scale of *War and Peace* is so great as to make it unlikely that it will be written – yet. The difficulty excuses none of us for retreating into a world made artificially static by excluding from it all the factors of change and the rumour of the real world.

Literature concerned with change and the changing world is concerned with revolution, and with all stages of revolutionary action. The type of socialist hero is a revolutionary (required reading is Ralph Fox's *The Novel and the People*), and here, if he is a novelist, the writer is not likely to be able to create a revolutionary hero under the eyes of the living Dimitroff. Even Tolstoi, writing fifty years after Waterloo, is not able to make a figure of Napoleon; Stendhal, a great writer, and a contemporary, does not try. It is perhaps necessary (this is not the place to consider it) for a really great figure to become diminished in time before he can be re-created by the imagination, which can tackle lesser men (a Baldwin, for example) easily enough. Note that in Ralph Bates's novels his heroes are least convincing when they are behaving as revolutionaries. In quarrelling, in gathering olives, in enduring, they appear as whole men. Compare the hero of Malraux's *Days of Contempt* with the figure of Dimitroff; he is a shadow. Compare him with himself – he begins to be alive only when he leaves the prison and is talking to his wife.

The use of the term 'proletarian novel' suggests, quite falsely, that socialist literature ought to concern itself only or mainly with working-class life.[4] In fact, a novel written about a Lord Invernairn, written from full insight into what this man actually is doing, a novel which exposed him, laid him open, need not bring on to the stage a single one of the people who do not exist for him as human beings. It would still be socialist literature. The process of change, of decay, of growth, is taking place everywhere all the time: it does not matter where you open up the social body if you know what you are looking for.

This misconception is not the worst of it. The worst is a dreadful self-consciousness which seizes the middle-class writer who hears the command to sell all he has and write a proletarian novel. He discovers that he does not even know what the wife of a man earning two pounds a week wears, where she buys her food, what her kitchen looks like to her when she comes into it at six or seven in the morning. It has never happened to him to stand with his hands in greasy water at the sink, with a nagging pain in his back, and his clothes sticking to him. He (or she) actually has to take a look into the kitchen to know what it smells like. At that he does not know as much as the woman's forefinger knows when it scrapes the black out of a crack in the table or the corner of a shelf.

The impulse that made him want to know is decent and defensible. If he happens to have been born and brought up in Kensington the chances are that he has never lifted the blind of his own kitchen at six in the morning, with thoughts in his mind of tumbled bed-clothes, dirty grates, and the ring of rust on the stove. But there is something very wrong when he has to contort himself into knots in order to get to know a worker, man or woman. What is wrong is in him, and he cannot blame on to his upbringing what is really a failure of his own will; it is still clenched on his idea of himself, given to him by that upbringing, but now to be cast off as the first condition of growth. Too much of his energy runs away in an intense interest in and curiosity about his feelings. 'What things I am seeing for the first time! What smells I am enduring! There is the woman raking ashes with her hands and here I am watching her!' This self-centred habit is not peculiar to the middle-class writer, but it is natural to him. If, as a child, he had escaped from the nursery and been found in some Hoxton backyard he would have been bathed and disinfected and made conscious of having run an awful danger, much as though he had been visiting savages. The mental attitude persists. Breeding will out!

The first thing a socialist writer has to realise is that there is no value in the emotions, the spiritual writhings, started in him by the sight, smell, and touch of poverty. The emotions are no doubt unavoidable. There is no need to record them. Let him go and pour them down the drain.

The writer living in one moment of time and in one society, and perpetually conscious of another trying to break through, has been set a task which calls for special discipline and effort. He must enquire into a revolution, but he cannot create a revolutionary hero as impressive as the still-living Dimitroff. If he could, he would be mentally of the size of Dimitroff and, at the present instant, that would lay on him the compulsion to work in other ways than as a writer. He must not, he ought not to indulge himself in self-analysis, since that is to nail himself inside his own small ego at a moment when what is individual to each man is less real, less actual, than that which he shares with

314 *History in Our Hands*

every other man – insecurity, the need to become a rebel for the sake of human dignity. What then should he do?

A task of the greatest value, urgent and not easy, is waiting to be done. George Orwell has begun on it in the first half of *The Road to Wigan Pier*. The instinct which drives a writer to go and see for himself may be sound. If a writer does not know, if his senses and imagination have not told him, what poverty smells like, he had better find out. Even if in the end he prefers to write about Invernairn or Krupp. But if he goes for his own sake, for some fancied spiritual advantage to be got from the experience, he had better stay at home: his presence in Wigan or Hoxton is either irrelevant or impudent. He must go for the sake of the *fact*, as a medical student carries out a dissection, and to equip himself, not to satisfy his conscience or to see what effect it has on him. His mind must remain cool; he must be able to give an objective report, neither superficial nor slickly dramatic. And, for pity's sake, don't let us have any 'slices of life' in the manner of the Naturalists of the 'eighties. In their determination to show life up they became as sentimental, as emotionally dishonest, as Miss So-and-so 'embosoming freely' with her readers in the columns of the women's magazines. For their own purposes they counterfeit reality as obtusely as she does.

The conditions for the growth of a socialist literature scarcely exist. We have to create them. We need documents, not, as the Naturalists needed them, to make their drab tuppenny-ha'penny dramas, but as charts, as timber for the fire some writer will light tomorrow morning. The detailed and accurate presentment, rather than the presentation, of this moment, and this society. A new *Comédie Humaine* – offered to us without the unnecessary distorting gloss of the writer's emotions and self-questionings. Writers should be willing to go and live for a long enough time at one of the points of departure of the new society. To go, if you like, into exile. Without feeling heroic, or even adventurous, or curious about their own spiritual reactions. Willing to sink themselves for the time, so that they become conduits for a feeling which is not personal, nor static.

They might, for instance, tell us what is stirring, if anything, in one of those Durham mining villages about which a staid report in *The Times* says that 'no hope exists for thousands of men and boys ever to lead a normal working life again'. A report made by two women doctors to the Council of Action on Motherhood in the Special Areas of Durham and Tyneside remarks, 'It was amazing that in this country people should be living in such dens, that mothers should go through their pregnancies there and infants be born.' I don't know who reads these reports with their ghastly 'cases'. They are not documents in the proper sense of the word; they are not full enough; they do not give the essentials of speech and action. They could not: the observation, however acute, is made from outside, too briefly, and as a stranger would report upon strangers after an hour's visit. We do not *see* the woman stripping the filthy, bug-ridden wallpaper from the thin wall of her attic; nor the pregnant woman waiting her turn at the lavatory which serves eight families (forty people); nor the gesture of the woman setting on the table the little pie she has bought for her consumptive child; nor the workless man looking at the soles of his shoes when he comes home. It is necessary that a writer should have lived with these things for him to record them as simply and coldly, even brutally, as if he chooses he can describe what has been familiar to him from his infancy. Something can be discovered in an hour's visit, but not the quick. Not the seed, if it exists here, of a different growth.

It is not necessary – in a great many instances it would be impossible or undesirable—for a writer to work alone. He might work with other writers, if it were decided to report on a district or a town (see the American classic in this sort, *Middletown*).[5] He can enlist the help of social workers to supplement his own experience of such specifically modern horrors as the effects on girls and young women of 'rationalisation' in the factory. (When Charlie Chaplin goes mad, in a recent film,[6] unable to stop himself jerking at anything that looks like the top of a screw, he is caricaturing a horrid reality: the girls from one of these rationalised factories cannot keep their hands still; they walk round the club room nipping off the heads of flowers, turning off the heating; they jerk and twitch and scream.)

A writer living in a Nottinghamshire mining village could not possibly do his job properly without the help of confidential reports from the workers themselves which he would have to wait for and deserve by his behaviour. He could not expect the wife of a miner living in one of the new 'compounds' to tell him at sight how she likes shopping in an employer-owned store. Why, he might be in the pay of the Economic League.[7] (The connections and activities of this organisation deserve a document to themselves – more than one.)

A well-placed novelist might bring out a double-sided record: one day or one week in the life of a family living in one of the wealthier residential districts of the West End (if he or she can find one which has so far forgotten itself as to breed), set down opposite the life during the same length of time of a similar (in ages, size, etc.), of a Paddington, Hoxton, Lambeth family. Again, this might be team work.[8]

The number of documents to be got is infinite. How are they to be presented? This is the crux. A journalist can observe and report. No writer is satisfied to write journalism, nor is this what is wanted – visits to the distressed areas in a motor-car. Nor must the experience, the knowledge waited for and lived through, be counterfeited, in the sense of making up a story or a novel on the basis of facts collected (e.g. *The Stars Look Down* [1935], by [A. J.] Cronin). Perhaps the nearest equivalent of what is wanted exists already in another form in the documentary film. As the photographer does, so must the writer keep himself out of the picture while working ceaselessly to present the fact from a striking (poignant, ironic, penetrating, significant) angle.[9] The narrative must be sharp, compressed, concrete. Dialogue must be short – a seizing of the significant, the revealing word. The emotion should spring directly from the fact. It must not be squeezed from it by the writer, running forward with a 'When I saw this, I felt, I suffered, I rejoiced . . .' His job is not to tell us what he felt, but to be coldly and industriously presenting, arranging, selecting, discarding from the mass of his material to get the significant detail which leaves no more to be said, and implies everything.

And for goodness' sake let us get some fun out of it. Nothing is less to our taste, and less realist, than the inspissated gloom of Naturalism. A novel by Ignazio Silone, *Fontamara* [1933], offers itself as a model – this tragic, bitter story of a village is extremely funny, and sticks faster in the memory by it. Let us write decent English, too; not American telegraphese. Social documents are familiar in our literature. The sermons of preaching friars are still alive where the preacher threw in a scene that was under his eyes as he walked about – often a savage indictment of poverty created by greedy merchants and landlords.

For the sake of comparison – the field to be covered is, after all, enormous – and for the sake of sharpness, much must be left out that a writer will be tempted to put in. For one thing, 'atmosphere'. It has been overdone, too – all those novels in which infinite pains have gone to the evocation of rain and moonlight, novels 'set' in Cornwall, in Sussex, in Paris and Patagonia. For another thing, the static analysis of feeling, and thought. No more peeling of the onion to strew the page with layer after layer. No stream of consciousness – that famous stream which we pretend to see flowing, as in the theatre we agree to pretend that the stream on the back-cloth flows. No commentary – the document is a comment. No aesthetic, moral, or philosophic enquiry – that is, none which is not implicit. To say this is not to say that a novel such as [L. H. Myers's] *The Root and the Flower* [1935] is of no value. It is of the greatest value and it is concerned with those human values we are trying to to save. It offers – in a form entirely unsuitable to our present purpose – a criticism of social values which is just and suggestive. Its method is useless to us – for a good reason. We must be field workers in a field no smaller than England, our criticism of values implied in the angle from which we take our pictures. By choosing this detail, this word, rather than another from the mass offered us, we make our criticism, our moral judgements.

Writers write to be read. If they are not read, by as many people as will do to keep them vigorously alive, they have failed as *writers*. People will listen even to what is disagreeable to them if the speaker's tone takes them by the ear. The Naturalists flung tear-sodden lumps of raw life in the public's face and complained because the public went home to amuse itself in its own way. There is a technical job to be done. It can't be done until the instruments have been made and improved, as astronomy had to wait on a lens. How to make people listen to what they don't want to hear. How not to bore the people who do want to hear. If they want to hear, you say, they'll take anything. But why should they? Why should they be bored by what is nothing more or less than incompetence or amateurishness? It is not a question of setting out to be a best-seller – if that is what you want there are shorter and easier ways – but of learning a craft. Again the relevant comparison is with the documentary film. It takes a sharpened and disciplined mind to handle a mass of material in such a way that only the significant details emerge. We're confronted by the extreme difficulty of finding phrases which are at once compressed and highly suggestive. It's hardly a job for an amateur unless he happens to be a genius. (When a genius arrives he can and will look after himself.)

The isolation of writers from each other is almost as deadly as their isolation from the life of farmers, labourers, miners, and other men on whom the life of the nation depends. If something of this unnatural apartness can be broken down, by writers working together, by their coming into relation with their fellow-men and women, they may, between them, provide the conditions, the warmth, for a new literature. We have been attending the death-bed of an old one for some time; a birth is about due. It may actually be the birth of a great writer, and the documents we have collected, the activity we have stirred up, will form the conditions into which he is born. They will shape him and he will use them. A great writer has more than one father and mother, as well as more than one nurse.

One technical difficulty remains to be solved. The solution may turn up one day, in the course of the experiments going on all the time. This is the frightful difficulty of expressing, in such a way that they are at once seen to be intimately connected, the relations between things (men, acts) widely separated in space or in the social complex. It has been done in poetry. At certain levels of the mind we see and feel connections which we know rationally in another way. In dreams things apparently distinct are seen to be related (but Surrealism is not the solution).[10] We may stumble on the solution in the effort of trying to create the literary equivalent of the documentary film.

Notes

1. Friday, 25 November 1923. *Diary of the Thirties*, p. 110.
2. On her differences with Brittain over this, see Berry and Bostridge, p. 403.
3. See below, p. 325.
4. See above, p. 12.
5. Cf. F. R. Leavis's mention of *Middletown* in *Mass Civilisation and Minority Culture*, p. 6. See above, p. 19.
6. *Modern Times* (1936).
7. The Economic League was formed in 1919 to promote private enterprise and undermine the advance of socialism. In particular it provided a focus for anti-union campaigns.
8. Jameson here imagines what was in fact the programme of the Mass-Observation movement. See above, pp. 289–94.
9. Cf. John Grierson's 'First Principles of Documentary', laid out in *Cinema Quarterly* in the Winter 1932 and Spring 1933 issues (see above, pp. 301–10). Also interesting in relation to Jameson's caution about artists making use of the personal testimony of workers and their wives is Arthur Elton's account of the making of *Housing Problems*. See Elton, 'Realist Films Today' (pp. 319–23 of this book).
10. Jameson's disagreement with surrealism is laid out in another essay, 'The Novel in Contemporary Life', *Civil Journey*, pp. 275–309.

37 Arthur Elton   *Realist Films Today (1937)**

Elton read English Literature and psychology at Cambridge, entering the film industry as a script-writer for Gainsborough Studios in 1927. When the studio was destroyed by fire, he joined Grierson's team at the Empire Marketing Board. The film for which he is perhaps best known is *Housing Problems* (1935), which he made with Edgar Anstey, and which he discusses briefly but usefully below. Like Grierson's *Drifters*, *Housing Problems* was a work with an obviously progressive, left-wing agenda, yet subsidized by a party with a vested economic interest: it was the first of a series of films commissioned by the British Commercial Gas Association. Anstey remarked that in the film there 'was a sort of political thing coming out which had been suppressed a bit, because we were all in a way politicians, but we were operating very indirectly. We were trying to show things as they were, people as they were, and there was a lot of indignation about unemployment, about malnutrition, about the bad housing at that time'.[1] In his essay included in this volume, Arthur Calder-Marshall draws attention to the ways in which films of this type could be hampered by their sponsors. On the style of *Housing Problems*, Elton commented that it 'was like a television presentation, only long before television. It pioneered the interview. It pioneered all that kind of thing' (Anstey and Elton in Sussex, p. 62).

Realist films in England really date from 1929, when *Drifters* and *One Family*[2] were produced by the Empire Marketing Board,[3] though before that date Bruce Woolfe had produced a few documentary films which were mostly reconstructions of war-time events, and also, under his guidance, there had appeared the first few films of that magnificent series *Secrets of Nature*. But 1929 dates the parting of the ways between the studio conception and the realist conception of the treatment of natural material. The Empire Marketing Board embarked simultaneously on two productions. The commission of the Board was to 'bring England alive' – in Sir Stephen Tallents's phrase. Its job was to create in the general public an understanding of the problems and activities of science and invention, of industry and commerce.

Of the two films, *One Family* sprang from the tradition of the studios. The treatment was artificial. Events of the British Empire were seen through the eyes of a small boy wandering in Buckingham Palace. The film had a certain success in a fashionable West End run.

* Reprinted from *Left Review* 2 (1936–7): 426–30.

Drifters was made from a very different point of view. Grierson believed that the events of the world could be interpreted without the vicarious addition of small boys and effigies of Britannia. It was his belief that if you could show the energies and humanities of the fishing fleet at first hand, without filtering them through the mannerisms of the studio, you could bring to the screen a vivid experience of reality. So he went boldly into the world of the herring fleet (which he knew well) and used for his raw material the people he found there. His film *Drifters* has now become world-famous, and *Our Family* is forgotten.

Drifters helped to create a new school of cinema, drawing its traditions from such films as Turin's *Turksib* on the one hand, and [James] Cruze's *Covered Wagon* [1923] on the other. One is now sufficiently far away from the silent realist film to be able to look back in a detached way, and to examine the effect of the appearance of sound.

Though we did not realise it before the coming of sound, the silent film excluded half the world. It was a deaf mute. It was a fine medium for lyricism and poetics, and for the creation of lovely rhythms. In some ways it was a drug, for it gave the skilled director the power to retire into a world of lyricism and impressionism. The silent realist film was too often used as a decorative medium. Its powers of presenting reasoned argument and the perspectives behind events were limited. Though the silent film could force an audience into taking a definite point of view, such conviction was often produced in an emotional way by sheer force of imagery. The directors of the school were in danger of growing into an art for art's sake movement, without knowing it. We were beginning to be immersed in fine images and fine rhythms to the exclusion of human beings. People in our films were often not so much living, breathing individuals, as decorative attendants to shining machinery and the pastoral scene. Our workers were often romantic figures posed against wheels or clouds.

And then sound came. At first we were against it. It added nothing, we said. We disliked commentators. We did not at first see our way to articulate the sounds of the ordinary world. They fell on our ears as a jumbled, roaring blur, greatly at variance with our smoothly constructed visuals. It is interesting to note that two of the earliest realist sound films, [Paul] Rotha's *Contact* [1933] still retained sub-titles and had no commentary, and my own *Voice of the World* [1932] had only a few rhetorical bursts of speech, though it is fair to add that both films displayed some rudimentary attempts to handle natural sound. We did not then realise that commentary properly used could give a new terseness and perspective to our subject matter.

Fortunately, two men at least knew the dangers of romanticism – Grierson and [Alberto] Cavalcanti. Today, perhaps the most living sequences of *Drifters* are the intimate, friendly scenes of the sailors eating, going to sleep, getting up in the morning, and the shot of the stoker lighting a cigarette from a shovel of red-hot coals. Cavalcanti, too, clung with firmness to the human element, and because of his persistence *Rien que les Heures* can take its place beside its successors in sound today.

Realist films did not take seriously to sound for some years after its introduction. This was not so much due to inhibitions as to the fact that the realist film was almost wholly under the wing of the Empire Marketing Board, and subsequently of the Post Office, and sound apparatus was expensive. The realist directors, therefore, had the advantage of being able to study the development of sound technique before embarking on sound productions themselves.

Almost from the beginning, sound had violent effects. In spite of early inhibitions, we soon realised that the addition of sound was going to give us an important weapon for clear elucidation of technical process and presentation of argument. We were at last able to put forward the specialised point of view of the man on the job.

Sound took us by the seat of the pants and forced us to face up to real things. First experiments were in simple commentary. Instead of using a commentary of stagey wisecracks mixed with information, we went to the workers and invited them to write and speak their own commentary. An example of this is *Under the City* (Production: Elton-Shaw), where workers on a telephone cable described the processes involved, in their own language. The effect was immediately interesting. There was a quality of freshness in the slang, in the racy lively cockney, and in the breakaway from the orthodox B.B.C. accent. But we were still outside the everyday world. We took our commentators, and putting them beside us, invited them to comment from the outside.

The next step was to bring to the microphone the sounds and voices of the world. This was done in *6.30 Collection* (Production: Anstey-Watt). In this film the sound was still largely unco-ordinated, and although there sprang from the background vitalising remarks and jokes as the work was carried on, the sound was not yet really articulate.

For the sake of space, it is necessary to restrict this article to the consideration of a school of sound films which is slowly separating out from the main body, and which may conveniently be called 'reportage'. There is not time to deal with the other extremely important developments in the realist sound film, such as the reaching towards a poetic approach to the subject, or the use of sound to give background. Such things as the Beattock climb in Wright and Watt's *Night Mail*, with Auden's poetic commentary, the provincial broadcast sequences of [Stuart] Legg's *B.B.C.: The Voice of Britain* [1934–5], the sequence in Rotha's *Shipyard* [1934–5] where the workers are discussing their jobs, whilst faintly over the steel shell of the hull we see the swimming pools and luxury of the finished ship, and [Basil] Wright's *Song of Ceylon* [1934–5], all point to methods of treatment which will become of surpassing importance.

The next step in reportage was to take a group of workers and to get them to play definite parts in front of the microphone. This is exemplified in my *Workers and Jobs* [1935]. I approached the subject with some trepidation. Thirty unemployed men had been picked at random to play definite 'parts'. Rumbling round in my mind was still, I think, the idea that the workers would be inarticulate, shy, and lacking in expression; but from the first shots this feeling was dispersed. In point of fact, workers in front of a camera are articulate and far more simple in their film acting than people from so-called higher levels of society, who are often shy, nervous, and frightened of committing themselves.

A further step in the move towards getting inside the subject is to be noticed in *Housing Problems* (Production: Elton-Anstey). In this film, instead of directing the players to 'act' a scene, they were asked to address the camera, and to tell it in their own words, unguided and unrehearsed, what they felt their own problems of living in a slum to be. One found that after a preliminary hesitation the various people spoke easily and logically about their own surroundings. Here the audience was transported inside the skin of the subject. All technical adornments were deliberately given second place to articulation and clarity, and the film perhaps suffers from its lack of nuance. But I believe that it opens up a valuable field which will soon be further exploited.

In the silent days *Night Mail* would have been a rollicking symphony of a train, but the producers, with sound at their command, have brought alive the unknown world of the Post Office services with all the raciness and slang and individuality of its workers. Commentary has been used, not as pedantic description, but as a poetic means of giving perspective and background reference. In the silent days, *Housing Problems* would probably have been an elegant draping of washing in backyards.

The modern realist film has given up the loving caress of industrial process and statuesque treatment of workers,[4] for a racy intimacy with men and women which we hope will blow away the romantic cobwebs of an earlier vision. It will move, we hope, from introversion and love of process for its own sake, to an attempt to put audiences in touch with the people of the everyday world around them.

Notes

1. See Burnett, *A Social History of Housing, 1815–1985*, Part III, especially Chapters 8 and 9: 'Council Housing 1918–1939' and 'Speculative Housing 1918–1939. 'The Attack on the Slums' is discussed at pp. 240–9.
2. Directed by Walter Creighton.
3. See above, p. 301.
4. The example, par excellence, of this 'loving caress of industrial process and statuesque treatment of workers' is surely *Industrial Britain*, made for the Empire Marketing Board in 1933. The producer was Grierson, the director Flaherty (who also wrote and photographed the film), and the editor Anstey, who collaborated with Elton on *Housing Problems*.

This essay appeared in Cecil Day Lewis's well-known collection of leftist essays, *The Mind in Chains: Socialism and the Cultural Revolution*, published in London in 1937. In the oft-quoted conclusion to Day Lewis's introduction, we are told that '*The Mind in Chains* could never have been written were it not for the widespread belief of intellectual workers that the mind is really in chains today, that these chains have been forged by a dying social system, that they can and must be broken – and in the Soviet Union have been broken; and that we can only realise our strength by joining forces with the millions of workers who have nothing to lose but their chains and have a world to win' (p. 17). Among the other pieces included were Rex Warner on 'Education', Edward Upward's notorious 'Marxist Interpretation of Literature' (on this and the collection generally, see Cunningham, pp. 212–14 and 301–3), Charles Madge on 'Press, Radio and Social Consciousness', and Edgell Rickword's 'Culture, Progress and English Tradition'. Anthony Blunt contributed a piece on 'Art under Capitalism and Socialism', and there were essays by Alan Bush, Alistair Browne, J. D. Bernal and T. A. Jackson. Despite this formidable lineup, Louis MacNeice evidently fell asleep reading the book on a train,[1] and Evelyn Waugh argued in *Night and Day* that there was a 'natural connexion' between the schoolmasterly tone of the contributions and 'a taste for totalitarian government'.[2] The latter, Cunningham points out (p. 145), was an assertion Waugh would make again in 1939 in *Robbery under Law*. In a rather odd hyperbolic flight, Montagu Slater declared in the *Left Review* that the book left him with the impression of 'a discovery of the actual world. Here is a peak commanding the new country, and these writers, like Stout Cortez and his men, look at each other with a wild surmise: then begin to move down to an intelligible society.'[3]

The analogy is surely a regrettable one, that descent of Cortez being one of the most shameful in the history of European imperialism. And it is probably inappropriate in another respect, namely that the 'moral' of The Mind in Chains, as Slater infers it, is much less militant than the link with Cortez would suggest. He quotes from Rex Warner:

> Nowadays . . . one need not be a Marxist, one need only be an ordinarily decent person, to approve the immediate practical aims of Marxism. There is no longer, then, any need for us in our propaganda to adopt that aggressive attitude which is appropriate to one who drags people from great darkness into the light. The light is much nearer than it was. (p. 365)

---

* Reprinted from C. Day Lewis, ed., *The Mind in Chains: Socialism and the Cultural Revolution* (London: Frederick Muller, 1937), pp. 59–68 and 71–9.

One can see why Arthur Calder-Marshall, writing in the *New Statesman* of 15 February 1941, asserted famously that the 1930s was a pink, rather than a red, decade. Pink, I suppose, is appropriate to an age he insisted in 1937 was a 'time of transition'.[4] And yet in *his* contribution to *The Mind in Chains* there is a stout, Cortez-like aggression provoked by his subject: the film industry where, as Slater puts it, there is 'capitalism without weakness or division, of unsurpassed cunning and evidently invincible' (p. 363).

For a somewhat different assessment of 1930s cinema, see John Grierson's essay, 'The Cinema Today', included by Geoffrey Grigson in his collection of essays by various writers, *The Arts To-Day* (London: John Lane/Bodley Head, 1935), pp. 219–50.

To understand why modern American and English films are as they are, we must first understand the conditions under which they are produced. We must understand the intentions of the producers and the means by which they realise those intentions.

The first essential of film making is finance. Money plays a comparatively unimportant role in the production of books, of paintings, or of music. But the cost of buying the necessary film apparatus and running it demands heavy financial backing. As with the Press, and to a lesser degree the theatre, the cinema is the means of expression of powerful financial interests in the capitalist state.[5]

The financiers may be said to control the policy of the film industry to this extent. They are prepared to finance any film, provided, firstly, that it will appeal to sufficient people for them to recoup themselves and, secondly, that it will approve and if possible confirm the state of society in which it is possible for them to go on financing films and drawing profits.

In every case, films are made by the very rich to be shown to the very poor. On the other hand, films fall into three different classes, when we analyse their motives. Films are, firstly, made to entertain (that is, to provoke in the audience laughter, horror, sympathy, sorrow, joy or excitement), or secondly, to instruct (that is, to give what purports to be true information about public interest), or thirdly, to advertise (that is, to induce people to buy certain goods, or think certain thoughts in preference to others). The second and third classes are always merging into one another. A travel film, for example, may be a disguised advertisement: while a G.P.O. film may be incidentally instructional.

When we speak of the film industry, we mean the vested interests which produce films of the first class rather than of the other two. Advertisement and instruction are left usually to free-lance film-producers or small companies. The great film companies concentrate on story pictures and supply the subsidiary films usually as makeweights.

I propose to examine each of these three types of film, as they exist under capitalism, because an understanding of how they are produced under capitalism will help to show the changes which socialist production would make.

In the first class, the most remarkable fact is perhaps the salaries paid to the creative and administrative staff. The initial cost of a film must be great, but this inevitable cost is minute compared to the extravagant salaries paid to anyone connected with the film industry in a capacity of any importance. The reason for this is obvious. Though two or three years elapse before the initial expenditure is repaid, the eventual returns on a successful film are colossal. Everybody is out to get as big a share as he can. And who'd blame them for that?

In the earlier days of the film industry, the more money that was spent on a film, the better the film was likely to be. But very soon the cinema had all the financial backing that it wanted and the second stage was reached, where super- and super-super-films were made, the main attraction of which was the lavish expenditure in the making of the film. The public, the producers argued, will be dazzled at the huge figures. Colossal expenditure will argue genius.

Colossal expenditure may have argued, but did not prove genius. A pennyworth of sincerity, time and again, proved to be worth a pound of splendour. But the Hollywood producers could not learn the lesson. They were under the spell that they themselves had tried to cast on the public. What costs most must be best. So the costs were rocketing, in the hope that the quality would rise with them. But, if anything, it sank.

Hollywood and England are still obsessed with the big money fantasy. A few years ago, England thought ten thousand pounds a lot of money to spend on a film. And they made bad films. Today, they say glibly that you can't make a film under £125,000, and they still make bad films. Cost and quality are scarcely related at all. A certain amount of money is needed for any film, but over and above that what is necessary is talent and sincerity.

Here is a great problem. With all the money in the world, how are you going to tempt people of talent and sincerity – people, that is, whose intelligence and understanding of life is higher than the average – to produce films that will appeal not only to the man and woman of average intelligence, but to people who are below normal? One man's sixpence is as good as another, provided it's a good sixpence. The sixpences of fifty nitwits, according to this reckoning, are fifty times better than the sixpence of any one wise man. Anything that will drive people into cinemas is good enough. In Chicago they have given up trying to improve the quality of the films. Instead they have lucky tickets, and if you're in the cinema when your lucky ticket's announced, you get a thousand dollars. If you aren't, you don't.

The people who are most useful in capitalist films are for this reason those who are interested in means and not in ends. (The whole of capitalist training is devoted to teaching people how best to do what they are told, with questioning what they are told. The end, that is, must be accepted without criticism: the means may and should be criticised in order that they may be made more efficient.) Cameramen are needed whose interest is in photographing anything that's put before them. Actors, whose interest is in their role and not in the significance of the whole film. Scenario writers, who are interested in the straightforward presentation of excitement, suspense, or romance.

No artist is so immersed in the means of his craft that he can ignore the ends completely. He studies and works at his technique so that it should be the perfect instrument for what he wants to say. Great artists are usually technical innovators, not because they want to say something old in a new way, but because they have something new to say and the old technique won't say it.

Hollywood has need of artists. It can't get on without artists. Artists have new ideas, new ways of saying things. And Hollywood has found that even a nitwit audience demands something new. That is why, whenever an actor, producer or scenario-writer of talent or genius has appeared in other countries Hollywood buys him up. Probably he has been struggling along with little money. His ingenuity has not been stifled but stimulated by his poverty. In Hollywood he is given all the money he wants. But he's not allowed to be free. He has sold his liberty to Hollywood. He must make what he's told to make. He must exert the technical skill that he has already shown, not to say what he wants but what somebody else wants.

A relevant example of this is the case of Clifford Odets. Odets is a young American Jew, who made his name in New York by his plays. He is a communist, a revolutionary. Yet his plays, by their fire and their rich sense of drama, brought capitalists eager to see them. He had three plays running on Broadway simultaneously.

Clifford Odets was approached by Hollywood. There was big money in it. He decided he could stick it out in Hollywood without losing his integrity. He made *The General Died at Dawn* [1936], the first half of which was fine stuff about the Chinese Revolution, and the last half the usual romantic muck. His last play was a failure.

It remains to be seen whether Odets is tough enough to stand out against Hollywood. But whether he is or is not is irrelevant. What is important is that as soon as they heard about him the Hollywood producers were out after him. They wanted to buy not his ideas but his brains: his way of making characters talk, not what they said.

Under capitalism, the second-rater will be in his element working for the films: the first-rater will also be all right, provided that he will suppress the quality that makes him first-rate, his integrity. He must be prepared to deny what he knows to be true, emotionally and in every other way.

I don't like the cliché of the artist 'having to prostitute himself'. But it is a precise description of the writer's job in films. As a harlot pretends love for money, so the scenario-writer has to pretend sincerity for money: he has to exploit his gifts in the way the woman exploits her body. It is this pseudo-art which gives the novelty to those films which are supposed to mark a step forward in film history. The film public is titillated by fresh stars, fresh producers, and story-writers, like an exhausted sultan by an inexhaustible supply of unravished concubines.

If this systematic dilution of originality was presented to the artist crudely, he would revolt against it. For this reason the making of a film is put into the hands not of a single artist, but of a number of executives. The scenarist is given full rope: he is encouraged to put all his creative power into his scenario. Then the scenario is handed over to another executive who emasculates it. This happens at every stage in the production: so that the final film represents the resultant of the progressive, creative forces, countered by the forces of reaction. Hence, the paradox arises that under capitalism, which claims to respect individual effort more than mass effort, the individual creator, whether he be scenarist, producer, director, cutter, or actor, is frustrated. Under socialism, where emphasis is placed not on the individual but on society, where co-operative effort is valued as highly, or more highly than individual effort, the individual is given full rein. An American film is a hotch-potch of conflicting forces. A Russian film is the work of the producer. The films of Eisenstein, Pudovkin, or Room have an individuality, a personal style that cannot be found in any American producer except Chaplin. It is the difference between individual and mass production.

Proceeding from the lot of the film-worker to the nature of capitalist story-films, we find that they have a uniform basis. They are all fantasy-films. In the case of Walt Disney, the Marx Brothers, and Chaplin this does not matter, because they are openly and avowedly fantasies. They express the dream-life of all people – sadistic fantasies, power fantasies, impotence fantasies, anal fantasies: in fact, the unconscious fears, anxieties, and desires that we all have. For the most part they are reassuring and cathartic.

The films that pretend to deal with actual life are also fantasies of the wish-fulfilment type. Formerly, these wish-fulfilments were in the simple form of the rich man marrying the poor girl, or the poor man marrying the rich girl. It has been pointed out, usually rather contemptuously by capitalist critics, how crude and universal this fantasy is.

The reason why the fantasy is universal, or almost universal, is that under capitalism poverty is almost universal. Just under half the population of this country is grossly undernourished: and the number of people whose emotional life is starved is even greater. For a long time these wretched people found in the belief in an immortal life the compensation for their misery on earth. But science, the War, and the corruption and decadence of the Church have destroyed that belief in many people: and celluloid now gives them the relief from present trouble and the resignation to future servitude that they got formerly from the Bible and the confessional.

But to get relief in wish-fulfilments, at least a minimum of everyday comfort and security is needed. It is no good to pay threepence to dream away the afternoon in a fool's paradise if you have to return to a hell of discomfort afterwards. The contrast is too great. Presumably, box-office returns have shown that to be the case. There is an apparent change of face. Hollywood is pretending to be squaring up to things. Witness *Mr. Deeds Goes to Town*. This film was based on the old Cinderella *motif*, worked out in modern terms. It was witty, charming, and human. (The testing of the echo in the hall, for example, was a human touch that appeared to be refreshingly original, chiefly because most Hollywood films are so inhuman and unnatural.) But that wasn't enough, presumably. Mr. Capra, or his scenario-writer, suddenly thought of all the depressed, unhappy, ruined people in cinemas all over the world watching this gay and light-hearted comedy. So suddenly a bankrupt farmer appeared and made an attempt upon the life of the Cinderella man. His speech was magnificent. It was what hundreds of people seeing the film were thinking. 'What is all this to us?'

At this point emerges what the film critics called the 'satirical' element of the film. Longfellow Deeds decides to devote the whole of his fortune to getting bankrupt farmers back on to the land. The farmers are overjoyed. Here at last is a man who is going to help them. (Everybody in the audience who wants a job is going up to Longfellow Deeds' desk and is registering his claim.) *But* just as he is carrying out his scheme he is arrested at the instigation of unscrupulous relatives and is detained as insane.

The culmination of the film is the trial. Deeds will not plead his sanity. The girl who has held him up to ridicule now loves him to distraction, but Deeds won't say a word. Not until the very last moment, when the girl has declared her love in the open court and the farmers have clamoured to him as their saviour, will Deeds speak out. Then he defends himself very simply, but with great native wit. And the judge sums up that he is the sanest man who has ever been in that court, and all the farmers cheer like mad. The 'satire' rests on the idea that any man in a capitalist world would voluntarily give up £3,000,000, and that a charge of insanity should be made against him.

What the capitalist critics did not mention, however, was the falsity of Deeds' solution. Under the system of production for profit, the amount of farm produce that can be produced economically is far short of the amount needed for the adequate sustenance of the population of the world. The farmers whom Deeds was going to put back on the land had not been bankrupted through famine, but through overproduction (that lovely word, explanatory of capitalist-organisational incompetence). Deeds with all the goodwill in the world was going to put back these ruined men on the land in order to increase the overproduction which had already ruined them.

The reason for the trial is now apparent. The issue being between sanity and insanity, attention is drawn away from the merits and demerits of Deeds' scheme. The audience knows that he is quite sane. Will he defend himself? If he doesn't, he'll lose all his money and be put in the looney bin. If he does, he'll have his money and win his girl (both of which are true), and he'll be able to save all those bankrupt farmers (which is untrue).

When the audience's identification with the ruined farmers is taken into mind (not all the audience, but only that part which really matters) we see a further proposition. If only everybody was like Longfellow Deeds the world would be all right. That is to say, the difficulties of our time are not economic but moral. If men were good, then everything would go well.[6]

This argument, implicit in the film, is a direct counter to the socialist arguments, which are prevalent in America today. Namely, that there are good capitalists and bad capitalists, but that the central evil of society today is that it is capitalist: and however good the will may be, no capitalist is able to keep his own head above water and those of his workers. Socialists attack not individuals, but a system which makes even the individuals at the top into puppets. Hollywood answers in terms of morality. Seeing that it is impossible to deny the disease of modern society, it scatters its wrong diagnoses . . .

All story films are subject at least to the negative criterion, that they must not be in any way subversive. Most are submitted to a further test. They should be conducive to the pattern of capitalist enterprise. They should offer only those explanations of society, which capitalists are willing to publicise: and in order to do that, truth may be distorted in any way that is thought fit.

In . . . these examples, as in all capitalist story-films, the individual is used to plead the general case specially. This tendency, implicit in the capitalist approach to social questions, has led to the star-system deplored by film critics almost without exception. Under the star-system, the interest shifts even from the individual portrayed, to the individual portraying.[7] Acting, therefore, is doubly debased: firstly, the film is not regarded as a whole, but as an opportunity for the exhibition of individual performances: secondly, these performances are not impersonations, but 'starring vehicles'. That is to say, people do not go to see Laughton as Captain Bligh, but Captain Bligh as Laughton: not Shakespeare's Juliet, but Norma Shearer's.

Furthermore, the human face and form are used to express a standard of unreal 'beauty'. Joan Crawford's freckles are blocked out, because the idea of a girl with freckles losing her virginity is ridiculous to Hollywood directors: only a superb glamour-girl can fall with grace.

In Soviet films, the anonymity of the actors and the utilisation of every quality of a face (texture, shape and imperfections caught and made vivid and beautiful by the camera, not by the make-up man) expose the falsity of Hollywood technique. Yet this falsity is deliberate and inevitable, because of the false values imposed by the capitalist approach, the desire to lead the audience away from reality, rather than to interpret it.

A second paradox derives from this. Because the subject matter of capitalist films is fantastic, the treatment must give the appearance of naturalism. The camera and the microphone are used like a natural eye and ear, reproducing what is seen and heard. The possibilities of the film medium, which are broader and more fluid than those of any other art-form, must be limited to a fraction of their capacity.[8] Yet there is no aesthetic justification for this practice, naturalism in the studio being as artificial as any other means of expression.

The Soviet films on the other hand, because they are rooted in reality, are able to exploit the full technical possibilities of the camera and microphone, using every device that comes to hand.

The conditions governing news films are slightly different. News films are makeweights. Little money is spent on them and usually only those events are taken which are certain of providing the camera-man with pictures. Rallies, tattoos, garden parties, marches past, races of all sorts, sporting events and fascist jamborees are the mainstay of the newsreels. They give no pictures of the world. The audience is faced by a multiplex and incomprehensible series of events, without significance. (This is the same function as that of the gutter Press, to distract and bewilder with unrelated events, since in fact the understanding of the true significance of events immediately reveals the injustice and incompetence of capitalism.) The fascist jamborees, however, are reported for a specific reason. In our present stage of development, the National Government is able to disguise its own fascist tendencies, by opposition to Mosley and to the avowed fascist countries. If, therefore, Hitler and Mussolini are guyed on the screen, the audience is put in the temper to accept the positive propaganda. ('These people are anti-Hitler – Mussolini. Therefore they are not fascist.') The attitude can then be adopted: 'We are impartial. Fascist or socialist are extremes. We are moderates. Good, solid, honest-to-God, copper-bottomed capitalists. Here is the truth about Spain.'[9] And there follows a series of pro-Franco propaganda shots, ending up with a pious little pacifist remark about 'the horrors of civil war. Are they ever worth it?' And behind that piety is the threat: 'This is what happened in Spain when they had a United Front.[10] See to it that you don't have one in England.'[11]

News films are a potent propagandist force against socialism. And even the progressive *March of Time*[12] is used in this country for Government purposes. Anything that might be objectionable in the American version (which has already been modified by the American authorities, the exposures being of past not present abuses) is further censored in England. The English contribution is even more staid. The film executives controlling *March of Time* in this country are Civil Servants, workers for the G.P.O. film unit. In sheer technique they are the most progressive unit working in England. But they are paid by the Government to publicise Government services. The scandalous working conditions in the G.P.O. are not mentioned in their films. All we hear of is the wonderful efficiency, the huge expansion of business handled. We are told nothing of the way the staff is limited, so that the G.P.O. can make bigger and bigger profits. Even the *March of Time* sections are thinly disguised advertisements for the G.P.O., Imperial Airways, Recruiting, the Government's cure for malnutrition by physical jerks. (You're half starved? You don't want more food, but more exercise.) In the films, as elsewhere, progressive tendencies are muzzled, not by complete suppression, but by semi-suppression. The men working for the G.P.O. Film Unit feel that they are doing really good work, I have no doubt. Their attitude is, 'Our job is making films. The G.P.O. pays us for it. We go as far as we can in expressing discontent, in criticising faults in the system. But of course we're working for an official organisation, and we don't have very much rope.' If completely suppressed, that desire for reform would become revolutionary. As it is, it is kept tame. The official organisation sees to that. You can admit that anything was wrong six months ago, provided that you say at the end that something is being done about it now. 'In venting this discontent,' say the reformists, 'we have been doing good propaganda.' 'And in saying that we are really tackling this problem and everything'll be all right,' says the official organisation, 'you have been doing that propaganda not against us, but for us. Take a rise.'

Under capitalism, therefore, we see that the films are used for propaganda on behalf of vested interests and the form of government that supports those vested interests. The general public is distracted from the contemplation of present affairs, or if not distracted, misled and cheated in their interpretation.

The charge that is made against socialist films, that they are propagandist, can be returned with double force against capitalist films. The socialist interpretation of society takes full account of facts and explains them without distortion. A film based on socialist ideology is, of course, propagandist in the same way that a film based on capitalist ideology is propagandist. The difference between them, however, is the difference between truth and falsehood.

I referred earlier in this essay to 'films made for nitwits'. That phrase needs explanation. Under capitalism, films are made for the ignorant, with the purpose of keeping that ignorance. (The capitalist boast of 'having no axe to grind' is a nice way of saying that capitalism wishes to keep the ignorant in their state of ignorance.) Under socialism, films would be made with the express purpose of helping people to understand the world in which they live. For its accomplishment, socialism needs the highest possible level of education. For its survival, capitalism needs the lowest standard that is consistent with mechanical efficiency. Capitalism has to bribe its artists to prostitute their talents. Socialism can use the highest talents of its artists. It demands that consciousness and criticism of ends, that capitalism wishes above all things to suppress.

The effect of the cinema, even capitalist critics complain, is at the moment sedative. Under capitalism, it has to be sedative. The only thing the masses are wanted to do under capitalism is to join the army and train to shoot their fellow-workers in the next imperialist war. Any other activity is almost certain to be dangerous.

The effect of the socialist cinema is the opposite. It is dynamic. It calls on every man and woman for his greatest effort. It does not say: 'There's no work for you. There's no use for you. Do jerks and join the army.' It says to everyone: 'There's work, and to spare, for you and your children and your

children's children. You can be, you must be of use. There's a new society to
be built, a world in which we shall cure hunger by food and not gymnastics.
You must fight. Not against your fellow-workers, but against ignorance, greed
disease, war, tyranny and reaction.' It says: 'We do not offer you the
compensation of fantasy. We show you what is being done and what has got
to be done to build a world in which fantasy is not needed as the substitute
for reality. Don't go to sleep, wake up!'

We have already had examples of socialist films in this country. The work
of Pabst, Eisenstein and Pudovkin is acknowledged even by critics, whose
criteria are aesthetic and not political, to be in the very first rank.
Kameradschaft, The End of St. Petersburg, Potemkin, Mother, Turksib, Earth –
these films have qualities which distinguish them from capitalist productions.

In the first place, the emphasis is laid not on the individual, but on the group
or mass. This is because the good of the individual under socialism is
coincident with the good of society as a whole. The individual achieves his
fullness in co-operation. His own profit is bound up with the profit of others.
Under capitalism, on the other hand, the interest of the individual is in
competition, not co-operation. Society, instead of being highly organised for
the good of all citizens, exists as a power ready to assist a small class to exploit
the majority. Even with the exploiting class there is a natural division through
competition: and the exploiting class only unites against the common enemy,
the threat of militancy from the exploited.

Since the socialist film regards the group as a unit, the individuals chosen
to represent that group are classical. What is important is not what distinguishes them from others, their neuroses, their oddities and idiosyncrasies;
but what they have in common with their fellows – hunger and thirst, the
appetites of body and mind, a common direction.[13] Analysis of individual
character is of course out of place in such films. Men are portrayed by their
behaviour. They are loyal or treacherous, weak or strong, bold or timid,
resourceful or helpless. It is these qualities of behaviour which are important
in building socialism: rather than the analysis of motive. A man may show
conspicuous daring, we shall say because he wishes to prove to himself that
there is nothing to be afraid of. But that doesn't make him any less daring. A
man may steal because he is a kleptomaniac, but it doesn't make him any less
a thief. The romantic is interested in the motivation. The classicist, who is the
social revolutionary today, is interested in the conduct.

The same distinction applies to subject-matter. The capitalist film (except
in certain epic films such as *The Covered Wagon*) is concerned with the
fortunes of individuals: the socialist with group activities, the rising of masses

in revolution, the struggle to complete vast and ambitious plans, the construction of the Turksib railways (with which compare [the] Gaumont-British effort on the same lines, *The Great Barrier*).

This is not, of course, to say that interest in individuals disappears under socialism and that no art-forms will be concerned with individuals (*vide* Alexander Room's *Bed and Sofa* [1926], which ran for six months in a sadly mutilated form in London). But it is to say that at first society as a whole will be the object of study, because in the service of society as a whole the individual is most fulfilled.

But what is the most important distinction is between the pessimism of sincere capitalist films (the end of *Kameradschaft* [1931], for example, where, after all the speeches of the Germans and the French, the frontier grill is fixed again in the mine-gallery: or the entirety of King Vidor's *The Crowd* [1928], or the underlying mood of Chaplin's *Modern Times* [1936]), and the optimism of socialist films. Even Sir Walter Citrine[14] was struck by the fact that Russian workers, whom he thought ought to be seething with discontent at their standard of living, looked so happy. The struggle for socialism is hard, but there is always hope underlying it. The struggle for livelihood under capitalism is even harder and there is no hope. Hence the split between realism and fantasy in American and English films: the study of things as they are leaves no chance of hope for their improving within the scheme of capitalism. But under socialism, this hope is constant, realised in the present and discernible in the future.

Notes

1. This he confesses in *I Crossed the Minch* (1938): a charming instance, Cunningham notes (p. 34), of a 'leftist Cain' laying 'killing hands' on a 'leftist Abel'.
2. *Night and Day*, 8 July 1937. Quoted in Cunningham, p. 145.
3. *Left Review* 3.6 (July 1937): 363.
4. *Fact* 4 (July 1937), cited and discussed by Cunningham, pp. 211–12.
5. For example, the policy of London Films is substantially in the control of the Prudential Assurance, to whom they are indebted for a loan of £520,000. [AC-M]
6. In 'Life and Letters Today' (*Winter Quarter*, 1936) and in *The Changing Scene* (Chapman and Hall), I have analysed the political content of several other films. A careful observer will find that almost all films which have pseudo-reality basis contain similar political distortions. [AC-M]
7. When Clark Gable appeared in *Mutiny on the Bounty* cleanshaven, he received a storm of protest from admirers of his moustache. This, though his moustache is, in fact, an artificial one. [AC-M]
8. Film companies pooh-poohed the idea of the use of sound, until *The Singing Fool* forced them to follow suit. But even now, they have left the possibilities of sound

alone, apart from the reproduction of speech, natural sounds and background music. (Chaplin, however, is an exception, as so often.) [AC-M]

9. Although opinion polls in Britain revealed very little public support for the Francoist cause in Spain, the policy adopted by the National Government under Neville Chamberlain effectively ensured its victory. By abiding by its decision not to sell arms to either side in the Civil War, Britain sought to avoid offending the Italian Government – a government which was committed to providing extensive political and material support to Franco's campaign.

10. See above, pp. 274.

11. The cinema camera always selects and distorts. It can't help it. On the other hand, it has the impression on an audience of actuality, that can only be rivalled by the B.B.C. In a news film, a 'shot' is shown and an explanation given by the commentary; and the audience is prepared to swear that it has seen with its own eyes what the commentator tells it it has seen. The 'shot' of the Government troops shooting at the statue of Christ was used as devastating anti-Government propaganda. It was a fact. Government soldiers were shooting at a statue of Christ. But it was not revealed that the camera-man had offered the soldiers five pesetas each to shoot, so that he might get his atrocity picture. [AC-M]

12. See above, p. 292.

13. I use the word 'classical' deliberately, since the revolutionary attitude to individual psychology is very close to that of Pope and Dr. Johnson. The desire for people to be 'different' is a hangover from the romantic period that reached its climax in Joris Karl Huysmans and his contemporaries. The antipathy that many Marxists feel to Freud is due, I think, to the realisation that whatever the therapeutic value of psycho-analysis, it is too individual and separative for revolutionary purposes. The difficulty would disappear, I think, if they would realise that the psycho-analyst's function is not competitive with the economist's. As it is, the situation is like that of a painter and a dermatologist disputing, the painter being interested in the face of his model as a whole, the dermatologist being concerned with microscopic examination of the pores of the skin. The economist is interested in the shape and structure of society, the analyst in the composition of its various parts. The individual and society interact constantly, just as the body and mind interact. But to see this, one must be neither psychologist nor economist, but economico-psychologist or whatever the social equivalent of a psycho-physiologist is. [AC-M]

14. Walter Citrine was at this time general secretary of the Trades Union Congress, and a key figure in the Labour movement throughout the 1930s and 1940s.

39 Winifred Holtby *Cavalcade (1933)**

After graduating from Oxford, Holtby became an editor of Lady Margaret Rhondda's *Time and Tide* magazine, serving after 1926 as a director. On Holtby's premature death in 1935, Lady Rhondda wrote of her fierce yet good-natured loyalty both to the paper and to her friends; Holtby was, she said, 'passionately in love with life', and that love found its proper extension in her concern 'for justice, for mercy, [as well as] for her own work as a writer' (Rhondda, p. 213). Although admitting that she could 'never quite make up [her] . . . mind whether to be a reformer-sort-of-person or a writer-sort-of-person',[1] Holtby was in practice an outspoken and influential feminist; her importance to the women's movement during the 1930s is confirmed by Philippa Polson's respectful essay in disagreement included in this volume (see above, pp. 259–63). One contribution to the cultural work of the movement was her *Virginia Woolf: A Critical Study* (1932), but perhaps most important of all her writing on women's issues was *Women in a Changing Civilisation*, appearing in the same year (and in the same series) as Naomi Mitchison's *Home and a Changing Civilisation* (1934) (see above, p. 227).

It was not unusual in the 1930s to find writers on the left gesturing outwards from their local arena of contention with capitalism towards broader international questions – particularly towards the inhumanity and economic injustice of colonialism. Woolf, for example, identifies women with the colonized other in *Three Guineas* (see above, p. 266). Certainly, the deep impression made on Holtby by her reading of Olive Schreiner led her to see strong connections between the campaign for women's rights and the struggle for black rights in South Africa. But what is unusual about Holtby in this regard is that for her the latter was never merely an illustrative extension of – a helpful analogue for – her own specifically European problems. She grasped, in a manner that has only been widely understood since the advent of postcolonial studies in recent years, the *singularity* of the colonial situation, how there are ways in which the predicament of a subaltern people is really quite unlike that of a disadvantaged group *within* European culture. In her essay on Noel Coward's film of *Cavalcade*, released in England shortly before she wrote this, she offers what must be one of the 1930s' most trenchant attacks on British colonial propaganda. The further point needs to be made that Holtby was much more than an intellectual opponent of colonialism: apart from her work with her pen, she provided active personal support to the black cause in South Africa. On her visit there in 1926 she became involved in advising and sustaining the relatively new Industrial and Commercial

---

* Originally published in *Time and Tide*, 11 March 1933. Reprinted from *Testament of a Generation: The Journalism of Vera Brittain and Winifred Holtby*, ed. Paul Berry and Alan Bishop (London: Virago, 1985), pp. 285–9.

Workers' Union. Paul Berry records that in 1940 a Winifred Holtby Memorial Library was opened outside Johannesburg, the first constructed entirely for the use of black South Africans.[2] That it was funded from within as well as without the country confirms that she was held in high regard in the very world where she most wished to make a difference.

In the second essay included here she outlines, for the benefit of British women who might be toying with the idea of Fascism, the situation of women in Germany in 1934. It is a very typical piece of Holtby's feminist work, its style forthright, authoritative, and with an insistence on factual evidence. Interestingly, Philippa Polson's 1935 essay in response to Holtby makes use of the very same style, taking her to task for failing to make the kind of distinction between different subaltern groups in British society that she insists upon in her critique of colonialism.

After a performance of *Cavalcade* I stood on the steps of the Tivoli, listening to those snatches of conversation which were one of the most interesting parts of the entertainment between the acts of the stage version. As before, the younger people seemed a little puzzled by the whole affair, and, not least, by the emotion of their elders. 'It's got the atmosphere,' said a hard-bitten man in the late forties. 'Aye. It was like that.' 'My dear, horror after horror, wasn't it?' giggled a pretty young thing of 18 or so, in a pert little veiled hat. 'Surely piled on a bit thick?' asked her friend with chestnut corkscrew curls. And had I not been trained by long habit never to speak to strangers, I could have replied, 'But, my dear child, that is just what a big war does seem like to some of the people who lived through it – all the accumulated vengeance of world history, horror upon horror, descending upon the heads of just such pretty, innocuous, unsuspecting little creatures as yourself.' But, of course, I did nothing except powder my reddened nose and watch with sympathetic amusement the similar furtive repairs to mottled complexions made by most of the women over 30, who, like myself, can sit unmoved through tragedy and even face with comparative calmness the disasters of daily life, but who are moved intolerably by the tapping of feet to a half-forgotten melody, the picture of a troop-train leaving Victoria Station, or the gesture of a hand waving farewell beyond a barrier. And I congratulated Noel Coward, Reginald Berkeley and the Fox Film Company for so successfully exploiting those memories that now, after so many years, release the tears we could not shed when they were part of our lives – not shadows on a screen.

But, to counterbalance this inevitably effective exploitation of personal sentiment, the Tivoli offers the most rich and gorgeous nourishment for our instincts of irony and amusement. As we left the place, attendants thrust into our hands copies of a leaflet called *The London Pictorial*, in which we read that *Cavalcade* is 'the most inspired production of any age'. At other times we might, thinking of certain rumoured productions at Athens, in Elizabethan London, Bayreuth, or even Oberammergau, have been a trifle staggered by this flat statement. But after the goings-on inside the Tivoli, we were hardened to anything. For, as an integral part of the entertainment, before *Cavalcade* begins, we were shown one of those 'educational' films whose educative qualities sometimes take our breath away. It is called *Round the Empire*, and is accompanied by a lecture from a gentleman whose suave, complacent voice – the quintessence of post-BBC patronage – positively screams for caricature by John Tilley. He opens by announcing that he will take us on a tour round the Empire inhabited by so many diverse peoples 'all cherishing the same ideals'. With a few scattered thoughts of French-Canadian separatists, de Valera republicans, Indian Congress pickets, New Zealand loyalists, Transvaal nationalists and the Kavirondo Taxpayers' Association, to say nothing about the unanimous (?) agreements of Ottawa,[3] I sat back prepared to enjoy myself. And this was the next remark that stirred me; 'which the world's greatest dramatist, Noel Coward, has so brilliantly portrayed in his epic drama *Cavalcade*.' Now I took my notes in the dark, and won't swear before God that the lecturer did not say 'the world's greatest living dramatist' – though after *The London Pictorial*, I doubt it; but even so, that, I feel, should make Bernard Shaw, Sean O'Casey, Yeats and a few other inconsiderable triflers with the theatre sit up and take notice.

Those little shocks, however, were mild compared with what followed. We were shown Canada. The chief point of interest about Canada, apparently, is that the policemen resemble their English prototypes – a comforting thought, perhaps, when we think of a few of the little activities along the frontier. I recommend it for the greater ease of readers disconcerted by *Limey*, that strange account by James Spenser of what happens to gentlemen of easy conscience and British birth who cross that frontier into the United States without the sanction of an orderly passport. Then Australia – distinguished, of course, by Sydney Bridge, with a coy side-glance at pretty girls, and a complacent survey of the Air Force. New Zealand has scenery and Maoris, actually Maoris, 'now living peacefully under the flag' and bathing in hot springs. Note the Maoris well. We shall look upon their like again. For India recognizes only the British and Natives – native police, a fine body of men, for whom our gratitude is invited as a tribute to their self-sacrifice during the Great War. Not a word, naturally, about more recent lathi-beatings and so on.

Viceregal ceremonies, garden parties with Princes, and the fortifications of the Khyber Pass present a fine substitute for the courts of Merrut, the slums of Calcutta, the jute factories and barren villages.

But the masterpiece comes with Africa. 'Africa is, even now,' continues that cultured voice regretfully, 'predominantly native.' How sad! Just think of that, after all these years of British rule. In Australia and Canada our virile race succeeded admirably in reducing Red Indians or aborigines to quite insignificant proportions, but the tiresome Africans continue to increase and multiply. I could not help remembering a similar regret expressed by a gentleman named Elliot, a Natal farmer, who in 1927 was giving evidence before the Select Committee on the Four Native Bills at Cape Town. 'You ask whether it is my idea that things will have to be decided by force,' he replied to a rather startled question from the Commissioners, 'and that if we want to hold our own we must exterminate these people (the Africans). I think that it will either be that, or I do not know what is going to be.' Kenya followed, to which 'prosperity has come since it has been under British control' – an observation likely to surprise those settlers now petitioning against the payment of income-tax. Finally, after a glimpse of Gibraltar, we were shown the Royal Navy, 'the symbol, not only of power and majesty, but of universal freedom and justice.' Well, well, well, well. I wonder how many of our foreign friends, attracted to the Strand by the 'Come to England' movement, were present at the Tivoli to ask, 'Oh yeah?'

But after that really splendid vision of battleships steaming off against a sunset to the tune of *Rule Britannia* and the enraptured applause of Britons, came *Cavalcade* itself, with its interesting sidelights upon the behaviour of English natives. There are, apparently, two kinds of Englishmen – the Dignified Gentlepeople, whose partings and deaths and sorrows are tragic – and the natives below stairs – cooks and mothers-in-law and housemaids and the like – whose goings-on are invariably comic. When Diana Wynyard as Jane Marryot said 'Goodbye' to Clive Brook, her gallant and loving husband, we bit our lips and blinked our eyes in sympathy. When Una O'Connor as Ellen Bridges said 'Goodbye' to her equally gallant and loving husband, Alfred, we giggled in appreciative amusement, because low life in kitchens is, of course, always comic, and the scenes in the East End, with the Graingers and Bridges – though their content is no less poignant than the scenes in the Marryots' drawing room – are, naturally, farcical in tone.

To do justice to 'the world's greatest dramatist', Noel Coward, I must say that his notion that the poor are always funny was shared by his humbler predecessor, Shakespeare. And his equally odd idea that only in the past did our country know 'dignity and greatness and peace' finds honourable precedents in almost all the great mediaeval thinkers except Dante. Personally, I do not really think that the Edwardian era had quite so many advantages as he believes over our present one. Nor do I think that the Cowardesque glimpses of night-club life, homosexual fondlings and twentieth-century blues with which the film ends, present an entirely adequate picture of our society which, after all, contains smallholdings and health clinics, nursery schools and growing universities, village institutes and the Workers' Travel Association, hiking parties and bouncing gymnasium classes at the Polytechnic, busy little families planning suburban gardens, and secretaries of hundreds of inconspicuous organizations working conscientiously for the future without hope of gain. On the whole, I thought, as I walked down the Strand in the fine March rain, a more emotionally riotous and intellectually prosperous entertainment I have rarely seen. By far the sanest comment upon the political ideas of Mr-Noel-Coward-plus-Reginald-Berkeley-plus-Hollywood is the absurd and delicious Silly Symphony of naval warfare and Father Neptune which, quite appropriately, precedes both Empire Tour and *Cavalcade*.

Black Words for Women Only (1934)*

Any constant reader of Fascist literature must have been impressed by the frequent if uneasy references to the Importance of Woman.

Our island breed of blackshirts forms a fairly reliable barometer to Continental thought upon this subject. When Sir Oswald Mosley found the Labour Party too small to hold his 'New Hellenism' and broke away to create the new party, he established a weekly paper entitled *Action*.

Some of us may remember how, in October 1931, we were urged from walls and hoardings to 'Take Action', and how, when we took it, we learned that it stood for Volt, and 'What does Volt stand for? It stands for Vigour, Order, Loyalty, Triumph.'

Tucked away, on the twenty-fourth page, after Gardens, but before Architecture, was a section called 'Listen, Women', devoted to female interests. What women were to listen to were, first, reflections upon the possible fall of the pound and how little this immediately concerned

* Originally published in the *Clarion*, 24 March 1934. Reprinted from *Testament of a Generation: The Journalism of Vera Brittain and Winifred Holtby*, pp. 84–6.

housewives; and, secondly, an exhortation to follow French styles of cookery by making *ragoûts* and *bouillons*.

Next year Sir Oswald founded the British Union of Fascists and delivered his soul of its burden of conversion in a book entitled *The Greater Britain*.[4] Here, in one section of one of the twelve chapters, he said what he had to say about 'Women's Work'.

'It has been suggested,' he began modestly, 'that hitherto in our organisation too little attention has been paid to the position of women.

'It is true that in our political organisation we have hitherto concentrated on the organisation of men. This was not because we underrate the importance of women in the world; but because our political experiences have led us to the conclusion that the early stages of such organisation are a man's job . . .

'The part of woman in our future organisation will be important, but different from that of the men; *we want men who are men and women who are women.*'

The italics are Sir Oswald's; they are, I think, important. They seem characteristic of that Fascist inclination to dream of an eclectic Olympus of virile he-men (Romans, Britons, or Teutonic-Aryans) separated sharply from all lower forms of being. 'Fascism,' he continues, 'in fact would treat the normal wife and mother as one of the main pillars of the State', and is gently sportive about 'professional spinster politicians' whose one idea is to escape from the normal sphere of woman.

Two years later, in *The Fascist Week*, he returns to that attack, and declares, 'it will not be surprising to those familiar with *this distressing type*' (the italics are mine) 'that the interests of the normal woman occupy no great place in the attention of Parliament.'

When one remembers how 'this distressing type' has fought for maternity and child welfare services, improved education and better housing, one is driven to wonder precisely what Sir Oswald visualizes as the interests of 'normality', and how he proposes to deal with them in his corporate state.

It is not irrelevant to compare what Sir Oswald promises with what Herr Hitler has performed.

The German Constitution of 1918 granted equality before the law to all citizens. Women entered politics, the professions, the civil services. Between thirty and forty-two sat in each of the various Reichstags as deputies between 1919 and 1933 – a higher proportion than in any other country. They held high executive and municipal offices.

But the Nazi movement has reversed all that. Women may vote, but none may stand on the lists as candidates. Their associations are now directed by men; since July, 1933, all the girls' high schools have been controlled by men. Professional women are finding themselves compelled for one reason or another to resign from work. Married women are often persuaded to leave their employment, and unmarried workers are often asked to surrender their jobs to men, as in one Hamburg tobacco factory, where 600 girls were asked to hand over their work to fathers, brothers or husbands, or to retire, marry, and claim the State marriage loan.

There is little hope for ambitious young women in Nazi Germany, where the brightest contribution of constructive economic thought towards the solution of the unemployment problem appears to have been the expulsion of large sections of the community from paid work, as a penalty for being women, Socialists or Jews, and their replacement by unobjectionable loyal male Aryans. Individual women have protested against this mass campaign to restore their economic dependence and drive them back to the kitchen. But protests are penalized; public influence is strong, and there are women who have been temporarily persuaded to believe that Hitler's policy really serves their interests.

One such wrote recently to the *Manchester Guardian* declaring: 'The German people, led by their great Führer, are today labouring for the rebirth of the nation and of morals. They know perfectly well that this task invests women with at least the same importance as men. The young generation obtain their first nourishment and teaching from their mothers . . .

'Woman has again been recognized as the centre of family life, and today it has again become a pleasure and an honour to be a mother.'

No explanation is offered of why or when motherhood ceased to be a pleasure and honour – perhaps when children were driven to concentration camps?

But what is significant is the emphasis laid on the exclusively feminine functions of wifehood and motherhood. Throughout history, whenever society has tried to curtail the opportunities, interests, and powers of women, it has done so in the sacred names of marriage and maternity. Exalting women's sex until it dominated her whole life, the State then used it as an excuse for political or economic disability. The moment those disabilities were removed, women began to urge the claims of children, of health, of domestic welfare for consideration before the law; until they spoke, these claims were rarely heard.

Today, whenever women hear political leaders call their sex important, they grow suspicious. In the importance of the sex too often has lain the unimportance of the citizen, the worker and the human being. The 'normal' woman knows that, given freedom and equality before the law, she can be trusted to safeguard her own interests as wife, mother, daughter, or what you will.

Notes

1. Quoted by Paul Berry in his 'Introduction to Winifred Holtby's Journalism', *Testament of a Generation*, p. 19.
2. See his 'Introduction', p. 23.
3. On the Ottawa agreements, see above, p. 210 n.14.
4. See above, pp. 26–36.

In 1928–9 Dawson was involved in the short-lived journal *Order*, which had been founded as 'an occasional Catholic review' by a group of intellectuals and artists under the leadership of T. F. Burns. The aims of *Order*, writes Christina Scott,

> were both negative and positive: on the negative side it was directed against the old-time militant Catholic who was fiercely anti-Anglican and enthusiastic for material, temporal and visible triumphs of the Church; aggressive and rigid in argument showing no sympathetic knowledge of human character. On the positive side it aimed to encourage more interest in the spiritual side of Catholicism, to foster a love of the liturgy and to recognise the value of all intellectual and creative work irrespective of religion. (pp. 95–6)

Elizabeth Ward notes that the magazine 'galvanised its original personnel and readership into forming a loose but coherent discussion circle'. Harman Grisewood, one of the journal's founding editors, recalled that '*Order* was a bombshell . . . [but] its importance was not the explosion but the crater which remained and . . . drew to its rim a circle of people who for the next few years met together often to discuss certain manifestations of the twentieth century in relation to the abiding truths of Christianity'.[1]

Out of those discussions came the idea for a series of pamphlets that would make available in England continental as well as home-grown speculation on connections between Christian thought and twentieth-century life. Sheed and Ward, the Catholic firm, agreed to publish the series as *Essays in Order,* under the general editorship of Dawson and Burns. The booklets began to appear in 1931, the first (which included this general introduction) being *Religion and Culture* by Jacques Maritain. All *Essays in Order* carried the same cover illustration as had graced each issue of *Order* – an engraving by David Jones, who was a member of the original group – and the series included *The Russian Revolution* (Nicholas Berdyaev), *The Drift of Democracy* (Count Michael de la Bedoyère), and Dawson's own *Christianity and the New Age*, all in the first year of publication. Dawson was at that time one of the best-known horses in the Sheed and Ward stable, his *Progress and Religion* (1929) having been, in Ward's words, 'an immense sensation'.[2]

An interesting perspective on Dawson is provided by H. B. Parkes[3] in his *Scrutiny* essay of March 1937.[4] Dawson, writes Parkes, 'is the most persuasive of

---

* Reprinted from Jacques Maritain, *Religion and Culture* (London: Sheed and Ward, 1931), pp. vii–xxv.

contemporary Catholic apologists; unlike Mr. Belloc he is not guilty of distortions of fact; and unlike M. Maritain he does not resort to rhetoric or appeal to the snobbery of those initiated into the Faith'. As is not unexpected in F. R. Leavis's own critical organ, Dawson is admired for his opposition to the 'mechanization of human life' towards which Communism, Fascism and parliamentary democracy are all in his view tending: 'Mr. Dawson's belief "that every culturally vital society must possess a religion, whether explicit or disguised, and that the religion of a society determines to a great extent its cultural form" is a valuable counteractive to the materialism of nineteenth century historians, and is in harmony with contemporary anthropology, which finds that a culture must be regarded as an organic whole, every element in a cultural pattern interacting and interpenetrating with every other element' (pp. 365–6). Parkes demurs at Dawson, however, over the latter's belief in the superiority of Catholicism; and especially he rejects the notion that 'religion' (a vitalizing and unifying system 'system of beliefs', merely) is necessarily dependent 'upon a faith in God or in a divine revelation' (p. 368): 'Mr. Dawson's belief that we must maintain contact with the supernatural is a mysticism so far beyond the boundaries of reason that it can be neither defended nor refuted in rational terms' (p. 369).

For Parkes, Dawson's approach to contemporary problems is rendered suspect by such basic 'mysticism', and even more problematic by (a) his identification of Catholicism with Christianity *tout court*, and (b) his failure to acknowledge that while modern liberalism may be derived from a humanistic strain within Christianity, the Faith also includes a contradictory tendency. Thus 'Mr. Dawson, by inviting us to preserve our liberal ideals by returning to the Catholic Church, is therefore in reality inviting us to abandon them' (p. 371). Parkes is disturbed by some of the consequences of this paradox, as he sees it, particularly by Dawson's demonization of Communism and his evident attraction to Fascism in *Religion and the Modern State* (1935). Finally, though, it is the tendency to insist on 'otherworldly elements' that in his view vitiates Dawson's project. 'The problems of contemporary society' are best addressed on the level of *ethics*: 'If Europeans had less faith in their capacity to discover truth, they might be less intolerant; if they had a less acute sense of their own individualities, they might achieve a greater social stability; if they were less intent on creating a better future, they might be more capable of appreciating the present' (p. 373). 'It is on the level of practical activity that problems are urgent' (p. 374).

Western civilisation to-day is passing through one of the most critical moments in its history. In every department of life traditional principles have been shaken and discredited, and we do not yet know what is going to take their place. There are those who hold that Europe has had her day and that our culture has entered the first stage of an inevitable process of decay, while others believe that we are only beginning to realise the possibilities of modern science and that we are about to see the rise of a new social order which will far transcend anything that the world has known. One thing is certain – the old order is dead; and with the old order there has passed away that traditional acceptance of the truth of Christianity and that general recognition of Christian moral principles, which even in the nineteenth century still retained so strong a hold on the minds of men.

It is the aim of the present series to attempt to face the problems which arise from this new situation and to examine the possibilities of co-operation and of conflict that exist between the Catholic order and the new world. It will not confine itself to any single aspect of the question, but will deal with general principles and with the concrete problems of contemporary life. Indeed, it is impossible to limit the inquiry to any one field, since the present disorder and confusion of ideas shows itself in every department of thought – in literature and philosophy, no less than in sociology and ethics. Hence, it is clear that this series must be tentative and unsystematic in character. It cannot attempt to propound a definite solution or to embody a formal programme. For Catholicism has no *policy* nor can the Catholic compete with the Marxian Socialist in offering the modern world a panacea for its material ills. Yet it would be equally impossible to dismiss the problems of the modern world as though they had no meaning for those whose lives were based on the supernatural certitude of the Christian faith. The Puritan or the sectarian Christian can isolate himself from the age in which he lives and construct a private world in harmony with his religious convictions. But for the Catholic this should be impossible. Catholicism stands essentially for a universal order in which every good and every truth of the natural or the social order can find a place.

The disorder of the modern world is due either to the denial of the existence of spiritual reality or to the attempt to treat the spiritual order and the business of everyday life as two independent worlds which have no mutual relations. But while Catholicism recognises the distinction and the autonomy of the natural and the supernatural orders, it can never acquiesce in their segregation. The spiritual and the eternal insert themselves into the world of sensible and temporal things, and there is not the smallest event in human life and social history but possesses an eternal and spiritual significance.

It is the Catholic ideal to order the whole of life towards unity, not by the denial and destruction of the natural human values, but by bringing them into living relation with spiritual truth and spiritual reality. But this can only be achieved if Catholics are prepared to make the necessary effort of moral sympathy and intellectual comprehension. If they remain passively content with their own possession of the truth, they do not, it is true, compromise the divine and indefectible life of the Church, but they prove false to their own temporal mission, since they leave the world and the society of which they form a part to perish.

As [Jacques] Maritain writes in the following essay [*Religion and Culture*]: 'It is certain that some good and some truth are immanent in the new temporal forms which are emerging from the obscure chrysalis of history, and that they manifest in some way the will of God, which is absent from nothing that exists. They may in the same way serve eternal interests on this earth.' It is our business to understand all this, and in order to do so it is necessary to be equally on our guard against the weak acquiescence in current fashions of thought which would cause us to lose our grasp of the eternal principles and from that 'narrowness of heart which prevents us from knowing the work of man' and doing justice to the work of God in time and history.

Difficult as this task may be, there is, we believe, a greater opportunity for carrying it out than at any time during the last hundred years. The old barriers are falling, and though the destructive and negative tendencies in modern culture have destroyed much that was valuable in the traditions of the past, they have also swept away many of the inherited prejudices and fixed forms of thought which isolated the Catholic tradition from vital contact with the realities of modern life.

The present generation is intensely sensitive to the existence of a religious problem. It is true that the ordinary Englishman no longer goes to church and that his theological beliefs are so vague as to be practically non-existent. He does not take religion for granted, as he did in the last century, when church-going was a mark of social respectability and religion occupied a distinct and strictly limited place in the national life. But this is very largely due to a recognition of the unreality and narrowness of the old sectarian ideals. There is a justifiable reaction against a type of religion which imposed rigid restrictions on any kind of rational enjoyment, while it left men free to exploit one another and to make life hideous in the race for wealth. To-day men demand of religion that it should be in touch with realities. That it should offer some solution to the social and intellectual problems of the modern world and that it should be at the service of human needs, though at the same time they often fail to realise the absolute and transcendent element which is inseparable from any true religious ideal. Consequently, if the interest in religion is weaker to-day than in the last century, it is wider and more diffused. It has come out of the pulpit and the meeting house into the columns of the daily Press and the programmes of the B.B.C. Both in this country and America there is a constant stream of literature dealing with religion and the modern age and with the problems of Christianity in the light of modern knowledge.

Unfortunately, the greater part of this literature is of little positive value. It witnesses to a real need, but it provides no adequate solution. It is vitiated by a complete absence of philosophical principles and by a vague optimism which slurs over the real difficulties of the situation and offers good will as a substitute for clear thinking. In order to come to terms with the modern world it has jettisoned the theological traditions of Protestant orthodoxy, and it is left with nothing but moral ideals and social aspirations unsupported by any solid intellectual foundation. The writers of such literature can have neither sympathy nor understanding for Catholic thought. To them Catholicism seems entirely out of touch with the needs of the modern world. They regard it as a refuge for those shrinking souls who are unable to face reality, and its philosophy as a relic of medieval obscurantism. But in reality it is they themselves who are living in the past and who do not realise that a new age has begun. Just as the schoolmen of the seventeenth century went on discussing the problem of the fifth essence and the theories of Aristotelian cosmology when Galileo and Newton were creating their new physical synthesis, so to-day the representatives of modern religious thought continue to murmur their platitudes about the liberation of religion from dogma and the ethical genius of Christianity, when the world is turning away from subjectivism and idealism and once more seeks absolute standards and spiritual realities.

In the eighteenth and nineteenth centuries, it is true, the whole trend of western civilisation was hostile to Catholicism. The absolutism and realism of Catholic philosophy was incomprehensible to an age which followed Rousseau and Kant, or Bentham and Herbert Spencer. When Pius IX denied that it was the duty of the Church to come to terms with Liberalism and Progress and Modern Civilisation, his pronouncement was greeted with a chorus of execration from every country in Europe. It seemed as though the Papacy was pronouncing its own sentence of death, for the triumph of material progress seemed inevitable and no one could conceive the possibility of its failure.[5]

To-day all this is changed – Liberalism and Progress and Modern Civilisation appear in a very different light from that of seventy years ago. We no longer believe that progress is a necessary and automatic process, and that if men are left free to follow their own devices they will inevitably grow wiser and happier and more prosperous. We admit the reality of modern progress as a vast material achievement, but it means something very different from what our predecessors believed. Human life, like animal life, depends on a balance of forces, and if the balance is upset by the removal of restrictive factors, the process of readjustment is full of danger and difficulty.

Thus the rapid growth of wealth and population which followed the Industrial Revolution does not continue indefinitely; it creates its own limits by calling into existence new restrictive forces. Machinery makes possible a vast expansion of industry, but it also leads to overproduction and unemployment. Science increases man's control over disease, but it also adds to the destructiveness of war. Colonial and economic expansion gives Europe the hegemony of the world, but it also awakens the hostility and rivalry of the oriental peoples. Capitalism creates new sources of wealth, but it also involves exploitation and social unrest.

It is now generally realised that we cannot progress indefinitely by drifting with the current, for the same current which has brought us to prosperity and power may equally drag us to destruction. Order and guidance are necessary if disaster is to be avoided, for civilisation is not the result of a natural process of evolution, it is essentially due to the mastering of Nature by the human mind. It is an artificial order, governed and created by man's intelligence and will. There is no question to-day of the necessity of order; the only question at issue is whether the order we create shall be exclusively a material one, or whether it must also be spiritual.

This is the vital issue of the modern world. On the one hand we have the Communist solution which is the only thorough-going and consistent attempt to create an order on exclusively material foundations. But there is also the American solution which is less uncompromising, and also less inhuman. It is based on a combination of the political tradition of Liberalism and democracy with the material order of a standardised mass civilisation. As a working system it is infinitely more successful than the Russian experiment, but there is a latent contradiction between its political ideals and its economic practice, which produces intellectual dissatisfaction and moral unrest. There is no organic connection between the mechanism and materialism of the new mass civilisation and the old ideals of political liberty and social democracy which have their origin in the simpler conditions of an earlier period. Consequently, the American solution is not an absolute one. It is bound up with local and temporary conditions, and its evolution is still incomplete.

On the other side we have the historical tradition of European culture. That tradition has never been a purely material one, for in the past it was bound up with the Christian religion, and during the last century it has been largely identified with the ideals of liberal humanitarianism and liberal nationalism. The French Revolution and English Liberalism, the Italian Risorgimento and German Nationalism, Parliamentarianism and Socialism – all these movements have contributed to the making of modern Europe and all of them possess a spiritual element. Yet they are not of themselves capable of producing a spiritual order. They are essentially *impure* phenomena, mingling idealism with selfishness and spiritual aspirations with materialistic aims. During the last half century, however, they have all been undergoing a kind of negative purification. The nationalism of Mazzini and Young Italy has become transformed into the nationalism of Mussolini and the Fascists. English Liberalism has passed from the hands of Lord John Russell and Gladstone to those of Mr. Lloyd George. Socialism has descended from the visions of Utopia to the realities of Westminster. The making of a world safe for democracy has involved four years of intensive slaughter and a peace that is in danger of ending peace.

In every case it has been the ideal element that has suffered, and to-day all the ideals that inspired the nineteenth century are shattered and discredited. Liberalism is everywhere in decline, and Parliamentarianism and democracy have suffered a general loss of prestige. Nationalism alone is still powerful, but in a grim and menacing shape which bodes little good to the cause of civilisation.

This decline in the forces of idealism does not, however, necessarily prove that Europe is ready to accept a purely material order. On the contrary, our confidence in material order is diminishing in proportion to our loss of faith in nineteenth-century ideals. We feel the need for spiritual order far more acutely than did the prosperous and self-confident nineteenth century, but we no longer believe that it will be the inevitable result of the political and economic evolution of the modern world. For behind all these various disappointments and disillusionments there is something still more profound – we have lost our faith in humanity, and that faith was the central dogma and inspiration of the whole modern development. This is somewhat surprising when we consider that the modern world is supposed to have begun with a revolt against the anthropocentric *weltanschauung* of the Christian world, but as T. E. Hulme trenchantly says, 'The change which Copernicus is supposed to have brought about is the exact contrary of the fact. Before Copernicus man was not the centre of the universe; after Copernicus he was. You get a change from a certain profundity and intensity to that flat and insipid optimism which, passing through its first stage of decay in Rousseau, has finally culminated in that state of slush in which we have the misfortune to live.'[6]

But during the present century there has been a general reaction against this idealisation of man. The psychologists have sounded the depths of the human soul and have found nothing there but a little mud. The men of letters have blasted the romantic view of life with ridicule and scorn. The artists have substituted abstract for naturalistic ideals. The physicists have abandoned the naïve empiricism of the old scientific materialism for the mathematical abstractions of relativity. Even the philosophers have begun to desert the tradition of subjectivity and idealism and are returning to realism and ontology.

This philosophical reaction is particularly marked in Germany, so long the stronghold of the opposite tradition. Even the neo-Kantians are retracing their steps and re-interpreting their master in the light of the older traditions of European thought. The Philosophy of Aristotle and St. Thomas is no longer relegated to the limbo of dead systems, and there is a distinct tendency in German thought towards metaphysical and epistemological realism.

It is obvious that these changes have a profound effect in the attitude of the European mind towards religion. The exaltation of man and the idealisation of Nature led to the depreciation and the denial of spiritual reality. Protestantism succeeded in accommodating itself to the modern environment by the abandonment of metaphysics and dogma and a concentration on ethical ideals. But Catholicism could not live in an atmosphere of subjective idealism and moral pragmatism. It was forced to go into the desert. To-day we are witnessing what [Peter] Wust has called 'the return of Catholicism from exile'.[7] Once more Catholic thought can find a place in European culture and can give its message to the modern world. For Catholicism is not compromised by the bankruptcy of nineteenth-century idealism. It has never denied – as sectarian Christianity tends to deny – the existence and the good of the natural order, but it recognises the limitations of human nature and maintains that spiritual order is only attainable in the light of absolute spiritual principles.

Hence the remarkable revival of Catholic intellectual life that has taken place during the last twenty-five years. Half a century ago it was taken as a matter of course in France and Germany that the intellectual should be an unbeliever, and that the practising Catholic should be an exile from the living thought of the age. To-day this is no longer the case, and it is among the intellectuals and the men of letters that the influence of Catholicism is most marked. This is most strikingly exemplified in respect to philosophy, where the Thomist revival inaugurated by Pope Leo XIII has been justified by results. In France we have Père Sertillanges and M. Maritain, both of them brilliant interpreters of St. Thomas to the modern world; M. Gilson, the historian of medieval thought; and the late Père Rousselot, S.J., the author of that remarkable book, *L'Intellectualisme de St. Thomas*. In Belgium there is the school of Louvain, which has been for forty years a pioneer of the Catholic revival of philosophical studies, and which has recently produced a work of the first importance in Père Maréchal's *Point de Départ de la Métaphysique*. In Germany the revival of Catholic thought first showed itself in the historical work of scholars like Denifle, Ehrle, Baümker, von Herlting, and Grabmann, who have done so much to restore our knowledge of mediaeval thought in all its branches; but the influence of Newman, as well as that of modern German thinkers like Max Scheler also contributed to the renewed activity of Catholic thought. It is true that Scheler's personal adhesion to Catholicism was incomplete and temporary, but his criticism of Kantian ethics and his return to objective spiritual values in his treatment of ethical and sociological problems made the intellectual world conscious of the spiritual riches of the Catholic tradition and aroused Catholics themselves to a new consciousness of their intellectual mission. Consequently, the last few years have seen a remarkable development of religious thought; and to-day it is in Germany that Catholic philosophy is most in contact with the tendencies of modern thought and most alive to the needs of the present age, as we shall see in the work of such writers as Przywara, Wust, Carl Schmitt,[8] Theodor Haecker and von Hildebrand.

At the same time there has been an equally striking revival of Catholic activity in the field of pure literature. This is most obvious in France, where so large a number of the younger writers have devoted themselves to the service of Catholic ideals. The movement had begun before the war with Péguy and Claudel and Psichari, and it owed much to the influence of Maurice Barrès, although he was not himself a Christian. To-day it is represented by poets and dramatists like Claudel and Henri Ghéon, critics such as Henri Bremond, Charles du Bos, Gabriel Marcel and Henri Massis, and novelists such as François Mauriac and Julian Green – these, with many others, contributing to such series as the *Roseau d'or*, the *Cahiers de la Nouvelle Journée*, the *Questions Disputées* and *Vigile*.

In Germany this movement is more recent and is far less known in this country. This is regrettable, since the German situation has many points of similarity to our own. The central tradition in German literature is derived from a Protestant culture, and Catholic writers in the past have suffered from the restricted atmosphere of an opposition minority culture. To-day, however, these disadvantages are being overcome by a new spirit of confidence and intellectual energy, and one has only to look at modern Catholic reviews, such as *Hochland* or *Der Gral* to realise the vitality and activity of the new movement.

In England, Catholics suffer in an even greater degree from the same unfavourable conditions that exist in Germany, yet here also there is a noticeable revival of literary activity among English Catholics; indeed, their achievement is greater than we should expect from the social and numerical weakness of the Catholic element.

Nevertheless, the Catholic intellectual revival, as a whole, is predominantly a continental movement, and its significance is not yet realised in this country. The existence of Catholic philosophy is hardly recognised except in academic circles, and it is still possible for writers like Dr. Coulton and Bishop Barnes, whose own mental outlook is entirely that of the past, to treat Catholicism as an exploded superstition which is completely out of touch with the mind of the present age.

It is one of the chief aims of the present series to make the contemporary movement of Catholic thought on the Continent better known in this country. In an age when England is ceasing to be an island, and when the external forms of civilisation are becoming everywhere more uniform and more cosmopolitan, it is necessary for all of us to do what is in our power to restore the intellectual community of European culture – and for Catholics before all, since they stand almost alone to-day as the representatives of a universal spiritual order in the midst of the material and external uniformity of a cosmopolitan machine-made civilisation.[9]

We must not, of course, exaggerate the importance of the intellectual element in the Catholic revival. It would be a great mistake on the part of Catholics to claim for themselves a monopoly of intelligence. Catholicism makes its appeal, not to those who demand the latest intellectual novelty nor to those who always want to be on the winning side, but to those who seek spiritual reality. Our advantage lies not in the excellence of our brains, but in the strength of our principles. Like the proverbial conies, we may be a feeble folk but we make our dwelling in the rocks. Our thought is not 'free' in the sense that it is at liberty to create its own principles and to make gods in its own image. But it is just this 'freedom' which is the cause of the discredit and anarchy into which modern thought has fallen.

The attempt of the nineteenth century to prescribe spiritual ideals in literature and ethics, while refusing to admit the objective existence of a spiritual order, has ended in failure, and to-day we have to choose between the complete expulsion of the spiritual element from human life or its recognition as the very foundation of reality. In so far as the modern world accepts the latter alternative, it can no longer disregard the existence of the Catholic solution, for Catholicism is the great historic representative of the principle of the spiritual order – an order which is not the creation of the human mind, but its ruler and creator.

Notes

1. Harman Grisewood, *One Thing at a Time* (London: Hutchinson, 1968), p. 79. Quoted and discussed by Ward, pp. 43–4.
2. Quoted by Patricia J. Anderson in 'Sheed and Ward Limited', *DLB* 112: 305.
3. Parkes and E. W. F. Tomlin were two writers in the Leavisite stable who attempted, at different times, a technical critique of Marxism. Francis Mulhern suggests that they were 'basically at one with Leavis: ostensibly revolutionary, Marxism was in fact *not radical enough*, in its analyses of the contemporary era or in its programmatic solutions' (p. 71). Mulhern argues that Parkes's essay on Dawson is a 'most striking expression of *Scrutiny*'s ambivalent relationship with socialism' (p. 91): 'if he was convinced that some kind of socialist option was economically inescapable, Parkes placed no confidence in its capacity for political or cultural advance' (p. 92). Parkes's *Marxism: A Post-Mortem* appeared in 1940.
4. H. B. Parkes, 'Christopher Dawson', *Scrutiny* 5.4 (March 1937): 365–75.
5. Cf. Maritain, *The Things That Are Not Caesar's*, Appendix V, 'On Liberalism'. [CD]
6. T. E. Hulme, *Speculations*, p. 80. [CD]
7. See Wust's *Crisis in the West*, another one of Sheed and Ward's *Essays in Order*, published later on in 1931.
8. Schmitt was also to publish in *Essays in Order: The Necessity of Politics* (1931).
9. Cf. above, p. 19. Dawson's solution to the problem of mass civilization is very different from Leavis's.

41 Eric Gill *Art and the People* (1932)*

This is the text of Gill's address to the Royal Institute of British Architects, Manchester, 1932. At the age of fifty he was, despite failing health and his notorious eccentricity, a figure of considerable – controversial – public eminence. In 1929 he had been commissioned to produce three 'winds' for installation on the walls of the St. James's Park Underground Station in London, and this led to further commissions. For example, in 1931 he completed several sculptures for Broadcasting House; in autumn 1933 he was invited to produce ten sculpted panels for the outside wall of the new Palestine Archaeological Museum in Jerusalem; and in 1935 he was approached for a sculpted panel to adorn the front of the new League of Nations building in Geneva. Robert Speaight notes that for Gill the 1930s was 'a decade of compromise with a world that Eric denounced in proportion as he was obliged, economically, to come to terms with it' (p. 204). 'The marginal Fabian of 1910 [became] . . . the marginal Communist of 1930.' The Catholic Gill leaned increasingly towards Communism, and this 'would bring him into conflict with ecclesiastical authority as the Catholic Church, in one country after another, cemented its disastrous alliance with Fascism' (p. 239). The decade saw him exploring social credit economics, becoming active in the Peace Pledge Union and in the founding of the Artist's International Foundation to Oppose Fascism and War (1933). For a contemporary perspective on the man, see Graham Greene's 1941 essay 'Eric Gill' (Greene, *Collected Essays,* pp. 260–2).

The following essay invites comparison, in particular, with Leavis. Gill frankly acknowledges the difference between 'highbrow' sensibilities and others, and like Leavis he sees no reason to be pleased about industrialism and the advent of mass culture. But unlike Leavis he argues that art is possible in the modes of production that typify a machine age, the key being to acknowledge those modes, 'to rid industrial art of its pretence to be anything but what it is'. That pragmatism is what lies behind his description of himself as a 'realist': 'Architects, as well as sculptors, have got to work according to the conditions of their time.' This philosophy would be elaborated by Gill at the end of the decade in *Christianity and the Machine Age* (1940).

A rt is in the first place skill, and whatever other associations have come to attach to the word, skill is the necessary physical basis of art. But it is the skill of men – not of ants or elephants, and man is from his own point of

* Reprinted from *Beauty Looks after Herself* (1933; Freeport: Books for Libraries Press, 1966), pp. 141–51.

view (whatever philosophers, or scientists with microscopes may say about it) a creature having free will – a creature responsible for his actions and responsible for the use he makes of his skill. Hence the thing called art is skill with human will behind it, and the object of the will, from man's point of view, and even from that of the scientist, the object of the will is the good. Hence the object of art is the use of skill in the making of good things. And this is the object of all the arts – from the lowest to the highest – from cross-sweeping (a lost art?) to the painting of pictures and the writing of poems and symphonies.

Now powers develop with use – this is scientifically observable! – and conversely, they decay with disuse. A society which preserves among its people a strong sense of responsibility (for responsibility is the concomitant of free-will) and at the same time a clear notion of good (and a knowledge of good is bound up with a knowledge of truth; for you cannot will what is good without knowing what is good) – a society which preserves among its people a high level of responsibility and a clear notion of goods to be willed, will be a society in which the arts will develop strongly and it will be a society in which all ordinary workmen, as well as the more intellectually gifted ones will be, in a true sense of the word, artists – that is 'responsible workmen'. The people, in fact, will be 'artistic' – history, both written and that which we preserve in museums, proves this conclusively.

On the other hand, a society which, under whatever influence of philosophic or religious or political change, fails to preserve full human responsibility among its members will be one in which the arts will languish among ordinary workmen and will become the accomplishment of specially gifted or rebellious individuals. Apart from the production of these extraordinary and eccentric persons, the only arts which will flourish will be the arts of engineering. Every kind of mechanism will be developed with enthusiasm and efficiency because such things are 'patient', as the Philosophers say, 'of dialectical exposition'. They are patient of measurement, they can be drawn on paper and expressed in figures; above all, they can be ordered. You can tell a mechanic what to do and exactly how to do it. Nothing need be left to the workman except his obedience. The enormous and magnificent development of applied science which we witness to-day (and of which cities like Manchester are the product) is absolutely dependent upon the suppression in the ordinary workman of all intellectual responsibility. It has been said that 'Industrialism has released the artist from the degradation of having to make anything useful'. I may say Industrialism has deprived the ordinary workman of the exaltation of being anything of an artist. And the result has been brought first by the destruction of the peasantry and the small property owner – by the destruction of the power of economic resistance, and, second, by the development of machinery.

In the absence of machinery the slave, however economically bound, remains a responsible workman. He cannot do otherwise. (There is about two miles of Greek pottery in the British Museum – as beautiful as such work has ever been – it is all the work of slaves.) Slavery has existed in all periods of human history, but no slavery has been so absolute as that of our own time, because no previous slavery has been operative at the same time in both the economic and intellectual spheres.

I said powers develop with use. And so it is with all human faculties. Eyesight, hearing, all the senses, are so developed. So also are the faculties of the mind – the intellect and the will. People who do not use their eyes and ears remain childish and half animal. Sensibility needs training as much as common sense. But training means doing things. You can't train yourself as a cricketer merely by paying subscription to the club, or as a musician by listening to the 'wireless', or as a painter by going to picture galleries, or as an engineer by receiving either a dividend or 'the dole'. You can't be an unskilled labourer by merely looking on. We are all trained by what we do, and no other way exists by which men may get either skill or cunning or culture.

But when we glibly join the words 'art' and 'the people' we are probably not meaning by the word 'art' anything so commonplace or universal as mere human skill, and by the word 'people' we mean anybody except artists. We take it for granted that artists are a special class; we regret their eccentricity and the immorality of which we have heard stories, but we do not regret – it does not occur to us to regret – their specialisation. We either assemble as benign 'welfare workers' – moved by a desire to bring separated people into friendly relations – or, like some of our leaders of commerce, we desire to bring artists into touch with manufacturers simply in the interests of salesmanship. (I read in the paper only yesterday, that Sir ___ had said, at another conference, that it was no use urging people to 'Buy British' unless artists and manufacturers got together to make 'British' synonymous with 'artistic'.)

But I take here another line altogether. Like most artists, I am a realist. I deal with real things and not more or less imaginary possibilities. I take it that we live in an industrial civilisation – and not in another kind. I know what an industrial civilisation is quite well. I am not under any illusion about it. Nor am I under the illusion that any but a very small minority of white men wants anything else. From the point of view of the great majority there's nothing whatever wrong with our civilisation but shortage of money. Very few persons are aware that the shortage is entirely due to the fact that the banks hold a monopoly for the issue of that convenience, but the majority are quite agreed that the shortage of money is the only evil in our otherwise admirable state of enlightenment. I say I am under no illusion about the nature of Industrialism. Industrialism means production for profit. It means a proletariat, i.e. a working class owning nothing but its labour power; it means the mechanisation of whatever can be mechanised and the mass production of whatever can be produced in mass. It means the specialisation of the arts of entertainment, whether the entertainers be professional cricketers and footballers or painters and poets. The West End picture gallery is just as much the showplace of professional entertainers as is the green grass at Old Trafford. Neither the working life of the rich nor that of the poor is a means to culture – both alike demand simply to be entertained in their spare time. The ideal of Industrialism is to produce short working time and high pay to spend on entertainment in a long leisure time. Industrialism means that whatever is deemed a necessary thing shall be made by machinery and in quantity, and only what is deemed unnecessary shall be allowed to remain in the sphere of those eccentrics called artists – eccentrics because in a world of slaves they choose to remain responsible for what they make. And those things only are allowed to express the mesh of mass-production because, being deemed unnecessary, the demand for them is small, and there's 'no money in them'. Such is, in brief, the thing called Industrialism. We may regret it or we may not. That does not matter here. This is neither a religious nor a political meeting.

Architects, as much as sculptors, are artists, and therefore responsible workmen, and therefore realists. Architects, as much as sculptors, have got to work according to the conditions of their time. You can't build a Gothic or classic cathedral to-day, even in Liverpool, without making a fool of yourself. It is said that function is insufficient for inspiration. It may or may not be so. The point is that no other inspiration is now available. All architecture which receives its inspiration in an industrial civilisation from any other source is pure play-acting, and the product is just stage scenery – the mere application of entertaining surfaces to things whose real nature is physical utility. Let such play-acting be confined to our places of entertainment – at Earl's Court or Blackpool. The people – the 'people' go to the pictures to see the pictures, not to see the picture palace. And when it's not play-acting it's simple publicity – like a gin palace. The brighter the glare the less the other 'pub' shows. So it is with the buildings of 'big business'; they aim at imposing effects in order to 'get away' with their impositions. You can't impose on people without being imposing.

'Art and the people', then, means two things: it means, first, the art *of* the people – the art they actually produce; and, second, it means that which is produced for their entertainment or 'uplift.' As to the first: we know that under Industrialism the art of the people is the art of making things by machinery. That's what they do in their working time. Now what's to be said of machine-made goods? Just this: that they must be starkly plain – plain building to start with – nor ornaments or sculptures, plain furniture and plain household utensils. Here's where the designer needs training, and first of all training in ordinary common intelligence. In Germany and Sweden they have got much farther in this than we have, and have shown that plain buildings and plain things are not only endurable, but much more endurable, i.e. when produced by machinery and in mass, than ornamental or ornamented buildings and things. The art of the people in an industrial civilisation should be plain art – the application of skill and obedience to the making of what is necessary in the way that machines necessitate and utility demands. But all bread and no jam is dull – the people won't stand it. That brings us to the second thing, the art of Entertainment. To enjoy plain necessities demands a highbrow mind. The people are not highbrow – 'the People,' not only the working class but their employers as well. Therefore, as a set-off, the people must be entertained. But we must remember it must be entertainment suitable to people whose work demands nothing from them but skilful obedience and often obedience without skill – people whose work is no longer their means to culture – people whose tastes will necessarily be almost purely animal. And I mean 'animal' in quite a good sense – healthy animal – football and games, including golf, lovemaking, and simple and sweet and rather noisy music with simple and exciting rhythms, plentiful and almost innocuous beer, cheap tours in charabancs. None of these things need be bad things. I'm not saying they need be anything but first-class in their kind. I am only saying that it is absurd to attempt to foist high aesthetics on people whose working life does not develop in them any intellectual responsibility. Nor am I saying that the things they produce in their working life, in the factory, or the things they deal with as clerks or shop hands, or transport workers, are or need be bad things. Plain things and plain buildings need not be anything but first-class.

Art is not just a few pictures in museums and picture galleries – any more than architecture is just the few buildings built by Fellows and Associates of the Royal Institute of British Architects. Art is *all* the things made in our time. Architecture is *all* the buildings. The Exchange Station in Manchester is as much art as the Royal Exchange in London, or the new *Daily Express* building.

Sculpture is not only the works of a few well-known sculptors, but also the works of the church furniture shops.

But we are still making things and still building buildings according to the dregs of the fashions of pre-industrial times. We've got an industrial world, and we are proud of it (are we not?), and we have got industrial art – but it is nothing to be proud of. The thing to worry about is not whether the people get lectures on Shakespeare or conducted tours round the City Art Gallery; nor need we worry as to whether they have intelligent views on the merits of Gothic or Roman architecture. The thing to worry about is how to rid industrial art of its pretence to be anything but what it is. Industrial art must be plain – devoid of ornament. If people want ornaments they can make them themselves in that spare time they're so keen on (naturally factory hands and shop assistants don't want to stay in the factory or the shop after the whistle's blown or the blinds are down), or they can save up and buy the produce of the independent artist. It's not 'the people' but the architects and manufacturers who need educating. They've got to learn that Corinthian columns and moulded stonework are as absurd on steel-framed buildings as arts and crafts wrought-iron work would be on the Forth Bridge. They've got to learn that hand-made ornament on machine-made furniture and pottery and household utensils is as absurd as inlaid mother-of-pearl would be on a motor-car bonnet. Moreover, it is unjust to the independent painters and carvers and metal workers to deprive them of their livelihood by supplying the people with necessarily bad machine-made imitations and reproductions. Above all, we must learn to leave out the word 'art' – except as meaning simply skill – the skill to make well what needs making.

Two Letters on the Artists' International (1934)*

The Artists' International held its first exhibition in Britain between 27 September and 10 October 1934. 'Paintings, drawings, sculpture, photographs and architecture have been invited from artists throughout the country,' ran the advertisement in the first issue of the Left Review, 'under the general heading of: "The Social Conditions and Struggles of To-day."' Works to be exhibited had been 'executed with a definite social purpose', and the exhibition itself would be complemented with lectures and meetings to 'discuss the position of the artist in Society and the effect of environmental influences on his work'. An attempt would

---

* Reprinted from Left Review 1.9 (June 1935): 341–2.

be made at a 'Marxian analysis of one or two periods in the history of art'. The initiative was, of course, not universally welcomed. G. M. Godden wrote in *The Catholic Herald* (27 October 1934) that 'Marxist propaganda is being launched in Europe, England and America', and 'under cover of a society calling itself the "Artists' International" Marxism has recently invaded the domain of art . . . Let there be no mistake about this British section of the so-called Artists' International. It is neither British nor International; nor is it primarily concerned with art.' Gill was one of the exhibitors, and Godden's review – and other comments it elicited – drew from him the following letters, which the *Left Review* saw fit to reprint 'as showing currents of thought among English intellectuals which ought not to be ignored . . .' For background on the Artists' International, see T. H. Wintringham, "Artist's International" (*Left Review* 1.2 [November 1934]: 40–1), and Morris and Radford, *The Story of the Artists' International Association 1933–53*. On Gill's relation to the Association, see Speaight, pp. 179–81.

S IR, – As one of the exhibitors at the exhibition of pictures arranged by the society called the Artists' International, held in London recently, you will perhaps allow me to comment upon the remarks of your contributor, G. M. Godden.

I visited the exhibition rather expecting to find many 'anti-God' paintings, as I had been told I should do, but in half an hour's walk round I could see none. All I saw were various works depicting the hardships of the proletariat, the brutality of the police, the display of armed forces against street orators, starving children, and slum conditions generally. There were also a few works in the vein of Van Gogh's famous 'Yellow Chair', that is to say, works depicting simple workmen and scenes of working life.

It was not a big exhibition. It was not held in a fashionable quarter. It might be described as a pathetic affair compared with the exhibitions of what your contributor doubtless calls 'Art' in fashionable West End galleries and art dealers' shops.

Suppose it to be true that the Artists' International is primarily concerned to propagate Communism; even so, there was nothing, in the terms under which we exhibited, which made it obligatory. And there was nothing to hinder any Catholic artist from showing that he could stand up for social justice as well as any Marxian.

So much for that aspect of the affair. But I am less concerned to defend the exhibition than to defend the principle governing it. Your contributor says that the exhibition was 'neither British nor international nor primarily concerned with art'. Further on she says that the Union was not created 'to promote good art but as a section of the army of propagandists'. Further, she quotes Lenin's saying that 'art must serve propaganda', and, describing a discussion which took place at the exhibition, she says: 'Speakers denounced the present English social system and the Sedition Bill – subjects familiar to Communist speakers but unexpected in a course of addresses connected with an exhibition of art.'

Now what, may I ask, is this extraordinary thing called art if it is not propaganda or at the service of propaganda? What are the sculptures on the medieval cathedrals and in modern churches but propaganda? What are the effigies of eminent politicians in Westminster Abbey and Parliament Square if they are not propaganda for the values and politics upheld by famous statesmen? What is the Royal Academy exhibition but propaganda for the bourgeois culture of modern England; just as Van Gogh's 'Yellow Chair' is propaganda for the values of simple people and simple things?

Art which is not propaganda is simply aesthetics and is consequently entirely the affair of cultured connoisseurs. It is a studio affair, nothing to do with the common life of men and women, a means of 'escape'. Art in the studio becomes simply 'self-expression', and that becomes simply self-worship. Charity, the love of God and your neighbour, which, here below, every work of man must exhibit, is lost. If you say art is nothing to do with propaganda, you are saying that it has nothing to do with religion – that it is simply a psychological dope, a sort of cultured drug traffic. I, at any rate, have no use for it. For me, all art is propaganda; and it is high time that modern art became propaganda for social justice instead of propaganda for the flatulent and decadent ideals of bourgeois Capitalism.

Every artist must be a preacher, a missionary. But it does not follow that he should make up his own sermons. What is wanted is precisely what Lenin said, with this difference: that, as Catholics, we are serving not the propaganda of Marxian materialism but the propaganda of the Kingdom of God and his justice.

– Yours, etc.   *Eric Gill*

SIR, – With reference to the letter of Mr. Edward Walters in your issue of December 29th, may I again protest against the implications in his sentence: 'The "Artists' International" exhibition was primarily concerned with communist propaganda and only secondarily with art'? Why do people persist in writing about art as if it were an activity performed *in vacuo*? (as who should say: 'I've eaten my breakfast, polished my boots, written an article on sunsets, and now I'm going to do some art'). Such and such, they say, is 'propaganda', but not art. Such and such is 'religion', but not art. An exhibition of gas cookers is not art, it is 'commerce' – and so on, and if you ask: What then is art? no two people give you the same answer. The truth is that there is no such thing. It's like the Snark – a Boojum. It's like the emperor's new clothes – not really there at all. There are, in fact, as many arts as there are human activities, but no such thing as art by itself.

All things made are works of art – from the art of stirring the Christmas pudding to the art of M. Picasso who stirs our aesthetic sensibilities; from the making of gas cookers which will cook to making houses for the Blessed Sacrament (i.e. cathedrals and such) – and painting pictures which stir us to rebel against capitalist exploitation is as much art, ART, as painting Madonnas to stir us to the love of God.

SIR, what I protest against is not your correspondent's objection to Communism but the frightful notion that people who make things are not concerned with propaganda – that when I make a statue of Saint Isidore it is bought by some connoisseur not because he loves the saint but because he likes the shape of my sculpture – that in Giotto's paintings of Saint Francis it is not Saint Francis who matters most but something called 'plastic form'. And if a statue means anything the connoisseurs won't like it – they say it's propaganda. They don't want to be disturbed in their complacency, they prefer what Mr. Aldous Huxley calls 'the feelies'. And our painters and sculptors accept this dope; they are proud to be free from any taint of propaganda, they talk about 'pure art'.

Can we not agree that pictures painted under the inspiration of Communism are as much 'art' as pictures painted under the inspiration of Christianity – that a picture painted in the service of religion (any religion) is no less a work of art than one painted simply to entertain? God forbid that all painters should start inventing new religions; but may God equally forbid the continuance of the notion that art has nothing to do with anything but aesthetics.

– Yours, etc.   *Eric Gill*

42 Frank (F. J.) Sheed *Catholics and the Social Problem (1938)**

This is an extract from Sheed's *Communism and Man*, published in 1938 by the firm he founded with his wife, Maisie Ward, in 1926. The editorial policy of Sheed and Ward, stated at the outset, was 'to express the whole Catholic mind',[1] and the firm's list grew rapidly diverse; among those whose books appeared under the Sheed and Ward imprint in the late 1920s and early 1930s were Alfred Noyes, Hilaire Belloc, Christopher Hollis, G. K. Chesterton, C. S. Lewis, Karl Adam and Jacques Maritain. Through projects like the series of inexpensive *Essays in Order* (see above, p. 345), Sheed and Ward managed to reach a fairly wide audience and to contribute to ongoing public debate. In the later 1930s their list began to include works by Sheed himself, as well as by Ward, whose study of *The Oxford Groups* appeared in 1937.

George Orwell, who was generally impatient with what he called 'the current drizzle of Catholic propaganda',[2] wrote positively about *Communism and Man*, a book remarkable, he said, 'for being written in a good temper. Instead of employing the abusive misrepresentation which is now usual in all major controversies, it gives a fairer exposition of Marxism and Communism than most Marxists could be trusted to give of Catholicism.' 'If all Catholic apologists were like Mr. Sheed, the Church would have fewer enemies.'[3] In *Inside the Whale* (1940), Orwell had much more to say about the 'sort of false dawn' of the late 1920s and early 1930s 'when numbers of young intellectuals, including several quite gifted writers (Evelyn Waugh, Christopher Hollis and others), had fled into the Catholic Church'. Like the Communist Party, the Church 'was simply something to believe in'.[4] For the full passage, see below, p. 387.

We have seen the views of the present Pope. Forty-six years ago Leo XIII uttered similar denunciations of Capitalism and a similar statement of the rights of the workers. Yet it would be idle to pretend that the Church is not widely associated, particularly in the minds of the poor, with the interests and the maintenance of the present system. In *Quadrigesimo Anno*, Pius XI says quite bluntly that many Catholics have embraced Socialism because they feel that 'the Church and those professing attachment to the Church favour the rich, and neglect the workers and have no care for them'. There is, therefore, a plain contradiction between what the Popes teach and what the Church is held to practise. The reasons for this are worth a closer examination

---

* Reprinted from *Communism and Man* (London: Sheed and Ward, 1938), pp. 195–204.

than can be given them here. A book would be needed to discuss all that the Church has done for the worker and all the reasons why so many workers tend to look elsewhere for guidance and support and even sympathy. I can do no more here than indicate what might be the subjects of some of the chapters of that most necessary book.

In the first place, there is no doubt that a large part of this general attitude towards the Church is due to her insistence upon doing her own special work and her consequent refusal to regard any task, however pressing in itself, as more urgent than the work she was actually founded to do. Her primary object is to bring men to their eternal destiny, and she will never allow that anything else should distract her from this. But men intent upon one thing are naturally impatient when they find others intent upon something else. There are great evils in the present social system; the needs of this life are more immediately obvious than the needs of eternal life, and once men are fully seized with the grave disease under which our social system is suffering, they are driven almost to frenzy by the sight of the Church preoccupied with other cares. Since, in the present dominantly non-religious atmosphere, most people have scarcely a suspicion that the Church's primary job carries with it elements which are indispensable to the proper performance of society's primary job, the Church seems to them like some Nero fiddling away at unrealities while the real world is in torment. Even those who pause long enough to realise that the Church does in fact claim that her work is necessary to social well-being, remain impatient. For great evils the unreflecting man demands quick solutions. Thus the average man, tormented by the present spectacle of social injustice, does not know enough history to realise what the Church's steady concentration upon her own job has meant in such matters as the disappearance of slavery or the emancipation of women; and he is too deeply rooted in the habit of taking familiar things for granted to realise the immeasurable advance in the state of the worker that was bound up with the Church's insistence upon one day's rest in seven. The arrangement of civil society is the business of citizens, not of the Church; and when men get themselves into a mess in what is clearly their own province – a province from which, usually, they have noisily excluded the Church in the days of their prosperity – it is a little hard that they should blame the Church for not producing a solution from up her sleeve. The individual Catholic as a citizen must work with all his might at the perfecting of the social order. But for the Church, as the Church, other concerns are primary.

All the same, the feeling that the Church is unnaturally remote from the realities of social life does here and there reach a point where even the Catholic is troubled. In a given Catholic society, the lot of the proletariat may be exceptionally hard and if there is no public protest by churchmen but apparent acquiescence, it is easy enough to feel that the Church is failing in a plain duty. And it might be so. In a given place, at a given period, there might be a devitalised Catholicism, for priests are men, and acceptance of an evil situation long-established is a temptation to human indolence. But this obvious explanation is not necessarily and in all cases the right one. A situation that is plainly indefensible to the onlooker does not always appear so to one who is born in it and all his life immersed in it; neither the rich Catholic who exploits the poor nor the priest who leaves him unrebuked is necessarily guilty of a grave fault in the will: blindness in the intellect accounts for much that looks plainly sinful – particularly that blindness which makes the familiar seem normal and prevents any questioning of a situation in which the poor always have had less than enough and the rich always have lived luxuriously; in support of this it is to be noted that in such countries, the poor themselves are as little disposed as the rich to question the only dispensation they have ever known. But this is not all. Frequently enough the Church has seen the injustice but has seen no spectacular way to remedy it. Thundering at the rich can be a relief to the feelings; but it does not necessarily bring any advantage to the poor. Where the rich are in strong and unshakable control, denunciation can affect nothing. The rich man who retains contact with the Church, is kept at least to half-awareness of his brotherhood with the poor, and for the Church to antagonize him totally would mean that even this minimum would disappear and the poor would not be the gainers. Nor is even this the only consideration that the Church has to weigh. She does not see men primarily as exploiters and exploited, with the exploiters as people whom it is her duty to overthrow; she sees men as saints and sinners, her own job being to help sinners to become saints and the saints to become greater saints. If she held the former view, the rich man as an exploiter would be the object of her hottest indignation, but from her own point of view the rich man as a sinner is the object of her most loving care. Where others see a strong man in the pride of success, she sees a poor soul in danger of hell, and she will do her uttermost to draw it from that way. Christ has told her that the souls of the rich are in special danger; and care for souls was her primary work.

The Church's interventions in the social order are always secondary to her work for souls; further they are invariably realist – she aims at what there is a reasonable chance of achieving and she will not act on half-knowledge or risk leaving essential factors out of her calculations. Thus it would be idle to pretend that Communism did not gain an immediate advantage by the forty-five years gap that lay between the *Communist Manifesto* (1847) and the first great Papal pronouncement on the Rights of the Workers – *Rerum Novarum* (1892).[5] In that half-century, individual Catholic leaders like Bishop von Ketteler were working steadily and unsensationally at the problem, which was after all a new one and changing from year to year as Industrial Capitalism grew to its maturity. When the Pope was ready, he spoke. The urgency of a problem is no reason for producing a quick solution that happens to be wrong. Karl Marx was forty-five years early – and wrong. Leo XIII was forty-five years after him – but right. But the relation between the two men is more profound than that. The work of Karl Marx, I firmly believe, helped to clarify the situation for everybody, Catholics included. What was of permanent value in Marx lives on, separated from his errors, in *Rerum Novarum* and *Quadragesimo Anno*.

I cannot pretend that in these few paragraphs the principles governing the Church's intervention in the conduct of the social order have been adequately treated. I have said that a book is needed, but I could not write it. It would need vast historical knowledge and a profound insight into the springs of the Church's action. All I can hope to have achieved is to have helped men realise that they and the Church approach every problem with totally different principles: and that snap judgements on her actions by those who do not understand her principles are foolish. But we Catholics must face the fact that the Church's action is almost incomprehensible to men of the modern temper; and that the modern temper is something from which even we Catholics are not wholly free.

Beyond the real misunderstanding both of the nature and present importance of what the Church is doing, there is from the Communist side a steady and unrelaxing propaganda against her. The reason is obvious enough – that if the Church is right about the existence of God and of a life after death, then Marxianism vanishes. The Marxian, therefore, can never be content solely with an effort to destroy the Church by undermining the belief in God, but here he also shows the modern passion for quick solutions. It might take centuries, he feels, thoroughly to uproot the belief in God from men's minds; it is easier and more promising to attack the Church as an enemy of the worker. And this he does very wholeheartedly. Yet one might search Marx himself through and through for a more deadly criticism of Capitalism than is to be found in the Papal Encyclicals. I have never met a Communist who so much as suspects that these Papal attacks upon the present system exist.

Given his ignorance of the teaching of the Popes, the Communist can appeal to a considerable number of arguments which seem to support his view of the relation between religion and the interests of the rich. The rich themselves have often, through plain stupidity or plain cynicism, used religion as a quarry for arguments to keep the poor submissive. In the great Capitalist countries, Capitalism has grown up since the Reformation and has usually been accompanied by fierce hostility to Catholicism. In England, for instance, Capitalism arose at a time when the penal laws against Catholics were still in existence. But other religious bodies have not spoken their minds about the evils of Capitalism with the clarity we have seen in the Papal pronouncements; the existing systems have even found a certain alliance with the various forms of Protestantism, and the Communist does not differentiate in this matter between one religion and another.

What is even a more powerful factor in convincing so many of the workers that the Church is on the side of the rich is her unfailing insistence upon the rights of the civil authority. A government has to be very plainly contrary to natural justice before the Church will admit a right of revolt. In plain fact, she does not like revolutions, and nothing will induce her to regard large-scale bloodshed as an agent for social betterment. She cannot adopt the painless word 'liquidation' for mass-murder. And if the workers should sit down calmly to add up the benefits they have ever received from bloody revolution, they would not be so sure that in her condemnation of these methods the Church is wrong. The workers have gained a hundred times more from the Trade Unions than from all the revolutions combined. But even if this were not so, the Church would still find incomprehensible and very horrible the attitude of so many peaceful Christian men, outside her ranks, who would excuse the murder of millions in such a movement as the Russian Revolution with some such formula as 'You can't make an omelette without breaking eggs.' The Church can never regard men as eggs with no higher fate than to merge their own personalities in some social omelette; and one would have to be very sure of the value of the future omelette to smash so many eggs – not in the making of it but in the preliminary experimentations which *may*, in some ultimate future, lead to the perfect omelette; or may not . . .

But again it would be blindness not to see that even with all these considerations running against us, there must have been faults in us too. Two thousand years ago the poor were given to us as a trust. It should have been impossible for anyone to arise in the nineteenth century and say: 'We, not the Church, are your friends.' Yet men did arise, making exactly that claim; and their claim was not drowned in the derisive laughter of the poor. There were faults in us, and the Popes have recognised it. In the Encyclical *Divini Redemptoris*, Pius XI speaks powerfully of the harm that can be done by 'an avaricious and selfish priest'. It is a plain fact of history that ecclesiastics have often been among the most unscrupulous of politicians, and that at given moments in given countries ecclesiastics have been found associated with governments under which the poor were oppressed. In a sermon preached towards the beginning of 1938 Cardinal Mundelein, Archbishop of Chicago, used very strong words: 'The trouble with us in the past has been that we were too often drawn into an alliance with the wrong side. Selfish employers of labour have flattered the Church by calling it the great conservative force, and then called upon the police to act while they paid but a pittance of wages to those who worked for them . . . Our place is beside the poor.'

Such cases as the Cardinal speaks of are on the whole exceptional. Yet the human defects of priests, whether on the grand scale of national politics or in the ordinary round of parish life, whether real defects of will or mere defects of vision, can have a totally disproportionate effect upon the minds of the poor. The Catholic knows that even if all priests were hard and selfish men (whereas the generality of priests are the very reverse) they would still have two great gifts that his soul needs – the gift of truth and the life that comes through the Sacraments. Thus, if he be a well-instructed Catholic, he is not likely to abandon his religious practice because of faults, real or imaginary, in the priests: if they were immeasurably worse than even their worst enemy thinks them to be, we should still need the gifts of truth and grace that come to us through them, and to turn away from those gifts would be to penalise ourselves. But many a Catholic, while continuing to turn to the Church for the supplying of his religious needs, might be driven to turn away from her social teaching by the feeling that this or that priest has not sympathy or understanding, while the less instructed Catholic easily goes the whole way in abandonment of the Church.

Far more serious in its psychological effect is the bad action of the Catholic rich. Where a Catholic employer shows himself rather worse than the general run of his class, and yet remains, to all appearances, a pious Catholic, the workers draw an instant moral. The Pope returns to this subject again and again. Thus in *Quadragesimo Anno*, he writes: 'There have been, and there are even now, some who, while professing themselves to be Catholic, are well-nigh unmindful of that sublime law of justice and charity which binds us not only to give each man his due, but to succour our needy brethren as Christ our Lord Himself;[6] worse still, there are those who, out of greed for gain, do not fear to oppress the workers. Indeed there are some who even abuse religion itself, trying to cloak their own unjust impositions under its name, that they may protect themselves against the manifestly just protests of their employees.'

In *Divini Redemptoris* he is even more insistent: 'It is unfortunately true that the manner of acting in certain Catholic circles has done much to shake the faith of the working classes in the religion of Jesus Christ. These groups have refused to understand that Christian charity demands the recognition of rights due to the working man, which the Church has explicitly acknowledged. What is to be thought of the action of those Catholic employers who in one place succeeded in preventing the reading of our Encyclical *Quadragesimo Anno* in their local churches? Or those of Catholic industrialists who even to this day have shown themselves hostile to a labour movement that We Ourselves recommended? Is it not deplorable that the right of private property defended by the Church should so often have been abused to defraud the working man of his wages and his social rights? . . .

'There are some who, while exteriorly faithful to the practice of their religion, yet in the field of labour and industry, in the professions, trade, and public offices, permit a deplorable cleavage in their conscience, and live a life too little in conformity with the clear principles of justice and Christian charity. Such lives are a scandal to the weak, and to the malicious a pretext to discredit the Church.'

These faults we see in ourselves. Rich Catholics have forgotten the implications of brotherhood; all classes of Catholics have in one way or another failed in their social duty. These defects are in us not because we are Catholics, but because we are men. Other men are as bad. But there is no spiritual profit in reflecting upon the sins of others. There is no spiritual profit in beating our neighbour's breast, or anyone's breast but our own. We have the true principles of brotherhood and the true motives for brotherhood. In so far as we fail, our defects are due to human weakness and so are remediable; the defects we have seen in Communism are of its very nature and are irremediable absolutely. May God help us to remedy the defects that are ours. And may St. Joseph, whom the Pope has given the workers of the world as their patron, pray for us.

The City of God (1937)*

The Communist who matters is a man who has seen a vision. If you want to know the essence of his vision, Our Lady said it two thousand years ago:

* Reprinted from *Sidelights on the Catholic Revival* [Sheed's selected writings from the 1930s] (London: Sheed and Ward, 1940), pp. 6–9.

He hath put down the mighty from their seat,
and hath exalted to humble.
He hath filled the hungry with good things:
And the rich he hath sent empty away.

It will go ill with us if we fail to see its splendour. For we shall go on meeting the Communist with our solemn arguments, showing this fact by statistics and that fact by psychology, confronting this statement of Marx with that statement of Stalin and both with some rigmarole from the local Communist party platform, destroying all his foundations with the ruthlessness of our common sense – and leaving him as firmly grounded as before, but angry with us and more passionately in love with his vision than ever. You cannot destroy a vision by nibbling at it or laying violent hands on it or throwing stones at it. You cannot meet a vision with arguments at all. You can meet a vision only with a vision. And we have one – one that includes the Magnificat – a vision of which the Communist's vision is actually one ray. The unanswerable answer to the Moon is the Sun: for the sun does not contradict the moon but accounts for it and to show its superiority has but to show itself. So that it should be easy for us. They have a vision but we have the Vision! But it is our tragedy that we have got used to our Vision – centuries and centuries ago. We scarcely think in terms of vision at all: visions are visionary; and we are as sensible as any agnostic. Use and custom have dulled the edge of the wonder of Catholicism. We even lay it as an accusation against the Communist that he is a visionary. For with all the Sun for our birthright we are cold, and they are aflame with their small ray.

This dimming of vision has not in us been complete. Some doctrines have held their radiance – as the Blessed Eucharist. Some have suffered more than others: but the greatest sufferer of all has been the Church. Read back and see how the Fathers apostrophised the Church, how the mere thought of the Church filled them with joy bordering on ecstasy: then think of our own cooler gaze. They saw her as the bride of Christ adorned for her bridal, we see her dusty and a little soiled with earthly polity. We see her through a haze of Popes and Bishops – saintly Popes obscuring our vision almost as much as bad Popes. We scarcely see the Church for her members. We go to her to receive God's gifts of grace and truth: and we do not see that she herself is God's greatest gift of all. Just as Christ is God as well as man, and too many see only the man, so the Church is Christ as well as men, and too many see only the men.

That is the great importance of Gertrud von le Fort's *Hymns to the Church*. Here is the Mystical Body of Christ as no *poet* has seen it for centuries. Here is no routine respectful Catholicism. Here is a powerful Catholic mind prostrate in the dust:

> I have fallen on the law of your faith as on a sharp sword
> Its sharpness went through my understanding, straight
>> Through the light of my reason
> Never again shall I walk under the star of my eyes and on
>> The staff of my strength.

She sees the living splendour of the Church, for the Church is Christ living in His members:

> But strength still goes out from your thorns, and from
>> Your abysses the sound of music
> Your shadows lie on my heart like roses and your
>> Nights are like strong wine.
> I will love you even when my love of you is ended.
> I will desire you even when I desire you no more . . .
> Where my feet refuse to take me, there will I kneel down.
> And where my hands fail me, there will I fold them . . .

We must meet the Communist vision with a vision: and men are so made that the most radiant other-worldly vision will not dim the radiance of a vision of this world: but with the Church seen as Gertrud von le Fort sees her, we have a Kingdom on earth to set against their kingdom on earth. Yet it is not only to counter Communism that we should see the Church as she is: but because she is what she is and we are what we are. And it may be, in God's providence, that the mission of the Communist with his flame is to remind us that our own fire is burning low.

Notes

1. Quoted by Patricia J. Anderson in 'Sheed and Ward Limited', *DLB* 112:304.
2. See his review of *The Spirit of Catholicism* by Karl Adam, *New English Weekly*, 9 June 1932. Reprinted in *An Age Like This*, p. 79.
3. *Peace News*, 27 January 1939; reprinted in Orwell, *An Age Like This*, pp. 383 and 385.
4. *An Age Like This*, p. 515.
5. It is interesting that in his essay on Eric Gill, Graham Greene also mentions *De Rerum Novarum*. He confirms Sheed's view of the document by noting that the Bishop of San Luis Potosi 'hid the Papal Encyclical . . . in the cellars of the Palace because he believed it would encourage Communism' (Greene, *Collected Essays*, p. 261).
6. St. James, Ch. 2. [FS]

43 T. S. Eliot *from The Idea of a Christian Society (1939)**

The lectures, which, 'with some revision and division', Eliot published as *The Idea of a Christian Society* in 1940, were first given in March 1939 at Corpus Christi College, Cambridge. 'My point of departure,' he wrote in his preface, 'has been the suspicion that the current terms in which we discuss international affairs and political theory may only tend to conceal from us the real issues of contemporary civilisation.' Towards the end of the preface he approvingly cites an anonymous writer in the *New English Weekly*[1] to the effect that

> Men have lived by spiritual institutions (of some kind) in every society, and also by political institutions and, indubitably, by economic activities. Admittedly, they have, at different periods, tended to put their trust mainly in one of the three as the real cement of society, but at no time have they wholly excluded the others, because it is impossible to do so.

The 'real issues' to be addressed in contemporary civilization, it becomes clear, involve not merely the tendency to *subordinate* spiritual to political institutions and economic activity, but also the more fundamental (and therefore more problematic) practice of regarding spiritual institutions as ultimately *separable* from those other 'secular' phenomena. When Eliot insists that 'this book does not make any plea for a "religious revival" in a sense with which we are already familiar', it is the 'possible separation of religious feeling from religious thinking' that he objects to in that phrase. Similarly, in closing, he remarks that what he is concerned with 'is not spiritual institutions *in their separated aspect* [my italics], but the organisation of values, and a direction of religious thought which must inevitably proceed to criticism of political and economic systems' (pp. 3–4).

Eliot's idea of a Christian society is based on a principle he was to develop even further in *Notes Towards the Definition of Culture* (1948) – namely, that 'unity' is both an abstract good and a civilizational imperative, and moreover that 'unity' is not incompatible with 'diversity'. In *Notes* it becomes clear that unity in the political or economic realms, though possibly valuable, cannot supply what 'culture unity' gives (p. 201).[2] In so far as we are concerned with the vitality of civilization, the latter is indispensable. But in Eliot's view 'the dominant force in creating a common culture between peoples each of which has its distinct culture, is religion' (p. 200), which explains why, in the preface to *Idea*, he insists on the continuity between politics, economics and religion, and yet also on the primacy

---

* Reprinted from *Christianity and Culture* (New York: Harcourt, Brace and World, 1968), pp. 30–5.

of the latter. 'No culture,' he was to generalize in 1948, 'can appear or develop except in relation to a religion' (p. 100); in 1939, however, he seems to have felt that in the propagation of culture the *Christian* religion had a pre-eminent and particular role to play.

That culture and the cultivation of philosophy and the arts should be confined to the cloister would be a decline into a Dark Age that I shudder to contemplate; on the other hand, the segregation of lay 'intellectuals' into a world of their own, which very few ecclesiastics or politicians either penetrate or have any curiosity about, is not a progressive situation either. A good deal of waste seems to me to occur through pure ignorance; a great deal of ingenuity is expended on half-baked philosophies, in the absence of any common background of knowledge. We write for our friends – most of whom are also writers – or for our pupils – most of whom are going to be writers; or we aim at a hypothetical popular audience which we do not know and which perhaps does not exist. The result, in any case, is apt to be a refined provincial crudity. What are the most fruitful social conditions for the production of works of the first order, philosophical, literary, or in the other arts, is perhaps one of those topics of controversy more suitable for conversation than for writing about. There may perhaps be no one set of conditions most suitable for the efflorescence of all these activities; it is equally possible that the necessary conditions may vary from one country and civilisation to another. The régime of Louis XIV or of the Tudors and Stuarts could hardly be called libertarian; on the other hand, the rule of authoritarian governments in our time does not appear conducive to a renascence of the arts. Whether the arts flourish best in a period of growth and expansion, or in one of decay, is a question that I cannot answer. A strong and even tyrannous government may do no harm, so long as the sphere of its control is strictly limited; so long as it limits itself to restricting the liberties, without attempting to influence the minds, of its subjects; but a régime of unlimited demagogy appears to be stultifying. I must restrict my consideration to the position of the arts in our present society, and to what it should be in such a future society as I envisage.

It may be that the conditions unfavourable to the arts today lie too deep and are too expensive to depend upon the differences between one form of government and another; so that the prospect before us is either of slow continuous decay or of sudden extinction. You cannot, in any scheme for the reformation of society, aim directly at a condition in which the arts will flourish: these activities are probably by-products for which we cannot deliberately arrange the conditions. On the other hand, their decay may always be taken as a symptom of some social ailment to be investigated. The future of art and thought in a democratic society does not appear any brighter than any other, unless democracy is to mean something very different from anything actual. It is not that I would defend a moral censorship: I have always expressed strong objections to the suppression of books possessing, or even laying claim to literary merit. But what is more insidious than any censorship, is the steady influence which operates silently in any mass society organised for profit, for the depression of standards of art and culture. The increasing organisation of advertisement and propaganda – or the influencing of masses of men by any means except through their intelligence – is all against them.[3] The economic system is against them; the chaos of ideals and confusion of thought in our large-scale mass education is against them; and against them also is the disappearance of any class of people who recognise public and private responsibility of patronage of the best that is made and written. At a period in which each nation has less and less 'culture' for its own consumption, all are making furious efforts to export their culture, to impress upon each other their achievements in arts which they are ceasing to cultivate or understand. And just as those who should be the intellectuals regard theology as special study, like numismatics or heraldry, with which they need not concern themselves, and theologians observe the same indifference to literature and art, as special studies which do not concern *them*, so our political classes regard both fields as territories of which they have no reason to be ashamed of remaining in complete ignorance. Accordingly the more serious authors have a limited, and even provincial audience, and the more popular write for an illiterate and uncritical mob.

You cannot expect continuity and coherence in politics, you cannot expect reliable behaviour on fixed principles persisting through changed situations, unless there is an underlying political philosophy: not of a party, but of the nation. You cannot expect continuity and coherence in literature and the arts, unless you have a certain uniformity of culture, expressed in education by a settled, though not rigid agreement as to what everyone should know to some degree, and a positive distinction – however undemocratic it may sound – between the educated and the uneducated. I observed in America, that with a very high level of intelligence among undergraduates, progress was impeded by the fact that one could never assume that any two, unless they had been at the same school under the influence of the same masters at the same moment, had studied the same subjects or read the same books, though the number of subjects in which they had been instructed was surprising. Even with a smaller amount of total information, it might have been better if they had read fewer, but the same books. In a negative liberal society you have no agreement as to there being any body of knowledge which any educated person should have acquired at any particular stage: the idea of wisdom disappears, and you get sporadic and unrelated experimentation. A nation's system of education is much more important than its system of government; only a proper system of education can unify the active and the contemplative life, action and speculation, politics and the arts. But 'education', said Coleridge, 'is to be reformed, and defined as synonymous with instruction.' This revolution has been effected: to the populace education *means* instruction. The next step to be taken by the clericalism of secularism, is the inculcation of the political principles approved by the party in power.

I may seem to have wandered from my course, but it seemed necessary to mention the capital responsibility of education in the condition which we find or anticipate: a state secularised, a community turned into a mob, and a clerisy disintegrated. The obvious secularist solution for muddle is to subordinate everything to political power: and in so far as this involves the subordination of the money-making interests to those of the nation as a whole, it offers some immediate, though perhaps illusory relief: a people feels at least more dignified if its hero is the statesman however unscrupulous, or the warrior however brutal, rather than the financier. But it also means the confinement of the clergy to a more and more restricted field of activity, the subduing of free intellectual speculation, and the debauching of the arts by political criteria. It is only in a society with a religious basis – which is not the same thing as an ecclesiastical despotism – that you can get the proper harmony and tension, for the individual or for the community.

In any Christian society which can be imagined for the future – in what M. Maritain calls a *pluralist* society – my 'Community of Christians' cannot be a body of the definite vocational outline of the 'clerisy' of Coleridge: which, viewed in a hundred years' perspective, appears to approximate to the rigidity of a caste. The Community of Christians is not an organisation, but a body of indefinite outline; composed of both clergy and laity, of the more conscious, more spiritually and intellectually developed of both. It will be their identity of belief and aspiration, their background of a common system of education and a common culture, which will enable them to influence and be influenced by each other, and collectively to form the conscious mind and the conscience of the nation.

The spirit descends in different ways, and I cannot foresee any future society in which we could classify Christians and non-Christians simply by their professions of belief, or even, by any rigid code, by their behaviour. In the present ubiquity of ignorance, one cannot but suspect that many who call themselves Christians do not understand what the word means, and that some who would vigorously repudiate Christianity are more Christian than many who maintain it. And perhaps there will always be individuals who, with great creative gifts of value to mankind, and the sensibility which such gifts imply, will yet remain blind, indifferent, or even hostile. That must not disqualify them from exercising the talents they have been given.

The foregoing sketch of a Christian society, from which are omitted many details that will be considered essential, could not stand even as a rough sketch – an *ébauche* – without some treatment, according to the same economy, of the relation of Church and State in such a society. So far, nothing has suggested the existence of an organised Church at all. But the state would remain under the necessity of respecting Christian principles, only so far as the habits and feelings of the people were not too suddenly affronted or too violently outraged, or so far as it was deterred by any univocal protest of the most influential of the Community of Christians. The State is Christian only negatively; its Christianity is a reflection of the Christianity of the society which it governs. We have no safeguard against its proceeding, from un-Christian acts, to action on implicitly un-Christian principles, and thence to action on avowedly un-Christian principles. We have no safeguard for the purity of our Christianity; for, as the State may pass from expediency to lack of principle, and as the Christian Community may sink into torpor, so the Community of Christians may be debilitated by group or individual eccentricity and error. So far, we have only a society such that it can have a significant relation to a Church; a relationship which is not of hostility or even of accommodation. And this relation is so important that without discussing it we have not even shown the assembled skeleton of a Christian society, we have only exposed the unarticulated bones.

Notes

1. 13 July 1939.
2. Page references are to *Christianity and Culture*.
3. A point made by numerous writers in this book, and within the context of numerous different political paradigms.

44 E. M. Forster *from What I Believe (1939)**

On 9 February 1938 Forster writes from Wallington, Hertfordshire, to William
Plomer: 'you are much more of a poet than anyone else I know, and . . . a good
deal of what we say or do must be irrelevant in your eyes, and indeed unnotice-
able. As for me, I am trying to construct a philosophy' (*Selected Letters*, vol. II,
p. 156). Forster had just been invited by the *Nation* (New York) to contribute
the first essay to its projected series of 'Living Philosophies'. The result appeared
under the title 'Two Cheers for Democracy' in the *Nation* on 16 July (pp. 65–8)
and made – so P. N. Furbank tells us – 'a considerable impression. It annoyed
many, both orthodox patriots and orthodox Marxists, but they felt out-
manoeuvred by it. And many others, sickened of "commitment" by the betrayals
and confusions of the Spanish civil war, found it a great support and recognized
a heroism in its facing of limitations' (p. 225). Nicola Beaumann has traced that
heroism to the influence of Forster's classical studies, particularly to the Greek
dramatist Sophocles, who helped 'to determine Morgan's loathing of tyranny and
implacability'; 'When he declared . . . that he would rather betray his country
than his friend, he was making direct reference, for those who could see it, to
Antigone's putting her loyalty to her brother before her loyalty to the State'
(pp. 77–8). Somewhat altered and with the title 'Credo', the essay was first
published in England in the *London Mercury* 38 (September 1938): 397–404, and
subsequently in 1939 by the Hogarth Press as a pamphlet in its series, *What I
Believe*. The essay finally became 'a key to the book' (p. 7) Forster brought out
in 1951 with the recycled title: *Two Cheers for Democracy*.

I do not believe in Belief. But this is an age of faith, and there are so many
militant creeds that, in self-defence, one has to formulate a creed of one's
own. Tolerance, good temper and sympathy are no longer enough in a world
which is rent by religious and racial persecution, in a world where ignorance
rules, and science, who ought to have ruled, plays the subservient pimp.
Tolerance, good temper and sympathy – they are what matter, really, and if
the human race is not to collapse they must come to the front before long. But
for the moment they are not enough, their action is no stronger than a flower,
battered beneath a military jack-boot. They want stiffening, even if the process
coarsens them. Faith, to my mind, is a stiffening process, a sort of mental
starch, which ought to be applied as sparingly as possible. I dislike the stuff.
I do not believe in it, for its own sake, at all. Herein I probably differ from

* Reprinted from *What I Believe* (London: Hogarth Press, 1939), pp. 5–10.

most people, who believe in Belief, and are only sorry they cannot swallow even more than they do. My law givers are Erasmus and Montaigne, not Moses and St. Paul. My temple stands not upon Mount Moriah but in that Elysian Field where even the immoral are admitted. My motto is: 'Lord, I disbelieve – help thou my unbelief.'

I have, however, to live in an Age of Faith – the sort of epoch I used to hear praised when I was a boy. It is extremely unpleasant really. It is bloody in every sense of the word. And I have to keep my end up in it. Where do I start?

With personal relationships. Here is something comparatively solid in a world full of violence and cruelty. Not absolutely solid, for Psychology has split and shattered the idea of a 'Person', and has shown that there is something incalculable in each of us, which may at any moment rise to the surface and destroy our normal balance. We don't know what we are like. We can't know what other people are like. How, then, can we put any trust in personal relationships, or cling to them in the gathering political storm? In theory we cannot. But in practice we can and do. Though A is not unchangeably A or B unchangeably B, there can still be love and loyalty between the two. For the purpose of living one has to assume that the personality is solid, and the 'self' is an entity, and to ignore all contrary evidence. And since to ignore evidence is one of the characteristics of faith, I certainly can proclaim that I believe in personal relationships.

Starting from them, I get a little order into the contemporary chaos. One must be fond of people and trust them if one is not to make a mess of life, and it is therefore essential that they should not let one down. They often do. The moral of which is that I must, myself, be as reliable as possible, and this I try to be. But reliability is not a matter of contract – that is the main difference between the world of personal relationships and the world of business relationships. It is a matter for the heart, which signs no documents. In other words, reliability is impossible unless there is a natural warmth. Most men possess this warmth, though they often have bad luck, and get chilled. Most of them, even when they are politicians, *want* to keep faith. And one can, at all events, show one's own little light here, one's own poor little trembling flame, with the knowledge that it is not the only light that is shining in the darkness, and not the only one which the darkness does not comprehend. Personal relations are despised to-day. They are regarded as bourgeois luxuries, as products of a time of fair weather which is now past, and we are urged to get rid of them, and to dedicate ourselves to some movement or cause instead. I hate the idea of causes, and if I had to choose between betraying my country and betraying my friend, I hope I should have the guts to betray my country.

Such a choice may scandalize the modern reader, and he may stretch out his patriotic hand to the telephone at once and ring up the police. It would not have shocked Dante, though. Dante places Brutus and Cassius in the lowest circle of Hell because they had chosen to betray their friend Julius Caesar rather than their country Rome. Probably one will not be asked to make such an agonizing choice. Still, there lies at the back of every creed something terrible and hard for which the worshipper may one day be required to suffer, and there is even a terror and a hardness in this creed of personal relationships, urbane and mild though it sounds. Love and loyalty to an individual can run counter to the claims of the State. When they do – down with the State, say I, which means that the State would down me.

This brings me to Democracy, 'even Love, the Beloved Republic, which feeds upon Freedom and lives'. Democracy is not a Beloved Republic really, and never will be. But it is less hateful than other contemporary forms of government, and to that extent it deserves our support. It does start from the assumption that the individual is important, and that all types are needed to make a civilization. It does not divide its citizens into the bossers and the bossed – as an efficiency-regime tends to do. The people I admire most are those who are sensitive and want to create something or discover something, and do not see life in terms of power, and such people get more of a chance under democracy than elsewhere. They found religions, great or small, or they produce literature and art, or they do disinterested scientific research, or they may be what is called 'ordinary people', who are creative in their private lives, bring up their children decently, for instance, or help their neighbours. All these people need to express themselves; they cannot do so unless society allows them liberty to do so, and the society which allows them most liberty is a democracy.

Democracy has another merit. It allows criticism, and if there is not public criticism there are bound to be hushed-up scandals. That is why I believe in the Press, despite all its lies and vulgarity, and why I believe in Parliament. Parliament is often sneered at because it is a Talking Shop. I believe in it *because* it is a talking shop. I believe in the Private Member who makes himself a nuisance. He gets snubbed and is told that he is cranky or ill-informed, but he does expose abuses which would otherwise never have been mentioned, and very often an abuse gets put right just by being mentioned. Occasionally, too, a well-meaning public official starts losing his head in the cause of efficiency, and thinks himself God Almighty. Such officials are particularly frequent in the Home Office. Well, there will be questions about them in Parliament sooner or later, and then they will have to mind their steps.

Whether Parliament is either a representative body or an efficient one is questionable, but I value it because it criticizes and talks, and because its chatter gets widely reported.

45 George Orwell *Why I Joined the Independent Labour Party (1938)**

This piece appeared in print only two months after the publication of Orwell's account of the Spanish Civil War, *Homage to Catalonia*. As he confesses in the final paragraph, his experiences in Spain – in particular, his deep disillusionment with the Communist Party's actions there – were the main cause of his returning to support the Independent Labour Party. The ILP had in fact arranged Orwell's introduction to the Spanish POUM (Workers' Party of Marxist Unification) with which he served in the first half of 1937, and his persecution as a member of that group undoubtedly strengthened his loyalty to the cause of an independent socialism.

What is interesting about this essay is Orwell's concern that 'the era of free speech is closing down', not only because of the threat of Fascism but also because of Stalinist Communism. The latter he had encountered recently in Spain, of course, but as a writer (and it is with a declaration that he is such that he begins to discuss his political allegiances) he had an even longer history of dispute with the Party. At the time of the publication of *The Road to Wigan Pier* (1937), for example, Harry Pollitt, the secretary of the Communist Party of Great Britain, had dismissed him in the *Daily Worker* as 'a disillusioned little middle-class boy . . . and late imperialist policeman.'[1] Victor Gollancz's attempts to suppress the second part of that book are well-known[2] and they mark a point in Orwell's career after which any real rapprochement with the orthodox left was for him impossible. Gollancz refused to publish *Homage to Catalonia* because he felt Orwell's critique of the Communists in Spain would 'harm the fight against fascism';[3] this comment, or perhaps merely the sentiment it expresses – common enough in the years of the Popular Front – is what seems to lie behind Orwell's remark that 'fatal danger' hovers over 'mere negative "anti-Fascism"'. It is furthermore part of the background to the extract from *Inside the Whale* which is also printed here, a trenchant appraisal of the whole period and the harmful consequences for literature of an 'atmosphere of orthodoxy'.

Orwell's changing reputation on the left makes for fascinating study. Raymond Williams's attitude to him, for example, hardened considerably after a first, affectionate appraisal in 1955; in *Culture and Society* (1958) and then in *George Orwell* (1971) and a number of later essays, Orwell became, as John Rodden puts it, 'the blameworthy elder on whom a radicalized Williams and New Left could

* Originally published in *New Leader*, 24 June 1938. Reprinted from *An Age Like This: 1920–1940*. Vol. I of *The Collected Essays, Journalism and Letters of George Orwell*, ed. Sonia Orwell and Ian Angus. New York: Harcourt, Brace and World, 1968. pp. 336–8.

lay the dashed dreams of their generations' (p. 199). See Rodden, pp. 188–200; Norris, *passim*; and Zwerdling, pp. 3–37.

Perhaps it will be frankest to approach it first of all from the personal angle.

I am a writer. The impulse of every writer is to 'keep out of politics'. What he wants is to be left alone so that he can go on writing books in peace. But unfortunately it is becoming obvious that this ideal is no more practicable than that of the petty shopkeeper who hopes to preserve his independence in the teeth of the chain-stores.

To begin with, the era of free speech is closing down. The freedom of the press in Britain was always something of a fake, because in the last resort, money controls opinion;[4] still, so long as the legal right to say what you like exists, there are always loopholes for an unorthodox writer. For some years past I have managed to make the capitalist class pay me several pounds a week for writing books against capitalism. But I do not delude myself that this state of affairs is going to last forever. We have seen what has happened to the freedom of the press in Italy and in Germany, and it will happen here sooner or later. The time is coming – not next year, perhaps not for ten or twenty years, but it is coming – when every writer will have the choice of being silenced altogether or of producing the dope that a privileged minority demands.

I have got to struggle against that, just as I have got to struggle against castor oil, rubber truncheons and concentration camps. And the only régime which, in the long run, will dare to permit freedom of speech is a Socialist régime. If Fascism triumphs I am finished as a writer – that is to say, finished in my only effective capacity. That of itself would be a sufficient reason for joining a Socialist party.

I have put the personal aspect first, but obviously it is not the only one.

It is not possible for any thinking person to live in such a society as our own without wanting to change it. For perhaps ten years past I have had some grasp of the real nature of capitalist society. I have seen British imperialism at work in Burma, and I have seen something of the effects of poverty and unemployment in Britain. In so far as I have struggled against the system, it has been mainly by writing books that I hoped I would influence the reading public.[5] I shall continue to do that, of course, but at a moment like the present writing books is not enough. The tempo of events is quickening; the dangers which once seemed a generation distant are staring us in the face. One has got to be actively a Socialist, not merely sympathetic to Socialism, or one plays into the hands of our always-active enemies.

Why the ILP more than another?

Because the ILP is the only British party – at any rate the only one large enough to be worth considering – which aims at anything I should regard as Socialism.

I do not mean that I have lost all faith in the Labour Party. My most earnest hope is that the Labour Party will win a clear majority in the next general Election. But we know what the history of the Labour Party has been, and we know the terrible temptation of the present moment – the temptation to fling every principle overboard in order to prepare for an imperialist war. It is vitally necessary that there should be in existence some body of people who can be depended on, even in the face of persecution, not to compromise their Socialist principles.

I believe that the ILP is the only party which, as a party, is likely to take the right line either against imperialist war or against Fascism when this appears in its British form.[6] And meanwhile the ILP is not backed by any moneyed interest, and is systematically libelled from several quarters. Obviously it needs all the help it can get, including any help I can give it myself.

Finally, I was with the ILP contingent in Spain. I never pretended, then or since, to agree in every detail with the policy the POUM put forward and the ILP supported, but the general course of events has borne it out. The things I saw in Spain[7] brought home to me the fatal danger of mere negative 'anti-Fascism'. Once I had grasped the essentials of the situation in Spain I realised that the ILP was the only British party I felt like joining – and also the only party I could join with at least the certainty that I would never be led up the garden path in the name of capitalist democracy.

from *Inside the Whale* (1940)*

Orwell left the Independent Labour Party in late 1939 for the same reason Storm Jameson left the Peace Pledge Union: he thought the party's anti-war position futile in the face of Hitler.[8] His departure coincided, more or less, with the publication of *Inside the Whale*, the essays for which he had begun writing at Wallington, Hertfordshire, in May 1939.

In 1930 the English Communist Party was a tiny, barely legal organisation whose main activity was libelling the Labour Party. But by 1935 the face

---

* Reprinted from *An Age Like This*, pp. 514–19.

of Europe had changed, and left-wing politics changed with it. Hitler had risen to power and begun to re-arm, the Russian five-year plans had succeeded, Russia had reappeared as a great military power. As Hitler's three targets of attack were, to all appearances, Great Britain, France and the USSR, the three countries were forced into a sort of uneasy *rapprochement*. This meant that the English or French Communist was obliged to become a good patriot and imperialist – that is, to defend the very things he had been attacking for the past fifteen years. The Comintern slogans suddenly faded from red to pink. 'World revolution' and 'Social-Fascism' gave way to 'Defence of democracy' and 'Stop Hitler!' The years 1935–9 were the period of anti-Fascism and the Popular Front,[9] the heyday of the Left Book Club, when red duchesses and 'broad-minded' deans toured the battlefields of the Spanish war and Winston Churchill was the blue-eyed boy of the *Daily Worker*. Since then, of course, there has been yet another change of 'line'. But what is important for my purpose is that it was during the 'anti-Fascist' phase that the younger English writers gravitated towards Communism.

The Fascism–democracy dogfight was no doubt an attraction in itself, but in any case their conversion was due at about that date. It was obvious that *laissez-faire* capitalism was finished and that there had got to be some kind of reconstruction; in the world of 1935 it was hardly possible to remain politically indifferent. But why did these young men turn towards anything so alien as Russian Communism? Why should *writers* be attracted by a form of Socialism that makes mental honesty impossible? The explanation really lies in something that had already made itself felt before the slump and before Hitler: middle-class unemployment.

Unemployment is not merely a matter of not having a job. Most people can *get* a job of sorts, even at the worst of times. The trouble was that by 1930 there was no activity, except perhaps scientific research, the arts and left-wing politics, that a thinking person could believe in. The debunking of western civilisation had reached its climax and 'disillusionment' was immensely widespread. Who now could take it for granted to go through life in the ordinary middle-class way, as a soldier, a clergymen, a stockbroker, an Indian Civil Servant or what not? And how many of the values by which our grandfathers lived could now be taken seriously? Patriotism, religion, the Empire, the family, the sanctity of marriage, the Old School Tie, birth, breeding, honour, discipline – anyone of ordinary education could turn the whole lot of them inside out in three minutes. But what do you achieve, after all, by getting rid of such primal things as patriotism and religion? You have not necessarily got rid of the need for *something to believe in*. There had been a sort of false dawn a few years earlier when numbers of young intellectuals, including several quite gifted writers (Evelyn Waugh, Christopher Hollis and others), had fled into the Catholic Church. It is significant that these people went almost invariably to the Roman Church and not, for instance, to the C of E, the Greek Church or the Protestant sects. They went, that is, to the Church with a world-wide organisation, the one with a rigid discipline, the one with power and prestige behind it. Perhaps it is even worth noticing that the only latter-day convert of really first-rate gifts, Eliot, has embraced not Romanism but Anglo-Catholicism, the ecclesiastical equivalent of Trotskyism. But I do not think one need look farther than this for the reason why the young writers of the thirties flocked into or towards the Communist Party. It was simply something to believe in. Here was a church, an army, an orthodoxy, a discipline. Here was a Fatherland and – at any rate since 1935 or thereabouts – a Führer. All the loyalties and super-stitions that the intellect had seemingly banished could come rushing back under the thinnest of disguises. Patriotism, religion, empire, military glory – all in one word, Russia. Father, king, leader, hero, saviour – all in one word, Stalin. God – Stalin. The devil – Hitler. Heaven – Moscow. Hell – Berlin. All the gaps were filled up. So, after all, the 'Communism' of the English intellectual is something explicable enough. It is the patriotism of the deracinated.

But there is one thing that undoubtedly contributed to the cult of Russia among the English intelligentsia during these years, and that is the softness and security of life in England itself. With all its injustices, England is still the land of habeas corpus, and the overwhelming majority of English people have no experience of violence or illegality. If you have grown up in that sort of atmosphere it is not at all easy to imagine what a despotic régime is like. Nearly all the dominant writers of the thirties belonged to the soft-boiled emancipated middle class and were too young to have effective memories of the Great War. To people of that kind such things as purges, secret police, summary executions, imprisonment without trial, etc etc are too remote to be terrifying. They can swallow totalitarianism *because* they have no experience of anything except liberalism . . .

Towards the end of Mr Cyril Connolly's recent book, *Enemies of Promise*, there occurs an interesting and revealing passage. The first part of the book is, more or less, an evaluation of present-day literature. Mr Connolly belongs exactly to the generation of the writers of 'the movement', and with not many reservations their values are his values. It is interesting to notice that among the prose writers he admires chiefly those specialising in violence – the would-be tough American school, Hemingway, etc. The latter part of the book, however, is autobiographical and consists of an account, fascinatingly accurate, of life at a preparatory school and Eton in the years 1910–20. Mr Connolly ends by remarking:

> Were I to deduce anything from my feelings on leaving Eton, it might be called *The Theory of Permanent Adolescence*. It is the theory that the experiences undergone by boys at the great public schools are so intense as to dominate their lives and to arrest their development.

When you read the second sentence in this passage, your natural impulse is to look for the misprint. Presumably there is a 'not' left out, or something. But no, not a bit of it! He means it! And what is more, he is merely speaking the truth, in an inverted fashion. 'Cultured' middle-class life has reached a depth of softness at which a public-school education – five years in a lukewarm bath of snobbery – can actually be looked back upon as an eventful period. To nearly all the writers who have counted during the thirties, what more has ever happened than Mr Connolly records in *Enemies of Promise*? It is the same pattern all the time; public school, university, a few trips abroad, then London. Hunger, hardship, solitude, exile, war, prison, persecution, manual labour – hardly even words. No wonder that the huge tribe known as 'the right left people' found it so easy to condone the purge-and-Ogpu[10] side of the Russian régime and the horrors of the First Five Year Plan. They were so gloriously incapable of understanding what it all meant.

By 1937 the whole of the intelligentsia was mentally at war. Left-wing thought had narrowed down to 'anti-Fascism', i.e. to a negative, and a torrent of hate-literature directed against Germany and the politicians supposedly friendly to Germany was pouring from the press. The thing that, to me, was truly frightening about the war in Spain was not such violence as I witnessed, nor even the party feuds behind the lines, but the immediate reappearance in left-wing circles of the mental atmosphere of the Great War. The very people who for twenty years had sniggered over their own superiority to war hysteria were the ones who rushed straight back into the mental slum of 1915. All the familiar war-time idiocies, spy-hunting, orthodoxy-sniffing (Sniff, sniff. Are you a good anti-Fascist?), the retailing of incredible atrocity stories, came back into vogue as though the intervening years had never happened. Before the end of the Spanish war, end even before Munich, some of the better of the left-wing writers were beginning to squirm. Neither Auden, nor, on the whole, Spender wrote about the Spanish war in quite the vein that was expected of them. Since then there has been a change of feeling and much dismay and confusion, because the actual course of events has made nonsense of the left-wing orthodoxy of the last few years. But then it did not need very great acuteness to see that much of it was nonsense from the start. There is no certainty, therefore, that the next orthodoxy to emerge will be any better than the last.

On the whole the literary history of the thirties seems to justify the opinion that a writer does well to keep out of politics. For any writer who accepts or partially accepts the discipline of a political party is sooner or later faced with the alternative: toe the line, or shut up. It is, of course, possible to toe the line and go on writing – after a fashion. Any Marxist can demonstrate with the greatest of ease that 'bourgeois' liberty of thought is an illusion. But when he has finished his demonstration there remains the psychological *fact* that without this 'bourgeois' liberty the creative powers wither away. In the future a totalitarian literature may arise, but it will be quite different from anything we can now imagine. Literature as we know it is an individual thing, demanding mental honesty and a minimum of censorship. And this is even truer of prose than of verse. It is probably not a coincidence that the best writers of the thirties have been poets. The atmosphere of orthodoxy is always damaging to prose, and above all it is completely ruinous to the novel, the most anarchical of all forms of literature. How many Roman Catholics have been good novelists? Even the handful one could name have usually been bad Catholics. The novel is practically a Protestant form of art; it is a product of the free mind, of the autonomous individual.

No decade in the past hundred and fifty years has been so barren of imaginative prose as the nineteen-thirties. There have been good poems, good sociological works, brilliant pamphlets, but practically no fiction of any value at all. From 1933 onwards the mental climate was increasingly against it. Anyone sensitive enough to be touched by the *zeitgeist* was also involved in politics. Not everyone, of course, was definitely *in* the political racket, but practically everyone was on its periphery and more or less mixed up in propaganda campaigns and squalid controversies. Communists and near-Communists had a disproportionately large influence in the literary reviews. It was a time of labels, slogans and evasions. At the worst moments you were expected to lock yourself up in a constipating little cage of lies; at the best a sort of voluntary censorship ('Ought I to say this? Is it pro-Fascist?') was at work in nearly everyone's mind. It is almost inconceivable that good novels should be written in such an atmosphere. Good novels are not written by orthodoxy-sniffers, nor by people who are conscience-stricken about their own unorthodoxy. Good novels are written by people who are *not frightened.*

Notes

1. 17 March 1937. Quoted in Selden, p. 253.
2. See Crick, pp. 309–12.
3. See Selden, p. 306.
4. A different perspective on this issue is to be found in A. J. Cummings, *The Press*, pp. 40–6. See also Keith Williams, *British Writers and the Media 1930–1945*, *passim*, but especially p. 22.
5. Orwell here refers to his *Burmese Days* (London: Victor Gollancz, 1935), to *Down and Out in Paris and London* (London: Victor Gollancz, 1933), and to *The Road to Wigan Pier* (London: Victor Gollancz, 1937).
6. An odd point, given that Mosley's British Union of Fascists was already six years old as Orwell wrote this.
7. See his essay, 'Spilling the Spanish Beans', *An Age Like This*, pp. 269–76; *Homage to Catalonia* (London: Secker and Warburg, 1938); and 'Looking Back on the Spanish War', *My Country Right or Left 1940–1943*, pp. 286–306.
8. See Selden, p. 328.
9. On the Popular Front, see above, p. 272.
10. OGPU (Unified State Political Administration) came into being when the USSR was constituted in 1923. After playing a key role in the mass collectivization of the kulaks, OGPU was in 1934 merged into the NKVD (People's Commissariat of Internal Affairs), which carried out Stalin's purges during the 1930s. By 1942 OGPU/NKVD had come to be known as the NKGB (People's Commissariat for State Security).

Bibliography

This bibliography comprises sources of material reprinted in this volume, works cited more than once, and general studies of interest to students of the period. Works to which only passing reference is made are usually documented in the notes.

Adam, Peter. *Art of the Third Reich*. New York: Harry N. Abrams, 1992.

Adams, R. J. Q. *British Politics and Foreign Policy in the Age of Appeasement 1935–39*. Stanford: Stanford University Press, 1993.

Aldgate, Anthony. *Cinema and History: British Newsreels and the Spanish Civil War*. London: Scolar Press, 1979.

Alexander, Bill. *British Volunteers for Liberty: Spain 1936–1939*. London: Lawrence and Wishart, 1982.

Almon, Bert. 'British Poets of the Thirties'. *Library Chronicle* 25.3 (1995): 77–109.

Annan, Noel. *Our Age: English Intellectuals Between the World Wars – A Group Portrait*. New York: Random House, 1990.

Armes, Roy. *A Critical History of British Cinema*. New York: Oxford University Press, 1978.

Ashraf, P. M. *Introduction to Working-Class Literature in Great Britain, Part II: Prose*. Berlin, 1979.

Auden, W.H. *The English Auden: Poems, Essays and Dramatic Writings 1927–1939*. Ed. Edward Mendelson. London: Faber and Faber, 1977.

Auden, W.H. *Collected Poems*. Ed. Edward Mendelson. New York: Vintage, 1991.

Baldick, Chris. *The Social Mission of English Criticism 1848–1932*. Oxford: Clarendon Press, 1983.

Barbera, Jack, and William McBrien. *Stevie: A Biography of Stevie Smith*. London: Heinemann, 1985.

Beaumann, Nicola. *Morgan: A Biography of E. M. Forster*. London: Hodder and Stoughton, 1993.

Bentley, Phyllis. *'O Dreams, O Destinations': An Autobiography*. London: Gollancz, 1962.

Benton, Jill. *Naomi Mitchison: A Century of Experiment in Life and Letters*. London: Pandora, 1990.

Bergonzi, Bernard. *The Myth of Modernism and Twentieth Century Literature*. Brighton: Harvester Press, 1986.

Bergonzi, Bernard. *Reading the Thirties: Texts and Contexts*. London: Macmillan, 1978.

Berry, Paul, and Alan Bishop (eds). *Testament of a Generation: The Journalism of Vera Brittain and Winifred Holtby*. London: Virago, 1985.

Berry, Paul, and Mark Bostridge. *Vera Brittain: A Life*. London: Chatto and Windus, 1995.

Beveridge, James. *John Grierson: Film Master*. New York: Macmillan, 1978.

Blaazer, David. *The Popular Front and the Progressive Tradition: Socialists, Liberals, and the Quest for Unity 1884–1939*. Cambridge: Cambridge University Press, 1992.

Bloom, Clive (ed.). *Literature and Culture in Modern Britain*, Vol. I: 1900–1929. London: Longman, 1993.

Bradbury, Malcolm. *The Social Context of Modern English Literature*. Oxford: Blackwell, 1971.

Bridson, D. G. *The Filibuster: A Study of the Political Ideas of Wyndham Lewis*. London: Cassell, 1972.

Brittain, Vera. *Diary of the Thirties 1932–1939: Chronicle of Friendship*. London: Victor Gollancz, 1986.

Burnett, John. *A Social History of Housing 1815–1985*. 2nd edn. London: Methuen, 1986.

Caesar, Adrian. *Dividing Lines: Poetry, Class and Ideology in the 1930s*. Manchester: Manchester University Press, 1991.

Campbell, Beatrix. *Wigan Pier Revisited: Poverty and Politics in the 80s*. London: Virago, 1984.

Campbell, SueEllen. *The Enemy Opposite: The Outlaw Criticism of Wyndham Lewis*. Athens: Ohio University Press, 1988.

Carey, John. *The Intellectuals and the Masses: Pride and Prejudice among the Literary Intelligentsia 1880–1939*. London: Faber and Faber, 1992.

Carpenter, Humphrey. *The Brideshead Generation: Evelyn Waugh and His Friends*. London: Weidenfeld and Nicolson, 1989.

Carpenter, Humphrey. *W. H. Auden: A Biography*. London: George Allen and Unwin, 1981.

Carr, Virginia Spencer. *Dos Passos: A Life*. New York: Doubleday, 1984.

Caudwell, Christopher. *Illusion and Reality: A Study in the Sources of Poetry*. 1937; London: Lawrence and Wishart, 1946.

Caudwell, Christopher. *Studies and Further Studies in a Dying Culture*. 1938; New York: Monthly Review Press, 1971.

Caudwell, Christopher. *Romance and Realism: A Study in English Bourgeois Literature*. Ed. Samuel Hynes. Princeton: Princeton University Press, 1970.

Clarke, Jon, Margot Heinemann, David Margolies and Carol Snee. *Culture and Crisis in Britain in the '30s*. London: Lawrence and Wishart, 1979.

Connolly, Cyril. *Enemies of Promise*. 1937; London: André Deutsch, 1938.

Cook, Judith. *Apprentices of Freedom*. London: Quartet Books, 1979.

Cornford, John. *Understand the Weapon, Understand the Wound: Selected Writings of John Cornford*. Ed. Jonathan Galassi. Manchester: Carcanet New Press, 1976.

Cowling, Elizabeth, and Jennifer Mundy. *On Classic Ground: Picasso, Léger, de Chirico and the New Classicism 1910–1930*. London: Tate Gallery, 1990.

Crick, Bernard. *George Orwell: A Life*. Harmondsworth: Penguin, 1982.

Crick, Bernard. *Essays on Politics and Literature*. Edinburgh: Edinburgh University Press, 1989.

Croft, Andy. *Red Letter Days: British Fiction in the 1930s*. London: Lawrence and Wishart, 1990.

Cummings, A. J. *The Press*. London: John Lane/Bodley Head, 1936.

Cunningham, Valentine. *British Writers of the Thirties*. Oxford: Clarendon Press, 1988.

Curran, James, and Vincent Porter (eds). *British Cinema History*. London: Weidenfeld and Nicolson, 1983.

Dawson, Christopher. *Progress and Religion*. 1929; reprinted Westport, CT: Greenwood Press, 1970.

Dawson, Christopher. *The Age of the Gods*. London: Sheed and Ward, 1933.

Day Lewis, Cecil. *The Mind in Chains: Socialism and the Cultural Revolution*. London: Frederick Muller, 1937.

Day, Gary. *The British Critical Tradition: A Re-evaluation*. New York: St Martin's Press, 1993.

Day-Lewis, Sean. *C. Day-Lewis: An English Literary Life*. London: Weidenfeld and Nicolson, 1980.

Deane, Patrick. *At Home in Time: Forms of Neo-Augustanism in Modern English Poetry*. Montreal and Kingston: McGill-Queen's University Press, 1994.

Dowson, Jane (ed.). *Women's Poetry of the 1930s*. London: Routledge, 1996.

Duparc, Jean, and David Margolies (eds). *Scenes and Actions: Unpublished Writings* [by Christopher Caudwell]. London: Routledge, 1986.

Eagelton, Terry, and Drew Milne (eds). *Marxist Literary Theory*. London: Routledge, 1996.

Eliot, T. S. *Christianity and Culture*. New York: Harcourt, Brace and World, 1968.

Empson, William. *Some Versions of Pastoral*. 1935; New York: New Directions, 1950.

Feather, John. *A History of British Publishing*. London: Croom Helm, 1988.

Ford, Boris (ed.). *Early Twentieth-Century Britain*. The Cambridge Cultural History, Vol. 8. Cambridge: Cambridge University Press, 1992.

Forster, E. M. *Selected Letters of E. M. Forster*. Vol. II: 1921–1970. Ed. Mary Lago and P. N. Furbank. Cambridge, MA: The Belknap Press of Harvard University Press, 1985.

Forster, E. M. *Two Cheers for Democracy*. London: Edward Arnold, 1951.

Forster, E. M. *What I Believe*. London: The Hogarth Press, 1939.

Fox, Ralph. *The Novel and the People*. 1937; London: Lawrence and Wishart, 1979.

Fox, Ralph. *A Writer in Arms*. New York: International Publishers, 1937.

Furbank, P. N. *E. M. Forster: A Life*. Oxford: Oxford University Press, 1979.

Fussell, Paul. *Abroad: Literary Travelling Between the Wars*. Oxford: Oxford University Press, 1980.

Gascoyne, David. *A Short Survey of Surrealism*. 1935; London: Frank Cass and Co., 1970.

Gill, Eric. *Beauty Looks after Herself*. 1933; Freeport: Books for Libraries Press, 1966.

Gindin, James. *British Fiction in the 1930s*. Houndmills: Macmillan, 1992.

Gloversmith, Frank (ed.). *Class, Culture and Social Change: A New View of the 1930s*. Brighton: Harvester Press; Atlantic Highlands: Humanities Press, 1980.

Graves, Robert, and Alan Hodge. *The Long Week-End: A Social History of Great Britain 1918–1939*. London: Readers' Union with Faber and Faber, 1941.

Greene, Graham. *Collected Essays*. 1969; Harmondsworth: Penguin, 1970.

Grigson, Geoffrey. *Recollections: Mainly of Writers and Artists.* London: Chatto and Windus & Hogarth Press, 1984.

Hardy, Forsyth (ed.). *Grierson on Documentary.* New York: Praeger, 1966.

Hardy, Forsyth. *John Grierson: A Documentary Biography.* London: Faber and Faber, 1979.

Harman, Claire. *Sylvia Townsend Warner: A Biography.* London: Chatto and Windus, 1989.

Harrison, Charles. *English Art and Modernism, 1900–1939.* London: Allen Lane/Bloomington: Indiana University Press, 1981.

Harrisson, Tom, and Charles Madge. *Britain by Mass-Observation.* 1939; London: Century Hutchinson, 1986.

Hawthorn, Jeremy (ed.). *The British Working-Class Novel in the Twentieth Century.* London: Arnold, 1984.

Heard, Gerald. *Pain, Sex and Time.* New York: Harper and Brothers, 1939.

Hibbert, Gerald K. (ed.). *The New Pacifism.* London: Allenson and Co., 1936; reprinted New York: Garland, 1972.

Hobsbawm, E.J. *Industry and Empire: An Economic History of Britain Since 1750.* London: Weidenfeld and Nicolson, 1968.

Hodgkinson, Anthony W., and Rodney E. Sheratsky. *Humphrey Jennings – More Than a Maker of Films.* Hanover and London: University Press of New England, 1982.

Hogenkamp, Bert. *Deadly Parallels: Film and the Left in Britain 1929–39.* London: Lawrence and Wishart, 1986.

Hone, Joseph. *W. B. Yeats: 1865–1939.* 1943; Harmondsworth: Penguin, 1971.

Hoskins, Katharine Bail. *Today the Struggle: Literature and Politics in England During the Spanish Civil War.* Austin: University of Texas Press, 1969.

Hynes, Samuel. *The Auden Generation: Literature and Politics in England in the 1930s.* Princeton: Princeton University Press, 1972.

Ingram, Angela, and Daphne Patai (eds). *Rediscovering Forgotten Radicals: British Women Writers 1889–1939.* Chapel Hill and London: University of North Carolina Press, 1993.

Jacobs, Lewis (ed.). *The Documentary Tradition: From 'Nanook' to 'Woodstock'.* New York: Hopkinson and Blake, 1971.

Jameson, Storm (ed.). *A Challenge to Death.* New York: E. P. Dutton, 1935.

Jameson, Storm. *Civil Journey.* London: Cassell, 1939.

Johnson, Paul (ed.). *Twentieth-Century Britain: Economic, Social and Cultural Change.* London: Longman, 1994.

Kermode, Frank. *History and Value.* Oxford: Clarendon Press, 1988.

Klaus, H. Gustav. *The Literature of Labour: Two Hundred Years of Working-Class Writing.* New York: St Martin's Press, 1985.

Leavis, F. R. *Mass Civilisation and Minority Culture.* Cambridge: Minority Press, 1930.

Leavis, Q. D. *Fiction and the Reading Public.* 1932; London: Chatto and Windus, 1965.

Lehmann, John, T. A. Jackson and C. Day Lewis (eds). *Ralph Fox: A Writer in Arms.* New York: International Publishers, 1937.

Lewis, Wyndham. *The Hitler Cult*. 1939; New York: Gordon Press, 1972.

Lewis, Wyndham. *Hitler*. 1931; New York: Gordon Press, 1972.

Lewis, Wyndham. *Men Without Art*. 1934; New York: Russell and Russell, 1964.

Light, Alison. *Forever England: Femininity, Literature and Conservatism Between the Wars*. London: Routledge, 1991.

Lucas, John (ed.). *The 1930s: A Challenge to Orthodoxy*. Sussex: Harvester Press, 1978.

MacKillop, Ian. *F. R. Leavis: A Life in Criticism*. London: Allen Lane/Penguin Press, 1995.

Meyers, Jeffrey. *The Enemy: A Biography of Wyndham Lewis*. Boston: Routledge and Kegan Paul, 1980.

Miller, David, Janet Coleman, William Connolly and Alan Ryan (eds). *The Blackwell Encyclopaedia of Political Thought*. Oxford: Blackwell, 1991.

Mitchison, Naomi. *The Home and a Changing Civilisation*. London: John Lane/Bodley Head, 1934.

Mitchison, Naomi. *The Moral Basis of Politics*. London: Constable and Co., 1938.

Montefiore, Janet. *Men and Women Writers of the 1930s: The Dangerous Flood of History*. London: Routledge, 1996.

Morpurgo, J. E. *Allen Lane, King Penguin: A Biography*. London: Hutchinson, 1979.

Morris, Lynda, and Robert Radford. *The Story of the Artists International Association*. Oxford: Museum of Modern Art, 1983.

Mosley, Nicholas. *Rules of the Game: Sir Oswald and Cynthia Mosley 1896–1933*. London: Secker and Warburg, 1982.

Mosley, Oswald. *The Greater Britain*. London: B.U.F. Publications, 1932.

Mowat, Charles Loch. *Britain Between the Wars: 1918–1940*. London: Methuen, 1959.

Mulford, Wendy. *This Narrow Place: Sylvia Townsend Warner and Valentine Ackland: Life, Letters and Politics 1930–1951*. London: Pandora, 1988.

Mulhern, Francis. *The Moment of 'Scrutiny'*. 1979; London: Verso, 1981.

Myers, Jeffrey. *The Enemy: A Biography of Wyndham Lewis*. London: Routledge, 1980.

Norris, Christopher. *Inside the Myth: Orwell – Views from the Left*. London: Lawrence and Wishart, 1984.

Orwell, George. *An Age Like This: 1920–1940*. Vol. 1 of *The Collected Essays, Journalism and Letters of George Orwell*. Ed. Sonia Orwell and Ian Angus. New York: Harcourt, Brace and World, 1968.

Orwell, George. *My Country Right or Left: 1940–1943*. Vol. 2 of *The Collected Journalism and Letters of George Orwell*. Ed. Sonia Orwell and Ian Angus. Harmondsworth: Penguin, 1970.

Orwell, George. *As I Please*. Vol. 3 of *The Collected Essays, Journalism and Letters of George Orwell*. Ed. Sonia Orwell and Ian Angus. New York: Harcourt, Brace and World, 1968.

Patai, Daphne. *The Orwell Mystique: A Study in Male Ideology*. Amherst: University of Massachusetts Press, 1984.

Pawling, Christopher. *Christopher Caudwell: Towards a Dialectical Theory of Literature*. Houndmills: Macmillan, 1989.

Pearce, Malcolm and Geoffrey Stewart. *British Political History, 1867–1990: Democracy and Decline.* London: Routledge, 1992.

Quinn, Patrick J. (ed.). *Recharting the Thirties.* Cranbury, NJ: Susquehanna University Press/London: Associated University Presses, 1996.

Rhondda, Lady (Margaret Haig [Thomas] Mackworth, 2nd Viscountess Rhondda). *Notes on the Way.* 1937; Freeport: Books for Libraries Press, 1968.

Richards, Jeffrey, and Dorothy Sheridan. *Mass-Observation at the Movies.* London: Routledge and Kegan Paul, 1987.

Riding, Laura. *The World and Ourselves.* London: Chatto and Windus, 1938.

Roberts, Michael (ed.). *The Faber Book of Modern Verse.* 1st edn 1936; 3rd edn London: Faber and Faber, 1965.

Roberts, Michael (ed.). *New Signatures: Poems by Several Hands.* London: Hogarth Press, 1932.

Rodden, John. *The Politics of Literary Reputation: The Making and Claiming of 'St. George' Orwell.* New York: Oxford University Press, 1989.

Rotha, Paul. *Documentary Film: The Use of the Film Medium to Interpret Creatively and in Social Terms the Life of the People as It Exists in Reality.* London: Faber and Faber, 1935.

Salter, Arthur (Lord). *Memoirs of a Public Servant.* London: Faber and Faber, 1961.

Samson, Anne. *F. R. Leavis.* Toronto: University of Toronto Press, 1992.

Scharine, Richard G. *From Class to Caste in American Drama: Political and Social Themes since the 1930s.* New York: Greenwood Press, 1991.

Scott, Christina. *A Historian and His World: A Life of Christopher Dawson 1889–1970.* London: Sheed and Ward, 1984.

Selden, Michael. *Orwell: The Authorized Biography.* London: Minerva, 1992.

Sheed, Frank. *Sidelights on the Catholic Revival.* London: Sheed and Ward, 1940.

Sheed, Frank. *Communism and Man.* London: Sheed and Ward, 1938.

Sisson, C. H. *The Avoidance of Literature: Collected Essays.* Ed. Michael Schmidt. Manchester: Carcanet, 1978.

Sisson, C. H., trans. *The Divine Comedy: A New Verse Translation.* Manchester: Carcanet New Press, 1980.

Skelton, Robin (ed.). *Poetry of the Thirties.* Harmondsworth: Penguin, 1964.

Skidelsky, Robert. *Oswald Mosley.* London: Macmillan, 1975.

Smith, Stan. *W. H. Auden.* Oxford: Blackwell, 1985.

Smith, Stevie. *Me Again.* Ed. Jack Barbera and William McBrien. London: Virago, 1981.

Spalding, Frances. *Stevie Smith.* London: Faber and Faber, 1988.

Speaight, Robert. *The Life of Eric Gill.* London: Methuen, 1966.

Spender, Humphrey. *Worktown People: Photographs from Northern England 1937–38.* Ed. Jeremy Mulford. Bristol: Falling Wall Press, 1982.

Spender, Stephen. *World Within World.* London: Faber and Faber, 1951.

Spender, Stephen. *The Destructive Element: A Study of Modern Writers and Beliefs.* London: Jonathan Cape, 1935. Reprinted Philadelphia: Albert Saifer, 1953.

Spender, Stephen. *The Thirties and After: Poetry, Politics, People 1933–1970.* New York: Random House, 1978.

Stannard, Martin. *Evelyn Waugh: The Early Years 1903–1939*. London: J. M. Dent and Sons, 1986.

Stansky, Peter, and William Abrahams. *Journey to the Frontier: Two Roads to the Spanish Civil War*. Boston: Little, Brown and Co., 1966.

Stevenson, John. *British Society 1914–45*. London: Allen Lane, 1984.

Sullivan, Robert. *Christopher Caudwell*. London: Croom Helm, 1987.

Sussex, Elizabeth. *The Rise and Fall of the British Documentary*. Berkeley: University of California Press, 1975.

Swindells, Julia, and Alice Jardine. *What's Left? Women in Culture and the Labour Movement*. London: Routledge, 1990.

Swingewood, Alan. *The Myth of Mass Culture*. London: Macmillan, 1977.

Symons, Julian. *The Thirties and the Nineties*. Manchester: Carcanet, 1990.

Taylor, A. J. P. *English History 1914–1945*. Oxford: Clarendon Press, 1965.

Thomson, David. *England in the Twentieth Century*. 2nd edn by Geoffrey Warner. Harmondsworth: Penguin, 1981.

Thorpe, Andrew. *Britain in the 1930s*. Oxford: Basil Blackwell, 1992.

Thorpe, Andrew. *Britain in the Era of the Two World Wars 1914–45*. Longman Companions to History. London: Longman, 1994.

Tolley, A. T. *The Poetry of the Thirties*. London: Victor Gollancz, 1975.

Tortosa, Francisco Garcia, and Ramon Lopez Ortega. *English Literature and the Working Class*. Seville: Publicaciones de la Universidad de Sevilla, 1980.

Ulrich, Mabel (ed.). *Man, Proud Man*. London: Hamish Hamilton, 1932.

Ward, Elizabeth. *David Jones: Mythmaker*. Manchester: Manchester University Press, 1983.

Waugh, Evelyn. *Robbery under Law: The Mexican Object-Lesson*. London: Chapman and Hall, 1939.

West, Alick. *Crisis and Criticism and Selected Literary Essays*. 1937; London: Lawrence and Wishart, 1975.

West, Alick. *The Mountain in the Sunlight: Studies in Conflict and Unity*. London: Lawrence and Wishart, 1958.

Williams, Keith. *British Writers and the Media, 1930–1945*. Houndmills: Macmillan, 1996.

Williams, Raymond. *Culture and Society 1780–1950*. London: Chatto and Windus, 1967.

Williams, Raymond. *The Long Revolution*. London: Chatto and Windus, 1961.

Williams, Raymond. *Orwell*. 1971; London: Fontana, 1991.

Woolf, Virginia. *Three Guineas*. London: Hogarth Press, 1938.

Worpole, Ken. *Dockers and Detectives: Popular Reading, Popular Writing*. London: Verso, 1983.

Yeats, W. B. *Essays and Introductions*. London: Macmillan, 1961.

Yeats, W. B. *The Oxford Book of Modern Verse*. Oxford: Oxford University Press, 1936.

Zhdanov, A, *et al. Problems of Soviet Literature: Reports and Speeches at the First Soviet Writers' Congress*. Moscow: Cooperative Publishing Society of Foreign Workers, 1935; reprinted Westport, CT: Greenwood Press, 1979.

Zwerdling, Alex.. *Orwell and the Left*. New Haven: Yale University Press, 1974.

Index